# INTERNATIONAL HISTORY AND INTERNATIONAL RELATIONS

This innovative textbook seeks to provide undergraduate students of international relations with valuable and relevant historical context, bridging the gap and offering a genuinely interdisciplinary approach. Each chapter integrates both historical analysis and literature and applies this to an international relations context in an accessible fashion, allowing students to understand the historical context in which these core issues have developed.

The book is organized thematically around key issues in international relations such as war, peace, sovereignty, identity, empire and international organizations. Each chapter provides an overview of the main historical context, theories and literature in each area and applies this to the study of international relations.

Providing a fresh approach, this work will be essential reading for all students of international relations and international relations theory.

**Andrew J. Williams** is Professor of International Relations at the University of St Andrews. His main research interests include international conflict resolution, international history and international organization. His book *Liberalism and War: The Victors and the Vanquished* was published in 2006.

**Amelia Hadfield** is Professor of European Affairs at the Vrije Universiteit Brussels (VUB), as well as Senior Research Fellow at the Institute of European Studies (IES). Her broad research interests include foreign policy analysis, diplomatic history, IR theory and the foreign policy of the European Union. Her research monograph, entitled *British Foreign Policy, National Identity and Neoclassical Realism,* was published in 2010.

**J. Simon Rofe** is Senior Lecturer in Diplomatic and International Studies in the Centre for International Studies and Diplomacy at the School of Oriental and African Studies, University of London. His research interests lie in the broad field of diplomacy and international relations, particularly in the international history of the twentieth century, and focus on US foreign relations with the rest of the world.

# INTERNATIONAL HISTORY AND INTERNATIONAL RELATIONS

Andrew J. Williams, Amelia Hadfield
and J. Simon Rofe

Routledge
Taylor & Francis Group

LONDON AND NEW YORK

First published 2012
by Routledge
2 Park Square, Milton Park, Abingdon, Oxon, OX14 4RN

Simultaneously published in the USA and Canada
by Routledge
270 Madison Avenue, New York, NY 10016

*Routledge is an imprint of the Taylor & Francis Group, an informa business*

*British Library Cataloguing in Publication Data*
A catalogue record for this book is available from the British Library

*Library of Congress Cataloging-in-Publication Data*
Williams, Andrew J., 1951-
  International history and international relations / Andrew J. Williams,
  Amelia Hadfield and J. Simon Rofe.
    p. cm.
  Includes bibliographical references and index.
  1. International relations—Textbooks. I. Hadfield, Amelia.
  II. Rofe, J. Simon. III. Title.
  JZ1242.W545 2012
  327—dc23

                                                    2011044822

ISBN 13: 978-0-415-48178-6 (hbk)
ISBN 13: 978-0-415-48179-3 (pbk)
ISBN 13: 978-0-203-11990-7 (ebk)

Typeset in Garamond
by Cenveo Publisher Services

FSC
www.fsc.org

MIX
Paper from
responsible sources
FSC® C004839

Printed and bound in Great Britain by
TJ International Ltd, Padstow, Cornwall

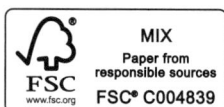

# CONTENTS

# ACKNOWLEDGEMENTS

We would like to thank a lot of people who have encouraged us in the writing of this book. Firstly, thanks to many students who helped us think through our ideas, and particularly at the universities where we have taught. In addition, and in alphabetical order, those who have encouraged us, read parts of the manuscript, given helpful comments, and in some cases plundered their libraries: Adnan Amkhan, Zeynep Arkan, Terry Barringer, Jeremy (Ken) Kennard, Tony Lang, Roger Mac Ginty and Tracey Morris, as well as three anonymous referees from Routledge. We would also like to thank Craig Fowlie, who never flagged in his faith in the project even when ours did, and Nicola Parkin from Routledge, who shepherded us through the editorial process with patience and good humour.

We would in particular like to thank Michael Fry, now Emeritus Professor at the University of Southern California, with whom Andrew Williams wrote a first version of part of what is now Chapter 1. Hence, within this chapter pages 20–32 are adapted from Michael Graham Fry and Andrew J. Williams, 'Diplomatic, International and Global-World History', in Jarrod Wiener and Robert A. Schrire (eds), *International Relations*, in *Encyclopedia of Life Support Systems (EOLSS)*, Developed under the Auspices of the UNESCO, EOLSS Publishers, Oxford, UK (http://www.eolss.net). In turn we would like to thank EOLSS Publishers for giving us permission to reproduce some of that original material here.

Finally we would like to thank our respective families, who were their usual supportive selves while this book took shape. The book is dedicated to Amelia's father, Alec Hadfield, who passed away during the final stages of completing the manuscript and who thoroughly approved of its rationale.

# Introduction

This is a book that originated as a result of 'customer demand', but also one that we consider is genuinely required by students of IR who generally (and rightly) complain that our discipline has become too ahistorical, too self-referential and generally lacking in 'roots'. It emerged from an eponymous module at the University of Kent that was taught by Andrew Williams (who now teaches at the University of St Andrews), Simon Rofe (who now teaches at the School of Oriental and African Studies, University of London) and Amelia Hadfield (who now teaches at the Vrije Universiteit Brussels). It was a very successful module in terms of the numbers of students who were taught – over three hundred a year for a good half-dozen years. Many of the ideas generated by the feedback we received from those students.

What we have tried to do, therefore, is to take a very different approach to most authors who have written books for IR novices who 'need some history'. This is not *histoire evénémentiel* – i.e. we have not provided a date-based encyclical, or indeed told many stories. What we have tried to do instead is to write interpretative essays arranged in *thematic* chapters that gather together the rich literature in a number of key areas. This literature includes both classic and contemporary texts and articles by both historians *and* IR scholars that we consider take historical method seriously enough to pass muster. We had lively discussions about which themes needed to be so treated, and the final choice (given the tremendous range available) was inevitably somewhat arbitrary. We hope that those themes chosen – war, peace, sovereignty, empire, international organization and identity – are sufficiently all-embracing as to give plenty of food for thought. To introduce readers of all stripes to the rationale of the text, we have prefaced these themes with a chapter on how IR and 'history', in its various guises, may be said to have a *terrain d'entente*: a common series of areas where both disciplines operate complementarily to produce a stronger, clearer understanding of the 'international' for both scholars of IR and those within history departments. The title, '"International" History and International Relations', therefore indicates our view that the 'international' in IR requires greater historical understanding. It is therefore *not* our intention to use 'international history' in the narrow sense of that term, though of course such literature is a very important part of our overall concern. We wish to push beyond the boundaries to a broader conception of the term 'international history' (IH).

This approach is inevitably subjective, but we do not mind that accusation. The essay is a format that we impose on our students, so why should we not use it ourselves? The main idea of the book, and the modules for which we hope it will be adopted, is to stimulate new avenues of approach for the many who remain baffled by the initially seemingly formless, even frontier-free, subject that is 'IR' and to generate debate about why we are right or wrong in placing emphases where we do by drawing on the insights of both historians and historically minded scholars of IR. If we subsequently see essays saying that 'Hadfield, Rofe and Williams have totally misjudged the importance of "X" or "Y" in their analysis of "Z"', we will be delighted (scholastically at any rate!), because a dialogue will have begun on the rather fretful relationship between IR and IH.

We have one advantage over the historian, who may feel that we are not doing a 'proper' historical job as regards the organizing principle of the text, an accusation that will wound slightly but is inevitable, [though it might be asked why IR courses tend to be more popular and are fuller than ones in 'straight' history?]. IR is a young subject, emerging only after World War I. As Oxford biographer Martin Ceadel has pointed out, the first real 'IR' text, Norman Angell's *The Great Illusion* (1910), came out at a time when there were few 'think tanks' on IR – the Carnegie Endowment for International Peace dates from the same year, as does the 'Round Table' group, who dedicated themselves to the promotion and study of the British Commonwealth, as does the Garton Foundation, a short-lived enterprise (Ceadel, 2009).

The lecturer or student who picks up this book may thus find that it responds to their needs in ways that are helpful or not, but our aim is to 'put the history back' into the initial (and later) stages of any degree programme in IR. It will not entirely satisfy historians, as we have had to elide and compact huge tracts of writing in many areas that we consider useful. Equally, it may not entirely satisfy IR theorists of all stripes, who will cavil at apparent omissions of undoubtedly brilliant insights into this or that aspect of the field. Drawing on both traditional and eclectic sources, our main mining has been done in the academic historical literature, including a few populist works, and (where appropriate) non-standard sources including works of literature, encouraged by Amelia Hadfield's own work on national culture and foreign policy. To understand, say, how naval warfare has been embedded into the British national consciousness, ignoring the novels of Patrick O'Brien or

C. S. Forester would be madness, as would that of the war poets for our under-standing of World War I.

One of the often-perceived problems of the social sciences is their lack of histori-cal depth. This is even more so with the social science that we call 'International Relations' – its proponents are less than clear about the need to acknowledge its historical working background so necessary for self-doubt and reflection. Until the end of the Cold War, many IR scholars acted as though history's cycles were somehow given, that the then presence of an immutable global system governed by the American–Soviet relationship meant that any 'history' had to explain only how it had arrived at that point. Texts that made sense of the apparent balance of power, the use of material force to maintain it, the foreign policy and security dilemmas it produced, and the high stakes created by nuclear weapons, were thus essential first stops on any IR101 course; as were the seminal realist foundation established by E. H. Carr's *The Twenty Years' Crisis, 1919–1939* (Carr, 1939) to the decision-making axioms of H. J. Morgenthau's *Politics Among Nations* (Morgenthau, 1948), Robert Jervis's books on perception and misperception, to the subsequent structural realist commentaries on the constraints imposed by the system like Kenneth Waltz's *Man, the State and War* (Waltz, 1959) or the administrative con-straints of imposed by bureaucratic structures in Graham Allison's 'Essence of Decision: Explaining the Cuban Missile Crisis' (Allison, 1971).

While all such texts (largely realist in pedigree) have their merits, an in-depth, nuanced history of the international system and its various iteration was sadly lacking, which led to some very strange attitudes to the past which are still evident, especially in the IR academy in the United States. Firmly allied with the deductivist merits of testing hypotheses against 'evidence' rather than an episte-mology based on verifying the emergence of political 'facts' from specific historical context, a clear attitude to the conscious use of history to shed light on broader historical patterns and thereby produce a firmer understanding of national interests cultural attitudes and decision-making was largely lacking.

Instead, axioms of political philosophy and 'classical theories of IR' were either subjected to deductive methodologies or awkwardly subsumed into various 'inter-paradigm debates' (Dougherty and Pfaltzgraff, 1971). History, and even the history of international relations, was relegated to a largely supportive area of study. Whilst explaining the flaws of past decision-making (e.g. Chamberlain's appeasement of Hitler or the 'failure' of the League of Nations) were favourite topics, there was little emphasis on the debates about these 'lessons' of history.

Contrast such conservative attitudes to the contemporary high praise lavished on interwar history revisionists like historian Niall Ferguson, who may have elicited howls of protest due to his very committed and controversial stance on some issues, but for us represents a very welcome development. It is to be doubted that he would have had much success had he published twenty years earlier; it is generally in times of major change and upheaval, like the present, that such histori-cal iconoclasm can have its just reward. Since 1991, considerable light and air has been let into the historical vacuum that was 1980s IR. There has also been a resurgence in what is often called 'normative' theory, not just moral philosophy, but also such esoteric areas as 'bio-politics', which in effect resurrect much older historical debates about the relationships between states and individuals, and individuals with each other. 'Classical' IR theory has been relaunched, often through such historical / legal frameworks as the 'English School' (Dunne, 1998), but also in the form of intellectual biographies (good examples are Ashworth, 1999; Ceadel, 2009). World history, and even 'detail' history, has made big inroads into IR conferences, not only through such subsections of the British International Studies Association as the British International History Group, but also through transatlantic cooperation, encouraging many more to think about what the *Annales* would have called '*les forces profondes*' (Ferguson, 2008; Lebow, 2008). It is nonetheless true that a CV loaded with history articles or political theory will meet with a frosty reception in most American IR departments, where the behaviourist revolution of the 1970s has never stopped. History may have made an emphatic comeback in the UK in IR departments, but not yet in the USA (Hadfield and Hudson, 2012).

As many historians have pointed out, it depends *what* you are looking for in order to determine what you find or think you have found. The dangers of what C. Wright Mills called a 'trans-historical straight jacket' (Wright-Mills, 1959, quoted by Skinner, 1985: 3) is particularly evident in many kinds of historical (and sociological) writing. To find, for example, evidence of 'class warfare' or the 'dominance of elites' as the driving force of history is very seductive but fundamentally flawed. In an excellent introductory historical text to the twentieth century, Richard Vinen points out that '[m]ost educated Europeans or North Americans probably know more about the couple of dozen people who lived around Gordon Square in Bloomsbury in the first decade of the twentieth century than they do about the whole population of, say, Serbia during the same period' (Vinen, 2002: 13).

This micro-focus on details of history sees 'agency', the particular role of individual actors and groups, even nations, as much more important than what the French historian Pierre Renouvin called '*les forces profondes*'. As the social theorist Quentin Skinner puts it, the French *Annales* school of historians were reacting against the 1930s prevailing 'cult of the detail ... distinguished above all by a view of human experience in which the individual agent and individual occurrence cease to be the central elements in social explanation ... it follows that the historians' time cannot be that of the linear narrative and his interest cannot be limited by the merely political' (Skinner, 1985: 180).

So history gives us a series of alternative explanations for everything; it cannot be strait-jacketed. That replicates exactly the *Zeitgeist* of the first decade of the twenty-first century. In time-honoured Chinese formulation, crisis gives us danger and opportunity; or, as per Antonio Gramsci's equally well-known maxim, 'History is at once freedom and necessity' (1971: 782). It is one of the underlying homilies of this book that contemporary IR must not only embrace the challenges of uncertainty through a retreat into clerical obscurantism, but also through a necessary exploration of the many diverse interpretations that the study of history opens up to us all.

The chapters in this book are therefore essays in the sense that we do not claim that the understanding of history we will present is the only possible one. We may not quite take the view, as Hilaire Belloc put it, that 'History is a matter of flair rather than of facts', but the 'ability to feel [oneself] into the past' is one that we feel to be an essential factor in and for IR training. Belloc's intellectual itinerary illustrates that his formulation can also lead to obscurantism of a different sort – in the case of Belloc and his associates, like Cecil and G. K. Chesterton, it led to some inspired observations about Western civilization but also, it must be said, to a repugnant anti-Semitism (Wilson, 1998: 13). However, we do believe that the essential element that is often missing in much of IR and is mainly to be found in the study of history is the sheer excitement of discovering multiple layers of meaning and action that need no mediating 'theory' or cleric to unwrap.

Each of these essays is thus unashamedly a personal and collective meditation on evidence that we have explored in archives, biographies and histories spanning many centuries. They are intended not to provide definitive answers to any of the issues raised, but rather to stimulate undergraduate students of IR to undertake the same kind of legwork that we have. As examined in Chapter 1, the 'cardinal concepts' around which this book is organized each give examples of the depth of historical circumstance by which key ideas are constructed over time into both political practice and cultural attitudes. IR, however, has a tendency to regard concepts like war, peace and sovereignty merely as organizing or attitudinal *categories* of behaviour rather than vastly challenging multi-layered social concepts. Simply because they exist in crystallized form as a 'self-evident' concept, or even a historical 'fact', does not mean they should be treated as unchanging abstract categories. Thus, to read history as merely the background leitmotiv of IR textbooks is to miss out on one of life's great adventures. We will, where we can, give a series of different questions and tentative answers which historians, and historically minded scholars of IR (of which there are many since 1991 or so), should find useful. Nonetheless we do not pretend to be all-encompassing in our analysis and in the sources used (to do so would be impossible), but rather to stimulate debates from seminars to bars, wherever IR is taught. (Note: Some of the chapters use the expression 'q.v.' to indicate where a concept is used elsewhere in the book.)

Chapter 1 will primarily look at the extensive literature that exists to explain how the approaches taken by historians regarding the nature of history, and what constitutes 'historical enquiry', vary greatly from those taken by students of IR. After investigating both gaps and overlaps between the methods of historical enquiry and those of political science, the chapter concludes by examining the various schools of thought within the history profession – especially 'diplomatic', 'international', 'global' and 'transnational' schools – that presently have much to teach the IR profession.

Chapter 2, 'War', looks at some of the incredibly rich historical literature on the causes, waging and consequences of war from the Roman Empire to the end of the modern era. It inevitably puts particular stress on the major conflicts of the twentieth century but aspires to show the antecedents in a more detailed light than is usually the case in IR textbooks. It also aims to show that war is as much a cultural as a military phenomenon, and one where we often refer to cultural concepts as 'honour' without fully realizing to what we allude. As with other chapters, there is some reference to the 'classical' IR literature to show how some scholars have demonstrated a keen historical imagination.

'Peace' (Chapter 3) is intended to complement the previous chapter and build on it by looking at some of the vast historical literature on the subject. It therefore seeks to examine peace in its own right while acknowledging the almost symbiotic overlap with 'war'. The chapter covers a broad swath of historical time since the seventeenth century, questioning notions of 'peacetime' from 'wartime' and what 'peace' really means for students and scholars of IR.

Chapter 4, on sovereignty, is a detailed, though non-exhaustive, overview of sovereignty, as both a political attribute and a legal status of the state. A thorough understanding of sovereignty is key to grasping not only the particularities of state behaviour in IR, but appreciating the driving force of much European and international history. The chapter thus surveys classical Roman and Greek interpretations through medieval, premodern and contemporary understandings to better appreciate the uneasy balance between its political and legal facets.

Chapter 5, 'Empire', again goes back to antiquity to examine the important legacy of Greece, Rome and other ancient empires in forming our historical imagination, one that has great importance for how we look at more recent imperial ventures. These include not only the great intercontinental European empires of the nineteenth and twentieth centuries, but also those of Soviet Russia and Nazi Germany and what are often referred to as the American and even European 'empires'.

Chapter 6, on 'International organization' (IO), examines an important liberal corollary to the political formations of the previous chapter. Current IR obsessions about 'humanitarian intervention' (for example) mean we need to look much more carefully than we do at the antecedents, institutional and normative, of current practices. The attempt here is to give a fuller overview of the historical literature on IO to better explain the current concerns of international society.

'Identity', Chapter 7, examines this most frustratingly fluid social and political category and its ubiquitously applicable attributes as a form of social and political analysis. Surveying both historical and contemporary definitions, the chapter examines how identity has operated in both history and IR, as a concept, a category and a legitimating principle.

# CHAPTER 1

# History and international relations

## Contrasts and comparisons

> The studious examination of the past in the greatest of detail does not teach you much about the mind of History; it only gives you the illusion of understanding it.
>
> (Taleb, 2007: 11)

> When it comes to understanding the past, historians are the acknowledged experts. But when it comes to understanding *how we understand the past*, there are no experts.
>
> (Martin, 1993: 31)

## INTRODUCTION

The central task of this book is to show how the discipline of history can be of cardinal use to the student of international relations (IR). While many IR scholars know they 'ought to take history seriously', they are also loath to do so. Are not historians prone to studying 'what one [foreign office] clerk said to another?' or to looking at extremely narrow areas of a state's activities, such as how Lord Lansdowne (British Foreign Secretary, 1900–1905) helped negotiate the Anglo-French Entente Cordiale in 1904 or how Sir Edward Grey (British Foreign Secretary, 1905–1916) got Britain involved in World War I? Such attention to detail has the effect on many IR scholars of inducing enormous self-doubt or overweening arrogance and disdain in equal measure. How could anyone *possibly* be interested in such ephemera when we have such huge problems as 'agency and structure' or 'hegemony' to worry about? Many IR colleagues would complain that not only was all that history 'a very long time ago', but they would also be unclear as to how or why we should care about it. So many of the judgements made by IR scholars rest squarely on the giant shoulders of diplomatic international historians like F. H. Hinsley and countless others who did the spade work in the archives so that they might draw their broad conclusions, and even founded entire theoretical dynasties on such 'obscure' work.

Acknowledging IR's debt to international history is a rarity. The great classical realist scholar Hans Morgenthau never denied his immense debt to his international and diplomatic historian colleagues. As we will see below, the 'English School' of IR theorists were either primarily historians (Herbert Butterfield being maybe the best example; see Dunne, 1998) or were overtly beholden unto them. So there should not be any problem with admitting historians into departments of IR, or for historians to accept those who (sometimes) play fast and loose with their scholarship to draw 'big picture' conclusions. This chapter illustrates how close the various schools of history that deal with the 'international' are to the key concerns of scholars of IR. After a study of 'diplomatic' and 'international' history, it shows that with recent developments like 'world' and 'transnational' history we are now beginning to acknowledge each other's presence in a less mutually hostile way and accept the reality of a cross-fertilization of what should never have been divided – history and IR.

## HISTORY UNCOVERED

First, a brief word about history itself. As we said in the Introduction, history comprises both a chronology of past events and a scholarly method of enquiry as to the nature of those past events. Historical enquiry itself has something of a 'history'. Commentators upon history are almost as venerable as the very events themselves. Over time they have taken various guises, depending on their role in recording or interpreting past events, from scribes and philosophers, to emissaries, politicians and professional historians. Our study recognizes nineteenth-century German historicism as dating the emergence of professional scholarly enquiry. This school included eminent philosophers and historians (including Michelet, Burckhardt and Fustel) who argued that history's purpose was to 'strive to understand each age in its own terms' and to bend both scholarship and imagination to 'the task of bringing the past back to life – or *resurrecting* it' (Tosh, 2009: 7). The Berlin university professor Leopold von Ranke (1795–1886) was foremost in the pantheon of historians seeking accuracy, description and completeness to explain, but also to thoroughly *understand* all aspects of a given historical event. Understanding, as in a high empathetic connection with past occurrences, loosely translated from German as *verstehen*, remains a key (if slightly antiquated principle) of contemporary historical enquiry.

Two things separate Ranke from later generations. First was Ranke's belief in the historian's overall ability to uncover history 'as it really was' (*Wie es eigentlich gewesen [ist]*), by believing that historical material comprised both verifiable and objective 'facts'. Second was his refusal to extend historical enquiry to the service of politics. His central criticism of earlier historians (and which applies to a swath who followed) was 'that they were diverted from the real task by the desire to preach, or to give lessons in statecraft ... in pursuing immediate goals they obscured the true wisdom to be derived from historical study' (Tosh, 2009: 8).

E. H. Carr's seminal work of 1961, *What is History?*, represents a watershed of early twentieth-century enquiry. In it, Carr suggested simply that no fact can be entirely value-free; it is always filtered through the interpretive forces of the original epoch, and again by the biases of the contemporary historian (Carr, 1961). A robust rejection of such relativist perspectives (i.e. that history is a product of its own time) then followed with G.R. Elton's 1967 *The Practice of History*, which not only championed the central role of objective truth about past events but argued that official documentary records (rather than other varied sources) comprised the best possible source of data. Philosopher Michael Oakeshott presaged the postmodernist wave that would shake historical enquiry to its foundations, and turned the tables once again by arguing not only the 'absolute impossibility of deriving from history any generalization of the kind which belong to a social science' (Oakeshott, 1990, quoted in Levy, 1997: 24), but criticizing any attempt at remaining objective in the face of historical 'facts'. From this perspective, any attempt to study or 'write' history was not only deeply interpretive but an exercise in remaking it once again from a different perspective, a process that ultimately renders history as 'a historian's experience' rather than something objectively verifiable (Oakeshott, 1990: 99, quoted in Levy, 1997: 26). Yet for many, total relativism was frivolous at best and dangerous at worst. Deconstructive trends would, in the eyes of Raphael Samuel, reduce history to fanciful storytelling, 'an invention, or fiction, of historians themselves' (in Evans, 1997: 7).

For those at either end of this broad and argumentative objectivist–relativist spectrum, the goal is ultimately still one of understanding the forces that explain events. This exercise is now a balancing act between the conscious cultivation of the mindset of a given historical era to accurately understand both the opportunities and constraints entailed in a given circumstance and an awareness that such cultivation prejudices both the historian's objectivity and end results.

Other key features mark out contemporary historical enquiry; Tosh, for example, suggests three principles that could guide such enquiry. First, the recognition of implicit *difference* created by the passage of time between the present day and the era under investigation. Thus one may identify the past, but avoid identifying *with* it to prevent 'the unthinking assumption that people in the past behaved and thought as we do ... the difference is one of mentality: earlier generations had different values, priorities, fears and hopes from our own' (Tosh, 2009: 9). Second, the *context* or accompanying information surrounding a given event or actor, which requires a rigorous effort on the part of the historian to place events accurately in their historical settings. Third, *process*, in which singular events – generally, the key focus of historians – are also appreciated as part of a wider chronological fabric. Developing a point first made by Fernand Braudel, Tosh suggests that this process is the 'relationship between events over time which endows them with more significance than if they were viewed in isolation' (Tosh, 2009: 11).

The point of this chapter is not to suggest that historical enquiry is itself a perfect scholarly art, or that the various generations of historical enquiry represent increasingly refined approaches. Historical enquiry is in some sense as precarious as political science, for two reasons. First, like political science, historical enquiry is a conglomerate discipline, one which has 'profited immeasurably from the invasions of neighbouring disciplines' including sociology, psychology, economics, anthropology and more (Evans, 1997: 8). Second, history – like political science – is in the business of selection and interpretation of past events (sometimes for present expediencies). As Braudel argued, 'All historical work is concerned with breaking down time past, choosing among its chronological realities according to more or less conscious preferences and exclusions' (Braudel, 1980: 27). Historical enquiry is thus selective in both the disciplines from which it can choose its raw material and the methodology by which it can choose to fashion its tools. In political science, however, the prime error is the ongoing failure to recognize difference, context or process. Its tendency instead is to create generalizations that compress past and present, rendering them similar in outlook; to remove or neglect key contextual details as extraneous; to see connecting dynamics merely from the requirement to discern broad and repeating patterns.

The 'cardinal concepts' around which this book is organized give examples of the depth of historical circumstance by which key ideas are fashioned across the generations into both political practice and attitudes. IR, however, has a tendency to regard concepts like war, peace and sovereignty as organizing or attitudinal *categories* of behaviour rather than multi-layered social concepts. Simply because they exist in crystallized form as concepts does not mean they should be treated as unchanging abstract categories.

## THE ORIGINS AND KEY CONCEPTS OF IR

From a disciplinary perspective, World War I can be understood as the seminal event of the twentieth century. In its wake emerged a clear need to determine both the causes of war and the methods of ensuring peace, major avenues of enquiry which up until 1919 had been tackled in the form of broad investigations into political history primarily by European political historians. 1919 saw the beginnings of a disciplinary approach, both the broad contours of European and American political science, and the more specific, theory-based approaches later to be referred to as international relations theory. IR as a specific subset of international politics was formally institutionalized in 1919 with the founding of the world's first Department of International Politics at the University of Aberystwyth, in Wales, with the intent of studying (and thus preventing) the source of political conflicts. The establishment of the Woodrow Wilson Chair of International Relations at Aberystwyth was thus the first step towards ensuring IR theory permanence, if not prominence, in transatlantic studies of international politics. Box 1.1 outlines in abbreviated fashion the paradigmatic tensions that accompanied the development of IR theories, grouped first into the four major paradigmatic debates. Suffice it to say that the majority of this book represents a detailed examination of the historicist ethos that largely informed the Second Great Debate.

## BOX 1.1 THE GREAT DEBATES IN INTERNATIONAL RELATIONS

### First Great Debate: realism versus idealism (1930s–1940s)

In attempting to deal with the rising threat of a rearmed, renationalized Germany, realist scholars pointed to the permanent requirement of states to safe-guard their own security and guarantee their survival arising from the immutably anarchic nature of international politics. Idealists, however, having placed their faith in the League of Nations emerging from the wreckage of World War I, felt that some forms of intrastate cooperation could still be rendered workable.

### Second Great Debate: the role of behaviourism in IR theory (post-World War II)

The Second Great Debate pitted vying methodologies against each other. Scholars who viewed IR as a political science remained committed to the scientific method in deploying hypotheses, quantitative methodologies and the requirement to test evidence to look both for generalizations and falsifying examples in an attempt to render IR a more predictable method of explaining state behaviour. Historicists keen on understanding the more detailed, bottom-up nuances dismissed 'scientific' approaches in favour of a historicist/interpretative approach by which the true origins and motivations of behaviour could be legitimately discerned.

### The 'Third' Inter-paradigm Debate

The inter-paradigm debate that arose in the 1980s and 1990s involved a pro-tracted debate between a wide variety of realist and liberal/institutionalist schools of thought as well as a range of emerging radical, poststructural IR theories.

### The Fourth Great Debate (1988)

Where the Second Great Debate featured spats over methodology, arguments over suitable epistemologies characterized the Fourth Great Debate, pitting ratio-nalist positivist theories against reflectivist post-positivist IR theories.

## ■ THE 'RAW MATERIAL' OF IR

The 'raw material' upon which IR has traditionally drawn is political history, which in a broad sense entails the array of conflictual and cooperative forces arising within the international and domestic spheres from varied sources. To be clear, history represents both the occurrences that took place in the past, and the method of historical enquiry, which is the analysis of that past in the research and writing of historians (Tosh, 2009: xviiii).

Historians often refer to political history as 'diplomatic history' (about which, more below), while political scientists refer to the same area as 'international politics', including the development of IR theory. This distinction, however, is not as profound as it may seem. As Stephen Haber, David Kennedy and Stephen Krasner suggest:

> Historians who study diplomatic history and political scientists who study international politics, despite some genuine differences, have always been engaged in a similar enterprise … What is most notable about diplomatic history and international relations theory are not their differences, but their similarities with regard to subject matter, and in the end, commitment to objective evidence.
>
> (Haber, Kennedy and Krasner, 1997: 34)

The development of political science and key aspects of IR theory owes much to the material uncovered and structured by diplomatic historians. Haber, Kennedy and Krasner have all accepted they are 'brothers under the skin' (Haber, Kennedy and Krasner, 1997). Other IR scholars that have successfully bridged the gap include Peter Katzenstein and J. G. Ruggie. The majority of contemporary diplomatic historians in turn have worked in the service of some policy agenda. American historians, in particular, 'emerged to shoulder the burden of convincing Americans that they had a stake in the Great War, and beyond it, in the long-term operation of the international system' (Haber, Kennedy and Krasner, 1997: 38), while anti-Vietnam and Cold War debates have animated subsequent diplomatic history. The post-Cold War era, however, suggests that diplomatic history has largely come to an end. In its place are a series of different types of history (as mentioned above), and the swath of political science approaches (comparative politics, foreign policy analysis, IR theory, etc.), whose appreciation and treatment of history remains imperfect. However, this apparent similarity of subject matter should be treated with some care; it does not assume an automatic foundation upon which to build. While both sides draw upon the same raw material, history serves three rather different purposes in terms of what it is explaining, the perception of this feature, and the method of its use.

First, the key feature to be explained (the 'what') are generally *singular events* in the history of a person or society; traditional historical research is dedicated to finding the historical data to explain an event in terms of its causes and the changes produced. They are not usually however, looking at a series of events. Political science, however, looks for cause and effect in terms of collective events that take the form of patterned behaviour.

Second, the key method of explanation (the 'how') for historians are factors that are wholly and utterly unique to the case at hand. Historians therefore focus on the particularist motivations explaining both human responses and societal changes. To explain a general principle of behaviour, political theorists instead look for broad connecting features by which many causes of change can be grouped together.

Third, with regards to the various tools employed, historians explain change by locating a specific, identifiable problem that suffered inattention or misinterpretation, and then assembling the necessary historical evidence to shed further light on the problem. Rather than the more rigorous theory-based methodologies employed in the social sciences, historians generally use multi-perspective or 'synoptic' judgements to determine the best method of integrating the problem within the available data. Historians seize on a particular dilemma and strive to make better sense of old and new evidence. Political theorists, however, stick to the key understanding and test the evidence *against* it, rather than attempting to find an understanding that 'best integrates the available evidence' (Haber, Kennedy and Krasner, 1997: 68).

From this perspective, the use of the same raw data by historians and political theorists alike is immaterial; differences over what history constitutes, its perceptions and its treatment are too dissimilar to be transcended and result in a profound and possibly permanent misfit between the two disciplines. From the historian's perspective, political theory is culpable of blind adherence to top-down methodologies that permit only 'highly restrictive assumptions without any empirical data' (Haber, Kennedy and Krasner, 1997: 35), looking solely for new connections and relationships. Here, historical material is either completely ignored or used in a sanitized manner that ignores its own context, the perceptions of those who have previously engaged with it, and which fails to verify its own validity as a source. Thus, while employing the primary material of history to construct and test causal claims, the heavy lifting goes into theory-building, not the analysis of the primary data. From the historian's point of view, 'parsimony postpones more than it provides'; in other words, elegant theory-building is fruitless if it requires a slapdash treatment of the building blocks (Gaddis, 1986: 99).

The outcome is an unpleasant misfit in which political scientists are twice guilty. First, when extracting data from original sources, they ignore the complex context that accompanies a given set of historical facts. Second, when using 'facts' as already treated and theorized by a given historian, they tend to forget that such primary data has already been selected and interpreted by a historian to answer the questions of historical enquiry, which may be wholly unrelated to the endeavour of political scientists. Thus, political scientists are ill placed to discern causal evidence of testable, patterned political behaviour when their basic data has been preselected to reveal the significance of historical change and human agency in a synoptic method (Schroeder, 1997: 71). The result is one of inaccuracy and distortion, misunderstanding and bias.

Historians, too, could benefit from a less parochial attitude to their own methods. G. M. Trevelyan exemplifies an early example of an enduring suspicion among historians in making generalizations (either quantitatively or qualitatively), arguing that 'The generalizations which are the stock-in-trade of the social historian must necessarily be based on a small number of particular instances ... but which cannot be the whole of the complicated truth' (Trevelyan, 1944: viii). As Gordon Craig has similarly argued, historians need to overcome both their 'congenital mistrust of theory' and their 'insistence upon the uniqueness of the historical event', looking to political science for evidence that one can with some confidence 'treat unique cases as members of a class or type of phenomenon ... discover correlations among different variables that may have causal significance' (Craig, cited by George, 1997: 47).

## FORM AND CONTENT

The most fundamental difference between IR theorists and historians lies in the basic method of organizing the raw material into a particular structure or form. In simple terms, traditional IR theorists (particularly from the US school) adhere to top-down, or deductive, methods to explain broad structures and processes. This approach applies to IR's key theories – realism, liberalism and (to a lesser extent) constructivism – and allows mainstream analysts to do three things. First, they examine the international structure in terms of generalizations; this in turn encourages them as look at states as abstract, unproblematic 'units', rather than as differentiated or detailed national societies. Finally, IR theorists look for the common features that characterize all 'state units' and their behaviour within the international structure.

Referred to as *nomothetic*, this top-down method allows political theorists to begin their analysis with a simple but strong generalization that can characterize all states and their behaviour (e.g. all states engage in confrontational behaviour when threatened; all states attempt to maximize their power and status; democracies do not war against each other). In pursuit of their own hypothesis, political theorists deductively test specific data against a given generalization to see whether it holds and why. Employed in mainstream political science for many years, this approach has some key virtues, including clarity, simplicity and possibly predictability.

Historians, however, generally examine past occurrences of history literally from the ground up, using bottom-up or inductive methods to assemble the data in its specificity. Its modus operandi is the *ideographic*: a method entailing the search for and examination of historical material associated with a singular event in order to understand that event as precisely as possible. Jack Levy argues that these different approaches result in two wholly difference disciplinary identities:

> Historians describe, explain, and interpret individual events or a temporally bounded series of events, whereas political scientists generalize about the relationships between variables and construct lawlike statements about social behaviour.
>
> (Levy, 1997: 22)

This difference, of course, informs the approach to the *content*. While political scientists look for regularities and patterns, historians focus on the 'richness of detail and scrupulous fidelity to the individual facts unearthed' (Schroeder, 1997: 65). Braudel clarified the implications of this distinction as a 'lively distrust' on the part of traditional historians who examine the history of single events with political history, which examines the drama of 'great events' (Braudel, 1980: 28).

The nomothetic approach common to political science data places within a pre-established conceptual framework, to see how well it proves (or disproves) a given 'law' or lawlike generality. Political scientists seek to answer how well data then explains a given generality. The ideographic approach employed by historians may well use the same historical data but it operates as building blocks by which to reconstruct a particular event or situation. Here, data does not *explain* external dynamics, but is the key to *understanding* as accurately as possible the precise forces at work in producing a past outcome. This high degree of understanding requires historians to subsume themselves within the data (rather than transcend it via abstraction) to the extent that they can quite literally empathize with past perspectives and forces. This allows them to gain the deepest possible connection with the event or personality under investigation, the process known as *Verstehen* (described page 8). Political theorists (and social scientists more broadly) are thus:

> more likely to emphasize general explanations of social phenomena, while the historian is more likely to emphasize particularistic, unique features of individual episodes of social phenomena.
>
> (Bueno de Mesquita, quoted by Levy, 1997: 24)

## BOX 1.2 HELPFUL DEFINITIONS

**Ideographic:** particularistic, the unique, the individual

**Nomothetic:** the general, the recurrent, the universal

## SIMILARITIES

The problem with these supposed differences between the two disciplines are the simplistic, unproblematic assumptions about the approach to knowledge (epistemology) and tools (methodology) employed by both political scientists and historians. First, there are analysts on both sides who have for years made use of perspectives and tools beyond the mainstream of their own school. Historians necessarily make use of inference as a result of absent data, while IR theorists (especially in European and British schools) have a good tradition of inductive methods and culturalist epistemologies. Indeed, if we take the top-down *versus* bottom-up perspective too far, we not only risk them turning into caricatures but assume that such grave differences will keep both sides permanently at odds – denying history the ability to obtain the methodological rigour of political science while assuming (perhaps even encouraging) political scientists to mistreat historical material.

A more nuanced approach suggests that political scientists and historians actually have three key aspects in common. First, *both* disciplines are looking for *causes* (rather than merely change). Indeed, it is history that has the greatest heritage in treating causes as the central imperative. As Carr himself famously argued in his seminal work *What is History?*, 'The study of history is a study of causes' (Carr, 1961: 81). From this, we can move to Carr's observation that:

> historians look for much the same things political scientists seek – clear assignable *causes* resting on evidence subject to intersubjective test and verification and capable of supporting broad, significant generalization and patterns.
>
> (Carr, 1961: 67, emphasis in original)

Second, in terms of understanding patterns, the nomothetic–ideographic distinction is a rudimentary reference point as to the major forms of separation between the two sides. It cannot denote the complex overlaps of subject matter and methodology that characterize both sides. The political scientist clearly relies on specificities and particularities available through historical data in their search for regularities and patterns. Likewise, the historian is indebted to the broad patterns that inevitably characterize the very details and unique characteristics under examination. In both approaches, therefore, one finds that 'broad patterns become clear only through a mastery of the details … the details are never there for their own sake, but for the sake of the patterns, the turning points, and causes they reveal and the broad interpretations and theses they undergird' (Schroeder, 1997: 65–66). Thus, while 'the primary goal of historians is to explain the particular, but they often do so with resort to the general', increasing amounts of political theory (for instance, neoclassical realism, see Hadfield 2010) explain the general by making specific use of the particular' (Levy, 1997: 25–26).

This uncouples the easy opposition between nomothetic and ideographic approaches, a division that emerged from the practices of German philosophers in the nineteenth century who sought to separate the study of history from the natural sciences. To be sure, this distinction does exist, and is a helpful starting point in grasping the basic differences between top-down and bottom-up methodologies, but it is not an unbending categoric division between the approaches of political science or history. Economic, social and demographic history all draw on quantitative data in a way that makes little or no use of individuated detail, but instead employs theories and hypotheses in testing generalities. The theory-oriented approaches of the French Annales school is a good example of historians who eschew the view of history as a simple narrative and use social science methodologies to explain specific historical phenomena under the deductive 'covering-law model'. Further, theory-building is as prevalent among historians as it is among political scientists; and that 'historians' ideographic orientation does not necessarily imply that they are atheoretical in their interpretation of singular events' (Levy, 1997: 25). Equally compelling is the increase of nomothetic international history in the late twentieth century in which leading historians use historical material to 'develop hypotheses, assign particular causes for events and developments, and establish general patterns' (Schroeder, 1997: 66).

Historical writing on political topics as wide-ranging as revolutions, imperialism, foreign policy, the origins and outcomes of the world wars and the Cold War all explain their outcomes in terms of discernible patterns and generalizations, and do in terms of generalizations about political behaviour. Overlaps regarding methodology now feature to increase the interdisciplinary dialogue. For instance, the increased use of a process tracing as a 'technique of historical explanation' has helped political scientists use ideographic data more effectively. As George explains,

> Political scientists who undertake to do historical case studies of a phenomenon such as deterrence in order to develop generic knowledge of it typically convert a historical explanation into an analytical one couched in theoretically useful variables.
>
> (George, 1997: 47–48)

Such 'conversions' represent the first step to genuine interdisciplinary bridge-building. Case studies take such developments even further, and symbolize a burgeoning interest in political theorists to appreciate both the historical content of a given episode and the need for its appropriate treatment when 'rendered' in political theory terms. The ultimate outcome may be a form of mid-range theorizing (something endlessly attempted in a number of IR's own subfields) in which 'conditional generalizations' are used as a method of continuing to explain patterns in behaviour while exercising a critical eye as to the visible dependence of such patterns upon key specificities and ungovernable factors. At this point, it is sufficient to observe that history and political science are not simply differentiated as to who 'does theory' and who does not. The outputs of both sides over the past fifty years are voluminous and sophisticated enough to demonstrate that they simply make use of history in different ways: 'Political scientists build general theories and test them, whereas historians use theory – or a set of theories – primarily to structure their interpretations of particular events' (Levy, 1997: 32). What is at issue is the lack of historical content in the theory of political scientists and that this gap is generally ongoing and largely unchallenged.

## THE FINAL BRIDGE

Both sides, as noted, have undergone significant twentieth-century shifts in terms of their broad worldview (ontology) and the appropriate criteria for looking at it. The 'ideational turn' has added values, norms and identities to IR's methodological arsenal, contributing inter-subjective qualities of a given society as a valid method of explaining (albeit only partially) political behaviour. This does not equate with full-blown *verstehen* as found in history; but it does represent an appreciably wider method of explaining general (and specific) forces, is now part of the IR toolbox alongside traditional theory-building and its customary focus on analytical coherence.

History enquiry, too, has undergone a 'linguistic turn', which can be traced back to Carr's observation of history as an 'unending dialogue between the past and the present' (Carr, 1961: 62). 'From Carr's perspective, all historical enquiry represents an interwoven series of events and perspectives in which 'the present intrudes on the reconstruction of the past' (Tosh, 2009: xii). The implications of Carr's 'unending dialogue' have transformed the methods and disciplinary boundaries of history; they have also had a profound impact in the social sciences, ushering in anxieties about the use of relativism, postmodernism and the disappearance of the subject/object distinction. The result for contemporary historians has been a healthy profusion of myriad strands of enquiry: social, cultural, urban, gender history among others, as well as area-based histories, all of which arose during the last half of the twentieth century.

The one exception to this disciplinary blossoming is diplomatic history, which has remained relatively isolated from methodological trends. As Levy argues,

> diplomatic history … has been consistent in its insistence on the empirical validation of its interpretations and in the utility of narratives and primary sources for that purpose. In important respects, it has also become more theoretical in the last couple of decades. Some historians are quite explicit about the analytical assumptions and theoretical models that guide their historical interpretations … Some historians are not only quite conversant with international relations theory or other social science theories, but have made important contributions to the theoretical literature, either by constructing theoretical generalizations or by contributing to debates on the methodology of international relations research.
>
> (Levy, 1997: 29)

Levy points to the work of Paul Schroeder (examined above), John Lewis Gaddis, Arno J. Mayer and Fritz Fischer as leading lights in interdisciplinary advances (Schroeder, 1997; Levy, 1997; Gaddis, 1986). In 'History, Science and the Study of IR' (in Woods, 1996), for example, Gaddis outlines how and why IR depends upon both the memory and methodology distilled from historical enquiry. Equally pertinent is the broader point made by Kavanagh in 'Why Political Science Needs History' (1991). Taken together, we find a quiet, contemporary current of scholars aware of the mutually reinforcing (and ultimately, indeed, co-constitutive) nature of history, political science and IR theory.

If we regard diplomatic history as the centerpiece for IR's raw material, the result is something of a perfect storm. Enlightened IR scholars have intersubjective tools at their disposal to explore ideographic forces, and a minority of historians have reinforced the theoretical backbone of diplomatic history, revealing the area to be highly conducive to both forms of analytic and narrative treatment. This is a good start, but it still does not equate to the overdue requirement for greater appreciation and use of history by IR scholars themselves. Whilst the perfect storm has yielded some shakeups, without a greater commitment to using history more frequently and more accurately in both its inbuilt assumptions, and its future theory-making, IR risks becoming becalmed on inconsequential seas.

This book forms part of this same commitment, namely to illustrate key features of internal and diplomatic history that are either misread by IR or overlooked entirely. The exercise is fundamental for IR theorists to better appreciate historical content in general and the specific implications of its use, particularly in terms of time and space (temporal and spatial), that constitute both history's singular events and its broader patterns. A second point – though not one continued in this text – is the visible requirement to develop a better method of integrating historical data into political theory. The question is not connected to how much or little historical data works to produce stronger or weaker hypotheses; that depends entirely on the overall objective of the research (though any approach that requires the complete elimination of key contextual and contingent features in service of an overarching hypothesis is to be avoided). The challenge is to recalibrate the contours of a 'generalization', requiring it to be a more flexible scope condition by becoming less universal and abstract and more conditional and inclusive. Indeed, the emphasis is upon the conditional. Conditional generalizations is the ideal middle ground in which the elegant simplicity of political hypotheses on war, peace, power, security, etc. are complemented by more detailed and contextualized understandings of these same features, as individual and recurrent forms of international history. Perhaps only in neoclassical realism has IR theory attempted such a challenge (Hadfield, 2010).

## DEFINING HISTORY, ITS FUNCTION AND POLITICAL/IR IMPLICATIONS

So methodological differences count for much, and will continue to do so. Political scientists (and IR theorists) concentrate on testing data against a given theory, while historians accumulate data to construct or support a thesis. But the manner of understanding history as the substantive driver of behavioural outcomes is shared by historians and political scientists alike. In both disciplines, *evidence* is the central feature in evaluating human or societal change, as well as broader generalizations about political behaviour. Diplomatic and international historians find their evidence in primary (usually archived) documents, while IR scholars are more wide-ranging in sourcing data. What ultimately renders both disciplines 'brothers under the skin' is that both require that claims – whether historical or theoretical – 'be justified by objective evidence' (Haber, Kennedy and Krasner, 1997: 43). How this interdisciplinary brotherhood can move forward will rest upon collaborative efforts in which political scientists renew their attention to the '*milieu et moment* that historians would bring to case studies', while historians can adapt any number of the analytical methods to strengthen their ability to conceptualize from gathered data (George, 1997: 47).

There are thus distinctive, but not irreconcilable, differences between history and political science. Carr's conclusions apply to both the existing chasm and the way across. His comment of 1953 suggested a gloomy prospect, with historians (and social scientists) 'balancing uneasily on the razor edge between the hazards of

TABLE 1.1

| Historian | Function of history | Implication for the discipline of history | Implication for political science |
|---|---|---|---|
| Ranke | To discover the unique, the particular | History must remain ideographic and not be forced to generalize. | There is an objective or 'authentic' knowledge of past events; history is the 'scientific' method by which to use detail-oriented investigation to uncover the causes of these events. |
| Carr | Interrelation of past and present | Historical enquiry changes over time in methods and priorities. | There is no objective or 'authentic' knowledge of past events; theorists are innately part of their own analysis. |
| Oakeshott | A relativistic mode of enquiry, history is simply a product of its own time | It is impossible to derive any comparisons or generalizations from history. | History 'is "made" by nobody save the historian'; interdisciplinary attempts are futile (Oakeshott, 1990: 26). |
| Stone | To reveal the contextual and the contingent | History is a discipline of context and provides snapshots of specific actors at a given time/place (Stone, 1991: 217–218). | The particularist features of actors, their time and place can likely be factored into broader analysis that uses such details to explain a conditional generality. |
| Levy | To explain the particular, if necessary, by resorting to the general | History can use theories to 'help explain and interpret behaviour in a particular case or a series or events that are temporally bounded' (Levy, 1997: 25). | History can be used in political science; all that separates the two sides is an emphasis on the particular use of concepts. |
| Tosh | Wide definitions, but accurate processes | Past denotes more than just current relevance. | History and subdisciplines are treated as open-ended applications. |

objective determinism and the bottomless pit of subjective relativity', asking only questions instead of providing answers (Carr, 1953: xiii). His later viewpoint, however, was more optimistic; namely, that both sides 'are engaged in different branches of the same study: the study of man and his environment' and, while the methods differ, both 'are united in the fundamental purpose of seeking to explain, and in the fundamental procedure of question and answer' (Carr, 1953: 80).

# DIPLOMATIC HISTORY

From the problems posed by the study of history in general and how it differs from the study of political science, we now turn to the subfields of how the 'international' has been understood by various groups of historians. This is important, as international relations is arguably not a 'subject'. It was, and it remains, a field of enquiry concerned with the large questions of war and peace, order, morality and justice, and contains several subfields such as foreign policy analysis and international political economy. Its intellectual taproots lie in history, law, geography and political theory. History can therefore claim to be both the central intelligence of the subject and, in Sir John Seeley's phrase, 'the school of statesmanship' (Wormell, 1980: chapter 4).

Diplomatic historians stood among the founders of international studies, and diplomatic history is a subfield of political history in the Thucydidean and Rankean tradition. Implicitly, for the most part it rested in the classical realist paradigm. Its axiom was anarchy. Its governing concepts were rationality, power and the state. Diplomatic historians set themselves two tasks – first, to understand how governing elites, in unitary states, generally free of popular forces, assessed risk, did the capabilities–goals analysis and constructed foreign policy; and second, to understand the behaviour of states and how they interacted with one another, i.e. statecraft. Great men ran the affairs of great powers and managed interstate conflict. Diplomatic history's issue areas were, therefore, essentially political and strategic, expressed in terms of security, national interest and great strategy. Its principal concerns were war and its origins, peace and its restoration, crises, alliance relationships and the sanctity of treaties. The sum of great power foreign policies constituted international relations, there being, therefore, no discrete international system. Governments dealt with other governments and scarcely at all with oppositions, or alternative, aspirant governments.

Diplomatic historians employed a methodology that rested on textual analysis of primary sources – manuscript and printed – preserved primarily in government archives. When bolstered by the record of public debate, in speeches, parliaments and the press, the archives were taken to reveal elite reasoning and state behaviour. Command of the archives, public and private, domestic and foreign, placing a premium on foreign language skills, identified the master craftsmen: Sir Charles Webster, William Langer and J. B. Duroselle, for example. Cumulation was determined more by the availability of primary sources (the opening of archives, often to serve political as much as scholarly purposes) than by puzzlement. Diplomatic historians wrote dense, analytical narratives chronologically, in a common vocabulary. They ranged over the historical record from classical times, and particularly from the Renaissance to what became their principal focus – the modern, industrialized, national security state. Historiography took on the familiar pattern of orthodoxy, revisionism and post-revisionism.

Diplomatic history gathered momentum in the late nineteenth century and flourished in the first half of the twentieth. World War I, total or not, but of unprecedented proportions and reach, required understanding – of its origins, causes, eruption, prolongation and consequences. So did the questions surrounding the peacemaking of 1919–1923. The 'War Guilt' clause of the Versailles Treaty, i.e. Article 231, written to justify the collection of reparations from Germany, stimulated scholarship, only to render much of it seemingly sterile by turning diplomatic history into a quasi-judicial process and historians into apologists and axe-grinders, waging scholarly war over war guilt. Luigi Albertini's monumental volumes marked the virtual end of the affair. The Nazi record, and that of imperial Japan, and the verdicts of Nuremberg and Tokyo, exempted World War II from a repetition. Orthodoxy, richly documented as the thirty-year rule became the norm, ruled. Revisionism in the 1960s, such as that attempted by A. J. P. Taylor, seemed eccentric, even perverse. The debate, such as it was, was short-lived. And diplomatic historians played an embarrassingly small role in the examination of the origins and course of the Cold War.

## INTERNATIONAL HISTORY

Diplomatic history continues to be written. Yet the term 'diplomatic history' has largely given way to the term 'international history'. It was not a case of diplomatic history ending in a particular decade and international history beginning, but rather, in the shadow of World War I, of the latter developing alongside the former and then, after World War II, rapidly outgrowing and displacing it. One can trace the process in several distinguished careers – those of Christopher Thorne, Fritz Fischer, Ernest May, Paul Kennedy and Donald C. Watt, for example. Self-examination and growth occurred in an environment that had turned hostile toward diplomatic history, in a history profession that was moving decisively in other directions. Diplomatic history was condemned as narrow, stagnant, impoverished, old-fashioned and ultimately irrelevant. The tides of historical scholarship were rising on other shores, the currents flowed in different channels, leaving diplomatic historians, derided as naive positivists, arid instrumentalists, lacking new frontiers of enquiry, to drown in their own deservedly obscure monographs. Social, economic, cultural, intellectual and new political historians scoffed at those who waited for the pendulum of relevance to swing back towards them. It never did.

International historians did not join frontally in the assault. Rather, they built on the considerable and enduring accomplishments of diplomatic history. The classical realist paradigm, maintaining a role for elites and agency and links with biography, had much to commend it, even as annalism and structural realism had their day. The state, being transformed conceptually, retained its centrality; its relations with other states and entities that were not states could not sensibly be relegated to the margins of enquiry. Politics and strategy, the security dilemma, held their relevance if not their primacy, assisted by a revival of military history. International historians played, therefore, a central role in the development of intelligence studies. Alternative, contending paradigms – idealist, progressive, radical, New Left and Marxist – had to be tested, inescapably, against classical realism. W. N. Medlicott, for example, in the introduction to his *Bismarck, Gladstone and the Concert of Europe* (1956), joined the realist–idealist debate. Diplomatic history's scrupulous empiricism and analytical narratives set standards that case-study writers did not emulate. Diplomatic history will always remind the international relations community not only of the relevance of statesmen, their beliefs, values, perceptions and information processing, but also that their understanding, the fruits of praxis, must be placed alongside the outpourings of theorists. After all, Woodrow Wilson, in his Fourteen Points, issued on 8 January 1918, set out the liberal interpretation of the causes of the Great War. Belatedly, political scientists are calling for 'Bringing the statesman back in' (Byman and Pollack, 2001).

From those foundations international historians selectively, even sceptically, found common ground with those who had flogged diplomatic history, i.e. principally economic, intellectual, cultural, new political and social historians (Joll, 1968; Cowling, 1971, 1975; Bentley, 1977), and with those who wrote business and institutional history. They also began to draw, equally selectively, even more sceptically, on the social sciences, principally economics, politics, anthropology, sociology, psychology and that intellectual conglomerate, international relations. The results are impressive, if uneven and controversial.

First, and providing a decisive normative foundation, there emerged what can be called a 'proto-Western' pan-European, North Atlantic and liberal consensus that war must be understood, its causes analysed, and alternatives (and even solutions) found for its consequences. This did not mean that war was necessarily seen as 'curable' – key 'realist' international historians like E. H. Carr (1939) and Henry Kissinger (1964) and political sociologist Raymond Aron (1962, 1966) were eloquent testimony to the belief that wars between states were inevitable, in a world characterized by a state of anarchy. Kissinger perhaps put it best:

> the attainment of peace is not as easy as the desire for it ... Those ages, which in retrospect seem most peaceful, were least in search of peace ... Whenever peace – conceived as the avoidance of war – has been the primary objective of a power or a group of powers, the international system has been at the mercy of the most ruthless member of the international community ... Stability, then, has commonly resulted not from a quest for peace but from a generally accepted legitimacy.
>
> (Kissinger, 1964: 1)

During and after World War II, Carr modified his previous view that cooperation between states was impossible, as he took his 'left turn' and became a strong supporter of the Soviet Union and advocated a generous settlement with Germany in his *Conditions of Peace* (1942) and *Nationalism and After* (1945), as well as the frankly pro-Soviet, the impressive *History of Soviet Russia* (1950–1978, 14 vols), which has been authoritatively praised and condemned in equal measure (with Isaac Deutscher, A. J. P. Taylor and Eric Hobsbawm in the 'pro' camp, and Robert Conquest, Richard Pipes and Hugh Trevor-Roper in the 'anti') – some sort of measure of greatness. Carr's importance to the study of international relations, sometimes crassly confined to a reading of *The Twenty Years' Crisis* (1939), has in recent years been recognized as immense, with a plethora of excellent biographies and collected essays (most notably by Haslam, 1999, 193; Jones, 1998; Cox, 2000). Maybe the most important lesson of Carr has been to confound the often watertight division between 'realism' and 'idealism' that was at one time seen to dominate the 'inter-paradigm debate' (Ashworth, 2002).

World War I provided the framework within which thinking was stimulated about the causes of war and its prevention in the future. Slavery was, in the nineteenth century, the great moral evil; war replaced it in the twentieth century.

International historians, liberal and others, began their subsequent reasoning about war principally with reflections on the causes and consequences of World War I. Risk-taking, loss of control, unanticipated consequences, multiple errors and unintentionality eventually elbowed aside war guilt as explanations of the origins of a war that was judged to be in the interests of none of the European protagonists. During and after the war, liberal history activists – E. D. Morel (1915), Goldsworthy Lowes Dickinson (1917, 1926) and Gilbert Murray (1928), for example – used history as a weapon to discredit those responsible for (and still conducting) the war, as a warning against a national self-congratulation.

After that war, liberal analysts such as Murray, Alfred Zimmern and Arnold Toynbee, and their European and US counterparts, gave international history a *pacificistic* bias (Ceadel, 1980, 1987, 1996; Morefield, 2005), which E.H. Carr characterized as idealist or utopian. The consensus was extended, nevertheless, to what seemed equally indispensable as the avoidance of war, i.e. the maintenance, the defence of liberal democracy. Quincy Wright's seminal *Limitation of Armament* (1921), *The Causes of War and the Conditions of Peace* (1935) and *A Study of War* (1942) demonstrated, however, that liberals and utopians were not alone in grappling with the problem of providing security for the democracies. After World War II, an important school of rather conservative international historians took up the interwar trend of international history writing, though not in the liberal *pacificistic* mode of Zimmern, Murray and Dickinson. This saw its most important development both for international history and IR in the 'English school', which stressed the emergence of an 'international society' (Dunne, 1998, 2005). Key among this 'school' were Charles Manning and Martin Wight (Porter and Wight, 1992; Dunne, 1999), who were all dominant figures at the London School of Economics. The volume of this school that has had the most longevity on IR reading lists is undoubtedly Hedley Bull's *The Anarchical Society* (1977/2002).

Those statesmen who constructed the 1919 peace settlement came, predictably, under attack from activists and historians. Woodrow Wilson was excoriated even more comprehensively than either David Lloyd George or Georges Clemenceau. The assaults mounted, as what were hoped to be the postwar years became, in the course of a twenty-year armistice, the interwar years. So did the counterattacks, led, in all his self-righteous indignation and his callousness, by Lloyd George (1932, 1938: see also Fry, 1977, 2011). He destroyed reputations in index entries. Peacemaking that did not contribute to the prevention of future wars and was judged actually to have made them more likely was examined almost as prodigiously as war itself (Lentin, 1984; Sharp, 1991; as well as, in French, Weill-Raynal, 1947). There was no doubting the seminal importance of World War I and the peacemaking at Versailles. Kissinger (1994), for example, came to see the debate on the Versailles Treaty of 1919 as defining US attitudes toward the world. Osiander (1994), Williams (1998/2007) and Knutsen (1999) conceptualized the whole period since 1919 as a quest, led by the United States and the other liberal powers, to develop a 'New World Order' agenda.

Second, international historians began to work within alternative paradigms to classical realism and thereby contributed to the debate about the potency of structural realism, idealism and progressive, radical and New Left alternative intellectual monopolies. In the process, they became, if only implicitly, more sophisticated and discerning theoretically. In their use of theory as analytical frameworks, as the source of patterns and regularities, they frequently outdid IR scholars in their use of history as a laboratory in their construction of case studies. Both agreed, however, if not equally so, that history was a principal source of theory and that, while history without theory was blind, theory without history was empty.

Third, international historians expanded their research agenda beyond politics and strategy, beyond the unitary state and elite behaviour. Charles Maier's (1988) political structures, cultural systems and economic arrangements were brought into play. Ideological dissent, foreign economic policies and inter-societal relations found a place in their work. Keynes, of course, in his *Economic Consequences of the Peace* (1920/2011), and those who followed him if only to reject his arguments (Mantoux, 1946; Weill-Raynal, 1947; Bunselmayer, 1975; Schuker, 1976; Trachtenberg, 1980; Kent, 1989), put reparations, war debts, economic policy and economic transactions in the international system at the centre of debate over the 1919 Peace Treaty and its consequences. Knock's (1992) biography of Woodrow Wilson demonstrated how international history could draw on the history of ideas. International historians, perforce, worked with a richer haul of concepts, beyond national interest, coercion and deterrence, including race, ethnicity, identity, dependence, interdependence, modernization, ideology and hegemony. International history became, consciously, more comparative across space, time and cultures, breaking with the focus on, and obsession with, the European great powers, the United States and Japan, and classical imperialism. Decolonization, neo-imperialism, north–south and core–periphery relations and the role of middle and small powers (in Afro-Asia, the Middle East and Latin America) in the international system drew more, entirely justified, attention.

Fourth, to make headway in these directions, international historians broke with the tradition of seeing the international system as the sum of great power policies and behavior. They recognized that the international system was neither an abstraction – a scientific metaphor and a 'metaphysical entity' – nor merely a context in which governments operated, but rather 'a series of intersecting outcomes not readily deducible from a summing up of individual policies' (Maier, 1980). Schroeder (1994) led the way in the realm of politics and security, demonstrating that the international system had dynamic properties, conflictual and cooperative behaviour; for example, structures and configurations such as distributions of resources and power, and thus polarities and regimes, and degrees of order. It also harboured paradox – the power, on occasions, of the weak and the impotence of the powerful. These developments paralleled the above-mentioned work of Hedley Bull (1977/2002), who had started to see states as part of a global system or even an 'international society'. It was a short but radical step to turn to the functioning of economic, cultural, ideological and social international and global systems and international civil society. Thorne (1985, 1988), addressing social structure, historical change and international relations, exploring the relationship between social structure and international history, developing a 'historical international sociology' (Scholte, 1994), was arguably the most creative in these 'border crossings'.

Fifth, international historians, as they joined in the redefinition of both state and power, looked inward to find the societal determinants of foreign policy that matched the sources and constraints emanating from the international system. It was a matter of constructing a social framework for foreign policy that demonstrated the relationships between government, the state and society. They examined how, in that space between the institutions of government and the boundaries of society, individuals, groups and the media helped define the nature and purpose of the state. Policy became an expression of social values and heritage, racial composition, political texture and economic structure (Kennedy, 1980). Electorates, the media, lobbies, pressure and interest graphs, publicists, business and organized labour wielded influence. Economic interests, political beliefs, values, cultural norms, intellectual fashion and configurations of power and privilege affected policy process and outcome. The concept of corporatism, examining the role of organized economic power blocs in harness with the state, flourished among US international historians as an analytical approach (Hogan, 1991; Iriye, 1979) described the state as a cultural system and international relations as interactions between cultural and power systems.

International historians also began to examine perhaps an equally important theme – the impact of foreign policy on state and society. Foreign policy became an independent not a dependent variable, a mechanism to reconcile, or drive apart, diverse interests and values within a state, and to justify extractions from and reallocation of resources between various segments of society. Foreign policy could thus contribute to or detract from political consensus, national unity and social harmony. International historians played a role, therefore, in the development of linkage politics, in exploring the reciprocal influences of the international and domestic spheres, and eroding the sharp distinction between them that had held up for so long (Fry and Gilbert, 1982). At the same time, international historians, drawing on institutional history and the social sciences, examined more thoroughly both bureaucratic and cabinet politics to improve their understanding of elite decision-making. The composition, organization and functions of foreign ministries, treasuries and military establishments mattered (Steiner, 1969; Schulzinger, 1975). Bureaucratic politics, the bargaining and negotiating between government departments, the Harvard view of Washington, did not travel well, however, beyond the United States.

These explorations by international historians enabled them to participate in the examination of three crucial considerations: (1) the nature of power, its economic and cultural dimensions, and the relations between those who wield or are deprived of it; (2) the nature of the state, its mediatory role between groups and forces in society, and its relations, beyond its borders, with states and entities that are not states; (3) and the relationship between structures, natural and constructed, economic, social and ideational, and prevailing patterns of authority and subservience, and agency. In so doing, international historians, wedded to a multi-archival approach, looked beyond the archives of the state, and beyond agencies of government concerned exclusively with political and strategic issues to plural sources from which to construct their data. Their methods evolved, often under the influence of the social sciences, and beyond the use of oral history techniques and counter-factual reasoning. Unmatched empirics and implicit theory produced rich historical tapestries which demonstrated, whatever the patterns and regularities, that international history is principally the study of uncertainty, complexity, the unanticipated, and of paradox, because relationships are contingent. Approaches to and debates over the origins, course and ending of the Cold War affirmed some of these trends in international history. Because the Cold War was the most truly global conflict, it also stimulated the development of global-world history. This will be further explored in Chapter 2 ('War'). One way of joining this debate is to look at it as largely a question of interlocking 'problems' – Russia's relations with the West, Anglo-American/French relations and Germany's relations with the rest of Europe.

## GLOBAL/WORLD HISTORY

There were attempts at writing global history in the aftermath of World War I, notably by Arnold Toynbee, who aimed at discovering the patterns of the rise of Western civilization. Oswald Spengler predicted the 'Decline of the West' in 1918. Barraclough (1979: 153) quoted Huizinga as saying in 1936 that 'our civilization is the first to have for its past the past of the world, our history is the first to be world history'. There was a partial rejection of national history in most of Europe, and certainly in Germany (Evans, 1997) after World War II as a reaction to 'nationalist' histories that had fed the warlike desires of the national socialist-fascist states of Europe and Asia. However, the roots of world history lie in many places, including historical sociology. Marxist history has always seen the world in global 'class' terms. The Annales school, led by French historians Lucien Febvre and Fernand Braudel, was also influential. Braudel's *The Mediterranean and the Mediterranean World in the Age of Philip II* (1972–1974) can be seen as the single most significant exemplar of the emerging synthesis that the writing of 'world history' was to attempt. He asserted that one must look at how the 'gentle rhythms' and 'deep-running currents' contributed to an understanding of change, that the history of 'events' had to be balanced by 'looking … at economies and states, societies and civilizations' and 'how all these forces came from the depths and came into play in the complex arena of war' (Braudel, 1980: 3). The forces that had 'come from the depths' in 1939–1945 had a profound effect on thinking about history.

It was not, however, until the 1980s and the work of William H. McNeill that 'world history' came to be taken more seriously. John Roberts' 'world history', as Moore puts it, was 'a history of the world embracing the entire globe from the history of man to the present day and addressed to an adult readership' (Moore, quoted in Bentley, 1997: 941–942). Other attempts, notably by Keylor (2000), Calvocoressi (1996), Ponting (2000), Bell (2001) and Wills (2001), have been made with varying degrees of success. Ponting did not merely look at a variety of regions over long periods of time, but traced common themes and connections between them. His principal themes were the nomad–sedentarist dichotomy, the transmission of culture, the spread of complex, structured and hierarchical societies, the origins and problems of modern industrial societies and the impact of Europe on the rest of the world. One area that was more than ripe for such treatment was that of the impact of empires, and this has led to a plethora of studies of the impact of the empires on subject peoples, such as Eliot's study of the Spanish and British in the Americas after 1492 (Eliot, 2007).

The Cold War, as a global conflict, provided a framework for, and invited the writing of, global history. David Reynolds, international-turned-global historian, accomplished that in his *One World Divisible* (2000). The Cold War unfolds through its major crises, from Berlin, via Cuba to Vietnam and beyond, providing the key to the analytical narrative. From the US–USSR rivalry, with all its forms of conflict, Reynolds examines the interactions of the national security states and their clashes with the non-Western world. 'Critical' history provides a very different view of those interactions. It views history as the domain of the conqueror, especially in the colonial period. It documents the need to rewrite history to tell the story of the victims and to explain the actions of the victimizers. Tzvetan Todorov is possibly the greatest living voice of moral outrage on the specific terrors of the twentieth century. His work has both placed the particular horrors of the impact of Western European 'civilization' in the first half of the twentieth century into its historical context, and made one appreciate the internal logic of that civilization's failings. For Todorov, the conquest of America in 1492 and the subsequent consequences of imperial conquest set the stage for the eventual turning in on itself of European civilization in the two world wars. What has truly distinguished the twentieth century from all others, he argued, is the emergence of totalitarianism and the largely successful defence against this made by the liberal democracies (Todorov, 1999). Africa, suffering through colonization and decolonization, experienced the same ordeal. The battle there between democracy and totalitarianism is far from over and represents the remnants of European influence (Todorov, 2000). His work points to crucial unfinished business – a world history of genocide.

No review, however brief, of global-world history can avoid reference to Felipe Fernandez-Armesto and his *Millennium* (1995), *Truth: A History* (1997) and *Civilizations* (2000) in the Americas after 1492 and Christopher Bayly of the impact of the European empires after 1780 (Bayly, 2004; Eliot, 2007). There is, as Fernandez-Armesto says, a lot of world out there and global history must help us understand more of it. Historians must see the world, as meteorologists do, as a system of interconnections. Yet the interconnections remain elusive and global theory, to explain them, inadequate. Organizing devices such as the grand narrative, tracing the contact between civilizations, comparative histories, incorporating non-Western historiography and adopting multiple, culturally sensitive perspectives have taken world histories only to part of the way. Unsure of current theories and methods, Fernandez-Armesto, in his *Civilizations*, attempts 'a radical cultural history of mankind's relationship with nature, which purports to advance a new understanding of what it means to be 'civilized' (2000: XX). It cannot but be both fascinating and controversial.

## TRANSNATIONAL HISTORY

'Transnational' history is not new in the sense that it looks at phenomena that have always been studied by historians, but new enough in that it merits its own 'dictionary' (Iriye and Saunier, 2009). It certainly tries to use a slightly new language – one definition has it that 'transnationalism is best understood not as fostering bounded networks, but as creating honeycombs, a structure that sustains and gives shape to the identities of nation-states, international and local institutions, and particular social and geographic spaces' (Clavin, 2005: 422), or even '[t]ransnationalism is about exploring connections (whether they attract or repel)' (Clavin, 2005: 427). It even uses expressions like 'border crossings' that were used some time ago, most notably by British historian Christopher Thorne, who used the expression in his 1988 book of the same title (Thorne, 1988), even if the credit is not given by Clavin (2005: 423). So it looks at the way that particular nations and regions are linked to each other in a myriad ways. Its aim in practice is to try and capture the dynamic of changes in these relationships over time by looking both at the domestic developments within any given state and the way they interact with changes in surrounding states and regions.

There is, of course, a history to this transnational history. Much of it overlaps and is claimed by our previous category, global-world history. If we include in it all 'critics of the national paradigm', then most of history since the 1970s, at least since Jacques Le Goff, is 'transnational' (Müller and Torp, 2009: 609). It has been driven, as these authors say, by a 'contemporary political debates on both European Integration and *détente* in East–West relations', added to which we could add postcolonialism and globalization (Müller and Torp, 2009: 609–610). This has led to the usual divisions about how to do it and what it should focus on, but that is the natural course of all intellectual debates. Others have claimed that it has made more traditional international history pay a severe price in terms of turning students away from tried-and-tested paths (in this case, in a criticism of Ian Tyrell) of understanding American 'exceptionalism' and creating 'a false antagonism between allegedly exceptionalist American historians and more progressive transnational writers' (McGerr, 1991: 1056). Others feel it is well worth it, with David Thelen believing that it has helped to greatly broaden both the historical understanding of the United States, but also to contextualize much of what the country does in (as well as to and for) the world (Thelen, 1999). It has also led to scholars like Heather Jones asking whether any particular phenomenon is international or transnational? What it does in this latter case, on 'Humanitarian Action during the First World War', is to show the tensions that exist between national and international (or transnational) efforts in any given field (Jones, 2009: 697).

One of the best examples of this, Ian Tyrell's analysis of the United States since 1789, *Transnational Nation*, accepts that '[t]he nation was deeply connected in the nineteenth century to world history and remains so today … There have been ups and down in this story of transnational connection, as the power of the American state has changed' (Tyrell, 2007: 229). Clavin's collection of essays on transnational history is particularly concerned to understand the way that international organizations work (the subject of Chapter 6 of this book) by looking at the networks of elites, and the way they interact within governmental, intergovernmental and non-governmental organizations in a series of issue areas (Clavin and Wessels, 2005). Even if she denies the desire to see 'elites' as anything more than parts of 'epistemic communities' (Clavin, 2005: 428), a term taken from IR, this time from Peter Haas (Haas, 1997), that is what they are, as scholars like Inderjeet Parmar have shown in studies of organizations like Chatham House and the Council on Foreign Relations (Parmar, 2004).

This is a very promising development for those who want to see a rapprochement between IR and international (or any other kind of) history, as it opens up the frontiers of both to promising cross-fertilization in some surprising ways. Clavin's collection accepts that it is covering ground that was initially explored by IR scholars like Robert Keohane and Joseph Nye in what she calls their consideration of 'the original understanding of "transnationalism"' or indeed Samuel Huntington's similar use of the term (Clavin, 2005: 425; Keohane and Nye, 1981; Huntington, 1973). Some of the seminal pieces in this transnational tradition rather resemble the way that IR scholars tend to use historical texts in a slightly promiscuous way to illustrate bigger issues. Covering US history from its origins to the present (as he admits) (Tyrell, 2007: ix) requires as much of a drawing on a vast array of archival historical work as does an 'IR' scholar like John Ikenberry, who is just as respectful of historiographical accuracy as Tyrell (Ikenberry, 2001) or even 'real' historians like Mark Mazower, whose recent brief book on the United Nations, *No Enchanted Palace* (Mazower, 2009b), is scrupulous in its attention to detail but covers a vast period and subject matter in ways that would leave all diplomatic, and even most international, historians worried. Among other notable contributions, Michael Mann, not strictly a 'historian', has shown how a sociological imagination can interact with historical scholarship in wonderful ways (Mann, 1986, 1993).

## CONCLUSION: POSTMODERNISM?

Diplomatic, international and global-world history have all suffered, and benefited, from scrutiny from within (i.e. from the history profession) and from outside (i.e. from social scientists). They could not hope to escape, moreover, assaults from postmodernists. As Michael Bentley says, early twentieth-century historiography was for a long time a kind of 'theology, the study of error', intent on sniffing out 'mistakes'. This has had some unlikely casualties, such as the great historians of the past like Gibbon or Carlyle, who were often fast and loose with the 'truth'. Until about 1960 this tradition persisted and then the citadel came under attack from those who believed that should be theorized, which as he says 'brought upon professional history an embarrassing sense of self-consciousness'. This in turn led to a denial that any kind of 'truth' could be established, and this is the trend that still makes the most ink flow (Bentley, 1997: xiii–xv). The main new, often very contested, influences on the whole of the social sciences and humanities over the past thirty years have of course been those of 'poststructuralism' and 'postmodernism'. The former was especially influential in transforming literary studies although the impact has been much wider. Even John Lewis Gaddis refers to a need to 'deconstruct' the title of his famous book, *We Now Know* (Gaddis, 1997: viii). But of course poststructuralism's influence has remained partial in history and IR, both because of the forces of tradition and because in some cases the insights are not conclusively damaging to the existing ways of doing things. It might be remembered that it was a liberal revulsion to colonialism as much as a Marxist or poststructuralist attack on it that finally led to the decolonization of the planet and also the fact that many of the great thinkers who are associated with this revulsion did so within a liberal educational system.

Robert Young has given us a useful synthesis of this in his *White Mythologies*, in which he reminds us that most of the poststructuralist thinkers derived their ideas from concrete experiences, so 'Sartre, Althusser, Derrida and Lyotard, among others, were all either born in Algeria or personally involved with the events of the war' (1990: 3; to this list we could, of course, add Camus). In this parade of French philosophers, Young points to the resurgence of the Frankfurt School and seems to agree with Vincent Descombes, who posits that the whole of French philosophy over the last hundred years has been a dialectic between the Hegelian German school, of which the Frankfurt School is the latest development, and the French emphasis on the experience of the individual. Poststructuralism thus challenges, for Young, the 'left' and the 'right' (Young, 1990: chapter 1, esp. 1–6).

This led to a rethinking of the colonial past and much else besides, and laid the ground for the postmodernist critique of all 'truth' and its supposed philosophical underpinning, the Enlightenment, which is now supposedly totally discredited by its products, colonialism and the Holocaust, among other disasters. So a study of history that was of nations in the nineteenth century and until after World War II became transformed into a much wider refection on the nature of humanity. Purely 'national' history had to change as a result of the horrors imputed to nationalism in the first fifty years of the century.

Selecting the key texts of postmodernist historiography in a sense goes against its entire ethos. But Hayden White is usually seen as the father of the new wave, with his *Metahistory: The Historical Imagination in Nineteenth Century Europe* (1975). Of this, Richard Evans comments that it was 'much-discussed but little-imitated', and was in any case more 'structuralist than post-structuralist in inspiration' (Evans, 1997: 290). Another major writer in this vein is Keith Jenkins, whose *Rethinking History* (Jenkins, 1991) and *On 'What is History'* (Jenkins, 1995) are useful summaries of the denial of the Establishment of Elton and Carr. Also interesting is Alex Callinicos, *Theories and Narratives: Reflections on the Philosophy of History* (Callinicos, 1995). The grand old man of historiographical postmodernism is the same as that of IR, Jean Baudrillard, whose *The Illusion of the End* (Baudrillard, 1994) crops up repeatedly in both disciplines.

Postmodernists would usually argue that 'a historical text … can no longer be regarded as having wholly fixed and unalterable meaning given by its author'. But, as Richard Evans counters, 'it is doubtful whether anyone, in fact, has *ever* believed that meaning can be fixed in this way'. Carlyle and Gibbon were well aware that they were interpreting history in their 'text'; history, after all, means 'story'. As Evans put it, even 'diplomatic history was largely built on the analysis of the ambiguities of diplomatic documents – not all of them intentional – and has taken much of its analytical power from its awareness of the possibility, even likelihood, that a treaty, or a protocol, could, and often would, be interpreted by different states in different ways'. But neither, says Evans, can we assume that we can 'impose any meaning we wish on such a text either ... Postmodern theorists are simply being unrealistic here.' The dialogue in any historical research is that between 'two different kinds of significances – the historian's and the document's' (Evans, 1997: 103–107). It is also true to say that postmodern historians themselves would probably accuse Evans of burning straw men in such comments (Jenkins, 1997 is a very useful summary and reader). The postmodern discourse is not one we can avoid thinking about, and we will on occasion use its language and evidence in this book. What is omitted ('closures' in postmodern parlance) are just as important as what is known, and it would be foolish in the extreme to deny that French poststructuralism, whence much postmodernism springs, is not as relevant a phenomenon as any other intellectual taproot.

But there's a growing awareness that all of us who deal with the 'international', however defined, have to move from the very narrow definition of the history of states while not throwing out that baby with bathwater that surrounds states, their regional, transnational and global relationships. But equally without some historians still studying what some French political scientists call the historians' *fond de tiroir* (by which they normally mean old-fashioned diplomatic history of two states over a short period, written in immense detail and based on diplomatic correspondence), there can be no 'bigger' picture history, or indeed political science. We need both the micro and the macro in order to make some sense of the world. The lesson may be that the more we enlarge the list of factors that matter in the study of history and IR the more we need to cross-fertilize the academic genres, and the more we need to accept that any picture will be approximate and to some extent subjective. In that we can accept the criticism of the postmodern critics, but also accept what Richard Evans has sagely said, it has always been understood to be thus; to say otherwise is to indulge in straw man criticism.

# CHAPTER 2

# War

The idea that every war has been different from the last is the delusion of those who know no history.

(Liddell Hart, *Thoughts on War*, 1932/1944: 24)

You will hear of wars and rumours of wars, but see to it you are not alarmed. Such things must happen but the end is still to come. Nation will rise against nation, and kingdom against kingdom.

(Matthew, 22: 15)

## INTRODUCTION

The discussion of what causes and motivates war and what can end it (as with peace, see Chapter 3) is a, maybe *the*, central obsession of students of IR and IH alike. It is also riddled with paradox. We are constantly told by some that it has changed its nature; especially since the Industrial Revolution, change accelerated by technology, even to the point of it being 'postmodern' (Nef, 1968; Gray, 1998), an evolution of global political systems and theories (Mitrany, 1943/1966) or even by a change in human nature. Religion is seen by some as making for very different views about why war should be fought *ad bellum* as well as how it should be conducted *in bello* (Popovski, Reichberg and Turner, 2009; Towle, 2009). There is much debate about whether wars can ever 'end' and huge discussions about the respective weight to be given to different factors in the causes and outcomes of war (Blainey, 1988, is a good place to start). There are others (like Liddell Hart, 1932/1944, above) who aver that it has not changed much, if at all (Gray, 2005). This chapter will explore these themes by looking at a number of wars and the way they have been interpreted. As with the other chapters in this volume, we will of necessity be very selective, even subjective, in which wars are examined, but all of them will be used to ask a number of basic questions of interest to the IR scholar and international historian alike. The key ones include:

- What weight can we give to the importance of the 'great man' (or rarely 'woman') as opposed to the structures in which these individuals operated in the success of failure of their efforts?
- What can war be said to be like to experience, and what are the consequences of these experiences, individual and collective?
- Do wars 'end', in both the literal sense that the fighting stops but also in the sense that they leave 'unfinished business' that leads to new wars and resentments that rankle to poison relations between states and peoples?

Several subsequent chapters, on peace (Chapter 3) and international organization (Chapter 6) will ask if there are alternative ideas, structures and processes that might be said to provide alternatives to wars in deciding the big questions that beset states and communities. Others, notably 'Empire' (Chapter 5), will explore notions that are of crucial importance for understanding war, and the concerns of IR more broadly, notably 'power' (q.v.). We will also look at the historical roots of some of the present wars since 1990, with Iraq as a key recent example. In Chapter 5, we will look at the origins and results of some key colonial wars, the logic being that many such wars might be said to be at least partly as a result of the unravelling of 'empires' – in these cases those of the Former Soviet Union as well as the Ottoman and British empires. It could also be argued that new forms of 'empire' are emerging, one being in the possibility (to put it no more strongly than that) of a future Islamic Caliphate, as advocated by the loose coalition known as al-Qaeda. Maybe we could also see the problems of European civil wars, of which those in the Former Yugoslavia are the most extreme example, as the birth pangs of a new European 'empire'?

## WAR AND THE STUDY OF INTERNATIONAL RELATIONS

It could be argued that that the whole study of international relations is ultimately directed at these questions: What is war? What causes war? What can prevent it? And How can we limit its effects? The first of these is difficult enough, but some of the best introductions for the student of IR are very historically informed. Our current favourites are volumes by: John Keegan (Keegan, 1994), because he gives one of the best accounts of war seen from the soldier's point of view; Michael Howard (1976, 2008), because he weaves a picture of war that embraces historical thought as well as global history; and Carl von Clausewitz's great classic *On War*

(Clausewitz, 1976), on strategy and warfare in general and war in European history in particular. On war outside Europe, the great classic is *The Art of War* by Sun Tzu, which dates from around 500 BCE (Sun Tzu, 1998).

The other questions constitute what Stephen Van Evera has called 'a philosophers' industry for centuries' where '[s]adly, though, scholars have made scant progress on the problem'. For Van Evera this is because:

> [m]ost of the causes that the [literature on war] identifies cannot be manipulated (for example human instinct, the nature of the domestic economic and political systems of states, or the distribution of power among states).' The 'stock of hypotheses' on solutions to war [he cites disarmament, pacifism and reliance on international institutions] are 'large but unuseful'.
>
> (Van Evera, 1999: 1–2)

Such is realist pessimism. It is intuitively understood by most of us. War is 'inevitable' because human beings are just the way they are, immutable and awful.

Indeed, one thing that strikes anyone who studies the history of war is that it has always been a terrible affair, striking down the innocent as much as the warrior (See Box 2.1).

## BOX 2.1 THE ENDURING HORROR OF WAR

The targeting of non-combatants as well as the gratuitous torment of vanquished foes is a constant of all warfare, and not a 'new' feature of the wars associated with 'failed states' noted by IR writers like Kaldor (1999). Thucydides writes of massacres and worse in the Peloponnesian Wars (Thucydides, 1954, also see online). The ideals of *Virtus*, and 'honour' more generally, a concept that is often now translated into the medieval idea of 'chivalry', gave certain protections to the weak – to kill an 'easy victim' has no honour attached to it, after all. But in what we would now call the 'ethnic wars' between, among others, England, Scotland and Ireland over many centuries, civilians were often primary victims (Macdonald Fraser, 1971). In the English Civil War (1642–1649) there were widespread atrocities against the Irish, with prisoners being thrown into the sea tied up and routinely hanged (Braddick, 2008: 317–318). In the Thirty Years' War (1618–1648) that devastated Europe (for once, the word is not hyperbole), the thinly veiled memoirs of Johann Grimmelshausen, *Simplicissimus* (1668, 1999), show that rape, appalling torture and other horrors were routine. How *killing* is carried out by modern warriors, and how it affects them, has been explored effectively by Joanna Bourke (Bourke, 2000). We now know of the atrocities visited upon Russian and other civilians by the German army (even the *Wehrmacht*) and by the

Red Army on German civilians in retaliation (Goldhagen, 1997; Beevor, 2002, 2007a). Some IR scholars (for example, Kalyvas, 2006) have shown us the widespread use of atrocities against civilians and enemy troops alike in civil wars before and since 1945 (Beevor, 2007b). It has to be said that the atrocities against children in Africa, where there have been many reports of up to 1,500 children *at a time* having limbs hacked off, make even historical examples pale by comparison (Machel, 2001), but they are far from being unheard of.

However, the *glory* and excitement of war are equally strong tropes in the Western, and indeed global, imagination. How else to explain the way the soldiers of 1914 marched off to battle (and, in many cases, death) singing and having flowers thrown at them? Many writers (Louis-Ferdinand Céline is a good example) have derided this, but it was deeply and widely felt at the time, even by Céline himself, who was decorated for bravery, though his celebrated book *Voyage au bout de la nuit* is a eulogy to cowardice (Céline, 1932/1999). War is closely associated with ideas of common purpose (nation building, commerce, technology); it has been the very stuff of the evolution of Western Europe and beyond (Howard, 1976; Nef, 1968; Preston, Wise and Werner, 1956).

There are, however, seemingly a few areas upon which all thinkers and practitioners of war of the last two hundred years can reasonably agree. The first is that the language of war and the language of peace are intimately linked. From the peace activist to the warmonger, it is accepted that war is a learned social activity. There is a perhaps astonishing agreement on this idea in IR, too, from critical theorists and feminists on one hand to strategists (generally of the Right) on the other (Jabri, 1994; Gray, 1999). This, of course, implies that we have to understand the *social context* in which war takes place. We might reasonably ask, therefore, if the context in which *Western* wars have taken place is the same as that in the Third World? The tacit assumption underlying most United Nations (q.v.) and other official instances is that we can use the historical examples of the West to determine what causes wars in developing countries and that the necessary cures for war are those that worked in the West – democracy, capitalism, etc. (see Williams, 2006, for one treatment of this problem, and Towle, 2009, for a critique of what that has meant for British foreign policy).

So the second major area of agreement is that history can be a good guide, but it is one that has to be handled with extreme care. History can and must provide a series of necessary contexts for thinking about war and war can provide the context for thinking about history. As W. B. Gallie says in the introduction to his *Philosophers of Peace and War*, 'we can perhaps best come to appreciate the distinctive structure of the international problem, centered on the causes of war and the possibilities of peace' by looking at them both in their historical context but also as 'participants in a time-transcending dialogue' (Gallie, 1978).

The mechanics of warfare itself have changed over the centuries. War has also arguably been the major vector in societal change, and has led to the creation of the 'West' in a variety of ways – politically (in terms of thinking and institutional structures), socially and economically. These paths of human endeavour have always been linked, and changes within them all have tended to accelerate in the crisis situations of war. War drives individuals and communities to examine their fundamental attitudes, beliefs and actions in ways that no other impetus can. Peace can seem 'boring' because its processes can be slow and ponderous, but there is nothing slow and ponderous about war.

However, we cannot give a good account of *all* the wars that have been fought, even those of the last century. A selection has had to be made, and that choice has come down on what we believe to have been the system-changing wars of recent times, but also those that have given us our major mythology of war itself. As we hope to make clear, we believe that wars in ancient times have to be studied as much as we would all accept the need to study the world wars and the Cold War of the twentieth century. IR is currently obsessed with these major events; one day it may not be and maybe it should not be. But for a beginner in the discipline it is a good place to start. Our 'new' (Kaldor, 1999) and our 'postmodern' (Kalyvas, 2006) wars have a great deal in common with 'ancient' warfare and are in many sense 'premodern', so reference will be made within the broader framework to what small and seemingly insignificant wars have to say about IR more generally.

# HISTORIANS AND ANCIENT WARFARE

## War and the study of strategy

The shadow of the wars of ancient Greece and Rome have always obsessed Western thinkers, about politics in general and war in particular. Herodotus is the inevitable starting point with his description of the wars between Greeks and between Greeks and Persians, which he described a century after the events in the fifth century BCE (Herodotus, 1996). The continuing relevance of Greek military tactics is explained wonderfully by Victor Hanson in *The Western Way of War* (Hanson, 2009). Although until the 1970s most schoolchildren in Britain were forced to read Livy on Hannibal's wars (Livy, 2006) and Caesar's *Gallic Wars* – the latter containing interminable accounts of the great man as he slew his way through the Celts and Gauls (Caesar and Hammond, 2008, 58–50 BCE) – they are still all a good read.

Most serious commentators on war will usually start with the paradoxes posed by the ancient Greeks and Romans, the most celebrated being '*vis pacem, para bellum*' – in the words of Vegetius (*De Re Militari*, 2001), 'if you would seek peace, prepare for war' (Luttwak, 2001: 3, and chapter 1, 'The Conscious Use of Paradox in War'). This is the classic definition of what we would now call *raison d'état*. There also exist excellent commentaries on the Roman way of war that have uncanny echoes of the way that warrior virtues are even today evoked and described – the need for discipline, courage and, maybe above all, organization (Campbell, 1994).

## Ancient wars and the notion of community and individual

Vegetius' dictum about preparedness for war during peace also held within it the idea that the citizenry of his day were, in the words of Richard Tuck, 'treated ... as defeated combatants' by the state structures that had finally emerged from a long period of civil war, the death of the Republic and a chaotic series of emperors in the first century BCE, described by Lucan in the first century CE (Lucan, 1999). His illustrious predecessors, Julius Caesar (assassinated 44 BCE) or Cicero (106–43 BCE) would have thought very differently about war, as their experiences had largely been in the Republican period. When Cicero wrote in praise of republican liberty and of the self-sacrifice of the republican heroes, he was assuming that men would subordinate their interests to that of their republic (Tuck, 1999: 11–12). We must thus remember that the history of the Roman Republic itself had much to do with why Vegetius wrote these words. This basic observation shows how notions of 'individual autonomy', Tuck's main concern, can be changed by the social context in which wars take place. From this basic dichotomy we might derive a narrative of individual rights, the behaviour of states and many of the broader concerns of the study of politics.

As another Roman historian, Sallust, pointed out, war is also an activity that links the domestic and the international spheres of a people's experience. In his writings on the subjugation of the Numidians and their King Jugurtha (111–105 BCE), Sallust emphasized the importance of a solid home front in the (then) 'war on terror' as Rome saw it – then, as now, 'some grieved for the glory of the empire, others – unaccustomed to the circumstances of war – feared for freedom' (Sallust, 2007: 82).

War is thus both the supreme *individual* experience, in that a man or woman can believe they will fight it as part of their duty, and are often then faced with a lonely death, and a *collective* one on the battlefield in that military units as small as platoons (in modern warfare) or *phalanxes* (in ancient Greek parlance) required total solidarity. John Keegan's *The Face of Battle* (Keegan, 1976) demonstrates the understanding that ultimately the warrior fights for his 'mates' in the trench or line of battle next to him, not for some higher purpose. The study of the history of war is therefore also vital to giving us an understanding of how societies fight wars. Clausewitz's dictum that 'war is politics by other means' (Clausewitz, 1976; Heuser, 2002: chapter 3) illustrates that war at most epochs, if not all, is a 'normal' activity, not an exception. It therefore requires some sort of basic societal code to be kept in place in any society, in case that society be called upon to fight.

## War and honour

Lebow usefully sums up the driving forces behind ancient societies, and by extension all societies, as 'fear, interest, honor and habit' – a short list but a serviceable one (Lebow, 2008: 4). So another key paradox that emerges from the practice and study of war in 'ancient' times that is still with us are the motivations of the warriors themselves, their conception of 'honour'. This is also a particular current concern in

IR (Sherman, 2006; Coker, 2007; Donelan, 2007; Lebow, 2008). Warrior 'codes' or 'honour' are embedded in any military and social establishment or, as Shannon French says, '[w]arrior cultures throughout history and from diverse regions around the globe have constructed codes of behaviour based on their own image of the ideal warrior' (French, 2003: 3). Equally, the importance of the warrior ethic is often evoked as a touchstone, not just for valour and honour (*virtus* in Latin) but for the vigour that states and communities are said to manifest through the ability to wage war. Lebow comments that '[p]ursuit of *Virtus* may explain why Rome was constantly at war' (Lebow, 2008: 206). The very existence of the Roman Empire was inextricable from its understanding of what war was for. As we will see in our discussion of the Roman Empire (Chapter 5), the most energetic and idealized Roman period was that of the Republic and of the Antonine emperors that succeeded them (Gibbon, 1830). Edward Gibbon is the main proponent of this in his *Decline and Fall of the Roman Empire* (Gibbon, 1776/[1981]). His successors, including Theodor Mommsen in his magisterial *History of Rome* (Momssen, 1996), made very similar play on the links between Roman *Virtus* and war (see also Chapter 5).

## The continued relevance of Rome in the imaginary of war

Hence a first observation we can make about the Roman attitude to war that has clear implications for our understanding of it is that the political and social context has a determining effect on how we read any given writer. It must also be said that those who write about Rome, and her wars in particular, often use it as an opportunity to talk about their *own* time. Mommsen in particular was keen to stress the democratic nature of the Republican period and wary of the impending (in 1854–1856) imperial tone that his native Germany was taking. He might have been warning about what liberal and socialist British and German opinion was later to call 'militarism', shorthand for an excessive reliance on military force abroad to deflect domestic unrest (Leibknecht, 1917/1973; Williams, 1998: 180–181). Gibbon was keen to draw parallels with the discipline of the Roman armies with the indiscipline of the British in CE 43, when the emperor Claudius started the campaign that finally conquered *Britannicum*:

> They took up arms with savage fierceness; they laid them down or turned them against each other with wild inconstancy; and while they fought singly, they were successively subdued.
>
> (Gibbon, 1776: 30)

The inhabitants of the new island conquest understood why they were being defeated: In a later campaign, in 83 CE the chieftain Calgacus told his army before the battle of Mons Graupius in Caledonia, now Scotland, that 'It is our quarrels and disunion that have given them fame. The reputation of the Roman Army is built up on the faults of its enemies' (Tacitus, *Agricola*, 98 CE). Another of Calgacus' most famous summaries of Roman success from the same account is: 'They make a solitude [or desert] and call it peace' (Tacitus, 1971).

Rome's reliance on disciplined but overwhelming violence was continued into much more recent times, when 'Roman ideas about the need for a city to use relatively unscrupulous violence in the pursuit of liberty and glory', as Tuck puts it (Tuck, 1999: 27), were also a feature of statecraft in early modern European city-states. This is reflected in the writings of Machiavelli in *The Prince* or in Pietrino Belli, whose *De Re Militari et de Bello* was a standard text for the aspiring or successful *condottieri* of the sixteenth century, and which make no sense without seeing the classical continuities.

# MODERN WARFARE, c. 1600–c. 1900

Even if the nature of war has changed drastically in the last hundred years, then the main political, social and economic vectors of that change can be said to have been already present in the few centuries before that. They were then accelerated by the rise of states, and the mobilization through economic forces and the emergence of the political 'mass'. The system that characterized medieval Europe, and the idea of a unified 'Christendom', one unified by political hierarchy and religious allegiance, was severely shaken by a series of secular movements that had their direct effect on the conduct of war. These were the Reformation of the sixteenth century and the Enlightenment of the eighteenth, which changed for ever the nature of man's relationship to God and to the pursuit of knowledge, both of which were increasingly individualized. To this must be added the revolutions, especially the 'Great' revolutions that changed both state and society in France (1789), Russia (1917) and China (1949), but also those in England (1641) and what became the United States (1776), and that led to popular sovereignty being seen as a norm of political organization (Armstrong, 1993; Calvert, 1997; Chan and Williams, 1994; Skocpol, 1979).

## State-building and interdependence

The modern nation-state, first in a few areas of the European landmass and then across most of the planet, saw its origins in the emergence of the French, Dutch and Spanish states from the fifteenth century on (Tilly, 1975) and in the 'Tudor revolution' in England in the sixteenth (Elton, 1953 – see also the debate on the 'Whig' theory of history: Coleman and Starkey, 1986). Many historians have noted the links between this phenomenon and war in both general and specific terms, and Michael Howard's classic text *War in European History* sets the tone for this literature: 'The origins of Europe were hammered out on the anvil of war' (Howard, 1976: 1). Charles Tilly probably did most to set the tone for war being an essential part of state-building with his often-quoted 'war made states and vice versa' (Tilly, 1990: 67). Contemporary historians agree and put the emphasis even more precisely. Hence Elizabeth Kier writes that '[w]arfare and the army are tied inextricably to the state-building process' (Kier, 1999: 3) and naval historians claim the same for their form of warfare.

The most recent comprehensive volume on British sea power makes it plain that 'the significance of sea power to British history lies at least as much in domestic politics and the growth of the state as in foreign policy and war (Rodger, 2006: 577).

The rise of the modern state is key to understanding why warfare changed so much in the period after 1815. As we shall see below, though, there was a much wider acceptance of 'just war' rules. A seeming 'civilization' of war and human relationships was seen as taking place, especially during the long and mainly peaceful nineteenth century in Europe, along with the rise of successful and powerful nationalistic and industrialized nation-states. Some, like Carl von Clausewitz, realized, albeit late in his life, that this was creating a false sense of security, but his warnings were drowned out in a tide of patriotic fervour. The Napoleonic Wars (1791–1815) had seemingly proved the power of the offensive, which was tied in the mind of, particularly, Prussian/German military thinking to the power of a nation, indeed a people, mobilized in a common cause, *la levée en masse*. The great statements of this came from Clausewitz, much quoted and much misunderstood (see below), as well as the future Marshal Foch and the Antoine Jomini in the 1860s (Gat, 1992). The emergence of a Romantic and anti-Enlightenment spirit in Germany has been blamed by many for the 'militarism' that drove imperial Germany to unify itself (mostly) by war and to defeat France in 1871 (Gat, 1992).

## War and globalization

The rise of the nation-state was succeeded by a gradual emergence of what is now called 'globalization', a political and economic tsunami that first really emerged in the colonization of large parts of the world after Columbus' discovery of the Americas in 1494 and their annexation to Spain and is propelled by the Dutch, Spanish, French and English colonizations and empires (see Chapter 5) of the sixteenth to nineteenth centuries (Wallerstein, 1974, 1980; Braudel, 1972–1974). John Darwin's wonderful rewriting of this thesis in a 'world history' context puts the Central Asian empire of Tamerlane in the fifteenth century as a much earlier impetus (Darwin, 2007), thus much reducing the Eurocentric punch of the original analysis. The growth of these political entities were driven by economic motivations but had important military aspects to them. War made these empires in conjunction with economic rapine and development. Some IR commentators rightly see the combination of war and economics as vital handmaidens in the creation of imperial states (Cramer is one such, on Africa; Cramer, 2006).

A discussion of modern warfare therefore requires an understanding of the 'hardware' of the emergence of a different kind of combat for different reasons, both in terms of the main types of commanders and of the armies they led, but also of the kind of societies that they both beget and were begotten by, in particular, the changing modern state. The 'software' is made up of the key thinkers and schools of thought that these elements of hardware both influenced and were influenced by, and foremost among these is Carl von Clausewitz, though we will also give due weight to other thinkers about war and its philosophies.

## Just war

As Chris Brown puts it, just war theory 'must be one of the only areas of contemporary moral philosophy where an essentially mediaeval theoretical construction still has common currency' (Brown, 1992: 132). Just war theory in medieval times was developed as a way of discriminating between those it was lawful (even desirable) to attack and destroy, 'the infidel', and those it was not. It also provided a way of reducing the impact of internecine conflict within Christendom, which was unified under the Church and the Holy Roman Emperor and subject to a web of intricate feudal rules and relationships. But with the Reformation, and the division of Christendom into warring sovereign states that allied themselves on the basis of 'national interest' and religion against each other, the feudal pattern dissolved in the Wars of Religion and the Thirty Years' War. It was only with the end of that war in 1648, and the signature of the Treaties of Westphalia (one of which was actually signed at Munster), that sovereign states were established in a way that we would now find more recognizable (Osiander, 1994).

By 1835, Alfred de Vigny was able to state in *The Military Necessity*, that:

> Formerly, the vanquished were massacred or enslaved for life, captured towns were sacked, their populations hunted or dispersed; while every state stood by, appalled, in constant, desperate readiness, prepared to be as cruel in defence as in attack. To-day cities have no more to fear than the levying of indemnities. War has become civilised.
>
> (de Vigny, 1953: 5–6)

One of the main explanations for this was the development, refinement and, most important of all, the general application of the law of war. The two central notions of the law of war (*jus ad bellum* and *jus in bello*) are so well-known that it would be superfluous to dwell on them at too great length. Just war originated in the many changes made in premodern societal practice, including warfare, and is generally claimed to have been the product of Christian thinkers, although recent scholarship is trying to redress the balance by pointing to similar traditions in Islamic, Buddhist, Hindu and even Sikh thought and practice (Robinson, 2003). It was based in all these traditions on the need to circumscribe the impact of war while generally not deeming it to be unacceptable practice. It has certainly never been far from the thinking of scholars of IR since the end of the Cold War, and even earlier (two key contributions being Walzer, 1992, and Bellamy, 2006).

## Carl von Clausewitz

The great chronicler of the rise of the modern state and its way of making war is naturally Carl von Clausewitz. No decent account of the development of war or of the rise of military doctrine (and thus strategic studies more broadly) can ignore the insights of *On War* (1830/1976). Many current gurus of strategic studies still take his views on war as essential (Gray, 1999; Moran in Baylis et al., 2002).

As Beatrice Heuser has pointed out, Clausewitz never properly finished his master-work, and a guide to the Guide is essential (Heuser, 2002). Heuser breaks his insights down into: the civil–military relationship, one of the key ideas in modern thinking about state-building (and disintegration); the role of generalship and serendipity (*Friktion*, see below); and the defensive–offensive debate, which became so important during and after the World War I and is still with us, i.e. how can 'Total War' help being as damaging to the attacker as the defender? She even gives us an insight into how Clausewitz has influenced several generations of guerrilla leaders. He is an intensely *contemporary* theorist of war and peace.

The most profound paradoxes of all are to be found in war. Clausewitz said that war 'belongs to the province of social life ... War is not an activity of the will exerted upon inanimate matter like the mechanical arts ... but against a living re-acting force' (Clausewitz, in Gallie, 1978: 43). He also claimed elsewhere that '[t]he introduction of the principle of moderation in the philosophy of war is an absurdity' (quoted by Amiral Lanxade in Sancery, 1999). So when war happens, it had the potential in Clausewitz's day, fully realized in the last hundred years, to include whole societies in its embrace, to destroy them utterly unless peace could be achieved by victory or the acceptance of defeat.

War is also full of pitfalls, most of them by their nature unpredictable, and so is the making of peace. The process that von Clausewitz identified as '*friktion*' in war, the chance for serendipity to upset the best laid plans, is as true in peace-making as in war-making (Cimbala, 2001). Clausewitz himself described it as 'The effect of reality on ideas and intentions in war' (Watts, 2006: 1, quoting Clausewitz, to his future wife, Marie Brühl, on 29 September 1806) and elsewhere as 'the force that makes the apparently easy so difficult' (Clausewitz, 1976: 68, book 1, chapter 7).

The idea of being able to predict with any real certainty what will happen if a certain strategic decision is taken in war is as hazardous as knowing what will happen if a certain path towards a lasting peace is taken after that war is (provisionally, at least) 'ended'. As Colin Gray puts it, 'defining and achieving decisive victory' is never a precise art. 'If "victory" unadorned is hard to corral intellectually, what sense can we make of "decisive" victory?' He points out that many states in powerful, even seemingly unassailable, positions have believed they could achieve that, and been destroyed along with their own hubris. They often saw themselves as the great 'peacemakers' with their own version of what 'peace' should mean (Rome, Imperial Japan and Nazi Germany, possibly now the United States). But they could not predict what the effects of their warmaking to bring about a lasting peace could be. Without a realistic political goal, war can simply not be successful.

## Naval warfare

Naval warfare, long considered the 'senior' service, is now largely relegated to a back-up role to the army and air force in all major nations. However, it gave birth in the modern era to understandings of war that go beyond the mere command of the seas that are of continued relevance today (Tangredi, in Baylis et al., 2002).

Not only can naval historians give us an understanding of purely naval tactics (Rodger, 2006; Davies, 2002), but they also have given much fruit for thought about what makes a 'great' military commander – Nelson being the obvious example (Lambert, 2004; Coleman, 2001). Two other key developments in the study of IR more broadly should also be considered – in particular, 'geopolitics'. Halford Mackinder's idea of the need for the dominance of the 'World Island' gave much food for thought to geopolitically obsessed political leaders (Parker, 1982). The absolute need for sea power divided these late nineteenth-century geopoliticians, with Mackinder coming to the belief that it was not absolutely essential for global empire, while Mahan and Friedrich Ratzel believed it was (Ashworth and Ashworth, 2010). American President Theodore Roosevelt and his successors, as well as American geopolitical theorist Admiral Mahan (Gat, 1992: chapter 4), saw Britain's claim to be the protector of the world's shipping as an attack on the 'Freedom of the Seas' about which Woodrow Wilson made much play (it figured in the Fourteen Points of 1918; see also British naval theorist Julian Corbett, 1914/2009) and the subsequent naval disarmament conferences in Washington in 1922 and 1932 (Williams, 1998). It also convinced Adolf Hitler, and his favourite geopolitician Karl Haushofer, whose notions of *Lebensraum* had a distinctly geopolitical slant to them (Herzstein, 1982).

## BOX 2.2 NAVAL WARFARE

The great exception to the emergence of land-based armies in the eighteenth and nineteenth centuries is, of course, that of Britain. The mastering of sea-warfare by the British was not, as the mythology would have it, instantaneous. The Spanish Armada (1588) was not defeated by the tiny and badly resourced Elizabethan navy. Cromwell's navy took a sound beating from the Dutch, and 'The Navy of the Restoration [the 1660s] was powerful, but bankrupt' (Rodger, 2004: 98). British sea dominance was still not a clear fact in the eighteenth century, as the fall of Yorktown in 1784 to the American colonists, aided by the French fleet, clearly showed (Rodger, 2004). The real opportunity for sea power to both cement British claims to statehood and to global dominance came with the emergence of a more competent civil service and to disruptions to the only viable opponent, France, as well as Napoleon Bonaparte's subsequent brilliance as a land commander, which starved the French navy of resources. The Royal Navy was thus a necessary condition for the development of a huge maritime commercial empire, but also needed an essential state to back it up. Its success can also be said to have been at the core of the development of a (particularly) British national identity (q.v.). Here we should not ignore the literary interpretations – Patrick O'Brien and C. S. Forester being the most notable – that have had, and continue to have, a major impact on Britain's view of itself.

## TOTAL WAR, C. 1900–1990

The expression 'total war' is often used about the era since 1914. It denotes a supposed transition from a world in which warfare was essentially between armies and where civilians were largely exempted from its effects. It also often connotes a move from the relatively low levels of casualties of the eighteenth and nineteenth centuries to the huge death totals of the world wars of 1914–1918 and 1939–1945, as well as the potential totals caused by atomic weapons. It contains within its logic the idea that technology can overcome and make largely irrelevant notions of courage and honour (Coker, 2007; Ignatieff, 1999). It is the warfare of the machine, projected in the modern and postmodern imagination into wars between machines (Wells, 1898; Pick, 1993; many films like the *Terminator* series; Virilio, 1989). All of these delimitations have their problems – war has always pitted more technologically advanced armies against those less so enabled; the supposedly more 'civilized' period before the last century often saw huge casualties and suffering among civilian populations, especially in civil wars and revolutions. But the rise of democracy as a dominant form of ideal political organization has made such horrors less acceptable in liberal societies and beyond (Norman, 1995; Williams, 2006).

Wherein lie the roots of these paradoxes of our collective understanding of the evolution of modern warfare? Partly it lies in our received understandings of what war is for. Liddell Hart saw in the 1940s that the problem of the late nineteenth-century military mind had been that it was still obsessed with the great thinkers of ancient times who had had their belief in the necessity of military glory reinforced by the romantic nationalist feelings of the period before 1914. He comments that '[this] was beneficial in so far as it led soldiers to imbibe the bottled wisdom of the Greek and Roman masters. But it too often produced an intoxication ... a revival of the phalanx, [and] ignored ... the modern fact of the bullet' (Liddell Hart, 1944: 110). When this hubris was observed in the enemies of the great imperial European powers, it could be an advantage to the conquerors.

The justification for the waging of war against colonial peoples in the modern period more broadly draws from the wellspring of classical justification by writers about Rome's treatment of 'barbarians', while also respecting Liddell Hart's 'bullet' addendum. For, as Hilaire Belloc wrote in *The Modern Traveller*, 'Whatever happens, we have got, the Maxim gun, and they have not' (1898). The lesson for the newly colonized peoples of the nineteenth century was that if you wished to be 'free' it was good idea to submit to the fealty of a great republic, a logic that sees its sequel in liberal imperialism in most Western states in the nineteenth and, indeed, in the twentieth century. This dialectic has pervaded modern thinking about war and statehood – and is one that we also see in non-Western thought systems like Islam. We are constantly torn between the idea of a single *Imperium* (or *Umma* in Islam) or that of more atomized, 'self-determined' nation-states (Williams, 1998).

But in the early twentieth century, the disequilibrium of the West versus the rest was soon to be turned on its head by the very same technology that gave the West an advantage in its colonial adventures. Individual courage arguably started being downplayed in favour of later developments in 'post modern war' (Gray, 1998) once the offensive gave away the advantage to the defensive, probably first really apparent in the American Civil War of 1861–1865 (McPherson, 2001; Keegan, 2009). In the trenches of World War I, machine guns made the taking of even a few yards of enemy territory a fruitless and bloody enterprise (Liddell Hart, 1944; Belloc, 1898).

## WORLD WAR I, 1914–1918

Such was, and is, the importance of World War I for the study of IR that it merits its own section. It has generated huge numbers of books and articles, quite often more than a hundred a year. Good recent summaries of this literature, including discussions of the diplomatic, social and cultural historiographical trends, include Jay Winter and Antoine Prost's *The Great War in History* (2005). There are many excellent overview histories of this war, but the best short introduction is probably by Gerard De Groot (De Groot, 2000) and a longer account by David Stevenson (Stevenson, 2005), though we could cite many more.

The reasons for this widespread obsession are many, among the most important was that it was the first truly *global* war. It had a particular *nature*, not reproduced in its entirety ever again (but nearly so in the Korean War, 1950–1953, and the Ethiopian/ Eritrean wars of the 1980s and 1990s). It was the first in which machines became arguably more important than manpower (Pick, 1993). And it was the first that pitted a variety of (mostly) democratically elected governments against each other and hence was the first war to really change the way public opinion played a role in the war and the peace that succeeded it (Knock, 1992). This has had profound effects for how we see the *mythology*, and how the (then) contemporary as well as succeeding generations have grounded it in a collective *memory*, with a corresponding change in the *iconography* of war and in its *commemoration* (Fussell, 1975; Winter, 1995).

Last, but by no means least, World War I was the first where, in the 'civilized' nations of the West – the main protagonists of the war – there was a shift in an understanding as to how the world could be profoundly changed by war. This reflection ranged from those who saw the war as a system-changing event (Polanyi, 1945; Carr, 1939 are the better-known examples), a move that in effect gave rise to the discipline of IR itself. Certainly the main 'thinkers of the Twenty Years' Crisis', as they have been dubbed (Long and Wilson, 1995) were often policymakers in 1914–1918, who often became academics after it, many of them great liberal figures who aimed to prop up liberal democracy or economics (notably, John Maynard Keynes and Friedrich Hayek). Others, like Lenin, Stalin and Trotsky, not to mention Hitler and Mussolini, drew the opposite conclusions and tried with all their vigour and military might to overthrow the alliance that had won the war and the 'Carthaginian' peace. IR was forged in that cauldron of war and has borne its mark ever since. But equally it gave birth to interests that are only now really surfacing in the study of IR. Feminism, for example, has had a huge boost from writers like Cynthia Enloe (1993/2000), but who has now heard of the prominent (feminist and pacifist) Labour Party woman delegate to the League of Nations from 1929, Helena Swanwick. Her statement of 1915 that:

> The adventures of women in war are solitary and full of horror … When aviators drop bombs, when guns bombard fortified towns, it is not possible to avoid the women and children who may chance to be in the way. Women have to make good the economic disasters of war; they go short, they work double tides, they pay war taxes and war prices, like men, and out of smaller incomes.
>
> (Swanwick, 1915: 8 and 1, quoted in Ashworth, 2011: 30)

The collective memory and representation of this war has had a more lasting effect than most. Historians, military commentators and cultural analysts have gone through a series of linked phases of observation. The phase of what might be called 'acceptance' was brief, in that there was no huge questioning of the way the war was fought until the late 1920s, in the words of the British Victory Medal (given to all surviving servicemen, including my grandfather, John Williams), which was described as the 'Great War for Civilization', although there was a natural regret about the huge loss of life. Ernst Jünger, a much-decorated and wounded German storm trooper, who later flirted with Nazism but was never a true convert, wrote an autobiographical account of his war experiences, *Storm of Steel* (2004), as a paean to the nobility of conflict but also as a realistic account of trench warfare that is still probably the best of its kind. Jünger's most moving chapter, about the fighting around Guillemont in September 1916, was the same battle where the prime minister's son, Raymond Asquith, was killed and where my grandfather's brother Charles (aged 20) was killed. Jünger later became a key figure in the reconciliation of Europe after 1945 and wrote a little-remarked-upon but important rejoinder to his own book, published in 1948 in the United States (but not in Britain), *The Peace* (1948).

## BOX 2.3 WORLD WAR I IN LITERATURE

In the late 1920s and 1930s a series of literary interpretations, notably Erich Maria Remarque's *All Quiet on the Western Front* (1929), Siegfried Sassoon's *Memoirs of an Infantry Officer* (1930) and Robert Graves' *Goodbye to All That* (1929), contributed to a growing revulsion with war, in Britain particularly. The positive view of the generalship, especially by Field Marshal Haig, was definitively punctured by the subsequent publication of a series of major works of poetry, notably the posthumous poems of Wilfred Owen (killed a few days before the Armistice in 1918) and several others of note. This was reinforced by later interpretations, notably Paul Fussell's *The Great War and Modern Memory* (Fussell, 1975). Fussell has summed up the case file against Haig and the politicians who let him do what he did: 'The disaster [in this case, the Battle of the Somme, 1916] had many causes. Lack of imagination was one … Another cause was traceable to the class system and the assumptions it sanctioned … A final cause … was a total lack of surprise. There was a hopeless absence of cleverness about the whole thing, entirely characteristic of its author' (Fussell, 1975: 13).

*What matters more – people or technology?*

The military criticism was arguably first concretized by Basil Liddell Hart, himself an officer in the trenches (Liddell Hart, 1932/1944), and followed up by other military figures like Major General J. F. C. Fuller (Fuller, 1948), who is quoted by Colin Gray as saying in January 1919 that 'strategy, command, leadership, discipline, supply, organization and all the moral and physical paraphernalia of war are nothing to a high superiority of weapons … no army of 50 years ago before any date selected would stand a dog's chance against the army existing at that date.' Fuller's bleak assessment of the impossibility of men fighting in a technological war is agreed with by Gray on the level of his emphasis on the importance of technology, but as 'monumentally wrong' in that technology can never determine wars, people do – 'strategic history tells us that people matter more than machines' (Gray, 2005: 99–100).

This debate is far from over. In between the wars there was a major change of heart in all the major combatant states about the way war should be fought, given the obvious advantage of the defensive on the Western Front. The names of Heinz Guderian in Germany and Colonel (later General) Charles de Gaulle in France revolutionized warfare and gave the advantage of war back to the offensive (Kier, 1999).

The reverberations of 1914–1918 go wider than this one war, though. Fussell quotes Corelli Barnett as saying that 'the pattern established during the Great War is still with us: great international questions are seen in simple moralistic and idealistic terms, as emotional crusades' (Fussell, 1975: 109). Philip Towle examines a variety of British justifications for standing up to 'tyranny' over more than two centuries. He reminds us that Britain has been involved in many more wars than most countries; that the evangelical side of British foreign policy has been more than evident since the time of Wilberforce at least in a 'synergy between national interest and faith' (Towle, 2009: 2). But history can also be used to justify the opposite. Historians and policymakers of the Balkans still evoke what Ambassador Richard Holbrooke called the 'Rebecca West effect' (Holbrooke, 1998) to warn against extrapolating the problems of one Balkan (or any other) war into another one. More recent novelists like Pat Barker, and Sebastian Faulks in *Birdsong* (Faulks, 1993), have added to this primary generation with similar presentations of war, but, as Niall Ferguson points out, more sex (Ferguson, 1998: xxxxi–xxxxii).

The role of memory in any war has, of course, always been important, but World War I took that truth to a higher level, both immediately after it was ended and since. In the immediate aftermath, the war elicited demands for revenge and reparation from Germany and its allies from the victorious Western Allies (Macmillan, 2001, and Williams, 2006, both have useful summaries of a vast literature).

That was followed by a continental-wide, even global, wave of grief and mourning and the erection of countless memorials to the war, as well as the reorganization and tending in perpetuity of war graves, both new phenomena of the last century (Winter, 1995) and continued for every major war since.

Partly as a reaction to the generally accepted interpretation of the unremitting horror of the trenches and the general futility of the conflict this has not gone unchallenged. Ferguson's *The Pity of War* (1998) was a not-uncontroversial milestone that made a number of (then) startling claims, notably about the widely accepted version of the 'evil [of] war', 'the myths of militarism' and German war guilt (though others had already begun questioning this long before in the 1930s). He even claimed how liberated many soldiers on all sides felt to be in the trenches and away from their jobs in factories or mines, as well as the sense of comradeship that such warfare engendered. This phenomenon was indeed mentioned by many survivors, mostly notoriously by Benito Mussolini and his 'trench aristocracy' and by many other interwar figures of the Right in Britain (notably Mosley and the British Union of Fascists: Skidelsky, 1990), Germany (Jünger, 2004; Hitler, 1924/1939) and France (Wohl, 1979). So it must be admitted that the evidence is quite strong that, in France and Germany at least, the 'Generation of 1914' did not universally remember the war with horror and distaste, and for every book like Henri's Barbusse's *Le Feu* (1916) and, after 1945, Roger Martin du Gard's many tomes, there were others, like Pierre Drieu la Rochelle's *La Bataille de Charleroi* (1915) and Jünger, who found war uplifting and renewing. We might also add the interest shown by international historians and historians of ideas in the 'modernist' aspect of this war and the creation of the 'new man' (one recent brilliant addition being Gentile, 2008, but see also Overy, 2009).

There has also been a spirited defence of the generals, especially Haig, by various scholars, notably Gary Sheffield and its 'forgotten victory' (2002, 2011) and Walter Reid (2006), who have written substantial biographies of Haig and (in Sheffield's case) edited Haig's *War Diaries* (Sheffield, 2002, 2011; Bourne and Sheffield, 2005; Reid, 2006). More populist writers like Gordon Corrigan have made even more extravagant revisionist claims, as in his *Mud, Blood and Poppycock* (2007).

The twentieth century in general and World War I in particular saw a large number of new developments in the variety and scope of methods for effective warfare against new populations. The much-criticized German 'militarism' of the period during and after German unification in 1870 perhaps sums this up best. In line with the previously described nineteenth-century military doctrine, the German High Command coined a doctrine of 'total warfare' and *Schrecklichkeit* ('frightfulness') in 1902, summed up in the *Kriegsbrauche in Landkriege* ('The custom of war in land warfare') thus:

> The conduct of war allows a belligerent state to employ any means which will facilitate the accomplishment of the aim of war ... A war waged with energy cannot be directed solely against the combatants of the hostile state and the positions which they defend, but will and *should* [sic] equally endeavour to destroy the collective intellectual and material resources of the enemy.

Humanitarian considerations, such as would protect individuals or their property, can only be regarded in so far as the nature and object of the war will allow … fortresses, but also every town and village which may be an impediment to military progress … may be besieged, bombarded, stormed and destroyed if the enemy defends them, and in some cases if he only occupies them.

(Hanson, 2008: 20–21)

Such logic saw its full development on land in the battles of the Somme and Verdun in 1916. They had seen their initial flowerings during the American Civil War and in the Franco-Prussian War of 1871. Hilaire Belloc, a prominent Franco-British poet, intellectual and critic of Germany throughout his life (1870–1953) never forgot that his family home in France had been desecrated by German troops in 1871 (Wilson, 1997: 9). In the same war, the French artist Camille Pissarro found that most of his paintings from the studio he had had to flee in 1871 before the same troops had been used by Prussian military butchers (the word is used here in the culinary sense) as meat chopping boards, which is why there are few Pissarros in existence from before that date.

Deliberate attacks on civilian targets were not a new feature in 1914–1918, but they assumed much more horrific characteristics. Belloc was not alone in seeing World Wars I and II as a struggle for the very soul of Western civilization, and with some clear reason. The first deliberate German bombing raids on British towns and cities took place in 1914 and there were plans, only stopped by the Armistice of 1918, for effective fire-storm raids on London, raids which did take place in World War II. As Prime Minister Baldwin said to the House of Commons on 10 November 1932, 'I think it is well also for the man in the street to realise there is no power on earth that can protect him from bombing, whatever people may tell him. The bomber will always get through … The only defence is in offence, which means you have got you kill more women and children quicker than the enemy if you want to save yourselves' (Hanson, 2008: 454–455). But this led the very self-proclaimed advocates of 'civilization' in London, Washington and elsewhere to use the same policies of 'frightfulness' through the bombing of civilian areas in Germany and Japan, with much greater effect in terms of casualties and damage (British Bombing Survey Unit, 1998; Lindqvist, 2001).

## WORLD WAR II, 1939–1945

Many traditional historians of this war have tended to concentrate on Grand Strategy, and the Conferences (Reynolds, 1981, 2006, 2007; Sainsbury, 1985, 1996) where this strategy was thrashed out. In particular, the three-way relationship between Churchill, Roosevelt and Stalin has been seen as key to understanding how and why certain political and military options were adopted and others dropped. France, a defeated power, has been seen as peripheral to these discussions, which has understandably rankled with the French and their historians ever since (Lacouture, 1991; Kersaudy, 1981). However, some French and foreign historians largely blame domestic French factors for *La Défaite* of 1940 (Duroselle, 1979; Adamthwaite, 1995), as well as for the aftermath, an orgy of internal reprisal (Shennan, 1989).

Quite a number of participants in these debates have written their memoirs or commentaries, notably Dean Acheson (1969), Adolf Berle (1961), Herbert Feis (1970), George Kennan (architect of postwar containment of the USSR and National Security Advisor under President Truman) (1951/1984), and Edward Stettinius (Secretary of State, 1943–1945) (1950). Their intentions and interactions, particularly among American policymakers, have also been subjected to much inquiry (for example, see Harper, 1996), and all stress what Robert Hathaway calls the 'ambiguous' relationship between the Anglo-Saxon and other Allies (1981; Reynolds, 2006; Williams, 1998). The actual conduct of the war has attracted huge attention from military historians, interested in both the personalities of generals on all sides, and especially Dwight G. Eisenhower (also later US president) (Ambrose, 1983) and field marshals Montgomery and Rommel (Kitchen, 2009), among others, as well as in the politicians.

## BOX 2.4 THE PERSONALIZATION OF WAR

At the level of human agency there have been many biographies of Hitler (Bullock, 1962; Kershaw, 1998, 2000a) and Stalin (most recently Boobbyer, 2000, and Service, 2004) and even comparative biographies (Bullock's [1991] dual biography of Hitler and Stalin, and Overy, 2004). Churchill (Gilbert, 1992; Jenkins, 2001), Mussolini (Mack Smith, 2001) and Roosevelt (Freidel, 1990; Schlesinger, 1957–1960). Roosevelt's intriguing way of doing business with Allies and the American people as a whole has been seen as crucial in holding the ultimately odd Alliance together (Dallek, 1979; Meacham, 2003). In recent times there have been investigations into their private social circles (Montefiori [2005b], on Stalin). Last but not least there has been the publication of the war diaries of key officials, which throw light on the office politics they generated – the British version being perhaps the most entertaining, with the Sir John Colville diaries (2004), and those of Lord Alanbrooke (2001).

## The rise of Nazi Germany

This next great system-changing war of the twentieth century took the developments of World War I to new depths of horror and promise – 'horror' because there is no disagreement among respectable historians or IR commentators that the systematic brutalization of populations by the German Nazi regime of 1933–1945 or, indeed, that by the Soviet Union before and after that period were terrible processes to live through or witness. But the explanation of the rise of a totalitarian system has been the major aim of most historians. Nazi Germany, Soviet Russia, and even Mao Tse-Tung's China and lesser dictatorships, have been the extremist touchstones of the last century, with Germany still being seen by most historians as the greatest of warnings from history; As Kershaw puts it:

> it has the quality of a paradigm for the twentieth century … it reflected, among other things, the total claim of the modern state, unforeseen levels of state repression and violence, previously unparalleled manipulation of the media …, unprecedented cynicism in international relations, the acute dangers of ultra-nationalism, and the immensely destructive power of ideologies of racial superiority … alongside the perverted usage of modern technology and 'social engineering.'
>
> (Kershaw, 1998: xix–xx)

This equivalence of the two great authoritarian regimes has seen its apogee in writing about 'totalitarianism' in general. Hannah Arendt is maybe the most celebrated figure in this tendency (Arendt, 1958). J. L. Talmon traces this political tendency back to the French Revolution and the idea of the 'popular will' (Talmon, 1952), a tradition that follows Edmund Burke's condemnation of the same revolution in 1792 (Burke, 1968). It could be argued that the French, Russian and Chinese revolutions form a tradition of 'popular' revolution that gave birth to socialism. This distinguishes them from the more 'bourgeois' revolutions of England and the United States that led to liberal political systems with better checks and balances to impede the rise of demagogues (Skocpol, 1979; Williams, in Chan and Williams, 1994: part 2). For the emergence of a Nazi 'empire', see Chapter 5 and Mazower (2009a).

In explaining how Nazi Germany was able to unleash the horrors of World War II, the majority of historians have concentrated upon either the emergence of the Nazi and Soviet political systems or on the mechanisms that were used by that system to dominate Europe during and after the war (in the case of Soviet Russia, see Applebaum, 2003). In the first category are (among many others) Michael Burleigh, Ian Kershaw and Richard Evans (Burleigh, 2000; Kershaw, 1998, 2000b; Evans, 2003). Richard Evans has emphasized the role of the study of history itself as a factor in the rise of an ultra-nationalist Germany, thus taking some blame for the outbreak of both world wars (Evans, 1987, 2000a). Others have looked at the cultural underpinnings and ironies of German cultural history: how can the people who produced Beethoven, Kant and Goethe have also produced Adolf Hitler and his ilk (Stern, 1974, 1999)?

## The Holocaust and the emergence of human rights

The extensive literature on the most remarked upon single atrocity of the Nazi period, the Holocaust (Hebrew 'Shoah' is often used interchangeably, as in Claude Lanzmann's magnificent documentary film of 1985) of the Jewish, homosexual and Roma populations of Europe, including in Germany, merits a section on its own.

There is so much that has been written about the events that made it up, especially the period of the 'Final Solution' (*Endlösung*, the Nazi euphemism for the extermination of the Jews), that books have been written to guide the reader through the maze of what has been written about it (good examples being Landau, 1998, 2006). Though it is invidious to have to choose, Saul Friedländer's *Nazi Germany and the Jews, 1933–1945* is usually accepted as the best overview (and now abridged in one volume: Friedländer, 2009). It is the particular collision of two nationalisms, German and Zionist, though not their equivalence, that gives the Holocaust its special meaning for global history and still affects any discussion of European or Middle East history (Laqueur, 2003; Fromkin, 2000; Fawcett, 2005). Any selection has to be subjective and we have chosen to concentrate not so much on the 'how' but on the 'why' aspects that have intrigued historians and what, if anything, can be said to have come out of it that is not depressing.

## BOX 2.5 THE 'INTENTIONALITY' OF THE HOLOCAUST

There are many and varied versions and opinions about the 'intentionality' of the Nazis to carry out the Holocaust, with a debate in particular as to whether Hitler's *Mein Kampf* of 1925/1926 (Hitler, 1939/1992) was in some ways a blueprint for what became the 'Final Solution' (Yehuda, 2002; Friedländer, 2007). There are also important commentaries on its domestic German roots (Goldhagen, 1997) and even how Germans might be said to have overcome them (Stern, 1999). There is also a 'Holocaust denial' literature in existence, though we will not dignify it with too much attention (indeed, it would be illegal for us to discuss this in any German edition of this book). One good summary of such views can be found in Lipstadt (1993). It has unfortunately come to some public attention due to the pronouncements of such pundits as Mahmoud Ahmedinejad (currently President of Iran) and other notable anti-Semites.

Why was not more done to prevent it? Historians have tended to be scathing about Allied non-efforts to help save the Jews of Europe during the Holocaust (Gilbert, 1991). Saul Friedländer's epoch-making *Pius XII and the Third Reich* (Friedländer, 1966) roundly indicted the Catholic Church for its passivity faced with the horror of Nazi actions (often reported to the Holy See by disgusted German officers). The International Committee of the Red Cross and the Swiss government had a wealth of knowledge of much that was going on in the extermination camps, and refused entry to many Jewish Germans, with fatal consequences for them, as Swiss historians have now amply documented in a Final Report and seven supplementary volumes edited by Jean-François Bergier in 2002 (http://www.uek.ch/en/index.htm). Britain's record in helping the Jews before, during and after the

Holocaust has not been seen in a very favourable light by some historians. In the interwar period British policy on immigration was unclear (to say the least) and that led to many Jewish Germans being denied entry (though many others were) on the grounds that it would stimulate domestic anti-Semitism, being fanned by Oswald Mosley's British Union of Fascists, a policy that was not relaxed even during the war, when evidence of the Holocaust was as clear in Whitehall as it was in Washington (Ceserani, 1998; London, 2001). French collaboration with their Nazi occupiers is even better documented and condemned, being described simply as 'bad faith' by Carmen Callil (Callil, 2006). Burrin and Calill's works on French views and actions towards French Jews make for difficult reading and still have resonance in French political life. Friedländer lost his own parents to Auschwitz thanks to the French and Swiss authorities (Burrin, 1995; Friedländer, 2007).

There are also few grounds to muster to defend the Allies' record towards the Jews of Europe adequately. Joseph Persico's account of Roosevelt's intelligence about Germany and Japan makes clear that the American and British administrations had ample access to top-secret German, Italian and Japanese cipher traffic that detailed the actions of the SS *Sonderkommandos* (special units) on the Eastern Front as they butchered their way through the Jewish, Roma and homosexual populations of their new conquests in their search to exterminate 'degenerate elements', as well as the setting up of concentration and extermination camps (Persico, 2001). Other Allied intelligence provided substantial supporting evidence (Hinsley, 1988). Michael Beschloss emphasizes the Allied desire to end the war as quickly as possible as a cover-all excuse for relative inaction on the camps, also pointing to the difficulties of bombing such precise targets without killing those who they were trying to help – there were no 'smart' bombs in 1943, and civilians, even in non-German parts of Europe, were often unintended casualties of carpet-bombing (Beschloss, 2002). But, mainly, the Holocaust was simply not seen as a priority by Allied military and political planners.

Last but not least the Holocaust has to be seen as perhaps the best example of the difficulties in history of remembering and forgetting. IR now has a burgeoning literature on this topic, often applied to postwar reconciliation and the like (Mac Ginty and Williams, 2009; Hayner, 2002; Rigby, 2001; Barkan, 2001). But the great impellers of this writing have been World War I and the Holocaust. Autobiographies of Holocaust survivors are our primary documents, along with the physical evidence, with notable examples being those of Primo Levi and Elie Wiesel (Levi, 2007; Wiesel and Wiesel, 2008) and collections (Whitworth, 2003; Zullo and Bovsun, 2005), but also in fictional accounts that try to explain what the Holocaust meant by those who were or were not participants. A recent moving attempt at this can be found in John Boyne's *The Boy in the Striped Pyjamas* (Boyne, 2007). But the 'truth' is one that is both too difficult for most people to comprehend and certainly difficult to explain. Such are the emotions deployed over these events that even those who wrote about them 'toned them down a bit' for a general readership, leading to a lively debate about 'truth and lies in Holocaust fiction' (Franklin, 2011).

## Genocide and human rights as by-products of war

One might have hoped that the Holocaust had finally made anti-Semitism into an unacceptable form of respectable political discourse, at least in the West among liberals, though the rise of neo-Nazism seems to indicate that we cannot count on that. Guilt among the Allied powers and a defeated Axis has led to the realization of 'genocide' (the word was first used by Raphael Lemkin in 1944) being a unique 'crime against humanity'. Others have reminded us that the term may be new, but the practice is as old as human history (Kiernan, 2007). The very term 'human rights' made its proper appearance in the aftermath of the Holocaust, though its roots can be said to be far deeper (Forsythe, 2006). In concrete terms the aftermath of the war saw an American-led drive to get human rights higher up the global agenda led by Roosevelt's widow, Eleanor Roosevelt (Borgwardt, 2005), though a cynic might see that agenda as having little traction during the Cold War years of US–Soviet confrontation.

# THE COLD WAR, 1947–1990

As with the two world wars, the Cold War needs a bibliographical introduction. There are a number of good overviews of the causes, course and results of the Cold War, with the works of John Lewis Gaddis being seminal. His *The Cold War* (Gaddis, 2005) will doubtless be bettered one day, but has not been yet, and with his *We Now Know: Rethinking Cold War History* (Gaddis, 1997) they are only the culmination of many books on the subject. There are some excellent collections of readings by authoritative historians, of which Melvyn Leffler and Odd Arne Westad's (2009) and Charles Maier's (1996) are a good place to start.

The Cold War, which succeeded a brief period of harmony between the Allies of 1941–1945, pitted two camps against each other after 1947 in a standoff that had strategic, ideological, even eschatological* roots (Kennedy-Pipe, 1995; Leffler and Painter, 1994). There are many accounts of the motivations for the various parties to start the conflict and much debate between 'traditionalists' (who blame the Russians for starting it), 'revisionists' (who blame the United States) and 'post-revisionists' (who blame both sides or who see the logic of war as being to blame). In the traditionalist camp we can place George Kennan, who coined the expression 'containment' to explain American desires to control ('contain') the Soviet Union (Kennan, 1968/1972, 1951/1984), but also many other actors on the American side (Nitze, 1989). The invention and use of nuclear weapons was naturally a backdrop to all of these debates (for the development of the American and British bombs, see Rhodes, 1998; De Groot, 2004; Gowing, 1964; for the development of the Russian atomic and hydrogen bombs, see Holloway, 1996; Zubok and Pleshakov, 1997).

In the revisionist camp we can place Gar Alperovitz (1965: 41), who saw the United States as using 'Atomic diplomacy' to intimidate its foes, Gabriel Kolko

* regarding the ultimate destiny of mankind or the world

(1990) and William Appleman Williams (1962), as using economic and military and economic pressure for the same effect. Containment and its 1950s successor, 'roll-back', was then seen by these historians as part of an overall conspiracy by what C. Wright Mills (1959) called the 'Military Industrial Complex' of the United States against the rest of the planet. Daniel Yergin's generally very sound historical research is perhaps the best example of more moderate interpretations. Yergin coined the phrase the 'Riga Axiom' to distinguish hard-line anti-Bolsheviks (like Kennan) from those who believed that a reconciliation between the USSR and the West had been possible after their cooperation in World War II. The more benign group followed what Yergin called the 'Yalta Axiom' (Yergin, 1977).

In the 'post-revisionist' camp, a good point of departure is Louis Halle (1967) or indeed Gaddis himself (for a good survey of all three schools, see Leffler and Painter, 1994; Dunbabin, 1994a; Maier, 1996; Gaddis, 1984; and for a rethink of them, Westad, 2000). The Post-revisionists blamed both superpowers for acting according to the rules of the Greek tragedy – that is, power diplomacy. Louis Halle's (1967) *The Cold War as History* and Diane Clemens' (1970) *Yalta* are models of their kind. They are essentially 'realist' interpretations based on sound archival research. Caroline Kennedy-Pipe (1995) quarried the Russian archives and concluded, against the revisionist school, that 'US attitudes toward Moscow were far from fixed in the spring of 1946'. Members of the Woodrow Wilson Foundation's Cold War project, directed by John Lewis Gaddis, also consulted the Soviet archives. Gaddis is the dean of Cold War historians. His reflections on the period in his (1997) *We Now Know: Rethinking Cold War History* shed doubt on the trenchant views of both revisionists and traditionalists alike.

A greater degree of perspective is now becoming possible. One of the lessons of the system-transforming conflict is to see that it was, as Halle is quoted as saying, 'a phenomenon not without precedent in the long history of international conflict; a phenomenon that, experience has taught us, has its own dynamics; a phenomenon that, typically, goes through a certain cycle with a beginning, a middle and an end' (Halle, quoted by Gaddis, 1997, vii) As Gaddis has also written, any new Cold War history 'will [have to] take ideas seriously', for there is a pressing need to show how ideas have evolved and to find a replacement discourse for that of the Cold War. Ideology has turned again to 'ideaology'. Along with Gaddis, students might consult Cox's (1998) *Rethinking the Soviet Collapse*, Booth's (1998) *Statecraft and Security: The Cold War and Beyond*, and Hogan's (1992) *The End of the Cold War: Its Meanings and Implications*.

It is now generally accepted that it was not one war, but rather an embedded nest of incidents, crises and full-on wars, where the 'superpowers' (the United States and the Soviet Union) never came to blows directly – mainly attributed to them both being nuclear powers capable of 'mutually assured destruction' (with the appropriate acronym, MAD).

It is also generally accepted that the root of all the problems lay in disagreements over the division of Germany (Acheson, 1969; Kennan, 1968/1972; Deighton, 1993; Trachtenberg, 1999). Whether that can be attributed to disagreements over reparations (Kuklick, 1972) or over wider arguments about spheres of influence that went beyond Germany to include Greece, Iran and beyond (Trachtenberg, 1999 is a good introduction to this idea), the 'front line' of the Cold War was most visibly 'Check Point Charlie' in Berlin, which has been immortalized in many spy thrillers by John Le Carré and other novelists. The resulting incidents ranged from disagreements about the division of power and influence in the different sectors of Germany, starting with the Berlin Airlift (1948), the declaration of a German Democratic Republic (GDR, 1949–1990; Fulbrook, 1995, 2005), the setting up of the Warsaw Pact and the North Atlantic Treaty Organization (NATO, 1949–present; Galambos et al., 1989) and continuing at various pitches of hostility through the building of the Berlin Wall in 1963 (Gearson and Schake, 2002), through a gradual thaw known as 'détente', which culminated in the signature of the 'Helsinki Final Act' of 1975 and went on till the Berlin Wall was dismantled in 1989 and Germany finally reunited in 1991 (for more on this, see 'Peace', Chapter 3).

There were other major conflicts, with a very destructive war in Korea (1950–1953; Stueck, 1997) that saw American, British and other United Nations forces in pitched battles against Chinese and North Korean troops. In Vietnam both the French imperial authorities (1952–1954), and the Americans found themselves losing a war of attrition against the North Vietnamese and Viet Cong (1964–1975; Smith, 1987, 1988; Daum, Gardner and Mansbach, 2003). In Afghanistan (1981–1988; Urban, 1988; Galeotti, 1995), the Soviet Union was finally forced to withdraw after attempting to occupy the country in support of a puppet regime. Other conflicts were long-lasting with, usually, the Soviet Union and its allies backing one side and the United States and its allies backing the other, overtly or covertly. This was the case in a number of African wars: Mozambique, Angola and Namibia (1975–1989; Anderson, 2009) and Eritrea-Ethiopia (1963–1993 and 1998–2000; Negash and Tronvoll, 2001), though in these wars no other state really backed Eritrea.

## Culture and the Cold War

Other lasting effects of the historiographical legacy of historians' musings on the Cold War might be said to be economic and cultural. David Caute rightly says that '[t]he "total" physical war [of 1939–1945] was followed by a "total" ideological and *cultural* war between the victors' and that for this '[t]here was no precedent' (Caute, 2003: 5) in the history of all warring civilizations. There were times in the interwar and post-1945 periods when Soviet film, music and literature was seen as the equal of, or even better than, anything coming out of Hollywood or Western concert halls or publication houses. Great Western philosophers dedicated their books not to Roosevelt or Churchill, but rather to Lenin or Stalin. This may now look preposterous, but at the time the soul of mankind was in the balance and tipping towards Moscow. Caute's previous books include *The Fellow Travellers* (Caute, 1988), about misguided Westerners who went to worship at the altar of Stalinism, and *The Great Fear*, about the McCarthyite persecutions in the United States. We need to remember that art and politics have always held up mirrors to each other, and especially in war. Bertholt Brecht, Arthur Miller, Jean-Paul Sartre and Albert Camus, as well as

Stanislavski, Eisenstein and Shostakovich, were all both stimulated by the Cold War and victims of it in many ways (Scott-Smith and Krabbendam, 2003).

## Economics of the Cold War

The counterpoint to military sabre-rattling and cultural counterattacks was the equally important attempt by the West to blockade the Soviet Union by denying it technological assistance and more general economic help. In the area of trade, 'economic containment' was started in 1947 with the 'CoCom', a shadowy committee within NATO that instituted an effective strategic embargo that gravely diminished Soviet technological achievement (Jackson, 2001). This process had predated World War II to some extent, with views ranging from British Prime Minister Lloyd George, who talked in 1922 about 'civilization though trade'; through US President Herbert Hoover, who was in favour of trade but no diplomatic recognition of the Soviet Union in 1928–1932; President Roosevelt, who advocated trade and recognition (Williams, 1992); and presidents after Roosevelt until 1990, who supported CoCom (Mastanduno, 1992).

## SOME CONCLUDING REMARKS

These concluding remarks are intended to ask if there are any broad lessons that what we loosely call the 'historical record', and specifically the history of war, can tell us for the future of such activity. Are the wars now being fought in places like Iraq susceptible to being explained using the 'lessons of history'? There are some obvious ones. Civilians have increasingly come to bear the brunt of the suffering that is war. It would, nevertheless, be ridiculous to claim that somehow wars have not always made them suffer. To read the accounts of the destruction of Jerusalem by Roman legions by the historian Josephus in 70 BCE (Goodman, 2007; Montefiore, 2011) or the sack of Constantinople in 1214 CE is to be forcefully reminded that atrocities have always gone hand in hand with military action (Angold, 2007). Equally, soldiers themselves suffer appalling privation, as well as wounds and death in war, and always have done. Journalist Anthony Loyd's account of the wars in the former Yugoslavia and former British Ambassador to Moscow Rodric Braithwaite's of the (Soviet) occupation of Afghanistan in the 1980s show that, as do accounts of the Crimean War in the 1850s or of the Thirty Years' War of the early seventeenth century (Loyd, 2000; Braithwaite, 2011; Grimmelshausen, 1668/1999).

## Postmodern war?

It is very popular at present to read in IR texts that the combination of hi-tech killing and low-tech brutality by non-state actors has somehow changed the rules of the game so fundamentally that we have to agree with Michael Clarke that 'the phenomenon of conflict and warfare is changing in ways that appear ... fundamental' (2001: 663–671). The fundamental dilemma of how to deal with war is thus made even more acute by the possible changes within it.

But equally a liberal observer of war and peace could claim the opposite – we have changed 'the nature of domestic economic and political systems' even if only the most optimistic liberal would claim to be able to change 'human nature', whatever that is taken to be. As Christopher Coker points out, the 'historical perspective' of the average German after 1918 was that the 'First World War did not end ... It continued on another front – the home front' (1997). He points to many wars not having been seen as 'ending', except in the view of those who had won them, and to the confusion of the very concepts of peace and war, much as Blainey did (1988; see also Introduction to this volume). Coker's answer is that we have a very 'nineteenth-century view of war', ones that do 'end', usually with a peace treaty, whereas most of the wars since then, and especially now, are the products of 'longstanding social conflicts' that flare up and dissipate in accordance with their own internal logic. We have, in other words, to understand why the participants are fighting their wars (Coker, 1997: 616–617, 626–627). We might even take Coker's logic further and ask if the idea of any 'end' is an illusion, a view proposed by Jean Baudrillard (1994).

## Fighting the last war

As generals get ready to fight the last war, so we as analysts get ready to project the 'lessons' of the last war on to the next. The best-known example of this is that the 'lessons' of the Treaty of Versailles were learned in the preparation of the end of World War II (Macmillan, 2001). Likewise, in the 1950s the further 'lesson' was learned that the betrayal of small states at Munich by the powers of the time in 1938 had led to the appeasement of dictators, and that this should never happen again. This lesson was then visited on the Soviet Union, which could not be appeased but had to be 'contained' or even 'rolled back', and on countries in the developing world, like Egypt, where Prime Minister Anthony Eden famously compared President Nasser to Hitler (Lucas, 1991, 1996). In August 2002, George Bush Jr's National Security Advisor Condoleezza Rice used the same kind of analogy about President Saddam Hussein of Iraq.

In the 1990s, the lessons of the last war(s) had to be learned bewilderingly fast. The intervention in Somalia in 1991–1992 taught the international community that it was rash to intervene in 'civil wars'. It was then decided that the wars in the former Yugoslavia (1992–1999) were largely of the civil war variety, in spite of much argument to the contrary. It is arguably the case that we will now 'learn the lessons' of Bosnia and Kosovo, as well as those of Afghanistan and then project them on to our attempts to end the next war, wherever that may be (Iran is a probable contender at the time of writing). Perhaps it could be said that the West in particular is looking at the wars in the former Soviet Union, especially in Chechnya, and in the Middle East (against Iraq), for such lessons. One policy response has been to declare that there is now a global terrorist conspiracy led by 'rogue states' (the American list has officially included, Iraq, Iran, North Korea and Syria) and by a religious fanatical organization led by Osama Bin Laden's al-Qaeda network. This, it might be said, is a classic projection of Western views of the 'other', in this case Islam – a view hotly contested by some and supported by many others. Equally, understanding why the United States and its 'coalition' in Iraq has been so resented locally can be better elucidated by reading even the work of Western historians on Iraq, and that is before we consider what local historians might further explain. As Sir Jeremy Greenstock – Britain's Ambassador to the United Nations in 2003 and UK Special Representative in Iraq, 2003–2004 – has asked: 'Is it too churlish to ask whether the leaders of a more modern administration might have profited from studying [former] experience?' (quoted by Nunn, 1932/2007: 7–8).

## BOX 2.6 THE 'LESSONS OF HISTORY' IN IRAQ?

There has been much written about the difficulties encountered by the American-led coalition since 2003. Some of these writings, like Ali A. Allawi's *The Occupation of Iraq* (2007), give a detailed, if somewhat biased, view of the background to the invasion, with brief references to the British involvement during and after World War I. Others, as in David Philips' *Losing Iraq* (2005), concentrate on the internal debates within the US Administration about what information to use in planning the invasion and its aftermath. *Revolt on the Tigris*, by Mark Etherington (2005), the British Administrator in Wasit Province in Southern Iraq after the invasion of 2003, gives a graphic view from the British side. Equally, if not more, interesting are those by Vice-Admiral Wilfrid Nunn, Commander in Chief British Naval Forces in the south of what became Iraq in 1914–1917, whose 1932 classic, *Tigris Gunboats*, has recently been republished (Nunn, 1932/2007), and a book by a Norwegian historian of the early period of British occupation after World War I, Reidar Visser (2005). Nunn's book is a tale of massive disillusion and defeat and inevitably draws the eye, as the names of so many places that have figured in our own headlines since 2003 are reported here – Baghdad, Nasiriya, Basra, etc. Visser's breathtaking range of sources (in Arabic, English, French and Ottoman Turkish) is drawn from many archives. What he found was that the elites of the 1920s were tempted into breaking up Iraq for economic and political reasons, whereas the majority of the ordinary populace wanted the surer protection of a central Iraqi authority based in Baghdad. The supporters of nationalism tended to be younger, often from the more highly educated sections of the populace, and, most significantly, Visser concluded that the Shia were not huge fans of the idea. Equally, the British were suspected by many locals of wanting Basra to break away so that they could consolidate their grasp on the whole Gulf, a claim that Visser says was true to some extent but not ultimately the view that prevailed in Whitehall (Visser, 2005: chapters 6, 11).

## 'Inevitability'

It is commonplace to read that such and such a war was 'inevitable'. Hence John Stoessinger's classic on war starts with an account of the opening gambits of World War I. War was inevitable, said German Army Chief of Staff General Helmut Von Moltke, so 'the sooner the better for us'. As Stoessinger comments, '[t]he theme of inevitability is a haunting and pervasive one' (2007: 1). Hence, also, one of the mainstay texts of basic undergraduate IR states that the Cold War was:

> inevitable, at the climax of a gigantic struggle such as the Second World War … the settlements and agreements arrived at by the victorious coalition would shape the primary conflicts of the years to follow. No matter what those settlements contained, some of the involved parties would be dissatisfied and their dissatisfaction would be the basis of future conflicts.
>
> (Ray, 1992: 43)

The same war was described by the historian Louis Halle as representing an 'historical necessity'. But it could be said, as do other historians, that the Cold War was in no way seen until around 1946 as 'inevitable'.

During World War II, many in the United States held the view that in the postwar period the main problem for peace would be the persistence of the British and French empires, and that the Soviet Union would work more or less harmoniously with the United States to preserve global order. Robert Skidelsky (2000) demonstrates that Harry Dexter White, main architect with John Maynard Keynes of what became the World Bank and the International Monetary Fund at the Bretton Woods conference in 1944, was absolutely convinced that the USA could work very successfully with Moscow. It is now apparent that White was actually passing information about the discussions with the British to Moscow through acquaintances in the American Communist Party. It could even be argued that Roosevelt held similar, if not so extreme, views about the viability of postwar US–British collaboration (Skidelsky, 2000).

The analyst therefore runs the risk of reading history backwards, in other words assuming that the current thinking about the Cold (or any other) War is that which was held at the time. Stoessinger agrees, on the grounds that, since it is 'mortals' that make decisions, everything about them is contingent – they are motivated by fright, misperception and they make decisions, which leads to unforeseen consequences (Stoessinger, 2007: 2).

## ▌ USEFUL FURTHER READING

### On the history of warfare

Howard, Michael (1976) *War in European History*. Oxford: Oxford University Press.
Howard, Michael (2008) *War and the Liberal Conscience*. London: Hurst.

Keegan, John (1976) *The Face of Battle: A Study of Agincourt, Waterloo and the Somme*. London: Penguin.

Keegan, John (1994) *A History of Warfare*. New York: Vintage.

## On what it might feel like to be in a war

Bourke, Joanna (2000) *An Intimate History of Killing: Face-to-Face Killing in the Twentieth Century*. London: Granta.

Jünger, Ernst (2004) *Storm of Steel*, trans. Michael Hofman. London: Penguin (memoirs of a German infantry officer on the Western Front, 1914–1918).

Sassoon, Siegfried (1974) *Memoirs of an Infantry Officer*. London: Faber and Faber (memoirs of a British infantry officer on the Western Front, 1914–1918).

## Online resources

Thucydides, *The History of the Peloponnesian War*, revised edition, ed. M. I. Finley, trans. Rex Warner. London: Penguin. At: http://classics.mit.edu/Thucydides/pelopwar.html

Sallust, *The Jugurthine War*: http://ancienthistory.about.com/library/bl/bl_text_sallust_jugurth_1.htm

For a contemporary account of Clausewitz, see Barry D. Watts (2004), *Clausewitzian Friction and Future War* at: www.clausewitz.com/readings/Watts-Friction3.pdf

To trace British military personnel of World War I, see: http://www.greatwar.co.uk/westfront/resources/trace.htm

The University of Oxford's World War I digital poetry archive (which has much more than poetry, including some information on French and Canadian archives) at: http://www.oucs.ox.ac.uk/ww1lit/education/online/family-history.html

Duncanson, Bruce (2002) The Great War: On Line Resources, *Organization of American Historians Magazine of History*, 17(1), *World War I* (October), 70–71. http://maghis.oxfordjournals.org/content/17/1.toc.pdf

Pictures and documents of US–Japan Peace Negotiations, 1945: http://www.jacar.go.jp/english/nichibei/negotiation/index.html

# CHAPTER 3

# Peace

He who wants peace must prepare for war.

(Vegetius, 2001)

Peace is our profession
(United States Air Force Strategic Air Command 1946–1992 motto)

## INTRODUCTION

Prime Minister Margaret Thatcher once poured scorn on one of our most prestigious universities for having the temerity to open a Department of Peace Studies. An article on the background to that controversy of the 1980s, the second head of that Department at the University of Bradford, James O'Connell, recalled that 'the Prime Minister had more than once asked her officials: "Has that department been dealt with yet?"' (*Peace Magazine*, 1997: 20). One of her objections lay in what she saw as the far less serious enterprise, maybe even subversive, aim of analysing the conditions necessary for peace, rather than in the much more important understanding of the necessary ways to wage war. But discussing peace invariably means thinking about war. The Roman military writer Flavius Vegetius recognized this inherent paradox almost two thousand years ago. More recently, Geoffrey Blainey has argued that 'war and peace are alternating phases of a relationship' (Blainey, 1988). Blainey's work *The Causes of War* is symptomatic of this linking of war and peace; war nearly always precedes peace (as in this book), and is also why the motto of an organization which had the capability to destroy the world many times over during the Cold War was 'Peace is our profession'.

This chapter investigates the relationship between war and peace and why peace is often considered as an afterthought to war. There is a compelling case for the exploration of peace in its own right.

In line with the overall aims of this volume, the focus of this chapter is to provide an understanding of peace, and its appropriate historical context. The strength of an historical framework in contemplating peace lies particularly in our belief that it allows multiple accounts to be presented and better expresses the contradictions and complexity of bringing it about, a central concern of theorists and practitioners of international relations since the inception of the discipline. Hence this chapter will build upon the previous concentration on war and show how these two key concepts intertwine. The analysis begins by explaining the differences in understanding peace by a contemplation of the classical distinction within international relations scholarship between liberalism and realism. We will then explore the relationship between peace and 'justice', and later peace and 'democracy' while asking: Is peace the normal state of affairs? and: Is peace invented? In contemplating these questions we will firstly focus upon the contributions of British military historian Sir Michael Howard (1922–) and Prussian philosopher Immanuel Kant (1724–1804) as two exemplars of our changing understanding of peace.

The chapter will then reflect on the development of the post-Westphalian system of states (1648 onwards) in international relations and its apparent propensity for war, which culminated in World War I (1914–1918). In the aftermath of the horrors of that conflict, many organizations hoped to make good on David Lloyd George's boast (though it has also been ascribed to Woodrow Wilson and H. G. Wells) that this was the 'war to end all wars'. The establishment of institutions like the Council on Foreign Relations and the Royal Institute of International Relations ('Chatham House'), and indeed the founding of the League of Nations and the academic discipline of international relations, are just a few examples of a new impetus for peace (Olson and Groom, 1991: chapter 4; Cortright, 2008). The peace settlement that followed has been subject to a vast range of different interpretations, at the time and since. These interpretations are examined and provide insights into the broader discussions of war and peace that took place in the 'interwar period' (1919–1939). That this twenty-year passage of time earns the title 'interwar' – as an interlude – is indicative of how far the two world wars overshadow the peace, in its many forms, that characterizes the period. It is also indicative of the language of war that is used to describe peace: we hear of 'peace Offensives', 'peace Enforcement' and 'peacekeeping' that may involve the tools of military force most often associated with 'war' fighting. Perhaps the most common – and also somewhat oxymoronical use of the language of war in the twentieth century is that used for 'Cold War', yet this contest between the US-led West and the Soviet-led East that dominated international relations in the latter half of the twentieth century is also known as the 'Long Peace' (Gaddis, 1987, discussed subsequently).

The chapter will then outline the efforts that were made during World War II to achieve distinct war and peace aims. In microcosm this period illustrated that they are not mutually exclusive phenomena, but that the relationship between them shifts across time and space so that they may be usefully considered in a symbiotic manner. We conclude by looking at the state of peace in its post-Cold War context, where its relationship with war has reached new levels of intimacy.

Given the scope of peace in both History and International Relations, this chapter cannot provide universal coverage. Instead its analysis of peace in history aims to provide insights into comprehension of International Relations and International History in the twenty-first century. George W. Bush was much lampooned for his language while forty-second president of the United States, but his remark of 18 June 2002 captures succinctly the difficulties faced here in distinguishing between peace and war: 'I just want you to know that, when we talk about war, we're really talking about peace.' The essential point is to recognize a synergistic and overlapping relationship between peace and war. A raft of issues cross over the two phenomena, as we shall see. To begin our discussion on the place of peace in history, we move from a recent former United States president to the first.

## PEACE IN HISTORY

In his first State of the Union address of 8 January 1790, President George Washington stated that 'To be prepared for war is one of the most effectual means of preserving peace' (Washington, 1790). But for many, peace is a simple phenomenon: it can be seen as the state of affairs when there is no war. Equally it is often seen as a utopia (Durrheim, 1997: 38–42) and derided for its quixotic nature (Morgenthau, 1945: 145). But understanding peace and its place in history requires us to look at it in a number of ways.

As with the opening to the discussion in Chapter 2 ('War'), a discussion of peace begins by considering the level of analysis, and what international relations scholars call 'actors' in the international system. By this we mean 'who' is involved when we talk of peace. The nation-state is the cornerstone of much analysis in International Relations, and its relation with peace will be discussed in due course, but the identification of the immutable causes of war, and the absence of peaceful solutions, can and often does lead us to the nature of the human condition (Van Evera, 1999: 1–2). International Relations scholarship often recognizes a delineation which translates human nature into a divide between realism and liberalism, where the former emphasizes aggressive qualities and conflict, while the latter plays on humanity's kinship and cooperation (Carr, 1939/1947; Dunne, Schmidt and Lamy, 2010: 63–91). Many commentators have concluded that war is an inevitable consequence of the human condition; wars happen because (some) people are violent and warlike (Walt, 1998: 31; Wendt, 1995: 75; Dunne, Schmidt, and Lamy, 2010: 71). In much the same way, ordinary parlance often suggest that there are two types of people: 'warmongers' and 'peaceniks' or 'hawks' and 'doves', and invariably we can recognize that elements of both types of tendency exist within us all.

Theories about the human condition are also influential in psychological studies of war and peace (Ashley, 1981; Mercer, 1995). Being told that your nation is 'at war' brings with it a raft of expectations as to what will follow. Michael Howard identifies a 'psychosis of war', suggesting that it arouses 'an immediate expectation, and demand, for spectacular military action against some easily identifiable adversary, preferably a hostile state; action leading to decisive results' (Howard, 2001: 1). In the contemporary world, while politicians and a 'rolling news' media, intentionally or otherwise, magnify being 'at war', there are also implications for peace. Simply, this is to emphasize a distinction between times of war and times of peace. The former heightens the senses, acknowledging the possibility for dynamic change to the status quo, while the latter implies order and stability. As we have already suggested, such a distinction is not always possible, or even desirable, for increasing our understanding of either phenomenon. It is therefore necessary to acknowledge that the language of war and peace is evident in everyday society and that figures in the worlds of politics, religion, media, sport and elsewhere all use metaphors of both 'war' and 'peace' to convey their message. As an example, with World War II imminent in 1939, the United Kingdom's Ministry of Information, as part of a campaign to stiffen resolve, prepared a poster for public display that stated 'Keep Calm and Carry On'. By implication, the message was that, in the event of war, and then possible British defeat at the hands of Nazi Germany, Britons should maintain their peacetime approach as the most effective means of contributing to victory. This approach reflected a widely held view in Whitehall at the outset of the war that the British people would be distraught at the prospect of defeat brought about by German attack. As events unfolded through to the summer of 1940, the government went to particular efforts to illustrate how exceptional the United Kingdom's plight was as it sought to galvanize the country to triumph in the Battle of Britain (Churchill, 1949; Seib, 2006).

The old adage 'Where you stand is where you sit' is true in many aspects of life and is evident in how we consider peace both in terms of human nature and of history. The history of nationalist movements in the twentieth century, associated with political violence and revolution, is populated by those who considered themselves to be 'at war' while other protagonists consider themselves to be acting peacefully in maintaining the existing order (as an example, Algerians seeking independence fought a bloody eight-year campaign against French Armed Forces before securing their goal in 1962) (Horne, 1978). The contrast between the perceptions of different parties raises questions as to the importance of power in being able to establish, maintain and enforce peace set against those who are seeking change.

Not all peace is 'peaceful'. Elsewhere in this volume, Rome's empire and its wars are discussed, but it is also instructive to consider how it sought to establish peace. The inhabitants of Carthage at the end of the Punic Wars felt the full force of Roman *peace*. They were either killed or forced into slavery as their city was razed to the ground. Put simply, not everything referred to as peace is 'peaceful'.

## BOX 3.1 CARTHAGINIAN PEACE

The term originates in describing the Roman Empire's imposition of a brutal and devastating peace upon the Phoenician city of Carthage at the end of the Punic Wars in 146 BCE. Subsequently the term has been used to describe peace settlements where the terms of peace are imposed by the victor on the vanquished. The Treaty of Versailles 1919 (q.v.) was considered by some, including the famous British economist John Maynard Keynes, to be a Carthaginian peace because of their reading of its harsh and prescriptive terms (it earned the moniker of being a 'Diktat' – a dictated peace). US Secretary of Treasury Henry Morgenthau's plan to deindustrialize Germany at the end of World War II was considered Carthaginian by many, including some (such as Secretary of War Henry Stimson) within the administration of President Franklin D. Roosevelt. After considerable debate amongst the Allies, it was usurped by a more benign and openly supportive approach to rehabilitating Western Germany. There is also an oxymoronic quality to the expression 'Carthaginian peace', if we consider that the causes of future wars lay in the ends of the last war.

Here, another important link can be made to the concept of justice and its relationship with peace, given its implications for the moral status of individuals, peoples and states. The 'peace' that the Carthaginians were subject to may not have been 'just' in their eyes. Nor was the peace that the German people were subject to after World War I 'just' according to Adolf Hitler. He railed against the *Diktat*, as the Treaty of Versailles was known in Germany, in his rise to power (Kershaw, 1998: 148). And the absence of justice in the peace meant many beyond Germany's borders acquiesced in 'appeasement' during the 1930s as Hitler moved against the peace settlement (Kershaw, 2000a: xxxvi). The two key elements of just war theory, *jus in bello* and *jus ad bellum* (q.v.) have been joined in recent times by the notion of *jus post bellum* (postwar 'justice') (Orend, 2007; Stahn and Kleffner, 2008; Williams and Caldwell, 2006). While the challenge of demarcating what is considered to be 'war' and what 'peace' is recurrent in this chapter, one interesting feature in furthering our understanding of peace is that the criteria for the ending of war align with the criteria for those before and during war ('proportionality' and 'intent', for example). In other words, what is 'just' in engaging in war is 'just' at other times, too. Seen also in the body of law that constitutes the Laws of Armed Conflict (LOAC), this is recognition that the conduct of war influences what follows: war can 'bleed' in many different, and often unexpected, directions and thus shape the peace and, importantly, subsequent wars. This will be seen later in this chapter, particularly in relation to the views of Immanuel Kant and the influence of World War I on the peace that followed.

## IS PEACE A 'NORMAL' STATE OF AFFAIRS?

War has dominated the historical record. Wars make for exciting history, and historical writing, but there is an important account of peace that also needs to be explained. Wars have a legal status and they should be declared, though increasingly this fails to happen, with politicians of recent vintage using language that avoids the word 'war' for all of the contested values it entails. Equally, peace can be identified by an armistice and a peace settlement, and such arrangements are often precarious and misleading (Goldstein, 1992).

## BOX 3.2 ARMISTICE

An armistice signals the end of war fighting signalling the cessation of hostilities. This may not mean the formal end of the conflict. An armistice may be broken and fighting resume. Armistices may be pre-empted by a truce or ceasefire, and followed by a peace settlement or agreement, which formally bring an end to conflict. The most widely recognized and commemorated armistice is the one which brought the end of fighting in World War I that came into effect at 11.00 a.m. on 11 November 1918 (leading to the phrase 'the eleventh hour of the eleventh day of the eleventh month'). The Armistice was signed by Commander in Chief of Allied Forces, Frenchman Marshal Ferdinand Foch and Matthias Erzberger, the German representative, in Foch's railway carriage in the Compiègne Forest. In June 1940, Adolf Hitler, the German chancellor, received the French armistice in the same location after Germany's defeat of France. Other armistices of note include the one that brought a cessation to active hostilities in the Korean War of 1950–1953. This armistice has held for almost sixty years, but has never been followed up by a peace treaty, and so in some respects considered in this chapter the war has not ended.

## BOX 3.3 PEACE AGREEMENT

An agreement to end a war conflict is known as a peace settlement or peace agreement. This may be distinct from an armistice, which brings about a cessation to hostilities. A peace settlement may be reached independently by the warring parties themselves, mediated by third parties or imposed by others. Typically the settlement will involve a gathering of delegations at a 'conference' or 'congress', with the settlement being known by the location of that event. The negotiations involved in reaching agreement are concluded in various fashions: 'final acts', 'protocols', 'exchanges of notes', 'accords', 'agreements' and, most commonly, 'treaties'. Well-known peace settlements include the Congress of Vienna (1815), which brought an end to the Napoleonic Wars, and the Treaty of Versailles (1919), which formally ended the state of war between the Allied powers and imperial Germany at the end of World War I (Boemeke, Feldman and Gläser, 1998). (Other treaties were signed subsequently with the other Central Powers at the end of the conflict: Austria – Treaty of Saint-Germain, September 1919; Bulgaria – Treaty of Neuilly, November 1919; Hungary – Treaty of Trianon, June 1920; and the Ottoman Empire – Treaty of Sèvres, August 1920, and then revised in the Treaty of Lausanne, July 1923). An example of a peace settlement known as an accord is the 1995 General Framework Agreement for Peace in Bosnia and Herzegovina, which brought a resolution to the conflict in the region. The agreement is commonly referred to as the Dayton Peace Accords. The Oslo Accords, or the Declaration of Principles on Interim Self-Government Arrangements, made a contribution to the resolution to the Palestinian–Israeli conflict in 1993 as part of the wider Arab–Israeli peace process (q.v.).

This reading of history would seem to suggest that war and peace inhabit different worlds. Mary Dudziak argues that wars and peace have been identified as discrete entities on the basis of time. In turn, this means distinct forces are at work during 'wartime' and 'peacetime'. Her analysis makes the point that the beginnings of wars bring with them ideas about them ending, through the coming of peace. Dudziak's particular focus is the application of laws that come into force during times of war that have a limited lifespan. By way of example, during World War II, President Franklin Roosevelt told Congress in 1942 that '[w]hen the war is won, the powers under which I act automatically revert to the people – to whom they belong' (Dudziak, 2010: 1670; Rosenman, 1950: 356–365). The powers Roosevelt used once the United States was at war, which included interning Japanese-American citizens, were those brought on by the crisis of war. However, many lingered into peacetime in the late 1940s and some became formalized in the National Security Act of 1947 (Stuart, 2008).

By then the world was facing a different challenge pertinent to our discussion of peace: the Cold War. As we saw in Chapter 2, historians, of different eras and varying political persuasions, have long disagreed about the origins of the conflict between the United States and the Soviet Union that dominated the geopolitical landscape of the latter half of the twentieth century. The 'dean' of Cold War historians, John Lewis Gaddis, entitled his 1987 book *The Long Peace: Inquiries into the History of the Cold War* (Gaddis, 1987). He makes the point that the Cold War had many of the characteristics of peace: the absence of large-scale conflicts and casualties between the major protagonists; agreements on weapons control (the Anti-Ballistic Missile Treaty, 1972), trade (the US–Soviet Trade Agreement, 1972) and Human Rights (Helsinki Accords, 1975). During most of the period after 1945, peace can be considered as war, albeit a 'cold' war.

Equally, declared war can appear peaceful. The outbreak of World War II in Europe saw German and Soviet forces invade and conquer Poland between 1 September and 6 October 1939. The Western Allies of France and Great Britain had responded by declaring war on 3 September, yet there was no fighting on the European continent between the Allies and Germany until the spring of 1940. The period between October and April was referred to as the 'phony war' (Lukacs, 1976; Smart, 2003). This reflected the standoff that ensued, particularly the absence of fighting of the mode that took place on the Western Front during World War I.

It is nonetheless important to nuance the view that the Cold War was a 'long peace'. Gaddis's outlook puts a good deal of emphasis on looking at the Cold War through a 'Western' and 'European' lens; but international history takes place over a broader geographical and temporal space. An alternative view is put forward by Odd Arne Westad in his *Global Cold War: Third World Interventions and the Making of our Times*. Westad argues that the battlefield of the Cold War, where casualties were high and conflict not restrained by the spectre of Mutually Assured Destruction, was the 'Third World', i.e. 'the former colonial or semi-colonial countries in Africa, Asia and Latin America that were subject to European … economic or political domination' (Westad, 2006: 3). The discussion of the Cold War as 'war' or 'peace' thus illustrates the difficulties in demarcating between war and peace on the basis of language and distinct periods of time: peace is more than just the *space* between wars.

Throughout history, and especially in contemporary wars, the line between what constitutes peace and war has been blurred. As we have seen, Dudziak argues that 'wartimes bleed into each other' (2010: 1672) and, we would argue here, so does peace. As war has an influence beyond 'wartime', peace has an influence beyond peacetime. The attempts to have rules for the conduct of war draw, to a greater or lesser degree, on peacetime notions that, for society to thrive and function, there are conventions that should be adhered to. (Examples include the Ottawa Treaty on Anti-Personnel Mines and the Law of Armed Conflict.)

Essentially, the point to be made is that thinking about war and peace should not be as mutually exclusive concepts. Indeed, International History offers further alternatives. Peace may also be considered as episodic or as a process. In the case of the former, often with war apparently the binary alternative, swift diplomatic action may be called for. In such circumstances individuals are often called upon to undertake peace missions as envoys of peace. Peace missions seeking to bring some measure of resolution to conflict may be either private or public affairs in terms of their public profile and/or the makeup of those participating. Those heading undertaking a peace mission are often referred to as a peace envoy. An example of a prominent 'peace envoy' in recent times is US Senator George Mitchell. Mitchell, a judge in Maine, and then the state's Senator for fifteen years up to 1995, became, by appointment of President Bill Clinton, the United States Special Envoy for Northern Ireland. Mitchell's role was critical in working with all parties and securing the 1998 Good Friday Agreement which marked a major step towards ending the 'Troubles' that had blighted Northern Ireland for over thirty years (Mitchell, 1999). Almost ten years after leaving this post, and just two days into his presidency, Barack Obama appointed Mitchell as United States Special Envoy for the Middle East.

As we have already learned, peace is rarely clear-cut. One peace settlement which may appear to bring closure may prove to be just a hiatus as the embers of conflict reignite. Acknowledging this, certain conflicts, and the efforts towards their resolution, have earned the term 'peace process'. Often applied retrospectively, this is used to describe long-standing, apparently intractable conflicts over fundamental issues that transcend generations. They operate without fixed beginnings and ends. Peace processes can create and maintain momentum: a key feature of diplomatic negotiation (Berridge, 2010: 56). Examples of peace processes can be found in addressing conflicts in Northern Ireland and the Middle East. In the case of Middle East, the peace process there refers to the moves that have been made to end the Arab–Israeli conflict since the mid-1970s. A number of 'peace agreements' have been reached during this period – between Israel and Egypt (1979) and Israel and Jordan (1994) – and numerous peace conferences at a variety of diplomatic levels held – the Camp David meetings hosted by US President Jimmy Carter (1978), the Madrid Conference sponsored by the US and the USSR (1991), the 'back-channel' meetings between Israel and the Palestinians that led to the Oslo Accords (1993), the summit back at Camp David hosted by President Bill Clinton (2000) and the Annapolis Conference, which saw mutual agreement on an outline for a two-state solution (2007). The United States has played a key role in the Middle East peace process, acting as mediator and instigator. Since 2002, alongside the United Nations, the European Union and Russia – the quartet – have worked on a 'road map' for peace. The situation on the ground remains tense, and violent episodes ranging from isolated acts of terrorism and retaliation to full military operations have typified the peace process: the First (1987–1992) and Second (2000–) Intifadas and the Lebanon war (2006) are examples.

In Northern Ireland the term 'peace process' was initially used to describe events leading up to the Irish Republican Army's ceasefire in 1994 as a measure of resolution to the 'Troubles' that blighted the region from the 1960s until the 1990s (Gilligan, 1997). The peace process led to the Northern Ireland Peace Agreement, also known as the Good Friday Agreement, given the day it was signed: 10 April 1998 (the document can be found at http://www.taoiseach.gov.ie/attached_files/Pdf%20files/NIPeaceAgreement.pdf). The term 'Northern Ireland Peace Process' has subsumed many of the subsequent moves (decommissioning of weapons) that have contributed to a more peaceful region. The peace process is considered by some to have 'ended' in the spring of 2007, with a joint government being formed by the two main parties (Sinn Fein and the Democratic Unionist Party). However, sporadic acts of terrorist violence do continue.

## 'Inventing' peace

As Michael Howard has put it, '[t]hroughout human history mankind has been divided between those who believe that peace must be preserved, and those who believe that it must be attained' (Howard, 2000: 6). This military historian begins *The Invention of Peace* by referring to the work of Sir Henry Maine, the jurist and historian (1822–1888). He quotes Maine as stating that 'War appears to be as old as mankind, but peace is a modern invention.' In his exploration of the relationship between war and peace Howard states clearly that peace 'is certainly a far more complex affair than war' (Howard, 2000: 2). It is clear that he believes peace is either worth protecting or worth striving for. Christopher Coker writes of Howard's work that it has 'a passion for peace informed by an understanding that to build peace one has to understand war fully' (Coker, 2001: 78).

Using the classical IR distinction we can identify the realist view of peace as 'when war was neither imminent nor actually being fought' as *negative peace*, in contrast to Howard's *positive peace* indicating a 'social and political ordering of society that is generally accepted as just' (Howard, 2000: 2). We can term the value added as *Peace Plus*. Efforts to strive for and maintain such a positive peace have a chimerical quality: peace requires careful management. Clearly evident in Howard's work, as he provides an openly Western-orientated account, is the influence of Enlightenment thinking. For Howard, within this body of thought one individual stands out and that is Immanuel Kant: 'if anyone could be said to have invented peace as more than a mere pious aspiration, it was Kant' (Howard, 2000: 31).

## Kant and peace

Immanuel Kant (1724–1804) was a key figure in the development of Enlightenment thinking, often known as the Age of Reason. Born in Königsberg, then capital of the Prussian Duchy and now Kaliningrad in the Russian enclave between Poland and Lithuania, Kant studied and then worked at the University of Königsberg (now the Immanuel Kant State University of Russia). He published widely on the philosophy of 'reason', but his major contribution to our discussion of peace was an essay entitled 'Perpetual Peace: A Philosophical Sketch' (original German title 'Zum ewigen Friede'), published in 1795.

## BOX 3.4 KANT'S PERPETUAL PEACE PRELIMINARY AND DEFINITE ARTICLES

The Preliminary Articles described the steps that should be taken immediately, or with all deliberate speed:

- 'No secret treaty of peace shall be held valid in which there is tacitly reserved matter for a future war.'
- 'No independent states, large or small, shall come under the dominion of another state by inheritance, exchange, purchase, or donation.'

- 'Standing armies shall in time be totally abolished.'
- 'National debts shall not be contracted with a view to the external friction of states.'
- 'No state shall by force interfere with the constitution or government of another state.'
- 'No state shall, during war, permit such acts of hostility which would make mutual confidence in the subsequent peace impossible: such are the employment of assassins (percussores), poisoners (venefici), breach of capitulation, and incitement to treason (perduellio) in the opposing state.'

Three Definitive Articles would provide not merely a cessation of hostilities, but a foundation on which to build a peace.

1. 'The civil constitution of every state should be republican.'
2. 'The law of nations shall be founded on a federation of free states.'
3. 'The law of world citizenship shall be limited to conditions of universal hospitality.'

The full text of Perpetual Peace can be found in Kant (1795/1793).

Kant's essay laid out six Preliminary and three Definite articles which, if enacted, could respectively reduce the likelihood of war and bring about a permanent peace. Kant's articles were, and remain, ambitious but it is worth noting how much progress has been made in the intervening decades since his 'Philosophical Sketch' was published. In respect of the Preliminary Articles, there is an acceptance of open diplomacy in contrast to secret treaty-making; a repudiation of Empire; while standing armies do exist, disarmament is prominent in international affairs; the UN Charter guards against foreign interference in 'matters which are essentially within the domestic jurisdiction of any state'; the idea of just war and the Laws of Armed Conflict mitigate to a degree wartime practices; though it is fair to say that incurring debts have been a recurrent feature of the prosecution of wars in the twentieth century. With regard to the first of the Definite Articles, Kant's aim for each nation to have a republican constitution has become increasingly prevalent, although a debate exists about how Kant saw the relationship between Republican and Democratic forms of government (which will be discussed presently). Of the second and third articles, the world has moved towards a 'federation of free states' – a League of Peace – in the form of the United Nations organization; and the rise of a human rights agenda in international politics is testament to the humanitarian concerns Kant raised. This is not to give Kant foresight that is not deserved: in the twenty-first century we do not have perpetual peace. There are numerous forces that mean the prospect is not imminent, but if nothing else the idea of perpetual peace is something that was given particular impetus by Kant and something that has a definite legacy in today's international affairs.

## Democratic peace

In 'Perpetual Peace', Kant gives particular emphasis to states with Republican constitutions being necessary for peace. Kant envisaged Republican states as those with a separation of powers between an executive and a legislature. Importantly he saw 'Republics' as distinct from 'Democracies' – given his concern for the tyranny of the majority, a fear reflected by his contemporary Edmund Burke (Burke, 1791/1968). Subsequent thought and events, however, have meant a greater focus on the relationship between democracy and peace. Crucial to this has been the development of the notion of the 'democratic peace' (Small and Singer, 1976; Doyle, 1983a, 1983b; Owen, 2005). The central tenet of this thesis is that democracies do not fight wars against each other. 'What is more,' John Owen IV argues, 'much research suggests that they are also unusually likely to sign and honor international agreements and to become economically interdependent' (Owen, 2005). Taken further, the logic of this argument is that if all states were democracies there would be no war amongst them, and universal peace would follow. The empirical evidence available bears out this line of thought. The major global conflicts of the twentieth century are characterized by democracies on the one side and tyrannical regimes on the other. Of course, the potential flaw in this analysis is that it does depend on what you consider a democracy to be; and it is on this that much of the debate about democratic peace has centred (Chan, 1997).

The link between the democratic peace and Kantian thinking was made explicitly by Michael Doyle in two 1983 articles which stressed how foreign relations amongst liberal democracies had been pacified to the point that war was barely thinkable (Doyle, 1983a, 1983b). In the case of Western Europe, for centuries riven by conflict, this was borne out. Political scientist Jack Levy's much-quoted remarks that the democratic peace 'comes as close as anything we have to an empirical law in international relations' (Levy, 1988: 662) point to an unusual level of consensus amongst academics on the issue. Importantly, in the world of policy the premise of the democratic peace has taken hold. By the turn of the twenty-first century, democracy was for some the *sine qua non* for peace long before the George W. Bush administration's openly stated policy of democracy promotion as the means to secure national security. Christopher Layne argues that US policymakers have been captivated by the democratic peace approach in seeing 'a link between American security and the spread of democracy, which is viewed as an antidote that will prevent future wars' (Layne, 1994: 5).

The approach has been critiqued in recent times by those who argue that it is not a democratic peace but one based on economic liberalization that promotes peace, and that the latter has a stronger historical record than the liberal democratic peace per se (McDonald, 2009). In *The Invisible Hand of Peace*, McDonald identifies 'liberal economic institutions – namely, the predominance of private property and competitive market structures within domestic economies' as fundamental to peace (McDonald, 2009: 5). Owen points to the importance of the liberal character of states that coexist in peace and that these are not always synonymous with democracy (Owen, 1997), arguing that it is liberal ideas allied to strong liberal institutions (the rule of law) that matter in states remaining at peace. Other critics would argue that democracy may make peace less likely. Mansfield and Snyder's point to the history of states transitioning to democracy as one which is replete with bellicose activity, regardless of whether the state eventually becomes a full-blown democracy (Mansfield and Snyder, 2005).

It is somewhat curious that the literature on the democratic peace, even allowing for its variations, and accepting its critique from realist quarters, is notable for its lack of optimism. Instead pessimism that peace is anything more than a utopian dream seems to have overwhelmed the aspiration of Kant's writings since the end of the eighteenth century. As such, it speaks to Owen's analysis that liberal states need an 'other' – illiberal states help to define liberal states. Nonetheless, there has been a huge rise in the number of states that can be reasonably described as democratic in the past sixty years, and with that many who feel that in the period the world has come 'closer than ever before to reaching a consensus … that only democracy confers legitimacy' (Gaddis, 2005: 265).

## The state and peace

Charles Tilly's maxim that 'war made states and vice versa' (1990: 67) provides an important dimension to the study of international relations and international history. Yet, the nation-state has also played a notable role in our understanding of peace. The peaces of Munster and Westphalia of 1648 were peace agreements which recognized the principle of sovereignty.

## BOX 3.5 PEACE OF WESTPHALIA

This peace of 1648, encompassing two treaties, signified a step-change in the conduct of international relations and marked the birth of the modern nation-state: a key component for international relations, and the central cast member in the international history of the past five hundred years (Croxton and Tischer, 2001). The peace signified the consummation of two treaties: the Treaty of Osnabruck (May 1648), which ended the Thirty Years' War (1618–1648) amongst the Holy Roman Empire; and the Treaty of Munster (October 1648), which concluded the war between the Holy Roman Empire and the French. Confusingly, a treaty signed in January 1648 is also known as the Treaty of Munster – this ended war between Spain and the Dutch United Provinces. The notable feature to these peace agreements was the number of delegations involved in the negotiations: over a hundred from various kingdoms, republics and princedoms, but the major delegations came from France, Spain, Sweden, the Netherlands, the princes and emperor of the Holy Roman Empire. The negotiations themselves were not restricted to 1648, with many of the delegations arriving from 1643 before the negotiations drew down in 1649. The net outcome of the treaty was that the princes of the Holy Roman Empire were given equal status and allowed to choose the religious denomination of their state, thus recognizing the principle of sovereignty over their own territory.

These agreements are a key marker for students and scholars of IR and IH, because they illustrate the demise of the Holy Roman Empire's influence over the internal affairs of its princedoms and the establishment of sovereign states (Osiander, 1994). So the contribution that these peace agreements made to the development of the state, to paraphrase Tilly, show that peace also made the state (Howard, 2001). The post-Westphalian system of states was hence one that provided for a measure of order in international affairs. The actors in international affairs were recognized as states and, within this, understandings were established that reinforced relations between them.

These agreements also led to a new kind of diplomacy (Der Derian, 1987; Berridge, 2010). Diplomats and diplomatists became the functionaries of relations between states and sought to provide for peace as measures short of war (Cull, 2008), while also seeking to secure their national interests in relation to other states. A burgeoning diplomatic system through the exchange of delegations had at its core what French statesman Cardinal Richelieu called '*négotiation continuelle*'. To ensure that diplomats were properly supported in fulfilling their role, ministries of foreign affairs were the 'inevitable corollary' (Berridge, 2010: 5) of continuous representation. This concept of permanent representation that developed from the seventeenth century meant the leaders of these states could be kept abreast of developments in other areas of Europe and gave prominence to diplomats as peacemakers in subsequent history. Importantly, as diplomatic missions (the term for those despatched to act as diplomats) were established in foreign capitals of Europe during the eighteenth and nineteenth centuries, the individuals involved found themselves in shared circumstances and the 'diplomatic corps' emerges on the basis of an esprit de corps (Sharp and Wiseman, 2007). In the post-Westphalian period this is how relations between the major European states, many still monarchies, have been conducted, a machinery that augured for peace. Further, the order that the Westphalian peace provided for also allowed for European states to establish Empire (q.v.).

The peaceful environment in which states found themselves gave birth to what scholars of the English School of international relations would identify as 'International Society' (Wight, 2005; Bull, 2002; Dunne, 1998). This is the recognition that states have similar interests in their self-preservation and conduct themselves in a mutually recognizable fashion. This does not preclude conflict, according to English School proponents, but helps to mitigate the anarchic nature of international affairs. In looking at the history of Central Europe since the Peace of Westphalia, clearly there have been numerous bloody conflicts but the prospect of decade-long wars has been removed.

Peace also provides space for economic activity, and in the first decade of the twentieth century levels of economic interconnectivity rose to unprecedented levels through trade centred on the industrialized nations. In an era before the term 'globalization' was in use, this suggested a level of interconnectedness that many believed made war impossible. So before an era of total war (q.v.) was identified we might talk of an era of 'total peace'. We know that World War I began in August 1914 with brutal consequences for those in Europe and its empires. It is ironic that it is the nation-state which carries the responsibility for being ready to fight wars and at the same time endeavours to avoid such a scenario.

## Peace and onset of World War I

As we have seen in the previous chapter, World War I is central to international relations, both as an academic discipline and more broadly, and more importantly, because of its impact on international affairs since (Carr, 1939/1947). Considerable and ongoing debates exist amongst historians as to the origins of World War I, and much of that discourse centres on the failings of the order, the peace and the system of diplomacy that allegedly underpinned it, that prevailed at the turn of the twentieth century; thus, the logic goes, allowing for the war to develop (Mombauer, 2002; Joll and Martel, 2007). Before the war broke out, the British socialist politician E. D. Morel railed against the system of diplomacy that had led to the colonial powers carving up Africa between them, and during the war itself enlarged that critique to attack the 'secret' nature of diplomacy itself (Morel, 1915). In the 1920s, in his *International Anarchy* (1926), Goldsworthy Lowes Dickinson, one of Morel's colleagues, also argued that the war could be attributed to the 'bankruptcy' of the entire European system of diplomacy, which instead of guarding against war made it more likely. Most famously Norman Angell, in his 1909 pamphlet *Europe's Optical Illusion*, later published and reprinted on numerous occasions as *The Great Illusion: A Study of the Relation of Military Power in Nations to Their Economic and National Advantage* (1910; see also Ceadel, 2009), argued that war was nonsensical, as the economic interdependence of the time meant belligerents would be worse off and that wars of territorial expansion would be 'economically futile' (Angell, 1910). Following the war, Angell rejoined the discussion with the often overlooked *The Fruits of Victory* (Angell, 1921), a classic of pacifistic philosophy. A more recent account (Mulligan, 2010) questions the inevitability of the conflict and argues that there were 'powerful forces operating in favour of the maintenance of peace'. What this illustrates succinctly is that what some consider as being conditions for peace, others would contend are portents for war.

We suggested in the previous chapter that the reverberations of the 1914–1918 conflict 'go-wider than this one war' and it would be equally true in suggesting that the implications for peace after World War I would have considerable future echoes. Thinking about the peace that would mark the end of the 'war to end wars' began long before the armistice of 11 November 1918, when the guns fell silent. Before war broke out, large sections of society in Europe and beyond opposed war as a means of settling international disputes. Instead they looked to 'arbitration' and sought to build upon the precedence of the Hague Peace Conferences of 1899 and 1907, where the principle of international arbitration was promulgated. Arbitration refers to a mode of resolving, peacefully, disputes, relying on the protagonists agreeing to abide by the decision of an independent body. Though the Hague Conferences failed to achieve agreement that an international court should have universal jurisdiction over all disputes, other notable achievements were made in the fields of voluntary arbitration, the rules of war and disarmament. Arbitration's critics point to a lack of enforcement powers. Instead it relies on the participants' will to adhere to the decisions taken by the arbitrator. The outbreak of World War I in August 1914 critically undermined the value of arbitration as a mode of resolving international disputes.

Equally important in the opening years of the twentieth century were debates about the utility of war and pacifism after the publication of Angell's *The Great Illusion*. Pacifism is a belief that war and the use of violence is an unsatisfactory and undesirable means of settling disputes. While often associated with the individual, 'Pacifism would … lose its inner drive without at least an implicit obligation to take a personal stand against war' (Brock, 2000: 90). Pacifism is a broad church and those who adopt its principles do so to differing degrees. At the outset of World War I, a clear distinction emerged between an absolute or pure pacifism (or pacifist), and pacificism (or pacificist), a less rigid interpretation identified by Historian A. J. P. Taylor. The latter term came to mean more traditional views, which were previously termed pacifism, and included the right to self-defence, while the stricter understanding came to mean a call for the absolute abolition of all armed forces and military capability. Some other pacifists would seek non-violent action or civil disobedience as a more effective means of instilling a change in their predicament. Considered to be a highly principled or moral approach to resolving issues, pacifism writ large has often been closely associated with religious beliefs such as those of Hinduism and Buddhism and, within Christianity, the Quakers or Religious Society of Friends, which grew out of the seventeenth-century English dissenting movement to have a global presence (Hirst, 1923; Brock, 2000). Conscientious objectors, those who refuse to perform military service, often cite pacifist beliefs in their rationale. Famous pacifists include Mohandas Gandhi, whose campaign of non-violent opposition led to Indian independence from British colonial rule in 1948.

But, while pacifism is itself a contested subject and while its later development in the twentieth century emphasized non-violent action, prior to 1914 many adherents incorporated a belief in wars of self-defence. So what Sir Rupert Smith would call in 2005 the '*Utility of Force*' was prevalent in many quarters of society. This included many religious and women's groups, trade unions across Europe and other leftist groups, and the peace societies that had been founded in the nineteenth century in the United Kingdom, the United States and Germany. In the United Kingdom the National Peace Council founded in 1908 brought together over 200 different groups from village peace societies to the national trade unions in a belief that an informed public would not countenance war, in peace and justice, and concerns for what we now call human rights and environmental issues (Vellacott, 1980; National Peace Council Archives). However, the outbreak of war changed the views of many. In the midst of the nationalist fervour that took hold in August 1914, many who called for peace to prevail across Europe supported their governments in the conflict: 'The peace journals attest to the fact that most activists did indeed change their position in August 1914' (Laity, 2001: 217). There were those who continued to champion peace, but from the outset the discussion of peace became intimately related to an anti-war movement, a pattern that would to varying degrees be repeated in subsequent conflicts.

Those who remained opposed to the war included Glasgow educator and social activist John Maclean (1879–1923), who organized anti-war demonstrations, for which he was convicted under the Defence of the Realm Act; and Helen Crawfurd (1877–1954), who founded the National Women's Peace Crusade in June 1917 after three years of anti-war campaigning. In other fields, the *Daily Herald* newspaper would remain opposed to the war throughout while providing an opportunity for anti-war views to be published from the likes of the Union for Democratic Control, in which E. D. Morel (q.v.), James Ramsay MacDonald and other prominent Labour politicians were involved, and the Fellowship of Reconciliation (Swartz, 1971; Robbins, 1976; Ferguson, 1995; Dekar, 2005). The former sought an early armistice; the latter had a Christian pacifist agenda. After 1917 and US entry to the war, opponents of the war were prominent there, too. Eugene Debs (1855–1926), leading American socialist and the Socialist Party of America's presidential candidate in 1904, 1908, 1912 and 1920, was tried and convicted under the 1917 Espionage Act for inciting Americans to avoid the draft. Also prominent was Jane Addams (1860–1935), founder of the Settlement House movement for social reform and later Nobel Peace Prize-winner (1931), as a leading pacifist and the international president of the Women's International League for Peace and Freedom (Linn, 1935; Addams 1922, 1960, 1964; Knock, 1992).

## BOX 3.6 PEACE PRIZE

The most famous Peace Prize is the Nobel Peace Prize. It is awarded annually by the Norwegian Nobel Committee, nominated by the Norwegian Parliament in accordance with the will of Swedish industrialist and inventor Alfred Nobel (Lundestad and Njolstad, 2002: 221). The terms of this award are that the winner 'shall have done the most or the best work for fraternity between nations, for the abolition or reduction of standing armies and for the holding and promotion of peace congresses'. The Nobel Peace Prize is one of a number of awards, given alongside Nobel Prizes in Physics, Chemistry, Physiology or Medicine, Literature and Economics. The prizes are widely recognized as the highest form of recognition of the contribution made by an individual or organization. Notable Peace

Prize-winners of recent times include Barack Obama (2009), Intergovernmental Panel on Climate Change and Al Gore, Jr (2007), Jimmy Carter (2002), Médecins sans Frontières (1999), Yasser Arafat, Shimon Peres and Yitzhak Rabin (1994), Mikhail Gorbachev (1990), Desmond Tutu (1984), Mother Teresa (1979), Mohamed Anwar Al-Sadat and Menachem Begin (1978). The prize, which is not awarded posthumously, has overlooked the likes of Eleanor Roosevelt and, most contentiously, Mohandas Gandhi. Critics claim the committee's decision has been politicised on occasion. Other Peace Prizes have been awarded. During the Cold War the USSR awarded the International Lenin Prize for Strengthening Peace Among Peoples, from 1957 to 1990.

Perhaps the ultimate manifestation of a desire for peace during the carnage of World War I could be found in Russia. Following the overthrow of the Russian monarchy in February 1917, the Provisional Government's failure to bring peace to the conflict provided an opportunity for the Bolsheviks under Lenin to seize power in October. They immediately sought peace negotiations with the Central Powers (Germany, the Austro-Hungarian and Ottoman Empires), which began in December 1917. Despite the punitive terms of the Treaty of Brest-Litovsk concluded in March 1918, by ending the conflict with the Central Powers it did provide the Bolsheviks with the opportunity to consolidate their position and bring a measure of peace to Russia. That it could not be considered anything more was because an often vicious civil war ensued for the next four years between the Bolsheviks (Reds) and opposition forces (Whites), supported by interventions from other nations (Figes, 1997; Mawdsley, 2008).

The key point from this brief account of World War I is that there was a diversity of opinion during the war over what it was being fought for and what the result should be. There was considerable debate over the aims of the war and the aims for a postwar world. This is hardly surprising given the complex history and disputed nature of peace and was to manifest itself in the peace settlements which resulted. It also meant for the generation that fought World War II that they had an immediate point of reference for ensuring there was no repeat of Marshal Foch's prophetic remark of the 1919 settlement: 'This is not peace. It is an armistice for 20 years' (Henig, 1995: 52).

## Peace at the close of World War I

The settlements that brought World War I to an end make a vital contribution to our understanding of peace since. This is because these peace settlements were contested and interpreted differently by those at the time and afterwards. International history can be read in many different ways and it certainly was in this case. For example, Foch's remarks are often used to illustrate that the Great War's denouement was illiberal, whereas the marshal himself had wanted a settlement that was harder on Germany. Already mentioned in this chapter, and with a vast literature covering their detail, it is important here to capture what we might call the 'Versailles moment' – the expectations for peace in 1919 and its legacy. Following the Armistice of November 1918, hope for a better world was widespread. Those who had seen the horrors of the war firsthand, or its shattering impact on those returning to civilian life, were determined to create a peace that would prevent such a calamity happening again. Succinctly put, 'Never again' was a guiding mantra that allowed for new ideas to be put forward and an acceptance to try new ways of doing things – for example, collective security which will be considered presently – and even a new academic discipline in International Relations (Macmillan, 2001; Williams, 1998 are good introductions to the Treaty negotiations).

Leaders of thirty-two states, representing almost three-quarters of the world's population, arrived in Paris in January 1919 to discuss the issues posed by the war and its somewhat abrupt end in the previous November (for detailed analyses of each of the major participants, see the series published by Haus, *Consequences of Peace: The Versailles Settlement – Aftermath and Legacy*; Alan Sharp, 2010). Integral to making peace in Paris was American President Woodrow Wilson, who arrived in Europe to much fanfare as a 'prophet of peace': he would win the Nobel Peace Prize in 1919 for his efforts. His country's intervention in the war was as an 'associated power' in April 1917 and not as an ally, which placed the United States, and its president, in a distinct position from the belligerents. Wilson had pledged to keep the United States out of the war after its outbreak in 1914, and won his re-election in 1916 on a slogan of 'he kept us *out of war*'. Nonetheless, the former Princeton professor surprised many in his address to the US Congress in January 1917 by arguing for 'Peace without victory'. Wilson buttressed himself to accusations of involving the United States by arguing that he was 'seeking only to face realities and to face them without soft concealments'. Wilson went on to articulate an understanding of peace that has antecedents in writings of Kant and speaks to dilemmas evident in achieving a meaningful peace. It would be a notable public pronouncement of thinking on peace in the era and subsequently (Knock, 1992; Morton, 2008). Wilson stated:

> Victory would mean peace forced upon the loser, a victor's terms imposed upon the vanquished. It would be accepted in humiliation, under duress, at an intolerable sacrifice, and would leave a sting, a resentment, a bitter memory upon which terms of peace would rest, not permanently but only as upon quicksand. Only a peace between equals can last. Only a peace the very principle of which is equality and a common participation in a common benefit. The right state of mind, the right feeling between nations, is as necessary for a lasting peace as is the just settlement of vexed questions of territory or of racial and national allegiance.
>
> (Woodrow Wilson, 22 January 1917, 64 Congress, 2 Session, Senate Document no. 685, 'A League for Peace')

In this speech Wilson articulated his views on what peace should be based upon: a common understanding mutually arrived at. A year later, with the United States a participant in the war, Wilson's annual message to Congress was notable for another contribution to the development of thinking about peace in the twentieth century. In this speech of 8 January 1918, he outlined Fourteen Points which sought to explain to the American people US involvement in the conflict by providing for the peace that would follow. The key aspects of the speech were an end to secret diplomacy, which Wilson believed perverted the cause of peace – instead, there would be open covenants of peace, openly arrived at; freedom of the seas at all times; disarmament; the right to self-determination; and, perhaps most importantly, was the fourteenth point, which called for a 'general association of nations' (that became the League of Nations).

The Fourteen Points were based on the 'Inquiry' that Wilson had established under the leadership of his close advisor Colonel Edward M. House, of approximately 150 academics, journalists, lawyers and experts on foreign policy (Goldstein, 1991; Williams, 1998). Building upon the breadth of views that abounded during the conflict on what form peace should take, the Inquiry illustrated the opportunity for different views to be incorporated into Wilson's thinking on peace at this stage. The Fourteen Points began by stating that international diplomacy should be based on 'open covenants of peace, openly arrived at' and went on to claim 'freedom of the seas', the removal of barriers to trade and offensive armaments, before arriving at the last point: 'a general association of nations' to preserve peace. The League of Nations, as the general association became known, is readily identified as Wilson's legacy, though he was not alone in discussing the idea at the time (for example, Viscount Bryce, British Ambassador to United States 1907–1913, and later twice South African Prime Minister 1919–1924, 1939–1948, Jan Christiaan Smuts, both influenced Wilson and the eventual outcome). The Fourteen Points collectively aimed to change the fundamental nature of international diplomacy that had failed to prevent the war. Importantly, in agreeing to sign the Armistice in November 1918 the Germans hoped and believed that the peace settlement that would result would be based on the Fourteen Points. The discussion in Paris the following year would centre on how far the promise of the Fourteen Points would come to fruition in the face of British and French opinion, which called for Germany to be squeezed 'until the pips squeak'. This reflected the disjuncture between the terms of the Armistice that was signed in November 1918 and the hopes that the German people had been stoked by Wilson's own rhetoric (Goldstein, 2002; Williams, 1998).

Buoyed by a cocktail of relief and euphoria in France and Great Britain, there was a call for Germany to accept responsibility for the war. In the United Kingdom the General Election of 14 December 1918 – known as the 'Khaki Election', given the numbers of returning servicemen – was fought amid calls to 'Hang the Kaiser'. At Versailles, the French premier Georges Clemenceau, known as *le Tigre* ('the tiger'), was receptive to his people's revanchist desires (Watson, 2008). What became known as the 'War Guilt clause', Article 231 in the Treaty of Versailles has been interpreted as a clear breach of Wilson's notion that, for peace to be lasting, it would be between equals. By fixing responsibility for the damage done during the war to Germany, this facilitated a belief that all of the war's ills could be 'blamed' on Germany. However, Wilson's intent may have been an entirely different outcome. By including Article 231 he sought to limit Germany's responsibilities to the damage done during the war – the terms of the Armistice – and avoid a more punitive settlement. Again the difficulties in deciphering history are evident, as is the importance of the peace at the end of World War I in interpreting the international history of the rest of the century. The differences here in the aims that the leaders of the Big Three powers (US, UK and France) brought to the peace conference illustrate the divisions in opinion that would be evident at Versailles.

The conference proceedings, which lasted six months until the final treaty was signed on 28 June 1919, while cordial, were often fractious when it came to specific terms. The issue of reparations, for example, was a particularly thorny one, with an Inter-Allied Reparations Commission being appointed to flesh out the final details. Importantly, also, the conference was covered voraciously by the world's media, providing another dimension to peacemaking for the delegates. 'It also ensured that the peace-makers at Paris, unlike their counterparts at Vienna a hundred years previously ..., had to negotiate in the full glare of publicity, knowing the details of their discussions would be carried the next day in newspaper columns throughout the world' (Henig, 1995: 3). To delve into those details is beyond the scope of this book but it is important to say that compromises were made on all sides. This meant most parties left Paris relatively satisfied (Sharp, 1991). However, the compromises that had been made would become contradictions as the treaty was enacted in the months and years that followed in confirming Foch's estimation of the settlement.

Germany's reaction to the Versailles settlement was immediately hostile (Hitler, 1924). The first democratically elected German chancellor, Philipp Scheidemann, resigned rather than sign the treaty, having been wholly excluded from the negotiations. A new government under Gustav Bauer did sign the treaty in June, but was quick to refer to the treaty as a '*Diktat*', given that its terms were dictated by the victors. Further hostility to the peace treaty came from nationalist elements in the military and their supporters. They accused politicians of the new Weimar Republic (so named after the city where Germany's first constitutional assembly took place in late 1918) of betraying the German military, as the German homeland had not been invaded, and so a myth that the German military had been 'stabbed in the back' was born. This cleavage typified the instability politically and economically of the Weimar Republic and ultimately provided the opportunity for Adolf Hitler to bring National Socialism to power in Germany (Hobsbawm, 1995; Patch Jr, 1998).

Even amongst the Allied powers criticism of the Treaty was fierce. The most famous, though subject to continuing historical revisionism, was composed by British economist John Maynard Keynes after he returned from Paris as part of the British Treasury delegation. Entitled *The Economic Consequences of the Peace*, Keynes' central argument was that imposing reparations on Germany above and beyond the 'damage done' would be a mistake: it would build resentment and, most importantly for Keynes, prevent Germany from recovering economically and contributing to a healthy international economy that would benefit everyone. Instead, the terms as Keynes saw them, and as Hitler was able to portray them, were 'Carthaginian' in their severity (Keynes, 1920/2011; Skidelsky, 2003; Markwell, 2006).

In the US, opposition to the Versailles Peace Treaty meant it was never even ratified. Senators such as Republican Henry Cabot Lodge opposed the treaty, as they feared US inclusion in the League of Nations would challenge US sovereignty. Wilson's conduct did not help the cause of ratification of the treaty (Link, 1979). His explanations of the merits of the new order he was proposing fell on deaf ears, and he refused to accept any of his opponents' amendments. Therefore the Peace Treaty was rejected by the United States. This meant that it was not until 25 August 1921, almost three years after the Armistice had been signed, that the United States signed a peace treaty with Germany confirming a Joint Senate resolution of 2 July 1921 'That the state of war declared to exist between the Imperial German Government and the United States of America by the joint resolution of Congress approved April 6, 1917, is hereby declared at an end' (*Treaties, Conventions, International Acts, Protocols and Agreements Between the United States of America and Other Powers* 1910–1923, vol. 3. Washington: Government Printing Office, 1923: 2596).

While additional peace settlements would be concluded with the other Central Powers (see Box 3.3 for further details) absent from discussions in France was Russia. In the midst of a civil war that was being fostered by many of the protagonists in Versailles (for example, the United States sent forces into Russian territory to fight against the Bolsheviks), and with an ideology that called for an end to international diplomacy, this was perhaps not surprising. Nonetheless, if peace was the outcome sought in Paris, Russia had a role to play. As it was the exclusion, voluntary or otherwise, of Russia, this meant a number of the issues would remain unresolved and led to a measure of collusion between Russia and Germany in the interwar period, as the two outcasts of the international system.

One further legacy of Versailles that had implications for the future of peace in the twentieth century is that the gathering in Paris brought individuals together who in a generation's time would again have to address the peace that would result from a global conflict. Individuals such as future US President Franklin Roosevelt and British Prime Minister Winston Churchill and a host of junior officials met in Paris (Williams, 1998).

The legacy of Versailles at the time and subsequently is contested (Beloff, 1950). Writing in 1998 in the opening to a German Historical Institute book reassessing Versailles after seventy-five years, the authors ponder: 'Even now, the reason for the ultimate collapse of the Versailles system remains disputed' (Boemeke, Feldman and Gläser, 1998: 2). The Versailles Peace Settlement – the Versailles Moment – framed the discussion of peace during the interwar period and into World War II. Writing in December 1939, one British Foreign Office official recalled of Versailles, as he pondered the outcome of World War II which had begun that September, 'I hope that we shall be less severe and wiser in many respects than at Versailles, but more severe and wiser in others' (Rofe, 2007: 74). Wisdom would be a sought after commodity for those seeking to achieve peace once World War II had begun.

## The peace of World War II

Even before World War II broke out, the idiom of peace was employed in efforts to avoid war. After engaging in diplomatic talks with Adolf Hitler to avert conflict in September 1938, British Prime Minister Neville Chamberlain declared that he believed the Anglo-German agreement would bring 'peace in our time'. Within a year Chamberlain would declare Britain to be at war with Germany.

As was argued in Chapter 2 ('War'), in one sense the peace of World War II was that *provided* by the Cold War in its aftermath. However, this outcome was not the intended peace that the protagonists envisaged in 1939. Had Germany and Hitler's National Socialism aim of *Lebensraum* ('living space') for the Third Reich and/or Japan's imperial forces in their quest for a Greater East Asia Co-Prosperity Sphere triumphed, then a different peace would have followed the end of the conflict. In making this statement, though, there may be a danger in conflating the stated war aims of the protagonists with their objectives for peace in the event of their triumph. We cannot know precisely how either of these states would have acted. What we do know is how the Allied powers who prevailed addressed both their war aims and their plans for peace. In light of our discussion thus far of the delineations and intersections of issues pertaining to peace and war, it is not a surprise that those who had seen the Versailles peace disintegrate wanted to align war aims and peace aims to best ensure that the peace that would follow would be long-lasting.

The endeavours of those in the United States to consider peace began before the nation was attacked at Pearl Harbor on 7 December 1941. At the beginning of 1940 Under Secretary of State Sumner Welles chaired the Advisory Committee on Problems in Foreign Relations in Washington, which aimed to 'survey the basic principles which should underlie a desirable world order to be evolved after the termination of present hostilities' (Notter, 1949: 20). The remarkable feature of this committee was the extraordinary and fantastic issues it covered such as a Regional Political, Economic and Security Organization for Europe, a Permanent Court of Justice, and even an International Air Force to ensure peace. The essential dilemma the committee faced in 1940, and one they would readdress once the United States was part of the war, was given expression by one of the committee members: 'The future is so uncertain, the course of the war so problematical, and the atmosphere in which peace negotiations may take place so unknown' (Rofe, 2012). While the dramatic events of the summer of 1940 put a sharp focus on what German victory might mean for the United States, it would nevertheless be these issues that would be addressed after Pearl Harbor. It was in the weeks after this attack that President Roosevelt commissioned the Advisory Committee on Post-War Planning, which would provide key support for the American efforts and result in the United Nations organization and the World Bank regime.

Before then, the United States, along with the United Kingdom and Russia and twenty-three other nations, had signed the Declaration by United Nations on 1 January 1942. This pledged the signatories – the 'United Nations' – not to pursue a separate peace with the Axis Powers and to uphold the Atlantic Charter of August 1941. This Anglo-American agreement was a blueprint for the postwar world. There is a worthwhile parallel to be drawn with the eight points of the Atlantic Charter, Wilson's Fourteen Points and, before then, articles of Kant's perpetual peace given how many from the former have their antecedents in the latter. 'Self-determination', 'Freedom of Trade', 'Freedom of the Seas' and 'Disarmament' are all common features and, where the other points differ, it is recognition that they may be expressed and dealt with more succinctly. As such the Atlantic Charter may be described as a statement of Allied peace aims in World War II (Williams, 1998).

The desire to 'learn lessons' from the Versailles experience was clear in the communication between the leaders of the key Allied powers (United States, Russia, United Kingdom and nationalist China) during World War II. They met with each other and exchanged their closest officials during the course of the war rather than rely on a set-piece conference at the end of the fighting. The wartime conferences at Casablanca (January 1943 – involving Roosevelt, Churchill); Cairo (November 1943 – Roosevelt, Churchill, Chaing Kai Shek); Teheran (November–December 1943 – Roosevelt, Stalin, Churchill); Yalta (February 1945: Roosevelt, Stalin, Churchill) were the venues for the discussion which shaped the postwar world. The issues that were tackled in smoke-filled rooms long into the night between these statesmen and their advisors meant that when it came to the gathering after the European war had ended in Potsdam in July 1945, key decisions had already been made. By way of example, in the first of the meetings mentioned above, at Casablanca, an announcement was made that had profound influence of the outcome of the war and the peace that would follow. While the wartime leaders put 'winning the war' first, appropriately, given its outcome was far from a foregone conclusion, what that meant was given substance when Roosevelt announced that the objective of the Allies would be unconditional surrender of the Axis powers. The call for 'unconditional surrender' was and remains controversial. It gave the Axis a propaganda coup at the beginning of 1943 to be able to portray to their peoples the Allies as wanting to crush them, and undoubtedly prolonged the conflict by stiffening resistance to Allied forces. While these were risks associated with announcing unconditional surrender as the goal of the Allies, Roosevelt was prompted to do so by his concern for the postwar peace. By pledging the Allies to this goal, the president, mindful of the 1919 experience, was seeking to remove any ambiguity that could arise from an armistice. The Allies wanted a decisive end to the war, which they believed would give them the best chance to establish a meaningful peace (Reynolds, 2006, 2007).

As we can see from the account above, it was the United States that provided much of the impetus for discussion of peace, but it was not solely an American enterprise. The British under Winston Churchill provided manpower and expert opinion, particularly emanating from the Labour Party as part of the National Government (Ashworth, 2007), to the efforts to address the postwar world across a range of issues. Other countries contributed, too. Individuals such as economist John Maynard Keynes and South African Prime Minister Jan Smuts would make their mark on the process (Skidelsky, 2003; Mazower, 2009b: 28–65). Also important was the army of civil servants and bureaucrats, many of whom had experienced the failings of the previous peace, who contributed to the 'war effort' by supporting the efforts for a 'better peace' in the postwar world. These were the kind of people who made up the 730 delegates attending the United Nations Monetary and Financial Conference (1–15 July 1944), more commonly known by its location, Bretton Woods, in New Hampshire. President Roosevelt's remarks to the opening gathering of delegates from the forty-four nations reflected a belief that the economic consequences of the conflict would be determinant of peace. Keynes was in the audience as the head of the British delegation and heard Roosevelt say, 'The economic health of every country is a proper matter of concern to all its neighbors, near and far' (Rosenman, 1950). The conference established the International Bank for Reconstruction and Development – known as the World Bank, the International Monetary Fund (IMF) and the General Agreement of Trade and Tariffs (GATT). Collectively they formed the Bretton Woods system that governed monetary relations and provided for an economic regime that transcended into the twenty-first century (Ikenberry, 1996).

In 1944, thought was also being given to the shape of political peace and an organization that could effectively provide order to international relations. While the United Nations declaration had been made at the beginning of 1942 in order for a lasting peace to result from the war, there was a desire that the nations united to fight the Axis should be more than a wartime alliance (Plesch, 2010). The Washington Conversations on International Peace and Security Organization, (21–29 August 1944), commonly known for the mansion in which they were held in Washington, DC, Dumbarton Oaks, was another of the wartime conferences that brought the major Axis powers together to discuss the peace that would follow. Representatives of the US, UK, Soviet Union and China agreed at this meeting on the foundation of the United Nations organization, with the Security Council as its executive branch that would emerged the following year in San Francisco. Representatives of fifty nations met at the United Nations Conference on International Organization (25 April–26 June 1945). By then President Roosevelt had died, although the address he had been working on, designed to provide impetus to the impending UN conference, clearly illustrated his desire that the peace that would emerge would be long-lasting. He wrote:

> The work, my friends, is peace; more than an end of this war – an end to the beginning of all wars; as we go forward toward the greatest contribution that any generation of human beings can make in this world – the contribution of lasting peace – I ask you to keep up your faith.
>
> (undelivered Jefferson Day Address, *New York Times*, 13 April 1945)

These words again reveal the philosophy integral to those fighting a war but looking to build a meaningful peace. That philosophy is evident also in the outcome of the conference in San Francisco: the United Nations organization based on the UN Charter. The opening line of the preamble reminds us again of the influence that war has on the formulation of peace: 'We the Peoples of the United Nations determined to save succeeding generations from the scourge of war, which twice in our lifetime has brought untold sorrow to mankind.'

# BOX 3.7 PREAMBLE TO THE UNITED NATIONS CHARTER

The importance of the Preamble to the United Nations is that it clearly outlines the shape of the peace that its authors wanted to achieve, while simultaneously giving credence to the notion that peace is the absolute opposition to war in stating first of all that the United Nation's primary aim is to 'save succeeding generations from the scourge of war'.

Given its relative brevity for such a defining statement of purpose, it is quoted in full here:

We the peoples of the United Nations determined:

- to save succeeding generations from the scourge of war, which twice in our lifetime has brought untold sorrow to mankind, and
- to reaffirm faith in fundamental human rights, in the dignity and worth of the human person, in the equal rights of men and women and of nations large and small, and
- to establish conditions under which justice and respect for the obligations arising from treaties and other sources of international law can be maintained, and
- to promote social progress and better standards of life in larger freedom,

and for these ends:

- to practice tolerance and live together in peace with one another as good neighbours, and
- to unite our strength to maintain international peace and security, and
- to ensure, by the acceptance of principles and the institution of methods, that armed force shall not be used, save in the common interest, and
- to employ international machinery for the promotion of the economic and social advancement of all peoples,

have resolved to combine our efforts to accomplish these aims: Accordingly, our respective Governments, through representatives assembled in the city of San Francisco, who have exhibited their full powers found to be in good and due form, have agreed to the present Charter of the United Nations and do hereby establish an international organization to be known as the United Nations.

Within the rest of the preamble one can see the influence of peace on the fifty nations who signed the Charter in the spring of 1945. This continues into the articles of the Charter. The first article of the first chapter outlines the UN's purpose as 'to maintain international peace and security'. Though the member states may not always have held to this, the Charter is a cornerstone to the body of international law that has provided for the regime of international relations since 1945.

An important element of World War II thinking on peace, evident in San Francisco and the UN Charter, centred on how a sense of justice could be instilled in the postwar world. The sense that the last peace had been unjust pervaded strategizing for a more just postwar world. In both of the major theatres of conflict, International Military Tribunals (IMT) were established as the war-fighting ended. Known respectively as the Nuremberg and Tokyo trials, they sought to bring to justice the leading individuals responsible for the war. The Tribunals' origins can be traced to the Casablanca conference in early 1942 and were discussed subsequently at each of the major Allied conferences. The first charge, significantly, was 'Crimes against peace', followed by 'War crimes' and 'Crimes against humanity'. Though a number of individuals evaded capture and trial, and the value of the justice has been questioned, the Tribunals established a notable precedent in bringing consideration of justice to bear in establishing peace (Charney, 1998; Katyal and Tribe, 2002; Overy, 2002).

The place of justice in the peace at the end of World War II was also evident on the cover of the UN Charter itself in the reference to the International Court of Justice. Chapter 14 of the UN Charter lays down that the principal judicial organ of the United Nations will be International Court of Justice (ICJ). The court is located at the Peace Palace in The Hague. Its fifteen international judges who make up the body are charged with settling 'in accordance with international law, legal disputes submitted to it by States and to give advisory opinions on legal questions referred to it by authorized United Nations organs and specialized agencies' (ICJ website: http://www.icj-cij.org/homepage/index.php). The Court has been criticized for lacking universal jurisdiction: its rulings only apply to issues submitted to it by member states, but nonetheless the Court's importance is in aligning justice with peace.

The point to take from this account of peace and World War II is the consideration given to peace as it unfolded. Looking back, the peace treaty that ended the Great War had a profound legacy on the protagonists' thinking. They started pondering the shape of peace and all of its implications at an early stage in order to learn lessons from their reading of the Versailles experience. Equally, the war was fought looking forward to the peace that would follow. Beyond its propaganda value, considerable efforts were made to establish a better peace: one that would be long-lasting and not contain the seeds of future conflict. Depending upon one's view of the Cold War as a period of prolonged peace or one of global conflict, the endeavours to inaugurate a more peaceful world were earnest and have endured.

## Post-Cold War peace – peace without victory mark II?

Identifying precisely the end of the Cold War is a troubling task to scholars of history and international relations; identifying when peace *began* even more so, though a number of International Relations scholars have tried. Francis Fukuyama's *The End of History and the Last Man* and Charles Krauthammer's 'The Unipolar Moment' both attempted to address the sudden and 'surprising' arrival of peace after 1989, but within a matter of years their concepts were challenged by the history that was unfolding (Fukuyama, 1992; Krauthammer, 1990/1991). Providing a counter-view G John Ikenberry argued that 'common wisdom' meant 'The end of the Cold War … was a historical watershed'. Ikenberry disagreed, putting it plainly:

> The common wisdom is wrong. What ended with the Cold War was bipolarity, the nuclear stalemate, and decades of containment of the Soviet Union – seemingly the most dramatic and consequential features of the postwar era. But the world order created in the middle to late 1940s endures, more extensive and in some respects more robust than during its Cold War years. Its basic principles, which deal with organization and relations among the Western liberal democracies, are alive and well.
>
> (Ikenberry, 1996: 79)

Ikenberry's final point sustains the argument of continuity in understanding war and peace made here. In light of the debates about peace to which the likes of Fukuyama and Ikenberry contributed during the 1990s, it is perhaps little surprise that the term became highly contested. During that decade it assumed a number of meanings and a number of new terms were born. Making sense of this development is challenging. Nevertheless, the overarching concept and the term most commonly used to describe it is 'peacekeeping'. Associated most closely with the United Nations, although never mentioned in the Charter, the UN's first peacekeeping mission was established to observe the 1948 ceasefire between Israel and its Arab neighbours. However, the UN's efforts at keeping the peace during the 1990s, in places such as Somalia, the former Yugoslavia and Rwanda, were often pitiful. As a result United Nations credibility in this field, and more broadly, suffered considerable damage. A considerable part of the problem was a lack of understanding between UN headquarters in New York, UN operatives in the field and, indeed, of the parties involved on the ground, of what peacekeeping meant. The term, used frequently in Western media, acquired a ubiquitous meaning as it was applied to a variety of missions, magnifying disquiet at the apparent failings of the UN to keep the peace. The UN, recognizing the challenge, established the Department of Peacekeeping Operations in 1992, but the challenging missions it faced, and the lack of operating procedures and institutional memory, meant it took much of the rest of the decade to become effective (Urquhart, 1987; Goulding, 2003).

Nonetheless, elsewhere during the 1990s attempts to further understand peacekeeping, and peace more broadly, were being made. Scholars, policymakers and militaries were distinguishing between different forms of peacekeeping (Bellamy, Williams and Griffin, 2010: 93–120). Peacekeeping became synonymous with post-Cold War peace and the efforts of the United Nations to remove its Cold War shackles. During the 1990s the language of peace evolved to describe a number of activities. These included: peacekeeping, Peace Support Operations, peacebuilding, peacemaking, peace enforcement, conflict resolution, Stability and Support Operations (SASO) and Stability, Security, Transition and Reconstruction (SSTR) operations. Each has a distinct meaning, though they are often confused and conflated with each other. Perhaps the most interesting developments could be found in militaries, not least because they were the people who had to operationalize peacekeeping on the ground. British Army thinking has evolved doctrine (i.e. aimed at the operational level) from Joint Warfare Publications entitled 'The Military Contribution to Peace Support Operations' (Joint Warfare Publications, 2004). The volume's origins and title illustrate its heritage, but nonetheless in its pages it is clear the thought given to the subject. For the British military the term 'Peace Support Operation' encompasses a range of activities with the 'peace' prefix, and others such as conflict prevention and humanitarian intervention. The trajectory of this thinking within an organization dedicated to fighting and winning wars was towards an all-encompassing methodology for the consideration of peace. The 'comprehensive approach' recognizes multiple lines of activity – diplomatic, economic and political – alongside a military one as a means of achieving strategic goals. For militaries, this may mean increasing deployments in the wonderfully abbreviated OOTW, standing for 'Operations Other Than War'. To return to our original delineation of peace between a negative Hobbesian peace and a positive peace, it is clear that peacekeeping, Peace Support Operations and OOTW exist in the space between the two constructs. In short, modern peace is often difficult to identify.

The peace of the twenty-first century is a chimera and as such has become ever more entangled with war and conflict. US President George W. Bush declared major combat operations in Iraq over on 1 May 2003, just eight weeks after the military campaign had begun in March 2003. In making his announcement he stood under a banner stating 'Mission Accomplished' on board the USS *Abraham Lincoln*, having flown on to the aircraft carrier while it was returning from the Persian Gulf. Over 4,000 US servicemen died as part of Operation Iraqi Freedom and 30,000 have been wounded in action (WIA). Only 139 were killed during 'combat operations', with 545 casualties during that phase. The vast majority of deaths and casualties have come in the 'post-combat operations' phase, i.e. since President Bush made his announcement. (Figures for US casualties can be found at http://www.defense.gov/news/casualty.pdf.) Figures for Iraqi casualties are less well accounted, though cross-referencing a number of sources would suggest that between March 2003 and December 2009, more than 100,000 casualties have been caused by 'violent deaths'. Bush later admitted to *Time* magazine as his administration drew to a close that 'Clearly, putting "Mission Accomplished" on an aircraft carrier was a mistake' ('Seeking a Legacy', *Time*, Mark Thompson, Washington, 12 January 2009; http://www.time.com/time/nation/article/0,8599,1871060,00.

html#ixzz0iYveTbkC). At a 1 May 2008 press conference in Washington, DC, Democratic Senator Jim Webb stated:

> This is the fifth anniversary of the day that President Bush arrived on an aircraft carrier in a flight suit and declared 'mission accomplished.' And in an ironic way, I think it can be said, when you look at the historic way that we use our military, that the Iraq war was over five years ago, in classical terms. And what began was a very contentious occupation that placed our military in what classically we would call a holding position, totally dependent on the ability of the political process to reach the type of solution that would allow this occupation to end.

Webb's remarks illustrate recognition of the difficulties of identifying, and achieving, a meaningful peace in twenty-first-century conflicts such as that in Iraq.

To conclude here, the increasing complexity of war, as has been described in Chapter 2 ('War'), is just part of the reason. This chapter has shown that peace deserves to be studied in its own right – not least because it determines the way wars unfold in a manner that escapes the attention of the casual observer.

## CONCLUSION

> 'All we are saying is give peace a chance' (repeat and fade)
>
> (John Lennon, 1969)

Composed during his 'bed-in' at the Queen Elizabeth II hotel in Montreal in 1969, John Lennon's anthemic comment on the ongoing war in Vietnam is a clear indictment of war as a means of resolving conflict. Lennon's words capture the view of many with a liberal bent who consider peace to be attainable if enough people want it. Equally, Lennon's words are utopian in the view of realist thinkers, as peace cannot simply be wished into existence. Yet the sentiment the words offer does exist in the real world of international relations: the preamble to the UN Charter – a foundation to our international regime – pledges states 'to unite our strength to maintain international peace and security'. Nonetheless, perhaps its most pertinent implication for our understanding of peace is that the final word is one that is unspoken: 'fade'. In the minds of many people, peace does indeed fade from prominence without its 'other', war.

While Lennon's words would seem to place peace as proffering hope, a directly opposite view was taken by American strategist Edvard Luttwak at the end of the 1990s. Luttwak stated, 'An unpleasant truth often overlooked is that although war is a great evil, it does have a great virtue: it can resolve political conflicts and lead to peace' (Luttwak, 1991). He argued in 'Give War a Chance' that, when wars end naturally, a peace of substance is the result. Further, he viewed intervention in a conflict as unlikely to help provide a resolution; instead, it had the capacity to make things worse. Published as it was at the end of a summer in which swift NATO intervention had seemingly righted the wrongs being done in Kosovo, and after the protracted conflict in the former Yugoslavia, Luttwak's comments were and remain controversial. Whatever your take on Luttwak, what is clear, again, is the interrelationship between peace and war that has been presented here.

Throughout this chapter particular thought has been given to the use of language in describing war and peace. Combined with the form of expression, in English at least, the language of war and peace is often unhelpful. We use words to distinguish between different things when there may be little distinction, and instead considerable overlap. There is a propensity, seen particularly in the contemporary media, to represent things in 'black and white' and we often understand things because of a contrast to something: the other. Within international relations literature, and broader historical writings, accounts of war and peace have suffered because of this. Wars, because of their capacity for far-reaching change, tend to be used as markers to begin and end chapters of history. This chapter has shown that the lines between war and peace are – to use another word – blurred. This is compounded when we factor in that long-standing axiom that 'history is written by the winners'. That history is characterized by ordered peace resulting from a heroic victory. In our discussion here we have seen how the objectives sought from war: the war aims and the motivations for peace may coincide without mirroring each other. This provides the opportunity for confusion, the interaction of people and events, and illustrates how important it is to think about the crossover between war and peace.

Eighteenth-century Historian Edward Gibbon (1734–1794) wrote in his seminal work on the fall of the Roman Empire (1776/1981), 'War was gradually improved into an art and degraded into a trade.' To twist his words and apply them to our thinking of peace in modern times, peace has become more scientific and been upgraded into a profession. The United States Air Force Strategic Air Command's motto is testimony to the latter, while the sheer scale of effort devoted to understanding peace has leant towards it being something that can be calculated. Sadly, the elements of the equation do not yet equal wholesale peace. To end this chapter, we can return to John Lennon, and stress the human dimension to our discussion of war and peace (*emphasis added*): 'War is over, if *you* want it' ('Happy Christmas [War is Over]', 1971).

## FURTHER READING

Carr, Edward Hallett (1939/1947) *The Twenty Years' Crisis: An Introduction to International Relations*. London: Macmillan.

Doyle, Michael (1997) *Ways of War and Peace*. New York: W. W. Norton.

Morgenthau, Hans (1948 and many subsequent editions) *Politics among Nations: The Struggle for Power and Peace*. New York: McGraw Hill.

Sharp, Paul (2009) *Diplomatic Theory of International Relations*. Cambridge: Cambridge University Press.

## WEBSITES

http://www.cfr.org/

Council on Foreign Relations: US-based thinktank focused on issues in contemporary international relations.

http://www.foreignaffairs.com/

The journal of the Council on Foreign Relations.

http://www.internationalrelations.com/

Website regularly updated by Professor Joshua S. Goldstein, Professor Emeritus of International Relations, American University (Washington, DC) and Research Scholar, Department of Political Science, University of Massachusetts, Amherst.

http://www.e-ir.info/

e-International Relations (e-IR) is an online resource for students of International Relations, containing useful forums and feeds generated by students for students.

# CHAPTER 4

# Sovereignty

The state is the central actor in both political science and political history. As Richard Evans argues, history as a university subject … was traditionally 'emphatically the political history of the nation-state and its relations with other nation-states. The history of high politics and international diplomacy was king' (Evans, 1997a: 161). Knowledge of sovereignty, as both a political attribute and a legal status of the state, is not only vital to a thorough understanding of state behavior in IR, but key to appreciating the driving force of much European and international history. The problem is that sovereignty itself encapsulates both political and legal facets. While much can be said (as evidenced by the Introduction) for using international history to obtain a deeper appreciation of international relations, law itself presents a very different perspective of the international system. As Charles De Visscher argued in the 1950s, international law is not an easy fit in explaining the imperatives of IR:

> There is no branch of law that lends itself less easily than international law to this reduction to a system of the mere imperatives of abstract logic. The dangers of schematic conceptualism are never more apparent than when it is applied to relations where particular situations are far more important than general situations and where, consequently, general norms are still far from occupying the place that belongs to them in the internal order.
>
> (De Visscher, 1957: 66)

This implies that our history, definition and conceptualization of sovereignty is bound to contain multiple levels of meanings, and internal tensions. As will be seen, sovereignty combines philosophy, political thought and legal reasoning, in addition to the comparative aspects of its development in key Western states. This chapter examines its historical origins and development, its operation as a feature of law, an attribute of the state, and a cause and consequence of state power. Doing so means tackling the various political, juridical and social components of sovereignty, in addition to the major contemporary challenges thrown up by patterns of postwar economic interdependence, examples of post-Cold War political integration in Europe and the increasing scope of international law, including the practice of intervention.

There is a particular need for historical accuracy when dealing with sovereignty; the concept undergoes a series of fundamental shifts in various incarnations, which can only be appreciated by looking back to the system of states developing in sixteenth-century Europe, and specifically to key contributions to political and legal thought. The bulk of this chapter examines watersheds in European political thought and practice that have shaped sovereignty; the second section explores the tensions between IR and customary international law in defining contemporary sovereignty; the third section concludes with a review of the internal oppositions that increasingly characterize sovereignty in law and complicate its ambiguous role in IR.

## BOX 4.1 ETYMOLOGY

**Classical Latin**: *super* (above); *superus* (being above)/*superbus* (being elevated above others).

**Middle Latin**: *superanus*; earliest record is 1000 CE, by St Victor of Marseilles, to denote 'that which is higher'.

**Early French**: *so(u)verain* (adjective); *so(u)veraineté*; records from 1100 to express supremacy; 1280–1283, Philippe de Rémy uses *souverain(s)* to denote the exercise of political control by those holding power over land and people.

**Medieval Latin**: *plenitude potestas*: sovereignty concentrated in the hands of one ruler or single institution.

## HISTORICAL WATERSHEDS

While the use of historical enquiry effectively 'bookends' any investigation with neat beginnings and endings, sovereignty is as much a reflection of core social principles regarding the development of humans as both individuals and groups as it is a feature of any historical era or civilization. Thus, while not all tribes or groups possess a sovereign, or a given structure of law, they do have an identifiable sense of the internal and external facets of their group. This in itself is enough of an organizing principle by which to produce internal cohesion and desire predictability and preservation in relations with others. What transforms rudimentary social groupings into political units is when the *seat of power* becomes coterminous with a given territory and an identifiable population according to observable precepts of law. Ancient Greece is by no means the first example of such a transfer but it is one of the best examples in which this transfer was first recorded and analysed. What emerges from the analysis is a clear vision of sovereignty associated not with the authority of a particular ruler, but with authority derived from, and enacted according to, the body of law. In other words, 'in Greek political theory the sovereignty of the law was a fundamental and perennial concept', in which Greek or Homeric kings were 'officer[s] of the community' not rulers seeing sovereignty vested in their own person (Larson and Jenks, 1965: 21).

Plato produced the first identifiably Greek concept of the sovereignty of law: 'I see that the state in which the law is above the rulers, and the rulers are the inferiors of the law, has salvation' (Plato, 2010: 4.715). Aristotle, Plato's student, helps to answer our two overarching questions (In whom does authority ultimately rest? What are identifiably 'sovereign' characteristics?). The supreme power of the state rests in the citizenry (Aristotle, 1995: 3.i), which may be found in one, or a few, or many. (For an excellent appraisal of moral ideas, behaviour and political concepts in classical context, see Herman, 2006.)

The identifiable characteristic is not the power emanating from this aggregate, but its sufficiency, a 'union of them sufficient for the purposes of life' (Aristotle, 1995: 7.4–7.8), wanting for nothing. This populace operates before the sovereignty of the law, and according to Aristotle, the truest relationship between people, their government and the law 'is secured by making the law sovereign and the government its servant' (Barker, 1906: 328). There is clearly some discomfort in the idea of giving full authority to a governing body that can use a body of law indiscriminately and abusively; for this reason, law must – in the eyes of Greek jurists – remain on a higher plane of authority than the government.

The Roman era provides the first real split as to where sovereignty resides, and accordingly produces two schools of thought. The first school is inherited from the preceding Greek era, and adheres to the idea of sovereignty vested in the law. Cicero, for example, argues that 'there exists a supreme and permanent law, to which all human order, if it is to have any truth or validity, must conform', with 'no other foundation of political authority than the consent of the whole people' (in Carlyle and Carlyle, 1950: 16–17). The people, or *populus* – themselves sovereign before the law – are therefore the source of true political authority.

However, this runs counter to the absolutist school of sovereignty propounded by the Roman emperors themselves. This school has two key precepts: first, that the emperor himself, and not the law, is sovereign; second, that what the ruler (prince or emperor) desires has the strength of law (*quod principi placuit legis habet vigorem*; Stein et al., 1983: i. 2.6). This is a serious division. Are the people themselves still the sovereign body? Or is the emperor's will law? The Roman jurist

Ulpian suggests that in practice emperors rule, but only because their power is bestowed upon them by the people. In other words, while the emperor's wishes have the strength of law, 'this is only because the people choose to have it so' (Carlyle and Carlyle, 1950: 56). As will be seen, this division over what sovereignty entails (power, authority, the law) and where it resides (the ruler or the *populus*) characterizes both the political practices and the commentary of the medieval period. Before understanding the theory of sovereignty of the state, as argued by Jean Bodin in 1576, we need to appreciate the two sides of this first division.

## The *populus* school

The *populus* school is dominated by the view that 'Medieval political thought inherited, and indeed was based upon, the concept of the ruler "as being bound by the laws of the nation, not as superior to them"' (Larson and Jenks, 1965: 22, citing Carlyle and Carlyle, 1950: 230). Here, we find the works of canonists like Augustine and Aquinas, who follow Aristotle's tradition of regarding authority not bound up in the wishes of the ruler but flowing from 'the habit of life of the community and that the law is supreme over every member of the community, including the king' (Larson and Jenks, 1965: 22). To this we can add insights from the jurist Gratian, that 'law is not an arbitrary command imposed by a superior, but rather represents the adaptation of the permanent and immutable principles of "nature" and justice to the needs of a community, under the terms of the circumstances and traditions of that community' (Gratian, in Carlyle and carlyle, 1950: 97). Another key view emerges from English jurist Bracton, and from John of Salisbury. Bracton, a lawyer himself, provides a clear view of medieval hierarchy in stating that 'where there is no law, there is no king, and the king is under God and the law, for it is the law which makes the king' (quoted in Larson and Jenks, 1965: 23).

As examined below, the medieval period is dominated by a three-way power struggle between the rise of the Church's authority directed by the pope, the rise of individual political units across Europe led by monarchs, and the rise of the Holy Roman Empire, led by an emperor. Who had authority over whom? The *populus* school rejects the idea of sovereignty as an absolute form of authority. As Carlyle argues, the only sovereignty recognized during this era 'was that of the law, and even that was subject to the law of God or nature' (Carlyle and Carlyle, 1950: 370). Whilst the Church may attempt to enforce its sovereignty over both spiritual and secular elements, and whilst early states may attempt to rebuff this power, there was not a clash between two systems of law; the only supreme authority was the law itself, not the State/emperor, not the Church/pope, or even Holy Roman Empire/ emperor. Other jurists and theologians subscribing to this view include Gerson, Nicholas de Cusa and Fortescue.

Medieval political theory turned into practice when key monarchs started modelling their states on this view. England, chiefly under Henry II, and Spain's Alfonso X are two notable examples of rulers who subscribed to the supremacy of law. These kings did not subscribe to the view of absolutism in which they as rulers literally embodied the law; they did, however, have a large – though not absolute and arbitrary – control over their territory and people.

## The absolutist school

During the early Middle Ages, the Church emerged as the key power over both spiritual matters regarding the faith of all and, initially, over secular matters, regarding the role of political powers on earth and their place under God. From this perspective, all of mankind formed a natural and unifying hierarchy. With the rise of the Holy Roman Empire, that hierarchy was separated between the *pope's authority* over the universal Christian Church, and the *emperor's authority* over the secular Holy Roman Empire, which comprised most of Western and Eastern Europe. Together, the result was a great Christian unity under God, known as the *Respublica Christiana*, or Christendom.

Where did sovereignty rest in the system of Christendom? Under God, Christendom itself was separate (but inseparable) between the religious authority of the Church on earth (*sacerdotium*) and the political authority of the Holy Roman Emperor (*regnum*), which emerged in the early medieval period and which – over a thousand years – shifted its secular seat from Rome to Constantinople to Vienna. Underneath the *sacerdotium* and the *regnum* was a range of lower authorities – both secular and sacred – from city-states to nobles, from monarchs to bishops. All, however, were regarded as members of the Christian community; none could declare independence from this community, for to do so would have been to flout God's law (Jackson, 2001: 157). What was confusing was the element of separation between the religious and 'worldly' authority on, and over earth, that the pope claimed, other forms of secular authority claimed by the Holy Roman Emperor, and still lesser forms of authority claimed by all beneath the emperor.

By the 1200s, however, increasing conflict arose over who held authority, the type of authority, and the area – or jurisdiction – in which that authority was wielded. The prime division was between the Church and a growing array of monarchs and secular rulers, as well as divisions between secular leaders themselves. This initially produced a neat hierarchy in which 'secular rulers might concede that on religious matters the pope "ruled", but in the secular realm the emperor increasingly challenged them'; this subsequently implied that 'kings had an exclusive right to rule' in their own realm, which undermined the universal authority claimed by popes (Holsti, 2004: 119). Gradually, an increasing number of monarchs refused to acknowledge the authority of the Church in secular matters. Such challenges to the pope, to the Church and, indeed, to the overall structure of *Respublica Christiana* emerged from Henry VII and King Robert of Naples. The Church responded by threatening to exclude the secular rulers from the religious authority that flowed through *Respublica Christiana* by excommunicating them, or by labelling such attempts as heretical – a trespass against the natural order and against God. These threats were increasingly ineffective and, by 1302, French kings publicly proclaimed that they alone were 'emperor in their own domain' (*qui est imperator in regno suo*) (Ullmann, 1949).

Robert of Naples used this precept to defy a series of imperial edicts, and to reject the power of both the pope and the imperial laws of the Holy Roman Empire, arguing that monarchs not only ruled in their domain, but had the right to make laws within it, including laws that ran counter to imperial laws. Monarchs had the right, or the authority, to do this (though not necessarily the actual power to make it happen). In other words, they had the sovereign authority to do so, by virtue of the fact that they personally were sovereigns, and that they held authority over their domain. In this way, Robert of Naples took on the emperor, and in 1312 was found guilty of high treason (*crimen laesae majestatis*) (Holsti, 2004: 119). Robert – ironically – had much in common with the Pope Clement IV, in wanting to limit the authority of the Holy Roman Emperor in key areas. Indeed it was Clement IV who supported Robert in the papal bull *Pastoralis Cura*, by arguing that the emperor had no imperial authority over any other monarch, and that (unsurprisingly) the pope himself had superiority over the emperor. As Holsti argues, the *Pastoralis Cura* 'effectively put an end to imperial claims of *dominus mundi* and thus to the idea of an organic, single Christian polity' (2004: 119; also see Ullmann, 1949).

From Clement IV's perspective, sovereignty was not only vested in the individual ruler, but vested in a ruler within a specific geographical area – the two together forming a polity. As will be seen, geography, and its internal/external dynamics, is a key facet of contemporary sovereignty (and identity, see Chapter 7). Clement IV also highlighted the universal vs particularist features of medieval Europe. The universalizing authority claimed of the emperor, and eventually the pope, gave way to the particularist authority actually wielded by key European monarchs in specific regions. Polities were different from each other, but also similar in that the majority of their rulers saw themselves as the unquestioned, absolute repository of sovereignty in their territory. Embodying the absolutist perspective, rulers, not the ruled, and not the abstract polity, and not the law, were sovereign. There are hard and soft interpretations of absolutism. Some European rulers (Peter the Great, Louis XIV, Louis XV) took absolutism to extremes in claiming not only supreme power over their realm, but arguing that this power was God-given and therefore undeniable, irresistible. Others felt it resided in them absolutely, in the sense that it simply did not rest in the law, or the people, or the overall polity.

The authority, and eventually the power, of the pope and the emperor were increasingly eroded as monarchs claimed sovereignty within their own realms. Francis I of France and Henry VIII of England successfully challenged papal authority by effectively nationalizing the Catholic Church in their own states. Francis took the authority granted to him by the Concordat of Bologna in 1516 and used it to appoint clergy and own church lands; Henry went further in 1533 by divorcing Catherine of Aragon in defiance of the pope, taking over (and destroying) church lands and property, and forcibly transforming English Catholic structures into a Church of England. Jurists like Vitoria and Suarez highlighted the increasing political particularism of late medieval Europe by commenting on the self-contained nature of specific polities, and the sovereign authority of their respective rulers.

The death knell for papal authority was sounded by Vitoria, who argued that princes – like the pope himself – derive their right to rule from God; this not only renders princes as 'vicars of the Church' in their own realm (undermining the local need for the pope as a universal figure), but places princes, and not the Church, in full control of their sovereign realm (eliminating the right of the Church to intervene in civil authority) (Holsti 2004: 121). Martin Luther, as the embodiment of the Protestant Reformation, took Vitoria's views to their logical conclusion, asserting that monarchs were sovereign in matters secular, and in matters religious, effectively granting them the freedom to declare independence from the Catholic Church in political and religious issues. This additional layer of authority to the form of sovereignty claimed by European secular rulers was encapsulated in 1555 at the Peace of Augsburg, which granted princes the right to freedom over the religion of their own subjects (*cuius regio, eius religio*). The first cracks in the formerly unshakeable edifice of the Church had appeared. Its ability to exercise political or economic authority over princes and polities was increasingly reined in. As J. N. Figgis argued a century ago, 'By the destruction of the independence of the Church and its hold on an extra-territorial public opinion, the last obstacle to unity within the State was removed' (1913: 72). Figgis continues, arguing that 'The unity and universality and essential rightness of the sovereign territorial State, and the denial of every extra-territorial or independent communal form of life, are Luther's lasting contribution to politics' (Figgis, 1913: 91).

## STATE SOVEREIGNTY

The concept of the *respublica* survived the medieval period, and transformed into the secular concept of a political unit, or polity. The polity that emerged in early modern Europe was a single, unified collectivity that possessed an identifiable population, was confined by borders to a specific geographical area, developed an identifiable set of political interests, ruled by a single authority. Monarchs held this authority in the medieval period on the basis of the early modern European definition of sovereignty (from which most subsequent definitions derive); that is, *supreme authority within a given territory*. The quality that defined early modern states, rather than individual rulers (including popes, emperors, kings, bishops, aristocracy), is sovereignty. As will be seen, contemporary 'vessels' of sovereignty include the populace in its entirety through the vehicle of a constitution, a given political party, and individual leaders (democratic, autocratic, military and religious).

In 1576, with the writings of the eminent French legal theorist Jean Bodin, Europe encountered for the first time a methodical treatment of the theory of state sovereignty. This in some sense brings together both the *populus* and absolutist schools, because, while these states are dominated by rulers with unfettered power over their own realm, the state itself is a wider representation – or emanation – of the prince, and is the vehicle for his authority, and embodiment of its sovereignty. In other words, the state, as an extension of the ruler and the ruled, is itself sovereign. Sovereignty itself 'is something more than mere superiority; it is at once the greatest force and the supreme authority within defined territorial limits'. That sovereignty emanates from the state rather than flowing solely from an individual illustrates one of the key generic aspects of sovereignty, namely its *permanence as an attribute of the state*, rather than just a quality of an individual ruler. From the political perspective, this consolidates the state as the key governing unit, granting states a measure of permanence and, consequently, a permanent attribute by which governments can justify the use of key policies, including security and warfare, necessary to secure the state itself. From the legal perspective, Bodin argues that sovereignty 'cannot be perfect unless it is absolute and indivisible … free of any subordination without and of any division within' (De Visscher, 1957: 16).

## BOX 4.2 BODIN AND SOVEREIGNTY

Jean Bodin's *De la république* is the first systematic study of sovereignty, and is worth investigating as a key text of both European history and European political thought. Contextualized by the upheavals in France during the time of Louis XI, Bodin articulated the juridical theory of sovereignty in which there is within the state unlimited one power: '*Majestas est summa in cives ac subditos legibusque soluta potestas*' (Bodin, 1576/1986: 1, 8). In other words, there exists within the state a central force from which all the subsequent powers which make laws are derived (*majestas summa potestas summum imperium*). This is, however, very different than the writings from or following the absolutist camp, in which the state, and its sovereign power, is manifested in the person of the ruler (for example, as argued by Bossuet, '*Tout l'état est en la personne du prince*'), and which monarchs like Louis XIV used to underwrite the theory of the divine right of kings, claiming famously '*L'état c'est moi*'.

As F. H. Hinsley observed:

At a time when it had become imperative that the conflict between rulers and ruled should be terminated, [Bodin] realized … that the conflict would be solved only if it was possible both to establish the existence of a necessarily unrestricted ruling power and to distinguish this power from an absolutism that was free to disregard all laws and regulations. He did this by founding both the legality of this power and the wisdom of observing the limitations which hedged its proper use upon the nature of the body politic as a political society comprising both ruler and ruled – and his statement of sovereignty was the necessary, only possible, result.

(Hinsley, 1966: 124–125)

Bodin, Machiavelli and Hobbes represent the triumvirate of theorists on state sovereignty. All are intellectual architects of the centralization of state power, the authority of the ruler, the role of the ruled. The writings of all three are contextualized by a period of violent religious and civil strife in their own countries. For Bodin, facing the growing anarchy of religious wars between Calvinist Huguenots and the Catholic monarchy, the procedural aspects of sovereignty provided 'the focus of order and effective administration' for the well-governed French state (Larson and Jenks, 1965: 25). Bodin's concept of *souveraineté* moves beyond medieval precepts of a feudal, fragmented society to one in which a single 'body politic' combined both rulers and ruled, and which embodied the very source of (human) law. Sovereignty referred both to the inhering of ruler and ruled into one body politic and the supreme authority vested in that body within a given territory. Whether the body politic was a democracy, monarchy or aristocracy, it was sovereign simply because it was subject neither to any external human law nor authority within its territory.

Niccolò Machiavelli observed both the spectacular cultural outpourings of the Renaissance and the vicious inter-city state and familial violence that repeatedly sundered Italy. The pinnacle of the absolutist school, *The Prince* was deemed to be supreme within the territory of the state, but with a heavy responsibility for its survival and wellbeing. As such, only a strong and effective administrative order, and its ruthless application was the correct and indeed only means by which to ensure the successful expansion of a state. The obligation of all rulers was *raison d'état*, that all actions must be taken in the interests of the state, and only the state (including disagreeable actions). Sovereignty was simply the justification for both such means and ends. Hobbes, reacting to the violence of the English Civil War, argued that men war against each other without mercy to the extent that authority must be taken from them, and moved from the remit of God's law to the permanent service of the state, where it could be exercised in unrestricted fashion.

The Dutch jurist Hugo Grotius represents a break from these views. He argued that sovereignty is more than the specific power, influence and authority of a leader; it is a legal status held by each state. This widens the jurisdiction and the role of sovereignty from a specific claim to authority made by individual monarchs, to generic legal attribute common to all states, regardless of their ruler. Further, the power entailed in a state being able to act as a self-contained unit internally, as a result of being defensible externally, also acted as a measure of sovereignty: 'that power is called sovereign whose actions are not subject to the legal control of another' (Suganami, 1996: 230, in Holsti, 2004: 121).

## 1648: the Peace of Westphalia

The secular power gained by German princes in 1555 at Augsburg to promote their own faith within their own territory did not guarantee peace; indeed it promoted bitter conflict and intense competition between a host of warring Catholic and Protestant powers. The first half of the seventeenth century thus saw protracted violence ravage Europe as sacred–secular and secular–secular antagonisms were fought during the Thirty Years' War (1618–1648). This era was especially bloody, ravaging the land, cities, towns, people and governments of High Medieval Europe in a manner not seen since the Roman conquests. The violence represented both the last gasps of the papacy and the Holy Roman Emperor (and their allies) to stamp their authority on European polities, and the first serious attempts by rising polities to consolidate their territory, extend their power and entrench their authority.

The peace negotiations concluded between 1644 and 1648 produced three significant treaties: one concluded at Osnabrück and two at Münster, known collectively as the Peace of Westphalia (now northwest Germany). The concept of sovereignty emerges not as a specific reference in these two treaties, but as a method of consolidating and conceptualizing the hundreds of claims which had arisen during and long before the Thirty Years' War by various authorities to particular lands, provinces, cities, towns, enclaves, castles, etc. As with most negotiations, there is both a desire to restore the status quo for those who enjoyed success under the previous regime, and a wish to create anew in order to avoid a repetition of the violence itself. Thus the Peace of Westphalia succeeded paradoxically in restoring a number of the ancient holdings of the Holy Roman Empire and long-standing dynasties while simultaneously establishing the freedom of princes old and new to govern on the basis of sovereignty, rather than on the basis of fealty owed to the pope or the emperor.

With the permanent marginalization of both the Holy Roman Empire and the Church, the first outcome of Westphalia was the *emergence of the sovereign state* as the singular mode of European constitutional authority. Not only did polities like Switzerland and the Netherlands gain uncontested sovereignty, but intra-state diplomacy and extra-European alliances formed all attested to the emergence of a genuine system of sovereign states. Pope Innocent X memorably condemned the Westphalian treaties as 'null, void, invalid, iniquitous, unjust, damnable, reprobate, inane, empty of meaning and effect for all time'. This symbolized the second major outcome of Westphalia, namely, the *ending of intervention on religious issues* or pretexts (generally the most common form of curtailing sovereign claims). While Westphalia did not prevent future wars, it did (with the exception of Ireland and the Balkans) largely stamp out religious wars in West European wars sparked by religion.

Westphalia had two further effects. It consecrated Bodin's principle of *sovereignty as vested in the state* rather than in the body of the ruler, and it heralded the equal application of sovereignty to all states. The *legal equality* of sovereignty is based on the understanding that a monarch who claims sovereign status in being able to promote, protect and secure their state must necessarily recognize the rights of other monarchs to claim the same. As sovereignty is vested in the state, and not actually within the ruler, this rendered all state units legally alike, despite material and constitutional differences. In sum, modern sovereignty had emerged, but with an uneasy blend of the absolutist leftovers and *populus* content. As Kreijen argues,

> Modern sovereignty is rooted in the profound changes – resulting in the centralization of power and a new social cohesion within certain territorial

units – that brought about the decline of traditional medieval society. This *essentially factual* transformation of the political scene had a direct influence on the excessive legal claims to universal power formulated by the two protagonists of the weakening Empire [the pope and the emperor]. It was the *de facto* situation that elevated the theory of sovereignty from its early youth to the full-grown legal doctrine that could sustain a new international order of *de jure* equal and sovereign States.

(Kreijen, 2004: 32)

## Deconstructing Westphalia

Following the example set by Osiander (1994), Krasner (1999), Philpott (2001), Kegley and Raymond (2002) and Holsti (2004), there is much merit in looking afresh at the treaties of the Westphalian peace, to get a clear picture of the key principles that still dominate the organizing principle of modern Europe. Five key points emerge:

- Denial of Church and imperial interference in the civil matters of European rulers. This clarified the actors at Westphalia as secular authorities with a right to 'international' representation.
- Prohibition of enforced religious conversion; whether Catholic or Protestant, princes were not to forcibly convert the subjects of another prince, or to aid the subjects of a prince in another realm against their prince in such a cause. This subsequently becomes the right of religious non-interference in the sovereign affairs of others, and applies to both monarchs and imperial authorities.
- (Article 64) Prohibition of interference; both princes and imperial authority (Holy Roman) were forbidden from interfering in the governing, taxing or religious affairs of other realms. This subsequently becomes the right of secular non-interference in the sovereign affairs of others.
- (Article 65) The restoration of rights to all monarchs to conclude treaty and alliance terms with other monarchs, provided they did not undermine the authority of the emperor. On the basis of legal authority, this subsequently becomes the authority of sovereign states to make and enter into treaties, with an accompanying prohibition to do so for non-sovereign entities.
- Clarification, on the basis of legal equality, that the above rights apply equally to states considered sovereign, whatever their physical, military, constitutional or religious difference.

## The social contract

As supporters of the absolutist school waned, so the concepts of sovereignty vested in the law, the people, the state or an intermediary vehicle like a constitution increased. Reflecting classical ideas that the populace itself, including its social habits and customary law, represented the supreme authority and not the will of the monarch, the early modern version of the *populus school* regarded sovereignty as a social contract struck between the populace, who agreed to be ruled fairly, and a fair ruler. The social contract suggests that individual members of society agree to be ruled; society transfers the authority to rule to one or a number of people. Whether they do so implicitly or explicitly, and whether this transfer is subject to qualifications or even revocation, is a subjective interpretation.

The medieval era accepted without question the concept of such an accord as the proper basis of the state; indeed this axiom is found again and again in the work of Thomas Aquinas (*On the Governance of Rulers*), Marsilius of Padua and Suarez, among others. As found in *Leviathan*, Thomas Hobbes' interpretation is as dispassionate as it is logical; the agreement between society and ruler is simply one in which absolute power is transferred irrevocably to the monarch, who then assumes (and possibly subsumes) the status of a sovereign, and the attributes of sovereignty. The jurist Pufendorf suggests, similarly, that this transfer of power entails first a *pactum unionis,* which is then followed by a *pactum subjectionis.*

However, it is Jean-Jacques Rousseau who emerged as the chief exponent of this form of plebiscite sovereignty: sovereignty as the public expression of will of a whole community, and the rightness of that general will (Bowle, 1961: 319–336). The precise terms of Rousseau's *pacte social* are as follows: 'Chacun de nous met en commun sa personne et toute sa puissance sous la supreme direction de la volonte generale; et nous regevons encore chaque membre comme partie indivisible de tout' ('Each of us puts in common his person and all his power under the supreme direction of the general will, and we still each member are an indivisible part of all'; Rousseau, 1964: I. c. 6). Thus, for Rousseau (as for Hobbes), 'the social contract was the title deed of sovereignty' (Larson and Jenks, 1965: 26). In other words, mankind's acceptance of a social contract between ruled and rulers legitimized the state as a unit, and justified its practices.

From the political perspective, the steady acceptance of sovereignty defined as the general will of the community cannot be overstated. From the 1700s onwards, attempts to oppose it almost always ended in war, whilst attempts to support and institutionalize it produced an increasingly clear structure – and eventually society – of European states. This doctrine both crystallized and catalysed the French Revolution, and the American Revolution. Taine exhorted the newly enfranchised French populace to believe that they themselves were not only kings, but greater than kings. Thomas Paine argued similarly, 'In republics such as there are established in America the sovereign power, or the power over which there is no control and which controls all others, remains where nature placed it – in the people' (Paine, 2010: i, 6).

With Hegel's metaphysical theory, 'the concept of the State as a harmony of the whole society is the absolute power on earth, and the denial of the existence of law in international affairs' (Bowle, 1961: 36–50). This suggests not only a forcible gathering of legal authority and material power into the state units of early modern Europe, but a parallel denial of any existing authority outside the state. Hegel's views can be a little misleading. He is clear that 'the institutions of political society are an expression of, and are maintained by, the general will' (2.409), but is unsure whether the general will is itself 'properly sovereign'. This suggests that it is not the quantitative majority of society that represents sovereign authority, but rather the genuine 'real' will of society, which is a more qualitative attribute. Further, the actual expression of this will is not necessarily articulated in words or acts of power; but rather a deeper bond by which a people's belief to be culturally bound to each other obtains politically:

> If the sovereign power is to be understood in this fuller, less abstract sense, if we mean by it the real determinant of the habitual obedience of the people, we must look for its sources much more widely and deeply than the analytical jurists do; it can no longer be said to reside in a determinate person or persons, but in that impalpable congeries of the hopes and fears of a people bound together by common interest and sympathy, which we call the common will.
>
> (Green, 1892: 2.404)

From this perspective, the state unit becomes increasingly regarded as a vehicle by which to translate sovereignty as the general will of the people on the *inside*, into a particularist set of laws, customs and culture, defensible in the form of sovereignty as power from those on the *outside*. However, one must not make the mistake of assuming a clear and categorical difference between states operating on the basis of the social contract, and states governed by more absolutist monarchs. The eighteenth century witnessed a tremendous variety of types of state, styles of governance and conceptualizations of sovereignty which existed concurrently but in radical contradistinction. What *can* be argued is that, from Westphalia until the defeat of Napoleon at Waterloo, one finds an increasing connection between sovereignty as a *series of legal and political concepts* and *sovereignty as state-based practice*. As Holsti opines:

> Monarchs used the arguments, vocabulary, and concepts of the publicists and scholars to buttress their claims to a monopoly of legitimate authority at home, and to disarm and subjugate lesser authorities within their realms, including free cities, duchies, and the like. They eagerly embraced the idea that sovereignty was complete and indivisible and used it to de-legitimize the constant rebellions, attempts at secession, and civil wars that raged throughout Europe in the early seventeenth century ... By the end of the eighteenth century, analysts had constructed long lists of sovereign rights and powers, including making war and peace, conducting foreign relations, appointing ambassadors, striking money, granting pardons and making final judgments, legitimizing bastards, naturalizing foreigners, and making laws.
>
> (Holsti, 2004: 127)

There was not only a connection between concepts and practice, in other words, but a growing unity in how these connections were made, justified and actioned. This unity is based on the norm of legal equality. Simply put, equality is the natural outcome of states that considered themselves externally autonomous from others by virtue of sovereignty. A major complicating factor of the Peace of Westphalia was the sheer number of polities that claimed not only sovereignty for themselves, but also legal equality vis-à-vis others. As Kegley and Raymond note, the patchwork quilt of Westphalian Europe included hundreds of sovereign polities, 343 of which lay in Germany, which in turn included 158 secular polities, 123 religious principalities and 62 imperial cities (Kegley and Raymond, 2001: 116). By the time of the Treaty of Utrecht in 1713 (used to settle the War of the Spanish Succession), legal equality between all states, including the Holy Roman Empire, was the external attribute of the internal property of sovereignty.

## 1815: the Congress of Vienna

Westphalia, Utrecht and Vienna do not represent sharp changes in state practice; rather, they represent three occasions when the rules regarding state claims to internal authority and external autonomy were consecutively consolidated. By 1815, a large number of the 'Westphalian polities' had been absorbed into larger areas, and the Church itself had radically waned in its proto-sovereign claims over key areas. From the hundreds claiming sovereign status in 1848, the Congress of Vienna reduced to a mere thirty-nine the number of states regarded as legitimately sovereign. From the use of *legal equality* as the norm denoting the equal status of sovereign states came another norm, came *recognition* as the principal method by which a state was first recognized *as* sovereign by another. Thus polities could come into existence, but 'would not enjoy the rights of sovereignty until recognized by other powers, meaning primarily the great powers of the day' (Holsti, 2004: 128–129). Together, legal equality and recognition transformed the political map of Europe from a multi-actor assemblage of different types of polities all with different statuses, to one with fewer (usually larger) state units. The result was the consolidation of sovereignty as both the pre-eminent legal status of European states and the paramount political attribute of their statehood.

Moving into and beyond the nineteenth century, two major forces need to be borne in mind.

*First, the dynamics of colonialism.* As a separate method of governing non-Western groups of people, nineteenth-century international law necessarily incorporated a variety of 'special doctrines and norms … devised for the purpose of defining, identifying, and categorizing the uncivilized' to be able to codify practices of '"conquest" and "cession by treaty" among the modes of acquiring territory' (Anghie, 1999: 4). The colonial encounter is of critical importance to both the extent of non-sovereign jurisdictions afforded to European powers and the changes imposed upon key assumptions of sovereignty as an organizing principle of governance. The most notable scholar in this area is C. H. Alexandrowicz, whose extensive and pioneering body of work includes *An Introduction to the History of the Law of Nations in the East Indies* (1967) and *The European–African Confrontation: A Study in Treaty Making* (1973).

Thus while the colonial confrontation is key to appreciating the character of sovereignty and the nature of international law, a sensible framework by which to understand non-European forms of self-government, and imposed governance, needs to examine the process by which order is created among entities belonging to non-Western cultural systems. As Anghie argues, 'Such an approach enables an exploration of both the relationship between ideas of culture and sovereignty, and the ways in which sovereignty became identified with a specific set of cultural practices to the exclusion of others' ... [as well as] an appreciation of the distinctive and unique character of sovereignty as it developed in the non-European context. Such an appreciation is important for an understanding of the subsequent histories of the non-European states, even after decolonization' (Anghie, 1999: 5). Scholars of IH and IR alike need, therefore, to be aware of the underlying historic currents from which sovereignty, as a comprehensive set of European precepts, first came into being, and then extended for the purposes of imperialism into Africa, Asia and the Pacific. Equally important is the subsequent feedback loop generated by the practices of instituting colonial control over territories and peoples, and in the process of transforming them into European possessions, identifying how sovereignty in turn was reconstituted and reshaped through colonialism.

*Second, the rise of international organizations as additional non-state entities.* Although states as sovereign political units moved around each other in increasingly sophisticated ways, there was insufficient diplomatic contact between states and national representatives, and even less recognition of the external consequences arising from increasing state interdependence, and as such 'no perceived need for institutionalized mechanisms to manage international relations' (Thompson and Snidal, 2000: 693). Thus, it was not until the nineteenth century that international organizations began to appear in significant numbers. Notable examples include the Congress of Vienna (1814–1815), which in the form of its pseudo-multilateral 'Congress system' represents a new development in the composition and conduct of international relations. The Congress system instituted two innovations; first, a systematized approach to managing issues of war and peace in the international system; and second, the requirement of state representatives to meet at regular intervals to examine diplomatic issues. Despite four major peacetime conferences held between 1815 and 1822, the Congress system was overtaken by more informal structures, limited only to tackling problems and crises as they arose, not a systematized attempt to anticipate or prevent diplomatic problems. As such, the Congress system was replaced by the 'Concert of Europe', featuring only sporadic groupings, generally prompted by the outbreak of wars rather than the deliberation of diplomacy or sovereignty. These include Paris (1856), Vienna (1864), Prague (1866), Frankfurt (1871), Berlin (1878, 1884–1885) and The Hague in 1899 and 1907. Congress and Concert outputs were focused both on the topos of sovereignty and newly arising cross-border dynamics. Thus, as argued by Thompson and Snidal:

> many of the most dramatic developments in international organization during the nineteenth century were not related to the goal of averting war but to an emerging mismatch between the geographic scope of problems versus the scope of state authority ... A new set of IOs was created to manage international economic transactions which were an increasingly important aspect of interstate relations but were difficult for national governments to manage on a unilateral basis.
>
> (Thompson and Snidal, 1999: 694)

After World War I, another watershed opportunity presented itself in the form of two key concepts: self-determination, to buttress the *content* of sovereignty; and a change in the criteria of sovereign recognition, which altered the *form* of sovereignty. The 1919 Treaty of Paris, famoulsy associated with self-determination, along with Woodrow Wilson's famous statement that 'Sovereignty resides in the community' (quoted in Reves, 1945). However, self-determination as a political norm had immediate implications for the legal norm of recognizing states as sovereign. Sovereignty was no longer simply defined as internal control over a given territory, and autonomy from and legal equivalence with other states. Instead, government itself became a criterion for recognition. States had to possess a democratic constitution that could guarantee both political freedom and protection for the rights of minorities. New criteria of *democracy, constitutionalism and minority rights* present three possible constraints on the formerly untrammelled status of sovereignty (Philpott, 2001: 37–38). Sovereignty came under additional constraints after World War II, when recognition norms were extended to all former colonies with no criteria whatsoever. Regardless of their internal capacity for governance or ability to maintain external autonomy, a cohort of newly sovereign states emerged to join the international state system.

## CONTEMPORARY SOVEREIGNTY

For IR scholars and students, sovereignty is the key attribute of statehood; the common possession of this attribute renders all individual states functionally non-differentiated in terms of their status and motivations. Sovereignty consolidates the state unit internally, though IR has generally less to say about this, apart from the issue of whether borders are hard or soft. Externally, sovereignty deters states from countenancing any higher external authority, and this renders the international structure precarious, with insecurity rather than cooperation as the behavioural constant. IR treats sovereignty altogether too lightly; there is an easy ambiguity at work in all mainstream theories that have historically damped methodical investigations of the principle itself, and its specific application to the structure, states and emergent international organizations. One reason for this may be that few in IR are aware (or indeed interested) in the detailed political history that refined sovereign concepts and practices. Fewer still take the time to appreciate the various components of sovereignty that exist within customary international law, or to understand how these definitions lay a burden of oppositional tensions on analyzing the definition, status and practice of sovereignty.

We ourselves need to be reasonably clear as to what contemporary sovereignty itself entails regarding state units. A number of eminent legal theorists have produced seminal works on this issue, of whom Ian Brownlie is particularly instructive. Brownlie makes the following three points.

- First, from the perspective of the international system, '*sovereignty and equality* of states represent the basic constitutional doctrine of the law of nations, which governs a community consisting primarily of states having a *uniform legal personality*' (Brownlie, 1998: 289).

- Second, from the perspective of states, all state units are understood to possess both *legal personalities and equality*; sovereignty simply represents the most fundamental aspects of a state's existence: namely, *its relation to other states* and organizations of states as defined by law.
- Third, there are three 'principal corollaries of the sovereignty and equality of states: (1) a jurisdiction (prima facie exclusive) over a territory and the permanent population living there; (2) a duty of non-intervention in the area of exclusive jurisdiction of other states; and (3) the dependence of obligations arising from customary law and treaties on the consent of the obligor' (Brownlie, 1998: 289).

In terms of competence (the authority and capacity to enact a given policy), sovereignty describes 'the legal competence which states have in general, to refer to a particular function of this competence, or to provide a rationale for a particular aspect of the competence' (Brownlie, 1998: 291). From this basis, sovereignty refers to two things: jurisdiction over national territory, and the actual 'power to acquire title to territory and rights accruing from the exercise of power'.

IR's focus upon sovereignty is rather different:

- First, IR focuses on the structural *consequences* of state sovereignty (anarchy, security dilemmas, pragmatic cooperation); as a result, IR fails to appreciate the nature of coexistence between sovereign states from the legal perspective, and the constitutive element of statehood that sovereignty plays in this respect. As Brownlie argues, 'the whole of law could be expressed in terms of the coexistence of sovereignties' (1998: 290).
- Second, IR has, since the post-Cold War era, been increasingly preoccupied with breaches of non-intervention by one or more states in the exclusive jurisdiction of another state, looking specifically at the causes, methods and consequences of such breaches. However, mainstream IR investigates these issues in the absence of a clear understanding of what constitutes the scope of non-intervention (not purely militarily), a state's jurisdiction, the qualities of its exclusiveness, the specific role of territory (rather than merely borders) and the role of a permanent population.
- Third, a preoccupation with the erosion of sovereignty. Again, however, IR has little sense of what a legal personality entails in the first place, its role in the process of states signing treaties, accords, bilateral or multilateral agreements, the nature of the various obligations arising from customary law, and the impact this has on sovereignty states including its power.

IR is confined to a simplistic and tautological understanding of sovereignty: states behave as states because states are sovereign. There is no sense of the key differences between internal and external sovereignty, positive and negative sovereignty, or a historical appreciation of how states have become the 'seat' of sovereignty. Westphalia is simply a paradigm for the ambiguous, almost mystic concept of sovereignty.

IR needs to be far more aware of the complications regarding the terminology and practice of sovereignty that have arisen both from its colourful European history and also from sovereignty's uneasy home in international law. Brownlie's neat definitions are a helpful start for all IR scholars, but there are a number of complicating factors that we now need to examine.

From the perspective of international law, sovereignty is a troublesome paradox. In large part, this is due to the history of international law, which itself is divided between universal and individual dynamics. As De Visscher suggests, 'the theory of international law oscillates between an individualist conception of the State and a universalist conception of humanity, between the subjectivism of State primacy and the objectivism of the primacy of the international order' (1957: 66). The consequences of this tension are reproduced in a double-sided (or Janus-faced) understanding of sovereignty as a concept with a severe internal tension between internal/positive features and external/negative ones. This produces a series of paradoxes that may render sovereignty as ultimately 'incompatible with a true international legal order' (1957: 66).

These paradoxes run as follows. Sovereign states were 'born of a claim for equality and a will for emancipation from a common supremacy', yet they are inherently exclusivist, and display deeply individualist tendencies in their behaviour' (1957: 17). Sovereignty is both vested in the law, and and yet defies law. Sovereigns (rulers or state) are supreme, yet must regard other sovereigns as equals. Formal sovereign equality suggests that states must treat each other on the basis of mutual respect, but the history of European sovereign states proves time and again that equality is unequal to the task of curbing national appetites for domination, or constructing a viable structure of enforceable international law. The end result is captured neatly by De Visscher: 'Obeying only the power impulse, sovereigns found in the unlimited right of war the means of harmonizing their ambitions with respect for legal forms. Thus they persisted in living in contradiction with the order of coordination which they invoked' (1957: 17).

The transformation of sovereignty from a principle in which power inheres in the ruler, to one in which it was vested in the state, is not necessarily a change for the better. The paradoxes inherent in sovereignty are inescapable whatever a state's style of government. While incidents of individual despotism have decreased in the modern era, sovereignty does not prevent the state from using its concentration of power to further its ambitions at the expense of its own populace, and others. Bodin and Hobbes conceived of sovereignty as a form of authority permanently transferred *from* the people to a supra-populace entity. The problem is that this ensures neither democracy nor accountability. The state as the 'seat of sovereignty' may not in fact represent the people or be held accountable to them, because sovereignty by definition transcends the people, thus making manifest the supreme and irrevocable right to rule them in a way that is *independent* of them, rather than representative of, and accountable to, them. The danger is that any government or ruler can construct his or her own moral creed, and direct the sovereign authority accordingly. Will redistributing sovereignty between states and institutions solve the problem of both concentration and orientation of power? Not necessarily. Hard interpretations suggest that sovereignty cannot be shuffled between international authorities; to do so undermines the legitimate validity of a government's authority as rooted in natural law. Soft interpretations suggest that absolute sovereignty can be trammelled with no ill effects to the state; such processes merely place certain limits on technically limitless power and authority.

# PROBLEMS AND OPPOSITIONS

## Internal and external

Simply put, internal sovereignty concerns the interior aspect of the state, and refers to the supreme power of the state to formulate laws in respect of its jurisdiction and population. External sovereignty concerns the exterior aspect of the state regarding its freedom to act with regard to other States, and the identical freedom held by all other states, which produces the principle of sovereign equality. If no state recognizes a superior, then all are in this sense equal.

Two points can be made here. First, internal sovereignty occurred in theory and practice before external sovereignty. As witnessed by the above historical survey, the declining *Respublica Christiana* compelled individual rulers to assert their own authority upon their own realms; those who were successful in doing so became 'the holders of the monopolies on economy and force' (Kreijen, 2004: 30). As demonstrated by Robert of Naples and others, like Philip the Fair of France, local rulers fiercely resisted imperial domination in their own jurisdiction. For both kings, this took the form of papal attempts to tax the local clergy, and various popes retreated on this issue, confirming the precept of the 'king being emperor in his own kingdom' (*rex in regno suo est imperator in regni sui*). The necessary but subsequent corollary of this is the requirement of rulers to likewise not recognize external superiors (*principes superiores non recognentes*). This precept was first used to separate states whose rulers had already declared themselves *imperator in regni sui* from the Holy Roman Empire, but which increasingly came to denote their general autonomy from each other in the emerging international system. The source of exclusive authority within a given domestic jurisdiction – i.e. one which will not recognize any superior authority – logically implies an independent position outside that jurisdiction. As Kreijen argues, 'Historically, therefore, external sovereignty or independence rests on internal sovereignty – the latter being a condition *sine qua non* for the former' (2004: 32). Second, contemporary sovereignty assumes both internal and external aspects to be simultaneously present and mutually constitutive for true sovereignty to inhere; this combination alone denotes the attribute of statehood.

## Positive and negative sovereignty

This opposition is symbiotically connected to internal and external sovereignty in dealing with liberty and freedom of action, and is probably a good deal more familiar to IR audiences. Following the work done in 1990 by R. H. Jackson on

*Quasi-States: Sovereignty, International Relations and the Third World*, the two can be defined accordingly:

> the positive aspect of sovereignty presupposes capabilities which enable governments to be their own masters: it is a substantive rather than formal condition. A positively sovereign government is one which not only enjoys rights of non-intervention and other international immunities but also possesses the wherewithal to provide political goods for its citizens … Positive sovereignty is the means which enables states to take advantage of their independence … it is not a legal but a political attribute if by 'political' is understood the sociological, economic, technological, psychological and similar wherewithal to declare, implement, and enforce public policy both domestically and internationally.
>
> (Jackson, 1990: 29)

Negative sovereignty, meanwhile, is a 'formal legal condition', which entails 'freedom from outside interference'. As Jackson makes clear,

> Non-intervention and sovereignty in this meaning are basically two sides of the same coin. This is the central principle of the classical law of nations: the sphere of exclusive legal jurisdiction of states or international *laissez faire* … It is a formal legal entitlement and therefore something which international society is capable of conferring. Negative sovereignty is the legal foundation upon which a society of independent and formally equal states fundamentally rests.
>
> (Jackson, 1990: 29)

As 'the distinctive overall feature of a "developed" state' (Jackson, 1990: 29), positive sovereignty is an excellent method by which to understand more precisely the nebulous process of globalization and the dynamics of international organizations from the EU to NATO in charting the actual impact that such processes and entities have on sovereign states, and the capabilities that states possess in either capitalizing on opportunities or reducing risks. Positive sovereignty presumes domestic coherence and capabilities in order to acquire external political goods. Negative sovereignty, meanwhile, as 'the central principle of public international law and the main focus of international jurisprudence', is a far better starting point for examining states' external dimensions in general, and specific issues of non-intervention than broad analyses of human rights. IR investigations on the uses and abuses of non-intervention must, like Jackson, 'think of independence and non-intervention as the distinctive and reciprocal rights and duties of an international social contract between states', a compact that requires merely 'observance and forbearance' (Jackson, 1990: 29, 27). The observation by Van Kleffens neatly links the four concepts, and provides a good linchpin to the last set of oppositions:

> Sovereignty has two faces. One looks outward, towards the outside world, being concerned with foreign relations … it define[s] a free nation as 'not being subject to another nation's power'. But in addition to this negative side there is yet

another, a positive face, a face which looks inwards, and refers to a nation's power to regulate its own affairs; call it autonomy if you like. These aspects are what is currently known as external and internal sovereignty.

(Van Kleffens, 1953, in Kreijen, 2004: 106)

## Absolute vs relative sovereignty

Blending freedom of action with constraint, sovereignty is sometimes viewed as an attribute that can enable a state and, equally, be itself disabled. Absolute sovereignty implies that rulers possess the 'unfettered right to wage war and to engage in foreign conquests' on the basis of *raison d'état*; relative sovereignty explains that rulers are constrained by the numerous agreements and treaties (considered binding), and the various obligations and norms that flowed from them (Holsti, 2004: 122). The quality of absoluteness does not refer to the *quantitative extent* of sovereignty, but rather to the *scope/jurisdiction* of issues and powers over which authorities are sovereign. This point is frequently missed in IR; absolute qualities do not touch on whether sovereignty is supreme within the state or constrained via equality outside it, but rather the *qualitative scope* of a state's ability to maintain or alter its authority and capacity for power. What, therefore, can be seen to impinge on the latitude of a state's authority? From the perspective of international law, virtually nothing. However, the perspective of international relations, whose conception of sovereignty is generally more ambiguous, more readily supports the idea that the political power inherent in state sovereignty (rather than its legal authority) can be visibly truncated by all manner of processes, and has been since the end of World War II. Globalization, the rise of international organizations, the increase of international obligations, the frequency of humanitarian-based interventions in the jurisdiction of states and the progressive institutionalization of EU integration all impinge on the political, economic, military and social freedom of action enjoyed by various state authorities in a way that suggests that they are still sovereign. However, as all states are subject to the same attenuating forces, they are sovereign only in the same, truncated, conditional, limited sense that everyone else is. The question of sovereignty's conditionality must be carefully treated as either an issue of law, or an issue of politics. In international law, the mainstream view is of sovereignty as an indivisible principle; in IR, however, sovereignty is increasingly treated as one of a number of facets of statehood, subject to internal constraints and external challenges. A brief examination of EU integration makes this clear.

## BOX 4.3 THE EUROPEAN UNION

The EU is a treaty-based, multi-level polity in which decision-making processes on key policies operate in supranational fashion – i.e. beyond the domestic jurisdiction of states. The EU also possesses institutions like the European Commission, which has legislative initiative, and the ECJ, which has interpretive and enforce-ment powers to ensure national laws operate in conformity with European Community law. The standard argument is that, taking supranational policy-making, and the powers of the European Commission and ECJ together, the EU effectively 'pools' the sovereignty of its member states in key areas, constraining their freedom of action and permanently circumscribing core aspects of their sovereignty.

The 'hard' legal position is grounded in the principle that becoming a party to a treaty in no way undermines or limits the sovereignty of a state. Rather it does the opposite: it manifests and highlights the very authority of a state due to its sovereignty to enter into agreements with other sovereigns (as first estab-lished in the Peace of Westphalia). It follows, therefore, that the EU – as a series of interlocking institutions embedded in a treaty structure – cannot undermine the sovereignty of its member states. Sovereignty by definition is inalienable and indivisible. What EU integration entails is the pooling of certain powers and authorities in key policy areas originally enjoyed by member states as a manifesta-tion of their individual sovereignty. Member states – *by virtue of being sovereign* – transfer these powers and authorities to the EU. As long as the state retains its legal personality within the international legal order, it retains its sovereignty regardless of what it subsequently transfers regarding authority and power. The mere fact that member states can at any time withdraw from the treaty and all accompanying obligations, and reclaim these same powers and authorities bestowed on the EU, proves that sovereignty has not been compromised.

However, a possible political counterargument – and one which fits mainstream views in both IR and European Studies – is that the EU has to a degree eroded the sovereignty of its member states. Sovereign powers are unique to a state; all mem-ber states are equal as sovereign powers. If the powers and authority of each of the member states is viewed as a manifestation of their sovereignty, by allowing the EU to pool those same powers and authorities, both the aggregate manifestation of these powers and authorities by, and in, the EU vis-à-vis these member states, and the *transcendent nature* of this aggregate authority, are ultimately greater than the power and authority delegated individually by each member state. It therefore could be argued that this does indeed represent a limitation on their sovereignty. Again, a close reading of international law is enormously helpful in clarifying latent ambiguities inherent in political approaches to sovereignty. Brownlie identifies the challenge that states face in joining international organizations:

> Of course it can be said that on joining the organization, each member consented in advance to the institutional aspects, and thus in a formal way, the principle that obligations can only arise from the consent of states *and*

the principle of sovereign equality are satisfied. In their practice the European Communities, while permitting integration which radically affects domestic jurisdiction for special purposes, have been careful not to jar the delicate treaty structures by a too ready assumption of implied powers.

(Brownlie, 1998: 292)

What could be argued is that EU member states have consented to a limitation on their internal (and positive) sovereignty. But this does not itself imply a change to their external (and negative) sovereignty, as that would endanger their legal personality. Brownlie makes this clear: 'If an organization encroaches on the domestic jurisdiction of members to a substantial degree the structure may approximate to a federation, and not only the area of competence of members but their very personality will be in issue' (1998: 292). How far need the EU, or any international organization, go legally, as well as politically, to abridge state sovereignty? Among the criteria Brownlie suggests are 'majority decision-making; the determination of jurisdiction by the organization itself; and the binding quality of decisions of the organization apart from consent of member states'. Some could argue that qualified majority voting (now extended in the 2009 Lisbon Treaty), the legislative initiative and sheer scope of competence the Commission, and the enforcement regime of the ECJ, may slowly be pushing the EU in this direction.

## CONCLUSION: CRITICAL PERSPECTIVES

With more than a thousand years of political practice largely derived from understandings of sovereignty, two key points should now be borne in mind by scholars and IR theorists alike at the beginning of the twenty-first century. First, states themselves are largely at the mercy of political, economic and social needs and changes of the people who 'people' states domestically, and the groups and organizations that bind states into various international communities. Thus, all changes to statehood will continue to trigger consequential transformations to sovereignty. Second, and as a result, sovereignty – as the umbrella concept by which to describe the method of domestic organization and expectations of external representation of states – is a contested term. If the state can be both transcended economically and attenuated politically, then sovereignty, too, is rendered ambiguous, challenged, flux-ridden. Perspectives on this range from viewing sovereignty as a grotesque imposition of the collective will upon individual freedom, to full-blown 'organized hypocrisy', to a fundamental but merely technical rearrangement of legal competences.

Three contemporary forces herald the transformation of the state unit and the increased acceptance of critical (or at least adjusted) perspectives about the unbending nature of sovereignty. First, as discussed above, the rise of the EU as an increasingly integrated and demographically varied cross-border political and market entity. Second, the profoundly deep impact of globalization in the form of cross-border forces, including climate change, pandemics like SARS, avian flu and E. Coli outbreaks, regional and ethnic violence, and, most prominently, the 2008 financial crisis triggering widespread and ongoing instability from the US to Asia to the Eurozone. Third, the increased prominence of international governmental organizations (IGOs) like the ECJ, ICJ, WTO, WHO, the UN and EU, and NGOs like Amnesty International or Human Rights Watch or Oxfam, which not only bear witness to the rise of a viable non-state community of actors, but which are increasingly deployed by states themselves as collective responses to cross-border problems. Sometimes the responses are traditional ones, and steeped in the organizing structures and expectations of sovereignty, as with the EU's gradual enlargement policy to the changed political landscape of the Balkans. Equally, however, a cocktail of IGOs and NGOs are detailed (usually by states) to solve cross-border policy issues from famine to war to global warming.

What, therefore, are the lessons to be learned for historians and IR theorists alike when examining sovereignty? First, as outlined in Box 4.4, getting to grips with the multiple definitions of and within sovereignty will reduce the chances of error, misuse and conflation.

## BOX 4.4 HELPFUL DEFINITIONS

**Jurist/positivist**: each state represents one verifiable authority in whom sovereignty is manifested, and from whom all other authorities within the state derive their power and use their influence. Sovereignty itself is indivisible.

**Political/relativist**: legal authority is neither absolute nor centralized in one state authority. It rests among several individuals, agencies and actors. This perspective (as per Comte, Durkheim and Giddings) sees society as a living organism, the state as a living being, with authority distributed unevenly and impermanently throughout its elements. Sovereignty is the endpoint of social, political, economic and cultural forces, which, taken together, permit the internal governance and external recognition of a national society.

**Titular/symbolic**: Sovereign refers to a titular head of state (Her Majesty the Queen in the United Kingdom of Great Britain).

**Legal sovereign**: the person or persons who administer the government according to the law of the land.

**Political or constitutional sovereign**: (Gierke, 1880: 3.568) the community of people from whom sovereign power is first derived, and in whom it rests.

This collective sovereignty can denote either the actual or potential power of a national society in its entirety.

**Non-sovereign states**: as recognized by international law, there are both sovereign and non-sovereign states. The latter possess only some aspects of internal authority, and/or do not enjoy international recognition. This puts pay to the theory that all states are somehow equal, or that they all possess the same attributes of sovereignty in equal measure. There is a range of failed and failing states, and a range of non-sovereign federations, unions and alliances.

# CHAPTER 5

# Empire

To them I set no limits in space or time. I have given them dominion without end.
(Virgil, *The Aeneid*, 1.227f, quoted by Moorhead, 2001: 1)

… like stout Cortez, when with eagle eyes; He star'd at the Pacific – and all his men; Look'd at each other with a wild surmise – Silent, upon a peak in Darien.
(John Keats, *On First Looking into Chapman's Homer*, 1816)

[Nation states] are not the only, or necessarily the highest, principles of political life. Empires at their best stood for multiracialism and religious tolerance. They also allowed a great deal of devolution in practice.
(Robert Skidelsky, quoted in A. N. Wilson, *After the Victorians*, 2006: 41)

## INTRODUCTION

This chapter deals with a type of agency of huge interest to students of IR, that of the category of 'empire', one that is often used in an ahistoric, and certainly casual, way. Those who do not like empires use it as a epithet of disapproval, an insult even, as in 'imperialist', akin to that other epithet of dismissal, 'fascist'. Others are determinedly nostalgic for a period when imperial 'order' seemed to reduce anarchy to a necessary minimum. There is a need to be more precise about what different schools of historical thought mean by the term and what is encompassed by it in different contexts, theoretical and historical, and these two needs are at the core of the thinking that underlies this chapter. Inevitably some topics will be given undue weight in the eyes of some, and not enough in the eyes of others. We have tried to pick out some of the most written about by the generality of historians and students of IR, while also looking at a few (such as the Mongol Empire) that are not much examined. Again, the overall concern is to be suggestive and not comprehensive.

The structure of the chapter is as follows. First we will examine how the notion of empire has been explored in the IR literature to see the kinds of themes and questions that this has generated. Second, we will look at the body of literature that we think might be useful as a starting point in any further reader's investigation of particular imperial destinies, from the Greek Empire through to the American Empire. This will be done from different angles, depending on the empire in question, as some have generated a different kind of literature derived from their different contexts, whether premodern, modern or postmodern. Last, we will look at what broad lessons we can draw from such a study of empire and how it might be useful in future scholarship for a student of IR.

## WHAT IS AN EMPIRE? THE LITERATURE

History does not run in straight lines, and nothing illustrates this better than the history of empires. They all come and go, *hubris* of the kind illustrated by Virgil above is duly succeeded by *nemesis,* but none of them disappears without trace, even where there is little written record (as with the Inca civilization of South America). They leave myths and legends, which are constantly recycled to form the basis of much of what we understand of evolving human experience. Keats' poem above itself encapsulates this – an Englishman marvelling at Homer's poetry about Odysseus, reflecting on the Spanish Empire's conquest of the Aztec Empire from the perspective of a nation (England) about to realize the full costs and benefits of the greatest empire the world had then seen. Empires leave behind them cultural, political, economic, even social, legacies and they evoke strong condemnation and eulogy in equal measure, as the Skidelsky quote shows. They always seem to preface themselves with a reference to 'peace' – *Pax Romana, Pax Britannica,* etc. (Parchami, 2009: 1) but they have been condemned for always leading to war (Lenin, 1900/1916). It is also the case that the whole concept of empire has taken a very new and interesting turn in the years since about 1990 – the literature on an American 'empire', which would until at least 1945 have been seen as a contradiction in terms, has revitalized the wider debate in IR and imperial historical circles alike (e.g. Lundestad, 1998; Kupchan, 2003; Ferguson, 2004; Ikenberry, 2006).

It is these dilemmas and legacies that this chapter will explore. But it will also ask if the study of the history of empires does not give us a different way of studying IR. As Sanjay Seth has put it in a slightly different context, maybe we can 'retell the history of the emergence of the modern world in such a way that Europe no longer occupies a position of centrality' (Seth, 2009). Good introductions to how this is now coming to be the case can be found in a number of new readers. The obvious places where the history of empire is being rewritten are in the areas of gender, race, anthropology, even ecology – the so-called 'new imperial history' (Howe, 2010). The links between theories of race and empire have been extended in some cases to a consideration of how imperialism, capitalism and the dominance of particular kinds of (especially) liberal thought are (maybe) beginning to enter both the historical and IR mainstreams to make us consider the existence of 'multiple modernities' (McCarthy, 2009).

Obvious constraints on the successful writing up of these imperial themes are linguistic, cultural, and due to the gender or other perspective of the writer and observer. All we can do here is to note these problems. They have always been with us – who could now understand the mind of Genghis Khan or even (fully) Lord Alfred Milner, the great British imperialist? The dangers of reading the past as if it were the present has never been greater as the 'West' undergoes one of its frequent paroxysms of self-doubt.

As with all major terms, that of 'empire' is fraught with terminological difficulty and such terms define any debate. From the Latin (and therefore Roman) period English has adopted the root word *imperium*, used by magistrates to imply 'power'. But this relatively neutral term has also come to have major connotations of dominance and extreme negativity. The best definitions are the simple ones, so here we will copy one broad and one more narrow definition: those of Dominic Lieven, that 'empire is, first and foremost, a very great power that has left its mark on the international relations of an era' (Lieven, 2000: xiv), and Michael Doyle, that 'Empires are relationships of political control imposed by some political societies over the effective sovereignty of other political societies' (Doyle, 1986: 19). The danger is, of course, that we might end up calling everything an 'empire'. As Anthony Pagden has put it, 'defining it so widely as to include any kind of extensive international power runs the risk of rendering the concept indeterminate' (in Howe, 2010: 438). Should we therefore call China an 'empire'? On Pagden's or Doyle's definitions we would not; on Lieven's we would. On balance we agree with the first two and have decided not to deal with China (though Lieven makes a convincing contrary case, we fully admit), but to give the Mongols some space. We have also included the United States, as the use of the word 'empire' is often juxtaposed with that state, rightly or wrongly.

## IR – then and now?

There has always been a flourishing literature on empire within history circles, though it was for many years unfashionable – as Stephen Howe puts it, 'For decades, imperial history was seen as fusty, hidebound, backward-looking … Study empires as such … most often meant studying (and identifying or sympathizing with) imperialists' (Howe, 2010: 1). For some of these reasons it is also a relatively new interest in IR. But other reasons exist. Most of IR from World War II until the 1990s was concerned with states and non-state actors like international organizations (q.v.) and non-governmental organizations (q.v.). What William Olson and A. J. R. Groom have aptly called 'IR – then and now' (Olson and Groom, 1991) made for a clear distinction between the pre- and post-World War II obsessions. Why was this?

One reason is that, pre-1939, the empire(s) looked permanent, whereas after 1945 they looked all too vulnerable. Also, classical scholars of the Greeks and Romans made a huge impact on IR before World War II, when IR was a far from hegemonic subject and students were still expected to have read the classics. It is true that Alfred Zimmern's *The Study of International Relations* (1931) was one early IR text that says relatively little about empire. But both he and Gilbert Murray, who can together be seen as the most important of the British liberal thinkers of the interwar period, and who defined the early (and mostly misnamed) 'idealist' phase of IR, had backgrounds in the classics. They were good liberals, not merely because they were influenced by the great liberal thinkers of the nineteenth century like John Stuart Mill and T. H. Green, but also because they saw liberalism as 'a Roman idea, derived from the Greek' (Murray, quoted in Morefield, 2005: 77). They saw the Greeks and their empire of the mind, in particular, as the model of a 'good' society. Their heritage for Zimmern was to give a way to look at society and politics as a whole – 'It is only by the swing of the pendulum back to the medieval idea of Order, by putting the life of the community in front of the good life of private individuals and groups, that a way can be found out of our perplexities' (Zimmern, quoted in Morefield, 2005: 90). Many of the liberals of that period, and indeed for a century before, would have seen that ideal writ large in the 'civilizing' mission of the British Empire and the creation of a 'Greater Britain' (Bell, 2007). This view, expressed by Zimmern during the Great Depression of the 1930s, has an eerie ring in our new era of economic crash.

Other classicists have also had short shrift – in the past, at least – from scholars of IR of the Cold War period, perhaps analogous to how radical intellectuals of the early 1900s rejected the scholarship of the Victorians, the Bloomsbury Group being a good example. The historian equivalents of that group, like Arnold Toynbee, a contemporary of Murray and Zimmern, was a great student of comparative empire and also a major figure in pre-1945 British IR. His *Study of History* (1974) contains a huge amount of food for thought on IR obsessions such as the nature of order and justice and their relationship to the state. But he has tended to be dismissed as a crank, or even a charlatan, since the 1950s (Thompson, 1985). A reaction to this has now set in among some newer theorists (Long and Wilson, 1995; Bleiker, 2001; Becque, 2009) as a familiar part of the continual rewriting of the historical and IR canon. Hence one of the reasons for the neglect of empire (in the classical sense) by post-1945 IR scholars may be seen in part as a side effect of the rejection of liberal 'idealism' in general, a tendency much encouraged by Edward Hallett Carr's *The Twenty Years' Crisis* (Carr, 1939), which made 'ten references to Toynbee, all of them critical' (Becque, 2009: 9).

In addition, the study of culture (Greek, Roman or any other) per se in IR was also seen as slightly bizarre before 1990, though there were exceptions to this philistine rule (Bozeman, 1960). The renewed interest in empire in IR since 1990 may be put down to a number of factors, of which the main ones are related to a renewed interest in philosophical factors narrowly defined or 'normative' factors more broadly in the study of IR (Brown, 1992; Brown, Nardin and

Rengger, 2002) and in culture (Lebow, 2006, 2008). To discuss 'tragedy' or 'honor' in the context of war (q.v.) is to evoke the ideals of the Roman and Greek empires in current debates. So these approaches are not new, but rather a return to older considerations of morality, even meaning, in IR; considerations rather eclipsed in the overwhelming concerns of the Cold War and the threat of nuclear annihilation.

Ironically, these concerns were dominant during what was in effect a period of great inter-imperial (US–Soviet) rivalry, though neither would have liked to see their own 'empire' described as such, but rather as a term of abuse for the other. Hence President Ronald Reagan's reference to the 'Evil Empire' when talking about the USSR was routine and the epithet 'imperialist' routinely used to denounce the United States from Moscow. There were some notable exceptions to the neglect of empire as a concrete concept in IR, largely in the late 1980s, when the USSR looked increasingly shaky, with maybe the best examples being Michael Doyle's *Empires* (1986) and Lewis Feuer's (1989) *Imperialism and the Anti-Imperialist Mind*. However, Feuer confidently predicted in the year the Berlin Wall fell, if the 'American ethic and its power' were to fail, 'that controlling role will in all likelihood fall into the hands of the Soviet Union' (Feuer, 1989: 1). As John Lewis Gaddis pointed out, no school of IR theory predicted the end of the Soviet Union – his advice was: 'if you are a student, switch from political science to history' (Conquest, 1989, quoted by Gaddis, 1992/1993: 53).

Since the mid-1990s there has been a huge outpouring of new and often radical analyses of the underlying logic of IR and this has led IR back to empire as a justificatory (or condemnatory) explanation of the problems the world now faces. Obvious elements in this concern a support for or opposition to colonialism (q.v.) and its practices (see page 137); the study of culture and IR mentioned above; and the advantages of imperial groupings of states as an encouragement or discouragement of warlike behaviour. Possibly the best example of this tendency is found in the writings of Paul Kennedy, a historian who 'crossed over' into the political sphere with his *Rise and Fall of Great Powers* (Kennedy, 1988), a book widely believed to have influenced the US Presidential election of 1988. It tapped into a relatively forgotten imperial literature of 'decline and fall' that had until the late 1980s been largely the purview of historians of Greece, Rome and many other empires, but not one that could be seen as applying to the Superpowers, who by 1990 or so were seen as a permanent part of the woodwork of IR. The fall of the Soviet Empire (q.v.) was able to propel historical thinkers like Kennedy into the IR mainstream, with his detailed consideration of how military power is dependent on economic as well as strategic actors, where the Chinese Ming Empire, as well as those of Britain (q.v.) and Czarist Russia (q.v.) could be shown to have a contemporary relevance.

Interestingly, as we will discuss further below, that new interest in empire post-1990 in IR has been mirrored by a new awareness of it in History faculties. But before getting to that new turn we need to look at a fundamental problem that antecedes empire in both series of discourses. That problem is that of 'power'.

## Power and empire

Lieven makes the claim that, while scholars of IR have tended to be interested in 'power, often defining it in very narrow economic and military terms', political scientists have tended to be obsessed with 'problems of nationalism' (Lieven, 2000: 25). Some would, of course, claim that the only *good* scholars of IR are political scientists; we would obviously beg to differ. But given the importance to IR scholars of all kinds of the notion of 'power', we might ask how that has come to relate to that of 'empire'. Many references in IR are made to 'Roman' types of empire, in the sense of their being based on military power, territorial dominance and legal force, or 'Greek', in the sense of a dominance (or hegemony) of ideas. IR scholars (like Ikenberry, 2006; Lundestad, 1996, 1998a; Williams, 1998), some historians of IR (Robert Kagan is a prominent example), and politicians (Winston Churchill and Harold Macmillan, for example), can all be said to have used this distinction. We are never allowed to forget that in *any* imperial relationship force and persuasion are (potentially) equally used tools – it is hard to imagine the United States allowing France or Italy to go communist in the 1950s while also wooing them assiduously with Hollywood, Marshall Aid and lashings of good cheer. This might be seen as a 'liberal' or even 'conservative' view of how power and empire interrelate. These thinkers do not see any Manichean desire to dominate or repress; just how the liberal world order might be made to better function (Ikenberry, 2001, for example).

Michael Hardt and Antonio Negri have made many important contributions to this IR debate. First is their idea that 'empire' and 'world order' are, and always have been, essentially synonymous ideas and realities, now tied together by the cement of economic globalization, and that the current world order is based on 'Euro-American' ideas and practices, not mere military coercion (Hardt and Negri, 2000: xiii–xiv). Second, they contend that there was no clear passing of the torch of Empire from Europe to the USA, or even from Britain to the USA, the process was and is much more symbiotic and ongoing. Third, Hardt and Negri believe that American hegemony has not come about by some sort of conscious global conspiracy, and that the USA, powerful and dominant as it is, is not some sort of all-powerful spider at the centre of a web of its own making and that 'indeed no nation-state can today, form the center of an imperialist project'. They also assert that this 'Empire' will be, and indeed is being, slowly but surely contested by the very 'creative forces of the multitude that sustain Empire [and are] also capable of autonomously constructing a counter-Empire, an alternative political organization of global flows and exchanges' (Hardt and Negri, 2000: xv). The idea being expressed here is that all empires rise and they can fall (Duroselle, 1981).

Other writers, like Steven Lukes, see all change in the relative status of empires, states and other bodies as being to do with the exercise of power. For Lukes, power is multidimensional. He says three initial positions could be taken. First, power could be merely a question of forcing 'A' to do 'B', so that, as Lukes says, we could merely examine decision-making processes to find the locus for power in action (Lukes, 2005: 19). Second, it could be about a more subtle combination of 'coercion, influence, authority, force and manipulation' though he dismisses this as it only looks at the '*conflict*' (Lukes' emphasis) of interests (2005: 24–25). Third, it could be about how '*potential*' conflict issues are kept out of the discussion, a 'contradiction between the interest of those exercising power and the real interests of those they exclude' (2005: 28). So power, says Lukes, could be about domination and he asks us to consider Foucault's idea that such power in our society is constituted by a myriad of 'micro-practices' in everyday life, from control over our sexuality, health, family, even criminal impulses and other aspects of behaviour, what he refers to as 'bio-power', and that this is at the heart of the Western project. We are thus victims of our conditioning and imprisoned within a society from which there is no escape (2005: chapter 2).

Lukes further argues that since we cannot escape we also cannot give our consent to it (2005: 109). But this also implies that we are all locked together in an immensely powerful Empire of the Mind, and that (along with Hardt and Negri's notion of political Empire) has clear political and strategic consequences. The really important 'Empire' is thus that of ideas and practices, not of the mere exercise of physical power itself. As any parent, soldier, teacher or politician should know, when thinking about what power means we have to understand that, as the great Italian Marxist Antonio Gramsci knew, power is based on 'consent … a psychological state, involving some kind of acceptance – not necessarily explicit – of the socio-political order or of certain vital aspects of that order' (Femia, quoted by Lukes, 2005: 8).

## The 'other' and empire

But more radical scholars reach back to an older anti-imperial discourse of the old Left, the 1930s Frankfurt School, as well as further still to Hobson, Marx and Lenin's denunciations of empire (Hobson, 1902/2005; Molnar, 1975; Lenin, 1916/2000) as inevitably leading to war. Following on from this, and in common with other disciplines with which IR shares both roots and concerns, like postcolonial studies, probably the most important other current obsession where empires are evoked in IR is that of empires creating the problems of the 'other'.

This can take a number of forms. The most obvious is in the way that hegemonic powers and their idea structures and discourses create 'others' (variously described, but usually some form of inferior 'native'). The idea derives from Karl Marx's model of 'superstructure' (the hegemonic ideas and practices of a given ruling class) and the infrastructure (the productive material 'Base'), what he called his 'critique of political economy' (McLellan, 1976; Marx, 1999/1867). This was developed by the interest of both postcolonial literature and by some scholars of IR in such political figures and scholars as Gramsci (as mentioned above). In literary terms the concentration has been on resistance to empire, either of the political and military or cultural and psychological kind, with such witty titles as 'the Empire writes back' (Ashcroft, Griffiths and Tiffin, 1989). Frantz Fanon's works on Africa first brought such thinking into the fringes of IR in the 1960s and 1970s, and especially into development studies.

This was further cemented by the writings of Edward Said on *Orientalism* and cultural imperialism (Said, 1979, 1993; Aslan, 2011), and its importance as a nineteenth-century literary tradition for understanding the 'othering' of the Palestinian people and Arabs in general has had a profound influence on the progress of this literary discussion within IR. The reading of the Middle Eastern 'other', though a prism of security, particularly in the aftermath of the 'War on Terror' proclaimed by the neo-conservatives and President George W. Bush after 2001, shows how closely literary tropes and those of military action are linked, to the detriment of both.

So this is more than a rumination on identity (q.v.) and independence after colonization, important as these themes are. In particular it invites us to think about how discourses of empire have marked the experience of empire for rulers and ruled, and it replaces the study of culture squarely back at the centre of the study of IR in general. Samir Amin, another writer in the same tradition denounced *Eurocentrism* for its grip on IR and beyond (Amin, 1992). As Seth puts it, there are also some much '"thicker" histories that have mapped out the historically mutually reinforcing effects of "East" on "West" and vice versa' (Seth, 2009: 229). Some even claim, not without reason, that the 'East' in effect created the 'West', an idea that has still to find traction in mainstream IR (Hobson, 2004; Bernal, 1987). In addition, the theoretical writings of Gayatri Chakravorty Spivak (1988); Kapoor (2004); and Howe (2010: 14) to acknowledge the 'subaltern voice' that is repressed in much Western literature on imperialism, and Homi Bhabha (1994), have had an evident impact on poststructuralist scholars that will probably have a profound effect on the way we think about IR in the future, though this development has been accused of introducing some nigh-on-incomprehensible theorizing into the discipline.

## ATHENS

The oldest quoted imperial discussion in IR is the 'Melian' dialogue between Melos and Athens discussed in Thucydides in his *History of the Peloponnesian War* (Thucydides, 431 BCE/1954; Münkler, 2007). In that war, power and force were the prime movers of the relationship. The Greek 'empire' centred on Athens started as a combination of many Aegean city-states, the 'Delian League', in their collective efforts to counter the growing menace of an expanding Persian Empire. Not all of the key actors in this League were willing tributaries of Athens, and some played a major role in the wars against Persia, such as Sparta at Thermopylae, where about 1,700 men fought off many more thousands for days in 480 BCE (Herodotus, 440 BCE/1996; Kitto, 1992). This battle has been depicted many times as showing how a small group of dedicated patriots can defend their lands against an imperial giant, and recently figured as a Hollywood blockbuster (*300*, directed by Zack Snyder, 2007). But the Athenian Empire was based on a 'Thalassocracy', a seaborne entity to which Athens always provided the main naval contingents and expected reciprocal respect, which the Melians found to their cost. The decisive defeat of the Persians was arguably the sea battle of Salamis in 480, the same year as Thermopylae.

Later, Alexander the Great (356–323 BCE) conquered the Persian Empire and in effect created a pan-Hellenistic world that eventually helped nurture the rise of Rome, even though that then led to the formation of other leagues, like the Achaean League, to counter Macedonian domination. As Herfried Münkler puts it, '*hegemonia* [became] *arche*: supremacy turned into domination'. This in turn created enemies for Athens, but it was two and a half centuries before the disunity of the Greeks led to their subjugation by the much more organized and ruthless Romans (Münkler, 2007: 7). We might also emphasize, as does Thucydides, that the Athenian 'empire' started out as a 'league', so what began as informal cooperation in a common cause evolved into 'hegemony', which then turned to revolt against that hegemony. Maybe this is an iron law of imperial creation and destruction? As Doyle says; 'Empire requires both a metropole and a periphery' (Doyle, 1986: 81).

Nonetheless the Roman defeat of the Achaean League at the battle of Corinth (146 BCE) did not finish the influence of an empire that had existed since about 1100 BCE. Its heroes – Alexander the Great, in particular – made a lasting impact on the whole Middle East and beyond; many would argue its civilization has never been bettered in artistic or philosophical terms. Greek remained a key Mediterranean language until the twentieth century, and ancient Greece gave lasting institutions to the West and beyond, including democracy and the Olympic Games (Doyle, 1986: chapter 3; Pomeroy, 1999). The Greeks started a process of creating a Mediterranean culture, and even a 'Common Market' that was continued by the Phoenicians, Carthaginians and, ultimately, the Romans, with considerable contributions from other groupings like the Jews, with Jerusalem a dominant city until sacked by the Romans in 70 CE (Goodman, 2007).

Ancient Greece also left a legacy of history being written by the Victors, and many, but by no means all, of the main philosophers (such as Plato and Aristotle) and historians (such as Herodotus and Thucydides) that we still celebrate were Athenians or lived there for some of their careers, such as the last two historians – from Helicarnassus (now Bodrum, in Turkey) and Alimos in Greece, respectively. Greek culture remained dominant in Asia Minor until the fall of Byzantium (q.v.) and was still significant during the whole of the Ottoman period until the wars between modern Greece and Turkey, when the Greek influence was literally annihilated in the massacres and population exchanges of 1922–1924, before and after the Treaty of Lausanne in 1923 (Morgenthau, 2003; Freeman, 1996). Greece since 1923 has experienced a tortuous and often violent relationship with modern-day Turkey that continues to poison the two nations' relationships with each other and other states, arguably continuing to echo the problems of empire (Ottoman and British) in the eastern Mediterranean (Woodhouse, 1999; Mazower, 2008; Koliopoulos and Veremis, 2002).

## ROME

The Roman Empire can claim with some justification to be the archetype for all empires. It had longevity (700 BCE–400 CE, and until 1453 if we include the 'Eastern'

Empire of Byzantium), and it brought with it a form of 'order', if not necessarily '*pax*' (peace, q.v.) in the current meaning of the word, then more 'tantamount to hegemonic control' (Parchami, 2009: 7–8). It created institutions that were the most advanced of their time, and arguably the most imitated since; it possessed a military and organizational prowess that enabled it to sweep nearly all before it for an extended period; it left us with an enormous cultural and artistic legacy, including a family of languages, as well as the basis of much of the language I am using here and a lingua franca that is only now fading into obscurity. It also left a heritage that has left an indelible imprint on architecture, engineering and many other fields of endeavour. It also had its successful imitators (like the United States, a military and constitutional empire that models itself on Rome in many ways), as well as unsuccessful ones, like Mussolini's Italy of the interwar period. On the Eritrean/Ethiopian border, the remains of the bridge can be found, on which can still be seen the carefully excised shadow of the *fasces* (bunched rods and axe – in ancient Rome, the symbol of the magistrates) of Fascist Italy that had ruled the area until 1940.

Those who have written about ancient Rome – Edward Gibbon (1776/1981), Theodor Mommsen (1996, 2008) – or about the many historians of Rome (Feldherr, 2009) – are a roll call of modern classical writers, and no one can call themselves 'educated' without some exposure to these thinkers. Rome has definitely made its mark on the contemporary media era. Robert Graves' *I Claudius* (and a memorable performance by Derek Jacobi in a BBC drama series in the 1970s) deserves honourable mention alongside Lindsey Davis' series of books on the Roman detective Falco and Robert Harris's novels on the first century CE. Some of the best Hollywood films (*Ben Hur*, 1959; *Gladiator*, 2000) have Roman themes.

As for the Romans themselves, a brief survey of even the genius of the first century CE gives us reason to remember them. Pliny the Elder wrote a massive 'Natural History'. His nephew Pliny the Younger left us much of interest on the domestic arrangements of the Roman people and is fascinating for his insights into Roman mythology. Seneca left a legacy of philosophical stoicism and political commentary that can still be read with much profit today, especially given the similarities between many of the century's emperors (of whom he fell foul) and many recent sanguinary dictators. To this list can be added the chronicler of the *Aeneid*, Virgil, as well as historians (Tacitus), poets (Ovid) and satirists (Petronius and Juvenal). This rich cultural harvest was acted out against the actions of the most illustrious emperors of Rome, such as Augustus, and some of the worst, like Nero and Caligula. Western civilization itself can be said to derive many of its key cultural tropes from Rome.

The strength of an empire, we were reminded by Edward Gibbon, in the year of the birth of the American Republic in 1776, is not to be measured solely in terms of military might. The Roman Empire in the second century CE 'comprehended the fairest part of the earth and the most civilized portion of mankind' (Gibbon, 1776/1981: 27). This is more than reminiscent of what we call the 'West'. Military might was and is nonetheless important, especially if exercised without bravado:

> The terror of the Roman arms added weight and dignity to the moderation of
> the emperors. They preserved peace by a constant preparation for war; and while

justice regulated their conduct, they announced to the nations on their confines that they were as little disposed to endure as to offer an injury.

(Gibbon, 1776/1981: 35)

But what Gibbon also points to in his remarks on 'moderation' is a pointer to all empires' propensity to succeed or fail. As Hardt and Negri put it, '[a]s Thucydides, Livy and Tacitus all teach us (along with Machiavelli …) Empire is formed not on the basis of force itself but on the basis of the capacity to present force and being in the service of right and peace' (Hardt and Negri, 2000: 15).

The Romans saw themselves as the antithesis of 'barbarians' and the exporters of 'civilization' (Münkler, 2007: 98). Mommsen put great emphasis on the liberating aspects of the Roman Empire, especially under Julius Caesar and Augustus. One typical passage goes thus:

> Seldom has the government of the world been conducted for so long a term in an orderly sequence … The carrying out of the Latin-Greek civilising process in the form of perfecting the constitution of the urban community and the gradual bringing of the barbarians or at any rate alien elements into this circle, were tasks, which, from their very nature, required centuries of steady activity and calm self-development.

(Mommsen, 1968: 4)

Mommsen was sure that the expansion of the Roman Empire was inevitable. 'Barbarians' were attacking its border and, as Julius Caesar, not yet an aspiring emperor, felt, 'this state of things could not be allowed to continue', or was 'required by the general political situation' (Mommsen, 1968: 23). The Romans duly destroyed one 'brave and desperate tribe' after another (often 'a toilsome subjugation') and one after the other Gauls, Dalmatians, Macedonians, Moesians, Helvetii, Germanii and so on fell under Rome's control (Mommsen, 1968: 7–44). Only when there was a major setback, as when General Varus 'lost' Emperor Augustus's legions in 9 CE was there any real effective resistance to this onslaught of highly skilled, well-equipped and 'modern' troops against barbarian levies. It was also clear that when the barbarians had a chance they proved their utter brutality. Those of Varus's men who survived the debacle in Germany were 'fastened to the cross, or buried alive, or bled under the sacrificial knife of the German priests' (Mommsen, 1968: 49).

Such horror stories will, no doubt, have whipped up popular Roman disgust with the enemy and justified repression in the name of civilization, a recurring theme when barbarians 'have' to be punished.

## Rome and globalization

One of the most significant results of empire has been the parallel emergence of the phenomenon of globalization, about which, as Anthony Hopkins acidly observes, 'no previous period in recorded history has been so persuaded of the irrelevance of the past experience of the human race' (Hopkins, 2002: foreword).

This analogy of globalization has been taken up recently by Harold James, who argues that

> 'the Roman dilemma' – the paradoxical notion that while global society depends on a system of rules for building peace and prosperity, [is a] system [that] inevitably leads to domestic clashes, international rivalry, and even wars. As it did in ancient Rome a rule-based world order eventually subverts and destroys itself, creating the need for imperial action. The result is a continuous fluctuation between pacification and the breakdown of domestic order.
>
> (James, 2006: cover notes)

This subversion by an imperial power of its own liberal principles is what Rome, Britain and now America will do, says James. Such views certainly have echoes of the writings of Gibbon, Mommsen and many Romans themselves. Equally, and in our own times, the notion that the nation-state has been marginalized by forces of globalization, as capital and science have opened up new avenues for the pursuit of power, adding to the stresses on the American 'empire' (see below and Hardt and Negri: 2000), but maybe this is also an analogy of the Roman dilemma. As Rome became more successful and spread its reach, it created the idea of a Roman 'people' who went far wider than the people of Rome itself. The 'people' that represent American power, through multinational corporations, banks and the like, are just as likely to be British, Indian, Chinese or Russian in their ethnic origin, not just because of the 'melting pot' that is the United States but because American power operates on many landmasses, just as Rome did.

## Decline

Perhaps, therefore, naturally empire also always holds the seeds of its own dissolution? The decline of Rome has been endlessly (and maybe futilely) debated, with arguments ranging from lead in the water supply, the replacement of martial religions (like the worship of Mithras) with the softness of Christianity, through to the madness of certain emperors and imperial overreach (Gibbon, 1776/1981). Many recent writers have taken up Gibbon's cudgels in trying to explain its collapse, often pointing to themes such as civil war and internal decadence that are unfortunate leitmotivs for many parts of our own current world (Ward-Perkins, 2005; Goldsworthy, 2009). It has also been the subject of choice for a number of painters – Thomas Couture's *Les Romains de la décadence* (1847) in the Musée d'Orsay in Paris is one striking example – and shown in many 'sandal' films, like *Gladiator* (2000). It was long believed that the end of the Empire was short and bloody, with Rome being sacked in 410 by the Goths, and then the Lombards fighting a long war against the Byzantine remnants of the Empire in the East (q.v.). This then allegedly led to the 'Dark Ages', a kind of black hole that separates the Greeks and Romans from the Middle Ages where most people lived a kind of *Monty Python and the Holy Grail* (1979) existence.

This view is now more nuanced to one of the 'barbarians' certainly usurping Italy as the centre of Roman power and culture, but also keeping many Roman practices and norms alive, not least of which was the Latin language as the vehicle of civilized discourse (Brown, 1971; Cameron, 1993; Heather, 2005). There have been challenges to this view, notably from Bryan Ward-Perkins (2005), based on archaeological evidence of extreme violence and cultural extinction. But maybe the key point for the student of IR to note is that, as Joseph Vogt pointed out, historians like Gibbon have tended to use the awful tale of the end of Rome to accentuate our own allegedly superior grasp on power (Vogt, 1993: 3; see below for more on this point).

## Byzantium

The Roman Empire in the East, that of Byzantium, has been much studied by historians, but is only usually referred to in IR as a term of abuse – 'byzantine' being meant to indicate excessive, complex and ultimately self-defeating bureaucracy. It was often used to denigrate the Soviet Union and other Communist states during the Cold War, though Russians themselves have never been particularly concerned to receive the epithet. They rightly see Byzantium as one of the high spots of Western civilization. Judith Herrin's book *Byzantium: The Surprising Life of a Medieval Empire* (Herrin, 2007) is one good summary of its achievements. These may be said to include its sheer longevity (the original Roman Empire was divided into two spheres by Emperor Diocletian, 284–305 CE, and only defeated by Islamic forces in 1453); its guarding of, and building on, ancient Greek and Roman civilization, including Roman legal and military traditions that are still important today and, says Herrin most significantly, by 'protecting the Christian West in the early Middle Ages' (Herrin, 2007: xviii).

The sacking of Constantinople in 1204, by Christian 'crusaders', was ironically its major setback, and Byzantium never recovered its previous power and status, one that was immensely enhanced by the Ottoman Empire that replaced it. Constantinople, now known as Istanbul, is a symbol of how 'East' can meet 'West' and create wonderful synergies, as well as conflicts. As will be discussed in Chapter 7 ('Identity'), the notion of 'Europe' might be said to be the result. The 'rape' of Europa by the bull Zeus (Jupiter in Roman mythology) is one that happens in the waters of the Aegean Sea, giving Constantinople/Istanbul huge symbolic importance.

Other writers on Byzantium include: Whittow, on the early Byzantine Empire, from 600 to 1025 (Whittow, 1996); Michael Angold, on the period 1025–1204 (Angold, 1997), which is particularly concentrated on the political history of Byzantium; and John Julius Norwich's three volumes covering the period up to 1025 and then that until 1453 (Norwich, 1990, 1992, 1995). On the culture of Byzantium, see Khazhdan and Epstein (1985). Certainly, if culture is a vector of empire and integration, it has its supreme manifestation in religious culture, and most specifically in the cultures of Christianity and Islam. This theme is also discussed at length by Judith Herrin (1989) in *The Formation of Christendom*, as well as by Peter Brown (2003), *The Rise of Western Christendom: Triumph and Diversity, 200–1000*.

Its successor empire in the Middle East and Europe, that of the Ottomans, also merits treatment at length, but will have to wait for a subsequent edition of this book. There are many excellent treatments of its long (1300–1923) existence (Kinross, 1979; Faroghi, 2005; Finkel, 2006). Its successor in Anatolia, modern-day Turkey, has a rich and enduring tradition from both Byzantium and the Ottomans, as well as multiple Western influences, and makes it a fascinating crossroads for many cultures and influences of all kinds (Findley, 2005; Stone, 2011).

## Mongol Empire

The Mongol Empire (1206–1257 CE) is mainly remembered in the popular imagination as what Feuer calls the best extant example of 'regressive' imperialism. These 'genocidal … imperialists' brought in their wake massacres of the most horrible kind, with no 'parallel save that of the ancient Assyrians and the modern Nazis' (as Feuer quotes historian J. J. Sanders, 1971). Neither are they said to have 'brought [any] higher culture to the conquered areas' (Feuer, 1989: 5). But even Feuer quotes one main positive achievement for this seemingly barbarous race, quoting Eileen Power's dictum that 'they wrought one of the most startling revolutions in the history of the world up to that date by bringing into contact for the first time the two ends of the earth, Europe and Far East' (Power, n.d.).

Other historians have pointed to the long-standing achievements of the Mongol invaders, who adopted their conquered territories' habits and customs fairly rapidly. Their links to Chinese history are, of course, numerous (Meskill, 1973; Franke and Twitchett, 1994; Tyler, 2003; Biran, 2005). So are those to Russian history (Vernadsky, 1979; De Hartog, 1996; Christian, 1998). These nomadic raiders were also a force for other kinds of unity – Lieven points out that 'China was united by the Mongols and has remained united ever since'. It had been riven by disunity from the third century CE until the Mongols invaded in the 1500s. Equally, China was ruled by the often successful Manchu dynasty, another group of nomadic warriors, between the 1640s and 1912 (Lieven, 2000: 37). The best single account of the Mongol Empire and its influence on the development of Europe is David Morgan's account, which describes the Mongol 'hordes' as a terrifying military force but also as one that had a certain civilizing influence (Morgan, 2007). For the direct impact on the West, Peter Jackson's (Jackson, 2005) is the best source.

## EUROPEAN EMPIRES

The 'European' empires, all of which were outgrowths of modern nation states since about 1700, are those that mostly directly affect our contemporary world, and in a short chapter like this we have to leave quite a lot out. Here we have chosen the British Empire as it might be said to have the widest and deepest impact, though some might disagree. It also has the advantage of having most of its literature in English. Certain key parameters clearly also help us organize analyses of them, as they also divide them all. Key among these is the influence of the 'domestic' on the 'international', and vice versa. 'Globalization' owes much of its impact to imperial ventures and the results continue to reverberate, as they do for all the empires we have discussed so far. Historical thinkers like J. A. Hobson, who made the link between colonial expansion abroad and social control at home (Hobson, 1902/2005; Porter, 1968/2007), or Lenin (1916/2000), about the links between imperialism and war (q.v.), were not merely thinking about the British Empire, but the way that nexus played out was different from, say, the French experience of empire. The racial and gender politics of the great modern empires all had their roots and being in social Darwinist theories, but all of them manifested this in different ways. Decolonization was equally not the same in all imperial settings, but had the same roots in the decline of European power and rise of alternative centres, such as the United States.

So, while we have to be careful about making trite comparisons, it has to be said that the communal experience of the imperial powers and their imperial vassals have a certain synergy, often expressed in joint 'events', like the 'Scramble for Africa' after the Berlin Conference of 1878. On this 'partition' of Africa, see Förster, Momssen and Robinson (1988) and Wesseling (1996), while for those who would liked to further explore the imperial experience of the Netherlands, see Kuitenbrouwer (1991) and Israel (1995). For Belgium, see Anstey (1996) and Nzongola-Ntalaja (2002); for France, Aldrich (1996), Chafer (2002) and Thomas (2005); for Germany, Louis (1967); for Italy, Ben-Ghiat and Fuller (2005). A good short introduction to all of these can be found in Andrew Porter's (1994) *European Imperialism, 1860–1914*. A very good collection that looks at the relations between imperial regimes (and with the United States) can be found in Christopher Thorne's *Border Crossings* (Thorne, 1988). One that compares the decolonization of the various European empires can be found in *Crises of Empire, 1918–1975* (Thomas, Moore and Butler, 2008).

## The British Empire

The literature on the British Empire is vast. The best introductions are still by Denis Judd, Ronald Hyam and Bernard Porter (Judd, 1997; Hyam, 2002; Porter, 2004), while the most recent 'IR-related' accounts are by Niall Ferguson (2003a, 2003b). For the impact on Britain itself, see Andrew Thompson (2005) and David Cannadine (2001). Bill Nasson's book (2004) on how the British made a 'British World' is fascinating, and Ashley Jackson (2009) is both serious and amusing in the 'mad dogs and Englishmen go out in the midday sun' school of imperial reflection. There are, of course, also very serious tomes on the political and economic history of the Empire (Andrews, 1984; Cain and Hopkins, 2002 – to name but a few), as well as an Oxford and a Cambridge series on the history of the Empire (with volumes too numerous to mention, though Marshall, 2001, is a good, illustrated one-volume summary).

Great Britain saw its empire as a 'New Rome'. As Parchami says '[b]y the 1880s, the leading exponents of Empire proclaimed Britain to be the one and only heir to Rome's imperial mantle' (2009: 61). But the origin of the British–Roman relationship was not auspicious. Gibbon did not have an unduly high opinion of the Roman motivations for the conquering and holding of the province of *Britannicum* – 'the pleasing though doubtful intelligence of a pearl fishery attracted their avarice … After a war of about forty years, undertaken by the most stupid, maintained by the most dissolute, and terminated by the most timid of all the emperors, the far greater [but only as far as present-day Perth] part of the island submitted to the Roman yoke.' As for the natives, 'they possessed valour without conduct, and the love of freedom without the spirit of union' (Gibbon, 1776/1981: 30).

Britain has since remedied the 'union' part of that stricture, even if the said union is not as solid as it once was. What used to cement it was arguably threefold – an empire of its own, which gave gainful employment to many of its subjects, and in particular the troublesome Celts from Scotland, Wales and Ireland; a world-beating economy, that provided the rest of the world with, among other things, a model for industrial and trading development which still underpins the thinking of development economists today; and, most importantly, a robust dislike of foreigners and their ways. On a positive front this 'union' was a useful model for British intellectuals and policymakers (and especially Scots) when they looked to other forms of union, whether that be federal with the United States and the 'freedom-loving peoples' (see Williams, 1998, for a discussion of such luminaries as Clarence Streit), or within a League of Nations, or, for some, within a European Union.

The first of these unifying forces, empire, is what interests us here. It gave rise to a particular 'Britannic Vision', in the words of David McIntyre, which he describes as a 'world where independence and unity could be combined', or what Conservative British politician Leo Amery called 'independence plus'. McIntyre quotes Canadian Premier Robert Borden as calling the British Empire/Commonwealth a 'union in amazing diversity through governance, founded on freedom and co-operation' (2009: ix). But this empire was established at a time (the late nineteenth century) when many within the country believed Britain to be in rapid decline – the Empire was constructed to give Britain guaranteed markets and sources of raw materials in flagrant disregard for Britain's previous great economic invention of 'Free Trade'. It was done out of an 'urgent need to rouse the people from apathy or domestic quarrels in some larger purpose', in the words of Joseph Chamberlain (Fraser, 1966: xv) – in other words to galvanize the domestic political scene by looking beyond it to a greater purpose. The idea of creating a 'Greater Britain' was thus done partly out of a desire to protect the original one and to cement the world order that Britain believed it had created, not without reason (Bell, 2007). The implications of this for the notion of 'liberal internationalism' are further explored by Casper Sylvest (2009a).

However, the sad truth was that, by the 1890s 'Great Britain, for all her territorial pomp and splendour, was without allies and openly disliked by many in Europe and the United States. "Splendid Isolation" was in fact uncomfortable and costly; a rationalization of a predicament, not a calculated policy' (Judd, 1977: 188). By 1900, it was painfully obvious that Britain needed allies in its desire to stay free and to spread its influence, no matter how powerful it looked to outsiders. Where was this to come from? In two world wars, the *Pax Britannica*, or British world 'order', was maintained but hung by a thread in 1918 and was totally superseded by a *Pax Americana* in 1945 (Williams, 1998; Parchami, 2009). It was too dispersed geographically and based on ideas that were either too limited in their appeal ('Britishness') or too disruptive in their results ('parliamentary democracy', for example) to give the empire true longevity. Gibbon had believed in 1776, in *Decline and Fall*, that Britain had created a true 'Roman' empire, untainted by corruption and decadence – 'the reflections which illustrate the fall of that mighty Empire [Rome] will explain the probable causes of our actual security' (Gibbon, quoted by Vogt, 1993: 3). Within a few years America had been lost, the French Revolution had been unleashed and all seemed in chaos.

## Origins and results

The two major schools of thought on the origins and results of the British Empire see their exact reflection in the theoretical debate described above about liberal/ conservative and radical/ poststructuralist views of IR. The first, epitomised by historians like Robinson, Gallagher and Denny (1961), Peter Cain and Anthony Hopkins (Cain and Hopkins, 2001) and many others, shows an empire created almost 'by accident'. Some see the results in more beneficial than negative terms (Ferguson, 2003a, 2003b; Lal, 2004) as they created the '*Pax*' ('order') that is necessary for commerce and prosperity to grow. The second sees probable malevolent intent and, certainly, disastrous consequences. The leader of this group is difficult to select, but two clear candidates must be Edward Said and Noam Chomsky, whose many books decry the results of British imperialism in the Middle East for creating the problems of that area, though Chomsky does tend to blame the United States more than the British 'poodle' for the 'failed states' that have resulted (Chomsky, 2003, 2007; Said, 1979, 1993). It must be said that a number of 'non-radical' historians like Louise Fawcett (2005) and Margaret Macmillan (2001) agree that the British breakup of the Ottoman Empire has had disastrous consequences for the subsequent development of the region. Even the most dedicated supporter of the 'civilising mission' of the British Empire would have trouble justifying such acts as the Opium Wars of 1839–1842 and 1856– 1860 which did so much damage to (and also to create) China (Lovell, 2011), or the brutal suppression of the 'Indian Mutiny' of 1857–1858 (Fremont Barnes, 2007; Spilsbury, 2008). Historically there were many 'critics of Empire' within the ranks of the radical and socialist Left within Britain (Porter, 1968/2007; Claeys, 2010) who merit a solid chapter of any book on empire, had we the space.

## Ending and decline

The management of the decline of, and extraction from, empire was another particular trait of the British imperial experience, though not, of course, unique to it. Many historians have stressed the positive and negative sides of this experience (for one inspiring collection, see Louis, 2006). Others point out that it was in fact a 'decline, revival and fall' (Gallagher and Seal, 2004) as Britain lost one empire in the eighteenth century and gained another one in the next. Indeed, we could almost say Britain lost 'two' empires, as well as one in 1453 to the French, at the end of the Hundred Years' War. As Oscar Wilde might have said, 'to lose one empire may be regarded as a misfortune, to lose two looks like carelessness'.

On the positive side we can point to the idea of the ending of empire leading to the creation of a freedom-asserting 'Commonwealth'. The trope of 'Freedoms at Midnight' is particularly striking (for a good recent collection on this, see Holland, Williams and Barringer, 2010). Indeed some historians have accentuated the very success of the British spreading the idea of democracy for its decline. The (largely white or white-dominated) 'Dominions' – Australia, Canada, New Zealand, South Africa and, of course, what became the United States – broke away to form their own democratic states. Ireland demanded its independence on solidly democratic principles and it was Britain's shame to have flouted this demand. This was also the case with the United States, which was powerfully defended by British (and Irish) MP Edmund Burke in the House of Commons, which nearly ended the 'first' British Empire (Welsh, 1995; Simms, 2007). In many cases a respect for democracy contributed greatly in both cases to the world's then superpower bowing to the will of relatively few people (Lieven, 2000: 116–117). This was also true of India and virtually every former African colony.

The more troublesome side of this transition to democracy and independence has tended to be the focus of those who criticize all empires, and the British Empire in particular. It has been perpetuated in the IR literature on brutal 'counter-insurgency' policies, whether that be in the process of extraction, as in Kenya, or Aden, or in the need to maintain a successor government in power that was threatened by a regional superpower – the case of Malaysia's troublesome relationship with Indonesia is the best case in point. Joanna Lewis has memorably summed up the end of British rule in Kenya as 'nasty, brutish and in shorts' (2007); David Anderson (2005), as one of being the *History of the Hanged*; Caroline Elkins (2005), as *Britain's Gulag*. In the latter, the expression 'hearts and minds' has come to be used, often wrongly in most 'insurgencies' ever since the British experiences in Malaysia in the 1960s and 1970s (Carruthers, 1995). There are defenders of the withdrawal process on the grounds that it was far from being a 'mismanaged disaster' (Grob-Fitzgibbon, 2011). Critics of British imperialism will point to the colonial legacies of poverty, the destruction of endogenous cultural and political norms and the racial legacies of inequality (Morgan and Hawkins, 2004) and so on (Howe, 2010, has a large number of articles on such critiques).

What has remained of this can, on one account, be said to consist of a sadly shrunken institutional structure, the Commonwealth (McIntyre, 2001; Shaw, 2008 are good introductions), is widely seen as a worthy but ineffective shadow of its former self. But it has also left a lasting legacy of local institutional democratic traditions in many (if not most) African countries, India, Pakistan and (of course) the United States itself. Britain has been a beacon for the English-speaking peoples since the 1790s at least. So, although most of the real 'British Empire' was only consolidated in the late nineteenth century, and had been dismantled by the 1960s, the British Commonwealth is a living proof of the longevity of at least the ideal of democratic governance. So a contrary view is embedded in the above-mentioned historical analyses of both British *thinking* on Empire and World Order (as in Bell, 2007; Sylvest, 2009a), but also in the *institutional* results of the handover of power by Britain to the United States (q.v.) and the setting up of the League of Nations (q.v.) and the United Nations (q.v.). This thinking, now being ably led by historian Mark Mazower, gives us to reflect that the United Nations in particular has colonial origins and that these origins are therefore founding flaws in these institutions that still need to be addressed by policymakers and intellectuals alike (Mazower, 2009b), a theme that will be further explored in Chapter 6 ('International Organization') (q.v.).

## Russian–Soviet Empire

The emergence of the Czarist Russian Empire was one of the great creations of the modern period. It was created by an awesome mixture of brutal human agency and a lack of real opposition in its formative period, the seventeenth and eighteenth centuries, when the rival imperial power in the Baltic, Sweden, was decisively defeated in the battles of Narva (1700) and Poltava (1709) (Englund, 2002). In the south the Ottoman Empire was in rapid decline and the British were largely engaged elsewhere, though there were points of friction in South Asia (Afghanistan, India, Persia), collectively known as the 'Great Game' of the nineteenth century (Hopkirk, 1992). The architects of the Czarist Empire – Czars Peter the Great, Catherine the Great and her field marshal lover, Prince Potemkin, have had many biographers, the latter couple having been immortalized most recently by Simon Sebag Montefiore (2005a).

Some would dispute the claim that the Soviet Union (USSR) was, in fact, an 'empire'. It had an explicitly *anti*-imperial ideology; indeed, it claimed it was in fact 'socialist'. It was not a 'colonial' empire like the British or French empires, but it was nearly as big as both. But, as Michelle Birgerson points out, in many other ways it was such an entity: 'Empires consist of a center and a periphery ... Politically the center dominates the periphery ... Nationally the center represents the homeland of a nation that is distinct from the nations of the periphery. Empires are political systems based on a power relationship between the center and the periphery and involves the control of the center *over* the periphery ... Hence the distribution of power overlaps with the issue of nationalism.' In the USSR, the national question was thus key in both its development and the manner of its ending (Birgerson, 2002: 9–10).

In 1947, George Kennan, then a State Department official who had served for many years as a diplomat in Riga, Latvia (before the establishment of diplomatic relations with the Soviet Union), and in the 1930s and 1940s, latterly under Ambassador Averell Harriman, asked the key question in *Foreign Affairs* about 'The Sources of Soviet Conduct' (Kennan, 1947). He had previously asked it many times in private, notably in the 'Long Telegram' (Kennan, 1950), and came to epitomize the attitudes of 'the Riga Axiom', one of profound distrust for Soviet intentions throughout the Cold War (q.v.). Kennan the historian was well aware that the 'sources' were proximately to do with a Soviet ideological commitment to protecting the Soviet Union but also to the concept of world revolution. As many historians have pointed out since, the key to understanding why Russia has wanted, and been seen as, an 'empire' for a period since at least Czar (Emperor) Peter the Great (reigned 1682–1725) is that the key to its geopolitical existence and identity has been remarkably constant ever since the Mongol Empire (q.v.) was expelled during the reign of Ivan the Terrible (1533–1588), the first true Czar to establish Russia as a fledgling nation state (Perrie and Pavlov, 2003). Since then, as Dominic Lieven has put it:

> The demands of international power politics and of membership of the European and then global system of great powers were of overwhelming importance in Russian history. More probably than any other single factor they determined the history of modern Russia.
>
> (Lieven, 2000: ix)

The sheer extent of its contiguous borders meant that the defence of those frontiers against attack was always going to be difficult (and it was invaded many times, notably by Napoleon and Hitler), but also that its political strength directly affected its ability to expand or forced it to contract, in a process dubbed 'expansion and coexistence' (Ulam, 1968; see also Ulam, 1984). Hence Czarist Russia lost Finland, the Baltic States and Poland in the chaos after 1917, and regained the Baltic states in 1940 (and Poland as a 'protectorate' in 1947) and then lost them again in 1991. Geopolitical factors thus link into political actions in very specific ways and dictated the expansion of the Russian people into one of the greatest land empires the world has ever seen.

Ivan the Terrible set a standard for a centralizing and brutal state that has been lived up to many times since, both under the Czars and since 1917 and the Bolshevik Revolution. Rule by 'terror' was initiated by Ivan and imitated by all of his successors, with the Soviet 'Gulag' (complex of concentration camps) not fully dismantled until the 1990s (Conquest, 1968, 2007; Applebaum, 2003). Karl Marx saw Czarist Russia as 'asiatic', by which he meant brutal and backward, and only learned to read Russian in the last few years of his life (Molnar, 1975; Chan and Williams, 1994: 59). It is difficult to say what he would have thought of his disciples and successors in the Communist Party of the Soviet Union, and especially Leon Trotsky (the first Commissar for Foreign Affairs), Vladimir Ilyich Lenin and Joseph Stalin, who between them ruled Soviet Russia for most of the period 1917–1953 and who ruled with an iron ideological fist. This system of control allowed only for a dominant Communist Party of the Soviet Union (CPUSSR) that was frequently violently purged until the 1950s. Historians were not all negative about the USSR, with E. H. Carr's monumental *Bolshevik Revolution* series spanning most of the period until the Purges of the 1930s (Carr, 1952, 1954, 1959, 1971/1978) and R. W. Davies marvelling at the feat of social engineering that the USSR represented (for example, Carr and Davies, 1979; Davies, 1980).

As an informal arm of its foreign policy, the CPUSSR imposed a similarly hard discipline on foreign Communist parties affiliated to the CPUSSR through the Communist International (*Komintern*) from 1920 to 1943 and after to the similar *Kominform*. A complex and intrusive system of secret agents run by the successors of the Czar's *Okhrana* (Security) dictated both domestic and foreign conformity to ideological changes of often bewildering rapidity, satirized by George Orwell in *Animal Farm* (1945/2011). This enforcement had both domestic and foreign tentacles in Felix Dzershinsky's *Cheka*, which later had other acronyms like NKVD, OGPU and KGB. It might be noted that the first of these latter acronyms had the 'People' (*narodnii*) in the title; the second two make main reference to the state (*gosudarstvo*). In particular, the USSR pioneered the use of outside liberals and Marxists, such as H. G. Wells, George Bernard Shaw and Jean-Paul Sartre for use as 'Fellow Travellers' (Caute, 1988, 2003) as well as lower-profile 'agents of influence' (Andrew and Gordievsky, 1990; Andrew and Mitrokhin, 1999). The USSR in effect ran a direct foreign policy through the Soviet Foreign Ministry and an unofficial one through communist parties, fellow-travelling organizations (usually infiltrated like the PEN, an international writers' union) in what was termed by William Gillies, the International Secretary of the British Labour Party until 1946, 'the Communist Solar System' (Williams, 1989).

Dissidence, or internal opposition, was by no means expunged in any of the imperial phases of the various Russian epochs. There are cultural and literary overviews (Figes, 2003); and many on dissidents, from Maxim Gorki in the late nineteenth century (*Mother*, Gorki, 1907/1949, was a great favourite of the Soviet state apparatus) through to Solzhenitsyn in the 1970s and 1980s (banned in the USSR until the late 1980s: Solzhenitsyn, 1973, 2000, are good examples). One good recent overview of this phenomenon of cultural dissent under the Czars and Soviet leadership is by Philip Boobbyer (2005). Indeed with Russian or Soviet literature, art and other cultural forms, it is often impossible to distinguish the 'politics' of empire from the 'art'. Russian and Western literary contributions have added to the partial and yet rich imaginary of the Russian/Soviet imperial experience. Many writers have chronicled the treatment of dissent in the USSR, with punishment often being meted out, usually by Stalin, to some of the USSR's greatest leaders, notably Bukharin and Trotsky, but with many more examples (Cohen, 1971; Deutscher, 1954–1963/2003).

The dissolution of the Soviet Empire was, on the face of it, very peaceful. The whole of the old 'East Bloc', which had all fallen under Soviet influence in 1944–1945, declared themselves independent with scarcely a shot fired, even parts of what had arguably been the old Czarist Empire like Estonia, Latvia and Lithuania. Much of the credit for this has been given to the last General Secretary of the Communist Party of the Soviet Union, Mikhail Gorbachev (1999; Sakwa, 2008). There was a short and vicious war between the new Republic of Moldova and the break-away state of 'Transdniestr' in 1992, which left the new republic divided, as it still is at the time of writing (King, 2000). There has been an ongoing and extremely vicious war in Chechnya that shows no sign of abating, though that is strictly speaking not 'post-imperial', as the province is still part of Russia. Ironically, perhaps, there has also been a deal of what might be called a 'Cold War nostalgia' literature, linked to a feeling that empires are by their very nature more stable and orderly than a shifting system of smaller nation-states. Perhaps the best discussion of this is in Mearsheimer (1991). The 'bipolarity' of the Cold War standoff between the United States and the USSR did indeed have elements of 'stability', but it also carried with it the constant fear of 'Mutually Assured Destruction' (appropriately 'MAD') and a huge lack of freedom for all the subject peoples of the former 'East Bloc'.

## The Nazi Empire

The other main candidate for a truly European empire in the recent past came from the vision of the National Socialists in Germany. They also talked about a Greater Europe, in which all the peoples of the area could feel at home. The problem was that this empire excluded more than it included, and not merely 'undesirables' like Gypsies, homosexuals, the mentally challenged and Jews, but also Slavs and anyone deemed not quite up to scratch (Mazower, 2008). The Nazis and Italian Fascists deliberately used the iconography of the Roman Empire for themselves – eagles, the *lictors* (Roman magistrates), fasces, the standards, parades and architecture, but they denied the peoples of Europe (even after subtracting the above, who did not qualify) any proper rule of law, access to the potential wealth of a unified Europe or any kind of peace. George Kennan saw the probable demise of the Nazi Empire as early as 1940 when he was based in Oslo for the German invasion in its refusal to accept anyone who was not 'Aryan'. The Nazis themselves wiped out many of their best men and women in insane military expeditions that made the loss of the Roman legions in the German forests in 9 CE look like a White House Tea Party. Kennan did not believe that it could be a lasting victory because of the implicit lack of universality in a message of German racial superiority (Kennan Papers, Princeton, 1940). If war does not lead to an *inclusive* peace, can it be successful and lasting?

## THE AMERICAN EMPIRE

As will be seen below, the idea that we have an American *Imperium*, at least since 1945, has grown exponentially over recent years (Ferguson, 2008; Lake, 2008). But it might be remembered that until quite recently American historians would have denied any such claim, and indeed pointed to the *anti*-imperial roots of the American Republic. The founding myths of this republic, much discussed by its 'Founding Brothers' (Ellis, 2002), lie in part in the rejection of the 'old' Europe and took pride in vanquishing imperial tyrants like George III of Britain. A strong theme of civic and political pride in anti-imperial feeling also comes from contemporaries of George Washington, such as Thomas Paine (Paine, 2009). Starting in the 1950s and 1960s, to some extent in line with the 'revisionist' views of the Cold War (see Chapter 2), historians like Walter LaFeber reinterpreted American expansionism to see it as 'imperial' (LaFeber, 1993). Others prefer to still use 'expansionism' as the preferred term and others are still reluctant to accept the term (Maier, 2006).

However, some recent historians of the United States, including notable conservative American figures, including Robert Kagan and Walter Russell Mead (Kagan, 2006a; Mead, 2002) and British historians like Niall Ferguson and Andrew Roberts (Ferguson, 2004; Roberts, 2006), have made a robust case for the United States being obliged to take its obligations for international leadership seriously as the 'leader of the Free World' since the outbreak of the Cold War, and even more so since the end of that confrontation. Liberal historians and political scientists like John Ikenberry and Joseph Nye have made the same point in less historical mode, as defenders of Western values like human rights, as well as institutional structures like the United Nations, etc. (Ikenberry, 2001, 2006). The United States, says Nye, is 'bound to lead' (Nye, 1991).

## The rise (and decline?) of the American Empire

The iconography of the American Republic has always consciously echoed that of Imperial Rome, but that symbolism was largely confined to the North American and American continent until 1914. Kagan and Mead show how much this power was based on Roman and Greek forms of power and influence (Kagan, 2006a; Mead, 2002). Distinctions along these lines have been made as to whether Greek ('normative') or Roman ('military') power is most effective in exerting influence in any 'imperial' situation, no matter which power is hegemonic in any given configuration of the international system (Lundestad, 1998).

Be that as it may, it is clear that World War I marked a decisive breaking-free from this geographical constraint and President Woodrow Wilson gave the opportunity for a first demonstration of what American power could do on the world stage, though it must be said one of his immediate predecessors, Theodore Roosevelt, also harboured global ambitions for the United States. In 1917–1918, the United States played an important, and maybe even decisive, role in defeating Germany and forcing that country to sue for peace. Wilson's '14 Points' of January 1918 (q.v.) were one basis for what became the Treaty of Versailles in 1919. Wilson aspired to bring about the 'end of war', even a 'New World Order' (Knock, 1992; Williams, 1998). Subsequent writers have asked to what extent Wilson's ideas and actions were determinate, with some arguing that his legacy has left the world with 'the ideas that conquered the world' (Mandelbaum, 2002). Wilson has certainly been the most quoted American president in terms of being the main originator of a twentieth-century record of American 'democratic interventionism'. Scholars like Stanley Hoffman claim that 'Wilsonianism' is a force in American politics that defies neat compartmentalization into 'left' and 'right', but is rather rooted in a common understanding of 'American exceptionalism' (Anthony, 2008).

This project was certainly renewed by President Franklin Delano Roosevelt, who is widely accepted to have been a 'realistic Wilsonian' in the words of David Reynolds (1981, 1991, 2006). There has been much discussion among historians about the nature of American 'Post-War Planning' for an American-dominated international system, with some very interesting more recent work being done on the geopolitical thinking that was part of that, such as that of Isaiah Bowman (Smith, 2003). The role of the United States in the creation of a United Europe to simultaneously unite, pacify and render it prosperous has been a major benefit for both parties (Harper, 1996). Through such declarations as the Atlantic Charter of 1941 and the absorption of British bases as part of the 'Lend–Lease' agreement of the same year, Roosevelt laid the foundations for a United States with global reach, which still sees the country as the only power capable of fighting a war on at least two fronts and with full command and control capability, currently being demonstrated in Afghanistan and Iraq. So the United States is accepted as the leader of the West, the question that might be asked is whether that means it has an 'empire' or, if it has, whether that has been beneficial or destructive? After 1945, the United States has often been seen as a 'conqueror', starting with its relationship with Germany and Japan (Beschloss, 2002).

In terms of influence, it might be argued that American power has been most noticeable in successfully spreading its ideas and practices of a lightly regulated, but rule-based system of capitalist economic progress, linked, more vaguely, to the ideal of human rights (though arguably the European Union has done more to foster that). This was strongly linked to the use of the Marshall Plan in the 1940s and 1950s to get Europe back to prosperity with the implicit military guarantees provided by bases round the globe and organizations such as the North Atlantic Treaty Organization (NATO), which will be discussed in Chapter 6 ('International Organization') (q.v.). Such thinking has become received wisdom as in the following statement by Simon Bromley:

> We have seen that what began as a specifically American project of post-[1945] war reconstruction and Cold War inter-capitalist unification has become a constitutive form through which significant aspects of the world-wide capitalist order of many states are rule-governed and institutionalized.
>
> (Bromley, 2008: 202)

This reasoning, of course, has its merits, even if it assumes that economic power is the key, though Bromley also accepts that the world now accepts American ideas of democracy – he approvingly quotes Ikenberry's statement that we live in an era of 'global empire … not essentially an American empire but rather an empire of capitalist democracy' (Bromley, 2008: 203).

To continue and echo the imperial theme as applied to other examples, the USA has also been compared many times in recent years to a declining imperial power. Perhaps this is the fate of all empires, as they are said usually to be declining as soon as they rise. As far back as the 1980s, scholars like Robert Keohane were talking about 'the end of hegemony' (Keohane, 1984), and many others since have written about the 'decline of the West' (Coker, 1998). Much of this thinking is based on the relative shift in economic power attendant on the shift in economic numbers from the stratospheric heights of American dominance in 1945 to the relatively lower dominance of the 1980s and 1990s. Coker was also referring to a decline in the strength of the American link to Europe as well as the re-emergence of a number of 'sensibilities' within Europe and indeed within the USA itself – the USA would look increasingly to the West and South and forget the Old Continent (Coker, 1998). Others, such as Charles Kupchan, see American power as having reached the limits that always befall such enterprises through strategic overreach (Kupchan, 2003).

As for the prospects of imperial victory in Afghanistan and Iraq, maybe our leaders should take more notice of the problems of subduing 'barbarians' noted by Gibbon and Momssen, not to mention reading the Romans themselves. In his writings on the subjugation of the Numidians and their king, Jugurtha (111–105 BCE), Sallust pointed to the importance of a solid home front in the (then) war on terror – then, as now, 'some grieved for the glory of the empire, others – unaccustomed to the circumstances of war – feared for freedom' (Sallust, 2007: 82).

## A EUROPEAN EMPIRE?

Other see alternatives emerging (China, Brazil, India, etc.) and, most notably for the purposes of our discussion, the European Union. John Cormick, for example, argues that the United States has shown its essential weaknesses in the wars since 2001, and that 'power can transcend states, can be expressed without resort to force, and can just as likely be latent and implied as it can be active and explicit'. This he sees in the 'new confidence' of Europeans, the internal problems of the USA itself, economic particularly, and the evident decline of American influence abroad under the George W. Bush presidency. What we are now seeing, he argues, is the emergence of a European 'superpower' (Cormick, 2007: introduction). We might argue that what successful 'imperial' (or indeed 'dominant') powers do is galvanize the public of their day in enabling a coalescence of moral 'good' and their own 'interest' in periodic crusades to demonstrate their superiority in various ways. The Blair government of 1997–2007, that of George W. Bush in 2000–2008, and many others (Wilson and Roosevelt being very good US examples) have used, and continue to use, both force and the evocation of moral superiority in their leadership of imperial blocs in joint enterprises. However, whereas the Anglo-Saxon powers can point to their leadership/followership in the world wars, the Cold War, Afghanistan, Iraq, etc., what scholars like Cormick would have to show is how 'Europe' has played any such intellectual, moral or military role in global affairs. Where was such leadership in the Balkans (a part of Europe, after all), in Afghanistan or in the Middle East?

## CONCLUDING THOUGHTS

The first prime minister of India, Jawaharlal Nehru's, ringing declaration in 1947 that '[a]t the stroke of the midnight hour, when the world sleeps, India will awake to life and freedom' (Cannadine, in Holland et al., 2010: ix) might be said to be the leitmotiv for history's judgement on the whole concept of empire. Many thinkers, of Left and Right, would agree with Raymond Aron, in 1959, that imperialism was a 'name given by rivals or spectators, to the diplomacy of a great power' (Aron, quoted by Pagden, 2010: 437). So should we write them off as one of the great errors of historical experience?

## Why do empires always seem to decline/collapse?

In 1981, the great French historian Jean-Baptiste Duroselle wrote a not uncontroversial book entitled *Tout empire périra: théorie des relations internationales* (1981), partly out of his frustration at the ahistorical nature of study of IR (*plus ça change, plus c'est la même chose?*) but also partly because he believed, along with Paul Kennedy (1988) and Robert Keohane (1984), that the American 'empire' was also heading for the rocks. All of these writers pointed to the increasing *décadence* (Duroselle's term for France in the 1930s; Duroselle, 1979) of the political elites, their complacency and arrogance. All pointed to the growing feeling that the Vietnam War (which ended in 1975) had shown up the weaknesses of American political, economic and even social structures. But of course theirs was also a reference to the age-old observation of all historians, that nothing permanent seems to last. All empires have gone the way of Rome, and so will that of the United States.

One recurring theme in this and other 'declinist' literature is that of 'imperial overreach'. As we stressed above, that moment for Britain may have come at the time of the 'new imperialism' of the 1880s and 1890s, when there was a huge expansion of the territorial empire after the Treaty of Berlin in Africa, leading to the catastrophe of the Boer War in 1899–1901. It could have been when Britain entered World War I, losing vast numbers of its most creative young men and discrediting its political institutions in the process, and was subsequently bankrupted by financing its Allies with American dollars. It then had to fight for years to get that money back and to effectively hand over the Empire to the United States to save itself from Nazi Germany with the agreements on Lend Lease and the Atlantic Charter in 1941 (Reynolds, 1981; Williams, 1998). Economic historians like Immanuel Wallerstein point to the 'Great Depression' that started after 1873 for British decline setting in. They also draw the parallel of the decline of the United States starting as a result of the cost of the Vietnam War after 1967 (Wallerstein, 1987).

Duroselle, Kennedy and Keohane were all attacked for being too precipitate in their judgements (though many others made the same point in the aftermath of the collapse of the US financial system in 2007–2008). Samuel Huntington's rebuttal of the 'declinists' in *Foreign Affairs* (1988), and Henry Nau's, as well as Joseph Nye's, major tomes (Nau, 1990; Nye, 1990) claimed, as we have seen, that America was 'bound to lead'. All asserted that there were no real alternatives to the United States as a world hegemonic power but also that it still had dominance in the things that really mattered: technological creativity, military power and social impact (among other factors). The parallels with Rome are again striking between these two great empires, based on economic clout, constitutional law and military might – in the fourth century CE, Rome still had the greatest minds (many of whose writings have survived in print to this day); the most disciplined and well-equipped military forces, and their amphorae of olive oil (for which read 'Coca-Cola'), still dominated Western consumption patterns. And yet an undisciplined army of barbaric nobodies who had come to supplicate Rome for help was able to sack the city. Just as the United States has also withdrawn from its European bases and was effectively bankrupt by the end of the century, so was Rome. Maybe the progressive withdrawal from global commitments that we are now seeing in the United States will enable the building of a 'second Rome', a kind of American Byzantium, but maybe not?

Deepak Lal has the deceptively easy answer that 'the common cause for the decline of empires has been an increase in fiscal exactions which by provoking tax resistance, tax avoidance and evasion led to a fiscal crisis' (Lal, 2004: 206). However, it is difficult to see that high taxes brought about the end of the Roman or Byzantine empires or that of the Soviet Union – they were brought down by a combination of internal and external forces. Adam Smith had a clearer explanation. In the last sentence of *The Wealth of Nations*, in the chapter on how the 'towns improve the country', he states:

> The ordinary revolutions of war and government easily dry up the sources of wealth which arises from commerce only. That which arises from the more solid improvements of agriculture is much more durable, and cannot be destroyed but by those more violent convulsions occasioned by the depredations of hostile and barbarous nations … Such as happened for some time before and after the fall of the Roman empire in the western provinces of Europe.
>
> (Smith, 1776/1982: 520)

His view was that to rely too much 'upon commerce and manufactures' was 'slow and uncertain' and therefore dangerous, though his point above was based on his belief that 'the North American colonies, of which the wealth is founded altogether in agriculture' (Smith, 1776/1982: 515–516) had done much better than much of Europe to that date, which was dependent on its trade and manufactures. Maybe the main lesson for us is that imperial societies (and indeed states of all kinds) that do not forget the need to diversify their basic strengths survive and those that rely too much on one area of economic activity do not. Rome was too dependent on the economic institution of slavery, Britain on trade and finance ('pecuniary capitalism') and the United States, in Thorstein Veblen's words, on 'conspicuous consumption' (Veblen, 1912/1994). If the next (potential) imperial power, China, does not deal with its surplus of young men over women (Hudson and den Boer, 2006) and its immense imbalance between rural poor and urban riches, it will certainly feature in a future version of Smith's 1776 classic.

## So is empire a 'good' or a 'bad' thing?

This chapter shows yet again that the writing of history is a function of the obsessions of the day as much as a factor of 'pure' scholarship. It would take a far larger chapter than this to explain why empire is now getting a better press that it did during the Cold War. But since 1991, many more commentators are praising

the advantages of empire as a form of political, social and economic organization,
True, there has also been an upsurge of postcolonial literature (mentioned on
pages 126–27), which bears witness to the damage that imperialism did to local
forms of politics and culture and the long-lasting damage of postcolonial relationships. But we could also point to the widespread revulsion that has resulted from
the uses to which 'freedom' in many postcolonial societies has been put. National
independence in many parts of Africa, the Former Soviet Union and Yugoslavia,
and elsewhere, has led to death and destruction on a previously unrecorded scale.
At the head of this chapter, A. N. Wilson quoted Robert Skidelsky about the
scale of the mass slaughter in the twentieth century, which seemingly went hand
in hand with nationalism and democracy (Wilson, 2006: 41). To prove the direct
link is difficult, but there is no doubt that Woodrow Wilson's Secretary of State
Robert Lansing was not entirely wrong when he said in 1918 that self-determination
would turn out to be a dangerous idea to unleash, for (as Cherry Bradshaw puts it)
nation-building is indeed often 'bloody' (Heater, 1994; Williams, 1998; Bradshaw,
2008).

So is empire a better form of political, social and cultural organization than
the nation-state, itself a historically contingent phenomenon? Why choose one
new idea over a tried-and-tested old one? George Schöpflin identifies the key problems with empires as being ones of legitimacy, problems that democratic states
are supposed to solve. He points out that many empires claimed the 'mandate
of heaven' (the Chinese, for example) or the approbation of the Gods (or God), such
as the Holy Roman or Ottoman empires (2000: 138). But, of course, Friedrich
Nietzsche's 'death of God' meant the death of that justification, at least in the
now-secular West. The national principle put paid to the multinational empires
of the Russian Czars (and the Bolsheviks and their own form of secular religion),
a virus that was identifiably a result of the French Revolution, spreading across
Europe and the world (Skocpol, 1979, 1981; Chan and Williams, 1994). It also led
to the absurd situation where the old networks of commerce and cultural affinity
were broken up in the former British, French, Italian and other empires, as well as
in the former Soviet Union and Yugoslavia, only to have to be replaced by the
European Union (an 'empire' in all but name) and other ad hoc systems like the
Commonwealth of Independent States in the former Soviet space, again dominated
by Mother Russia (Birgerson, 2002).

Hence the supposed solutions to the problems of empire have run into a
challenge that was also a product of the rise of the nation-state in Europe, and the
West more generally. Europe itself found that its nationalisms contributed not
only (in many, but by no means, all cases) to a stronger sense of pride and identity
(q.v.) and economic progress but also to nationalist competition that led to dissolution and war. This dilemma was put most famously by Norman Angell (1910),
when he spoke of the 'Great Illusion' that states could ignore their interdependence
(Ceadel, 2009). The 'cure' for this, as proposed by President Wilson in 1918,
was the breaking down of national barriers, free trade and a set of international
organizations (q.v.) to regulate what we now call 'globalization' (q.v.). It could be
argued that capitalism, which knows no borders, has itself contributed to the rise of
nation-states and to their inevitable decline. The main problem for the would-be

imperial solution would seem to be whether there is a necessary corollary of an 'imperial' world, or at least 'regional' power, that must underpin and defend this economic 'empire'? Lal insists that empires need local understanding to flourish, citing the example of the United States, which has not understood Iraq as the awful example of how not to do empire – Americans are indeed 'crusaders' and see themselves as vectors of moral 'truth' (Lal, 2004: 210–213). The world, he suggests, can cope with a number of regional imperial players who collectively regulate global capitalism. That does, indeed, seem to be where we are headed now. Imperial urges clearly continue to haunt the planet, and are variously greeted by cries of support or of denigration. Zbigniew Brzezinski, President Carter's National Security Advisor (1978–1982) has said, 'America is acting as an imperial power. But the age of colonialism is over. Waging a colonial power in a post-colonial age is self-defeating. That is the fatal flaw of Bush's foreign policy' (Brzezinski, quoted in Ferguson, 2008: 272). But other scholars noted above, from the Right and Left of Western politics, see such 'imperialism' as necessary for the defence of democracy, human rights and global security. Such is the fine line that many powers have trodden over the past several hundred years.

## USEFUL FURTHER READING

Some useful introductions to the subject:

Lieven, Dominic (2000) *Empire: The Russian Empire and Its Rivals*. London: John Murray.
Münkler, Herfried (2007*) Empires: The Logic of World Domination from Ancient Rome to the United States*. Cambridge: Polity.

Good simple introductions to individual empires are:

### Rome

Baker, Simon (2007) *Ancient Rome: The Rise and Fall of an Empire*. London: BBC Books.
Kelly, Christopher (2006) *The Roman Empire: A Very Short Introduction*. Oxford University Press.

### Britain

Brendon, Piers (2008) *The Decline And Fall Of The British Empire, 1781–1997*. London: Vintage.
James, Lawrence (1995) *The Rise and Fall of the British Empire*. London: Abacus.
Marshall, P. J. (ed.) (1996/2001) *Cambridge Illustrated History of the British Empire*. Cambridge University Press.

*Africa Research and Documentation*, currently edited by Terry Barringer, is a treasure trove of a journal, containing ideas on all aspects of African history and current politics.

## Online resources

The full text of Kennan's famous article of 1947 about the USSR can be found at http://www.historyguide.org/Europe/kennan.html

# CHAPTER 6

# International organization

The world has reached such a degree of interdependence … that international cooperation has become essential … the only self-supporting region of the world is the whole world … Only one opinion and only one market cover the face of the earth.

(Salvador de Madariaga, 1929)

Liberal Internationalism is 'underwritten by expectations of intellectual, moral and/or political progress'.

(Sylvest, 2009b: 49)

The League of Nations … was an attempt to 'apply the principles of Lockean liberalism to the building of a machinery of international order … But this transplantation of democratic rationalism from the national to the international sphere was full of unforeseen difficulties.'

(E. H. Carr, 1939)

## INTRODUCTION

It has often been argued that the study of IR is the study of war (q.v.) and of peace (q.v.). The subject matter of this chapter, International Organization (IO), has often been claimed by those who are advocates of peace, or at least a 'cure' for war, implicitly or explicitly. The field of IO is vast, so we have decided to concentrate on where we might be said to have most 'added value' for a book like this, by concentrating both on the two main IOs of the last hundred years, the League of Nations (LON) and the United Nations (UN), and in particular the period up to the end of the 1950s. Very good surveys of the period beyond that can be found, and of course there is a vast theoretical debate within IR about the meaning and significance of IO, which we will also leave for others, with the exception of the theoretical debate that existed until the 1960s. What we aim to do here is to lay out the stall of (some of) the historical literature that is least likely to have been presented to IR students, and even those taking courses in IO. This chapter is again intended to provide the backdrop to what most IR courses already do well.

The history of IO really starts with the changes in thinking about peace (q.v.) and war (q.v.) that we have discussed in other chapters. Peace movements throughout the nineteenth century had called for such structures to be set up (Cortright, 2008: 3; Howard, 2000: 62). The historical antecedents of the discipline also show us that a major obsession linked to both of these is the question as to how we actually foster peace and discourage warlike behaviour. So IR theory and policymakers has often circled round the idea that humankind can somehow organize itself to discourage warlike behaviour and encourage peaceful endeavour. 'Realists' among policymakers, states, people and intellectuals alike have argued that such attempts will only ever mitigate the impact of violence in the international system, and the (often crudely told) story is that we cannot change 'human nature', which is inherently violent and warlike; the only actors that matter are states and the international system is by its very nature 'anarchic' and not amenable to good intentions thrashed out in committees of like-minded liberals. But of course this is a somewhat 'straw man' debate. Even a cursory examination of many of the key historical thinkers on IR more broadly, and IO more particularly, were hard-headed practical conservative 'realists', like the first Director of the London School of Economics and geopolitician Halford Mackinder and Conservative Minister of the Blockade in World War I, Robert Cecil (Johnson, 2011). Equally some who condemned IO as a fantasy were advocates of that ultimate 'idealist' fantasy, socialism, like E. H. Carr. Also, many liberal internationalists were from policy circles. This debate is one of the main themes of this chapter, one that contrasts and develops liberal internationalist thinking as one side of a coin, and praxis and realism as the other.

So at the head of the chapter we find this contrast expressed in the seemingly contrary statements of E. H. Carr in *The Twenty Years' Crisis* and that of Casper Sylvest (2009b). Carr's dismissal of all attempts at liberal world government as mere statements of the desires of status quo states and organizations, has to be set alongside his belief that IO as he knew it in the League of Nations by 1939 was not how he saw the potential for the United Nations if it was backed up by real hopes of support from the Powers (Carr, 1939/1947, 1942, 1945). That need for the exercise of power stands as a constant counterpoint to liberals who believe that the evolution of IO is for the common good of all mankind. This chapter might therefore be said to ask as its central question: Whether attempts at IO over the last century are anything more than statements of the desire for the rich and powerful liberal democracies to institutionalize their global power? Or, can we say that the support shown by many small states, non-governmental organizations, trades unions and the like for IO reflects their belief that IOs give them the opportunity to have a voice that can speak to power? Small states were the greatest supporters of the League of Nations, as were the decolonized states after 1945 for the United Nations.

In attempting to answer this question a more subtle and interesting story emerges when we look at the historical record of attempts by individuals, states and non-state actors alike to encourage international cooperation and organization, and it is to that record that this chapter will address itself. One of the key themes that will be explored here is a mapping of the evolution of thinking about the development of international political thought and action over the period since the French Revolution (q.v.), with a particular emphasis on the period since about 1900 as it pertains to IO. There will inevitably be some overlap with our other chapters, especially Chapters 2 and 3 ('War' and 'Peace' respectively). Another theme will be to examine the way that war has been the greatest recurring impetus behind the elaboration of international schemes and institutions, and, allied to this, the role that Great Powers have played in the concretization of such phenomena. It will be demonstrated that the emergence of IO has indeed, as Carr says, more often than not been due to the desires of these states to entrench their ambitions and their status quo positions, both by providing mechanisms through which they can better push their interests, but also by providing safety valves for the dispossessed at any given point in history. It has also been about both promoting and controlling the immense forces of what we now call globalization to make sure that they are both efficiently used and channelled in the direction desired by the liberal powers, a sentiment expressed above by Salvador de Madariaga, Chief of the Disarmament Unit in the League of Nations Secretariat from 1922.

This story will be told, as it was in previous chapters, by a brief overview of the debate in the literature of IR more broadly, and then a more detailed examination of the evolution of historical thinking about IO at particular points in the past, often in the context of the ending of a great war.

## INTERNATIONAL ORGANIZATION-GENERIC LITERATURE UNTIL THE 1960S

There are many good overviews of the historical evolution of IO by scholars of IR. These have tended to rise and fall in number and interest with the corresponding rise and fall of the influence of the League of Nations and United Nations. In the 1960s two books stood out. One is essentially historical – F. H. Hinsley's *Power and the Pursuit of Peace* (Hinsley, 1967) – and the other is Inis Claude's more political science interpretation, *Swords into Ploughshares* (Claude, 1964). In the 1990s, the best summary of thinking to that date can be found in Armstrong, Lloyd and Redmond (1996/2004), but the most interesting and challenging is Craig Murphy's *International Organization and Industrial Change* (Murphy, 1994), which reminds us that IO has played a key part in the global economic and social changes of the past two centuries. A recent summary of newer, purely historical literature on IO can be found in Amrith and Sluga's 'New Histories of the United Nations' (2008).

Though of course there is some crossover between genres, we can propose that IR as a field can be said to have split in how it examines IO as a phenomenon. One branch of IR theory has pursued what might be called the 'history of ideas' (or 'history of international thought') route, which examines in some detail the philosophical thinkers in their historical milieux, with Hinsley, maybe, as the 'Godfather' of this group. Another branch, to some extent following Claude, has indulged itself in an ever more complex theoretical debate about what IO is for and what it ends up doing in theory and practice. This next section will look at some of the key 'turns' in that theoretical journey. We will start with the period of World War II, as other pre-1945 theories of IO will be looked at in the context of the League of Nations.

## Integration theories

The evolution of Europe from a network of feuding states into the European Union is often quoted as a key example of how integration works to further the cause of world peace through the setting up of IOs. James Goodby claims that, to have this, there has had to be agreement on a variety of key issues: common values; 'almost certainly democratic values … a similar sense of identity or self-image, transparency and some denationalising of defense establishments, and a reasonably healthy economy' (Goodby, in Kacowicz et al., 2000: 239). But in order to get to this situation many wars have been fought, ended and started again.

The first of what Lucian Ashworth has referred to as several 'IR subcultures' on IO emerged largely from the thinking of one man, David Mitrany, whose work is still described in terms used for few other writers on occasion. Chris Brown has written that '[f]unctionalism is the most elaborate, intellectually sophisticated and ambitious attempt yet made not just to understand the growth of international institutions, but also to plot the trajectory of this growth into the future and to come to terms with its normative implications' (2001: 133). Mitrany was also a very significant player in the postwar planning in Britain during World War II (Williams, 1998), but then neglected for a long time after the 1950s, except by A. J. R. Groom and Paul Taylor (1975). He has attracted some notable intellectual attention of late, especially from Ashworth (1999); but also, in French (2003), and Devin (2008). Although much of his thinking had its roots in the liberal thinking of L. T. Hobhouse and Leonard Woolf (author of *International Government*, 1916; see Wilson, 2003), and the socialist thinking of the socialist 'planners' of the interwar period like G. D. H. Cole (Navari, 1995), he took this thinking a big step further. He was being fairly conventional when he stated in 1941 that '[c]entralized planning and controls, for both production and distribution are no longer to be avoided'. This was partly because of the exigencies of wartime and the examples being given by Roosevelt's New Deal and Stalin's Five Year Plans, but also because it was widely accepted by the 1940s that central controls were necessary to save capitalism from its own worst excesses to fend off the extreme nationalism that was widely seen to have caused the war (Williams, 1998/2007: 124). Within Britain itself, his intellectual trajectory is perhaps the best example of what the collaboration between 'Libs' and 'Labs' could produce before 1945. Mitrany's thinking was therefore just one aspect of a wider reflection on the nature and purpose of the state. This was a debate that the free-marketers like Friedrich Hayek (*The Road to Serfdom,* 1944/2001) lost until the 1970s to Keynesian ideas of demand control.

Mitrany's two main publications, *The Progress of International Government* (1933) and *A Working Peace System* (1943/1966), elaborated a theory of international politics that he dubbed 'functionalism'. This had a number of major tenets. First, he believed that economic, technical and other forms of 'functional' cooperation, or 'low politics', could in time encourage cooperation at a political level ('high politics'). The example of the LON's social and economic policy (see below) may be said to have encouraged the belief that such activity was a necessary base to build political cooperation. Second, he thought that this would in turn, and probably very gradually, lead to international government by a process of 'spillover' (or *engrenage*). Third, he coined the expression – linked to the first two – that 'form follows function', to indicate his belief that 'bottom-up' cooperation would lead to a diminishing power for the nation-state. As Barry Hussey (2010) and Ben Rosamond (2000) have pointed out this did not mean that Mitrany advocated regional organizations, as these were 'exclusionary' (Hussey, 2010: 129); neither did he much like federalism, which he also considered too narrow, indeed timid (Brown, 1992, 2001: 132). As Hussey has also pointed out, Mitrany stressed that IO must reply to basic human 'needs', as in 'an international community must grow from the satisfaction of common needs shared by members of different nations' (Mitrany, quoted in Hussey, 2010: 131). This idea was later echoed in the many writings of Groom and Taylor on IO (Taylor, 1964) and in the thinking of the celebrated conflict analyst John Burton.

As a sequel to his cited praise for functionalism, Brown also adds, 'which is not to say that all of its ideas, or even most of them, stand up to critical scrutiny' (Brown, 2001: 132). Ernst Haas, who followed most closely in his footsteps, took Mitrany's theory and tested it against two major developments of the 1950s in international politics in what he saw as more 'scientific' idiom. He tested Mitrany's main tenets against the development (to date) of European integration and also by studying the tripartite system of the International Labour Organization of the United Nations (Haas, 1964, 1968). The resulting theory he called 'neo-functionalism'. He believed that both these structures answered some of the criticisms of Mitrany's theories as being too ambitious – it made empirical testing of huge ideas possible (in line with the then, and now, obsession in American IR, for 'testable hypotheses') and it took domestic politics more into account. But Haas still kept the key idea that the nation-state might be replaced by IOs in the future and he was a key early enthusiast for the European Union, about which Mitrany, as we have seen, was not so keen. European Union studies, not really the domain of a chapter like this on global organizations, is still a key part of the intellectual discourse of IR (Hussey, 2010; Manners and Whitman, 2000).

# THE ORIGINS OF IO IN THE EMERGENCE OF THE MODERN STATE SYSTEM

The roots of the idea of IO still have to be sought in scholars of philosophy and international historical thought. Through them it is necessary to go back to the emergence of what is usually termed a 'Westphalian' state system, after the middle of the seventeenth and into the eighteenth century. The great thinkers of that period were all concerned to redefine the relationship of individuals to states, and states to each other. Many writers have stressed how much this relied on a rethinking of the Roman idea of *jus gentium* ('law of nations'), and many of them saw the future of the state as being in combination with other states. Hence Hinsley quotes Montesquieu's *De l'esprit des Lois* (1748): 'The state of things in Europe is that all states depend on each other … Europe is a single state composed of several provinces' (1967: 162). This was echoed in the next century by Voltaire, Rousseau and the international lawyer Emmerich de Vattel (*The Law of Nations*, 1758), who also referred to Europe as a 'single body', albeit one divided into sovereign states (Hinsley, 1967: 166). Earlier seventeenth-century lawyers, like Hugo Grotius, author of *De jure belli ac pacis* (*On the Law of War and Peace*, 1625), and Samuel von Pufendorf, author of *De jure naturae et gentium* (1672), laid the groundwork for the next several hundred years' thinking about the state, and thus of the possibility of IO (a good introduction to all of these thinkers can be found in Tuck, 1999).

We might see the emergence of what become institutions aiming at the creation and maintenance of what Kant called 'perpetual peace' in a reaction to the above thinkers. Most of them saw the notion of what Bruno Arcidiacono has called a 'hierarchical peace', one based on the necessity of monarchy, the 'supremacy of the strongest' to keep order and impose some sort of discipline on the normal state of international anarchy (Arcidiacono, 2011: chapter 1). This was a natural feeling among Romans – especially after the messy end of the Republic – as well as most Greeks, and all medieval thinkers. With Kant we find a first real reply to those like Grotius and Vattel, whom he dismissed as 'sorry comforters', but he had to find a response to many of his near contemporaries, like Jean-Jacques Rousseau (1712–1778), who found war to be a natural state of affairs between states, one that was 'born in the nature of society' (*naît de l'état social*) (Rousseau, 1964). But even Rousseau, as well as in his predecessors – such as William Penn (1644–1718), the non-conformist and Quaker founder of Pennsylvania – could find some solace in the idea of a union, or even a federation, of states. In the language of the Cromwellian revolution of the 1640s and 1650s, such an arrangement might be termed a 'Commonwealth'. This, said Penn, might restrain Princes and their 'Duels' (Penn, 1693/1912, quoted in Arcidiacono, 2011: chapter 3). In the early nineteenth century, and thus after Kant, the Marquis de Saint-Simon also talked of the 'reorganization of European society' in similar federalist terms (Saint-Simon, 1814), presenting his views for consideration by the Congress of Vienna of 1814. Many other near contemporary thinkers and writers of the American and French revolutions, including the Marquis de Lafayette and Benjamin Franklin, were agreed that Europe's problems could only be solved by some sort of federation, the origins of the later European Union, showing in particular its French and American ancestry (Marriott, 1937; Hemleben, 1943; de Rougemont, 1961; Hinsley, 1967). Kant was thus only a part of a wider reassessment of the notion of sovereignty, albeit an important one.

## Kant

Immanuel Kant, also discussed in Chapter 3 ('Peace'), is significant when we consider the federal ideas that played such an important part in the development of thinking about IO. His views have been well served by historians of ideas and IR scholars, especially since the end of the Cold War (Brown, 1992, 2001; Brown, Nardin and Rengger, 2002), and have been quoted by IR theorists, policy-makers and historians of IO alike, particularly in the context of the normative turn that IR took in the 1980s and 1990s. But his claim to be a father of IO is, on the face of it, rather slim. The main text that is always quoted, *Perpetual Peace* (Kant, 1795/1983), is really only a 'celebrated pamphlet', albeit one that sold out in several weeks and also that was published at a great moment in time – the immediate aftermath of the French Revolution (Gallie, 1978: 8). This work had been prefigured by an *Idea for a Universal History* (c. 1785), in which Kant had declared that 'the problem of establishing a perfect civil constitution is depen- dent upon the problem of a law-governing relationship between states' (Gallie, 1978: 13). This linking of law, constitution and state was, of course, very much a question of the IR of the day, with the United States breaking away from Britain and the emergence over the next few years of ideas such as '*le peuple*', 'human rights' and many other ideas that launched the need to rethink the relationship of the individual to the state and wider institutions. Martin Wight was also an early IR scholar to point to the ethical implications of Kant's more purely philosophical works, and his key concept of the 'categorical imperative'. If we all have what Kant calls a 'duty' to work for the happiness of others as much as for our own happiness, then, as Wight puts it, '[t]he end of man must be something universal and inclusive', and this must have, as he said in *Perpetual Peace*, a structure that will ensure that the philosophically grounded 'harmony of interests' (as Adam Smith, among others, put it at the same time), is assured in practice (Wight, 2005: 68–76). These ideas lay at the heart of a debate that resonated through the next century. It is still at the centre of IR today and has particular resonance in the study and practice of IO.

## The French Revolution and the emergence of popular sovereignty in Europe

The French Revolution (q.v.) gave rise to a number of key ideas that we have alluded to above – popular sovereignty, the new idea of the 'nation' and so on. The nineteenth century saw the apotheosis of the attendant ideology of nationalism as states formed largely on the basis of ethnic identity (q.v.) – mainly in Europe, but also in South America. But there were important moves towards international cooperation that also created what Mitrany was later to call 'functional' international agencies. The nation-state in Europe, as Montesquieu, Voltaire and Kant had realized, was necessarily linked to all the others. In order to prosper there had to be cooperation. At the Treaty of Vienna in 1815, many heads of state were also keen not to allow the rise of new 'Napoleons'. The autocracies of Europe, and especially the absolute monarchies, were also determined to make sure that the more wild ideas of 1789, such as popular sovereignty, were not allowed to take hold. They of course failed, and the ideas of 1789 were to sweep through Germany, Italy, Greece and many other parts of Europe, with greater or lesser impact. So we can say that the nationalisms of the nineteenth century, as well as the emergent institutions that are the forerunners of modern IO, were born out of war (Langhorne, 1982, 1986). They also responded to a deeply conservative view of the world, one that has been identified by Henry Kissinger as representing a 'world restored' (Kissinger, 1964), as an attempt to save the imperial powers of Europe not supersede them. The most important result of the Congress system is what is known as 'conference diplomacy' and the beginning of a never-ending series of good stories about it. One of the most celebrated has French delegate Talleyrand asking, after the Belgian delegate died, '[W]hat did he mean by that?' The subtleties of protocol were such that all the foreign ministers entered by separate doors. A more serious precedent was the importance of procedure, and the coalition ('group') behaviour that continues to this day. Harold Nicolson's (1946) account of the Congress of Vienna is a good source on this, as well as the increasing proliferation of conferences that has reached fever pitch over the past hundred years or so, as is Andreas Osiander's (1994) placing of it in a much longer tendency towards multilateralism. On the Congress of Vienna itself, a recent good account comes from Adam Zamoyski (2008).

The political cooperative response to the French Revolution by what came to be known as the Powers – Britain, Russia, Austria and Prussia – was the informal 'Concert of Europe' established at the Congress of Vienna in 1815. This created a mechanism where the Powers would meet as necessary to counter any threat to the peace, an early form of what would be called 'collective security'. But this was not a coalition of ideas so much as a coalition of interests; more of a consolidation of an existing balance of power. Alfred Zimmern summed it up as 'the medicine of Europe, not its daily bread' (Zimmern, in Taylor and Groom, 1988: 12). All the Powers were agreed that they needed, as it was stated at Vienna, to 'uphold the public order in Europe', but did not agree on exactly how they wanted that order to be (Hinsley, 1967: 194–197). As Andreas Osiander has put it (of the 1648 Treaties of Westphalia), '[t]he conviction prevailed among the peacemakers that, provided the rights of each of the participating actors could be established definitively, so source of conflict would remain' (1994: 48). On that occasion the 'rights' were said to be those of sovereignty itself and of sovereigns to determine the religion of their subjects.

As after Westphalia, the conferences that took place after Vienna rapidly revealed the cracks that could appear between the sovereign interests of the Powers. The Concert of Europe did not stop wars breaking out between them – most notably over the future of the Ottoman Empire, which led to hostilities between Britain (with France) against Russia in the Crimea (Troubetzkoy, 2006: Figes, 2010), but also over the future of Italy, where Austria and France engaged in substantial combat in the 1860s. There were conferences that did resolve major problems, notably the one at Berlin in 1878 that purported to settle differences in the Balkans (Medlicott, 1963), though this did not stop a series of wars breaking out before 1914 in the same region (Carnegie Endowment for International Peace, 1914/1993; also see below). Another Congress in Berlin in 1884 started what has been termed the 'Scramble for Africa' (see Chapter 5, 'Empires') by setting out ground rules for who could take what in the 'Dark Continent'. The locals were not consulted, of course. It was not to outlive the developments during this period of the alliances between Austria, Italy and Germany (The 'Triple Alliance') and the 'triple Entente' between Britain, France and Russia (Langhorne, 1981).

Some other relatively rare examples of inter-state cooperation in areas of global interests occurred (and which became more commonplace in the twentieth century), such as the Rush/Bagot Agreement of 1817, which led to the reduction of naval forces on the Great Lakes in North America after the Anglo-American War of 1812. The first proposal to limit national armaments was actually by Austrian Chancellor Von Kaunitz (to Frederick the Great of Prussia) after the Seven Years' War, a proposal that was not taken up (Wright, 1921: 9). 'Declarations of Neutrality' were also interesting harbingers of disarmament and other agreements – for example, the declaration of the neutrality of the Canadian–USA border in 1839, and the neutralization of the Straits of Magellan in 1881, the Suez and Panama canals in 1888 and 1901 and (a first between states) Norway and Sweden in 1912 (confirmed formally in 1914 – Scott, 1989: 468). For neutrality and 'neutralism', see also Lyon (1963), Karsh (1988) and Malmborg (2003).

Other examples of international cooperation were in the setting up of 'functional' organizations'. The link between these developments and the wider phenomenon of industrialization is again well developed by Craig Murphy (1994). The Universal Postal Union was founded in 1874, and the International Telecommunication Union in 1865 (Codding, 1952; Taylor and Groom, 1988: chapter 10) helped to facilitate the passage of information any mail, telegraph and then telephone, but they did not necessarily reduce international tensions. The International Committee of the Red Cross (1864) was set up to help wounded soldiers on the battlefields of the war between France, Austria-Hungary and Italy over Italian reunification in the 1860s (Moorehead, 1999). More substantial organizations and initiatives had to wait until 1899, and again war was the impetus.

## THINKING ABOUT IO: 1900–1914

The most important period the 'prehistory' of the modern IO, which we take to begin with League of Nations (LON), was therefore during the years between the Boer War (1899–1901) and the outbreak of World War I in 1914. This saw the development of 'think-tanks', of which the most important in Britain was the 'Round Table' Group (founded 1909) and the Carnegie Endowment for International

Peace (founded 1910). At the state level, the period saw two major conferences at the Hague (1899 and 1907) – to discuss measures for bilateral and multilateral disarmament and the establishment of a crude system of bilateral treaties to try to establish conflict resolution procedures through arbitration in the case of possible outbreaks of hostilities. This Permanent Court of Arbitration was set up in 1903. The Hague agreements are important for setting a new benchmark, not only for the attempted limitation of arms and the peaceful settlement of international disputes, but also because they mark an important awakening of public opinion (especially in the United States, where the conferences gave a major boost to the American Peace Society, which had been set up by Quakers in 1828). They most emphatically did not lead to their primary goal, the limitation of armaments, though exploding ('dum-dum') bullets were not used in World War I. As scholars like David Stevenson (1996) and Martin Van Creveld (2011) make clear, these pious declarations banning new weapon systems, particularly in the air, were the precursors to yet more developments in air power.

The period also saw the publication of a number of important tracts which attracted considerable public attention, of which Norman Angell's *The Great Illusion* (1910) is probably the best example (Miller, 1986; Ashworth, 1999; Ceadel, 2009), but also the significant writings of liberal and left-wing thinkers such as Henry Noel Brailsford and James Bryce. These writings found their echo among continental European thinkers and policymakers, of whom the most important is probably Léon Bourgeois (1851–1925), who was a prominent official at both Hague conferences and also played a key role in the elaboration in France of plans for a *Société des Nations*, which had some impact on the final LON (Bourgeois, 1910; also see below). His precursory ideas on 'Solidarity' can be seen as an important impetus for continental thinking about ideas for a League (Bourgeois, 1896).

The Round Table group, founded in 1909, emerged from a much wider reflection among the intelligentsia and policymakers of the British Empire (then the hegemonic Power on the world stage). Attempts to understand the dominant British philosophical liberalism of the early part of the twentieth century can only be understood in the context of the imperial era (q.v.). As Duncan Bell has pointed out, most late Victorian Englishmen were fervent believers in 'progress', and many 'supported the utilization of political violence in the struggle for national liberation.' They were almost to a man great supporters of Kantian and other ideas of federation, often (as with the Round Table group) through a 'federal Greater Britain and a re-union with America'. They saw the Empire as 'civilising and having within it a moral obligation to support [for example] the Indian people in the quest for progress ... The British, that is, were to act as the midwives of Indian modernity.' As Bell goes on to say, '[o]nce again, [there was a] heavily moralized concern with what we might now call "nation-building"' (Bell, 2001: 559–580; 2007). These themes were translated into British thinking about ideal future world orders, which had many of the supposed features of the British Empire, including progressive moves towards a federally organized Empire, with states that were linked by ties of language, culture and history. Cambridge historian J. R. Seeley argued in the last 1890s for a 'world state', of which he believed a 'Greater Britain' could be one element, 'composed of men who are in some sense homogeneous, and not only … in blood and descent, but also in ideas or views of the universe' (Seeley, in Bell, 2007: 109). He argued elsewhere in favour of other groupings, including a 'United States of Europe', though he thought that might well founder on the problem of incompatibility of race (Bell, 2007: 110).

In the USA before 1914, a number of famous successful entrepreneurs funded thinktanks. The most famous of these is that associated with the largesse of Scots steel magnate Andrew Carnegie, and its influential Presidents (former Secretary of State) Elihu Root from 1910 to 1925 and Nicholas Murray Butler, 1925 to 1945. The main aims of the Carnegie Endowment, then and now, were opposition to war and the encouragement of better IO. A 1914 study of the Balkan wars of the period reads with a certain freshness even today. It was republished in its entirety, with an introduction by George Kennan, in 1993. The then President of the Carnegie Endowment, Morton Abramovitz, wrote in the Preface: 'Yet again a conflict in the Balkans torments Europe and the conscience of the international community, and when our willingness to act has not matched our capacity for moral outrage' (Carnegie Endowment for International Peace, 1914/1993). In 1914, the then Director of the Carnegie Endowment, Butler, had written:

> If the minds of men can be turned for even a short time away from passion, from race antagonism and from national aggrandizement to a contemplation of the individual and national losses due to war and to the shocking horrors which modern warfare entails, a step and by no means a short one, will have been taken toward the substitution of justice for force in the settlement of disputes.
>
> (Butler, in Carnegie Endowment, 1914/1993: preface)

Another way of putting it is that, in order to have a 'positive peace', there has to be created 'a social and political ordering of society that is generally accepted as just'. So, whatever this may be seen as being (and there are many different definitions of 'just'), it is 'certainly a far more complex affair than war' (Howard, 2000: 2).

Such ideas, therefore, were already well in the air by 1900, and others took them up. J. A. Hobson saw the potential – for good as well as ill – of Seeley's ideas in his classic *Imperialism* (1902/2005). Beyond Seeley-esque unions of 'States … closely related by ties of common blood, language, and institution', he could foresee 'the best hope of permanent peace on an assured basis of inter-imperialism' (Hobson, 1902/2005, in Bell, 2007: preface). The Round Table group was inspired by, and largely merged from, Viscount Milner's Kindergarten, the body of young men that Milner recruited from Oxford University to oversee the development of South Africa after the Boer War tried to put flesh on such bones. John Buchan (author, among many other works, of *The Thirty-Nine Steps*) referred to the 'brilliant minds of the Round Table' in 1906 (May, 1995: 2). The *Round Table* journal was the most important-sounding board for British imperial and federal thinking until the 1950s. Lloyd George described it in 1921 as 'a very powerful combination – in its way perhaps the most powerful in the country' (May, 1995: 11). Prominent figures like Lionel Curtis and Philip Kerr (later Lord Lothian) had ready access to imperial government circles across the globe. This group was also important as a vector for a much wider network, including figures like Lord Robert Cecil (later the major British advocate of the LON), J. C. Smuts (South African Premier and main architect of the LON's mandate policy), Alfred Zimmern (probably the most important single interwar liberal thinker and LON advocate), as well as key imperial advocates like Leo Amery (Colonial Secretary, 1924–1929 and Secretary of State for India, 1940–1945).

The main product of such thinking was what we have come to call 'liberal internationalism', though by no means all of its adherents were members of a liberal *party*, like Amery. While not by any means a purely British phenomenon, until the 1930s British thinkers were its predominant contributors. Before World War I, another important precursor of LI was transmitted through the presence of James Bryce as British Ambassador to the United States between 1907 and 1913. He was very close to Republican President William Howard Taft (term of office 1909–1913), and had some influence on President Woodrow Wilson (terms of office, 1913–1921), who like Bryce was a prominent constitutional lawyer. In Bryce's thinking there are, yet again, elements of wider British imperial thought, and he wrote one of his most famous books as Professor of Civil Law at Oxford, *The Holy Roman Empire* (Bryce, 1864), which was greatly admired by Queen Victoria herself (Sylvest, 2009b: 154). The stress that he also put on the need for Anglo-American cooperation was another important pointer towards the future evolution of IO. This emphasis was also shared by the Round Tablers, and especially Kerr, who played a distinctive personal role during World War I as a go-between with Washington and (as Lord Lothian) was instrumental in getting Churchill and Roosevelt to cooperate. In both cases, this led to enhanced Anglo-American discussions about the LON and the UN.

## BOX 6.1 LIBERAL INTERNATIONALISM (LI)

LI has been defined as 'an ideology aimed at grafting progress, order and justice on to international politics, often through explicit analogy to domestic political practice and experience, in order to make possible full realization of liberal values, including freedom, individual and national improvement, and good government based on the rule of law.' In that LI was a project aimed at an ever-increasing cooperation between states, not their extinction, 'underwritten by expectations of intellectual, moral and/or political progress' (Sylvest, 2009b: 49), it was markedly present in both the British and American elites before and during World War I, and beyond (Parmar, 2004) making it the most important driving theme among the Western Powers for IO and other forms of international social engineering on vast and hitherto unheard of scale. Believers in LI think that the economic and social sources of war are paramount and require international cooperation to resolve. Others would have thought that Great Power manoeuvrings were more to blame.

The problem that confronted that, and subsequent generations, was how to go about operationalizing these opposite sets of insights.

Again, the impetus was war – this time, World War I.

# THE DESIGN OF THE LEAGUE OF NATIONS

## The apotheosis of public opinion?

World War I provided an important platform on which to discuss such matters in a live experiment, and the turmoil at the various fronts was matched by a frenzy of speculation about how to make this the 'war to end all wars'. A large number of thinktanks also sprang up at this period, some that lasted well beyond the end of the League itself, like the League of Nations Union (LONU) (Birn, 1981). The LONU was not against the war per se and garnered support across the political spectrum in Britain. Other groups that supported the idea of a League of Nations, like the Union of Democratic Control (UDC), believed that a league could actually replace the existing system of diplomacy with 'open' diplomacy, an idea that Wilson consecrated in the first of his Fourteen Points of 1918 as 'open covenants openly arrived at', and the last of them, number 14, as: 'A general association of nations must be formed under specific covenants for the purpose of affording mutual guarantees of political independence and territorial integrity to great and small states alike.' This idea, more generally referred to as 'collective security', is usually described as a 'one for all, all for one' idea, and has of course seen its apotheosis in the United Nations (Northedge, 1986).

But Wilson, though long on ideas, was by general consent not too good on implementation. His main biographer, Arthur S. Link, says he was a 'visionary, unrealistic, provincial and ignorant of European problems' (Link, 1971: 128). He has been thus lauded as understanding the nineteenth-century idea that the Balance of Power system was one of the key factors in constantly plunging Europe into war and wanting to see 'a community of power, not organized rivalries, but an organized peace' (as he put it in his 'Peace Without Victory' speech of January 1917), but allowing himself to be manipulated by devious British and French politicians into devising a League of Nations (LON) that suited these imperial powers much more than the cause of IO (Harper, 1996: 30).

## Historical sources on the League

Writings on the LON fall into a number of important categories. First there are biographies and autobiographies of some of the major players in the League. Probably the best of these are by the main British architect of the League, Robert Cecil (1941, 1949; Johnson, 2011), though there is no life story of its longest-lasting secretary-general, Sir Eric Drummond, but a very long one by his deputy, F. P. Walters (1952). There are also major autobiographies and biographies of some of the main players at the Versailles Peace Conference, such as Lloyd George (1932, 1938), Clemenceau (of which the best are Watson, 1974, 2008; Winock, 2007) and, of course, Wilson himself (Link, 1972; Knock, 1992). This has been helped greatly by a new series on all the major heads of delegation – Wilson (Morton, 2008), Clemenceau (Watson, 2008) and Lloyd George (Sharp, 2008a). Second, there is a fair amount published on the writing of the Covenant of the League, of which the most complete is that by David Hunter Miller (1928), and also Zimmern (1936). Recent surveys include books by Fred Northedge (1986), Ruth Henig (1973), Gary Ostrower (1996) and the work of Lorna Lloyd (in Armstrong, Lloyd and Redmond, 1996/2004). But, third – and maybe most important for the student of IR – there are the descriptive and theoretical musings of key thinkers of the time (Long and Wilson, 1995).

One stark contrast that emerges from reading the contemporary account is of course the split that emerges as a result of the Wall Street Crash of 1929 and the rise of Hitler in Germany in 1933, in many ways respectively sounding the economic and political death knell of the League. Before 1930, although Gilbert Murray, in a survey of the League, could talk (in 1928) about the *Ordeal of this Generation*, he still ends the book by saying that 'by acting on the principles of ... civilization we must inevitably move towards the abolition of war among the nations who share in it'. In another book of the same year, with a preface by James T. Shotwell of the Carnegie Endowment, John Spencer Bassett could say that 'it seems we are justified in thinking that the power of the League is slowly growing stronger' (Bassett, 1928: 377). The 1924 'Geneva Protocol' – in which the American activist David Miller, as well as Shotwell and Butler, played a prominent part along with Robert Cecil and British Labour Party IR specialist and academic Philip Noel-Baker – was an attempt to give the League more teeth in any coming conflict (Noel-Baker, 1925; Miller, 1925). This highlighted the fact that the United States might not be part of the League, a factor often cited in its demise, but that Americans nonetheless played a very important role. In 1928, the Kellogg–Briand Pact to abolish war as means of inter-state activity (officially the 'General Treaty for the Renunciation of War' or the 'Pact of Paris') was negotiated outside the League, but accepted by the League Council, and peace activists claimed they had the key to the end of violent conflict (Ferrell, 1952).

There was huge hope invested in the League idea, which could not help but exalt, but also disappoint, those who were in contact with it, a sense of elevated unreality even in the 1920s – Henry Morgenthau, later Franklin D. Roosevelt's Treasury Secretary, wrote that it was like 'going to Athens' (Morgenthau, 1929). The LON was most emphatically *not* a total failure. It did prevent a number of major conflicts from escalating into war in the 1920s, notably in the Aland Islands (between Sweden and Finland) and in the Balkans, the proximate source of World War I (Barros, 1970). The economic and social activities of the LON were by far its most successful activities, leading to a raft of legislation in the International Labour Organization and followed up in the United Nations by the Economic and Social Council (ECOSOC) (Lloyd, 1997). But by 1933, with the clouds of war gathering, Max Beer was talking at length about the *League on Trial*, though the book was written in 1932 (Beer, 1933). By 1936, even one of its great believers, Alfred Zimmern, was wondering whether the international rule of law that (for him) the League represented should talk about 'using the past or the present tense', although he did try and 'err on the side of optimism' (Zimmern, 1936: vii–viii).

## Disarmament

In line with the long-established thinking of both peace movements and the institutions that had resulted from The Hague agreements, disarmament figured prominently among Woodrow Wilson's Fourteen Points and has to be seen as a touchstone of the LON's long-term impact. The main institutional result was the Preliminary Conference of 1927 and its successor, the Disarmament Conference of 1932–1933, in which the United States played a full part as well as the Soviet Union (although neither were members of the LON at that point, and the United States never was). The best sources for the origins of this are to be found in Philip Noel-Baker's *Disarmament* (1926/1972) and Salvador de Madariaga's identically titled work of 1929. De Madariaga, Director of Disarmament at the LON between 1924 and 1928, wrote in the interwar period that 'the world has reached such a degree of interdependence … that international cooperation has become essential … the only self-supporting region of the world is the whole world … Only one opinion and only one market cover the face of the earth' (1929: 6). Armaments were therefore an economic absurdity; war, a tragic net cost to humanity and only of benefit to arms manufacturers.

The problem was that there were major 'spoilers' at work in the conferences. The Soviet Union, a member of this conference even though it only formally joined the League in 1934, professed to believe in total disarmament, proposing the first 'zero options' in such talks (Williams, 1989; Kitching, 1999), but only to stymie the seriousness of the talks. The United States would only deal with the issue bilaterally – especially in a series of naval arms talks, most notably in Washington in 1922. Germany pulled out of the talks in 1933, sounding their effective death knell. (The best documentary review of these actions can be found in Henig, 1973: chapter 3.)

## Was the League of Nations a 'failure'?

The bibliography that is most often quoted on the LON is a long litany of failure. Many writers on the League took their cue from the revulsion felt by many on the Left and Centre about the League's inability to deal with the Far Eastern crisis, with the *Geneva Racket* (Dell, 1937) vying with later titles like *Broken Star* (Joyce, 1978). It must be said that it was often also linked to mainly postwar, post-facto revulsion about the 'appeasement' of Nazi Germany by the democracies, and especially Britain and France's sellout at Munich in 1938 to a hubristic Adolf Hitler. We need to try and separate out myth and reality in this literature. What, for example, could the League have done in concrete terms to stop the Japanese invading Manchuria in 1932? The Lytton Enquiry, set up to investigate the invasion, was actually very critical of the Japanese government. Equally, how could the

League have stopped Germany reoccupying the Rhineland in 1935? Or stopped the Munich Agreement? There has been a revision of these harsh views in recent years, notably in the work of Lorna Lloyd and A. P. Dunbabin in the UK, and Gary Ostrower in the United States (Dunbabin, 1993; Lloyd, 1997; Ostrower, 1996). There has also been a wider appreciation of the impact of the League on Europe itself (Sarolea, 2009) and outside Europe, notably in the Far East (Thorne, 1973; Burkman, 2008), Africa (Callahan, 2004) and even Thailand (Hell, 2010).

But this cannot avoid the observation that the key problem for the League was that of the major Allies of 1919. The United States did not join the LON at all (though it had its major American defenders: see Kuehl and Dunn, 1997), and Britain and France were at loggerheads over it much of the time. Equally, although writers like Egerton (1974, 1978) and Williams (1998) have stressed the pivotal role of Britain and the United States in setting up the League, other historians, such as Brian McKercher (1990), have pointed to the fraught relations between the United States and Britain, particularly in the 1920s, over a series of issues, many of which had to do with the debt and reparations issues resulting from the Versailles Treaty (Williams, 2006). Much of what really counted in international diplomacy between the two world wars was achieved outside the auspices of the League, for instance, the Locarno Pacts of 1925.

In the League's favour, the Bruce Report of 1939 pointed out that the social and economic (or functional) agencies of the LON worked well and took up a large proportion of the budget. The International Labour Organization (ILO) passed a plethora of work-related international legislation that is still considered vital for workers' rights (Foggon, 1988). As we have seen, the tripartite structure of the ILO was seen as a neo-functionalist model of its kind by Ernst Haas in the 1950s. The League also passed legislation and implemented some very significant measures against sex trafficking and drug abuse. It continued the discussions at ambassadorial level that had given the Concert of Europe some real influence in the 'Conference of Ambassadors', a far more 'realist' body than Carr (for one) would have acknowledged (Pink, 1942).

The assault on what E. H. Carr has called the 'utopian' vision, presented both by supporters of the LON and British and American liberals like Zimmern, is worthy of a book in itself. The 'idealist–realist' or 'First Great' debate unleashed by Carr with his famous book *The Twenty Years' Crisis* (1939) has produced its own cottage industry (Long and Wilson, 1995, again, is the best summary). The debate hinges around whether the interwar liberals were indeed foolhardy 'utopians', as asserted by Carr, or whether they rather engaged in a search for new ways of understanding international politics with perfect cognizance of the imperfections of human constructions like the LON and a keen understanding of the problems of practical international political action. Carr was inspired by Karl Mannheim and Reinhold Niebuhr into thinking that, to be very summary, the interwar liberals had allowed themselves to be carried away by the belief that the LON and its instruments could actually change mankind, whereas in fact their ideas were 'historically conditioned, being both products of circumstances and interests and weapons framed for the furtherance of interests' (Carr, 1939/1947: 68).

In short he asserted they were representing their interests as being those of the rest of humanity, which they were not, and that they were rather apologists for an untenable status quo. Hence Carr was an apologist for those who wished to revise the Treaty of Versailles, an 'appeaser' of Germany and Adolf Hitler, as well as a great admirer of Bolshevik Russia (Carr, 1952–1979: all of the 'Bolshevik Revolution' series; Haslam, 1999).

Carr was not against the idea of IO as such; rather the idea that any economic, political or security 'harmony of interests' could be successful without taking into full consideration the workings of power. Carr's emphasis on what Charles Jones calls 'the rationalization by those in power ... of their privileged positions' (Jones, 1998: 236) has a clear echo in today's debates about the 'self-evident' benefits of the free market. But if IO can be made to represent and reflect both power and contrasting interests, then Carr was not against this per se. This is crucially laid out in chapter 14 of the *Twenty Years' Crisis*, which many IR academics do not seem to have reached in their reading of the book. As a career diplomat in the Foreign Office (1916–1936), and then as a journalist and academic, Carr disliked what he saw as 'utopian' theorizing that ignored the dictates of the real world. Hence his 'realism' was tempered in ways that many subsequent IR theorists did not notice. He was not entirely wrong either, as a reading of Gilbert Murray's rather maudlin peroration, *From the League to the UN,* rapidly makes clear (Murray, 1948). There was wishful thinking among prewar liberals of Carr's acquaintance.

A new wave of scholars can be said to have understood this paradox and begun re-examining the underpinnings in Carr's work (Cox, 2000; Jones 1998, Haslam, 1999), and this has had a knock-on effect on thinking about the 'failure' of the interwar thinkers to grasp the nettle of power. Some recent scholarship in IR, especially by Wilson and Long and Lucian Ashworth, has taken the view that in fact *none* of the interwar theorists were 'idealists' in the way they were painted by advocates of the 'realist–idealist' distinctions of the 1980s. In short, the 'idealist–realist' debate was a 'myth' that led IR astray for far too many years, helping to drag down the LON in its wake (Schmidt, 1998a, 1998b; Ashworth, 2002, 2006). In turn, this impacted on revisionist thinking about the LON and its supporters, especially in Britain (for a discussion of this in the British Labour Party, see Ashworth, 2007). Carr was, it is safe to say, misunderstood at the time and for a long while afterwards. Here we can show a clear interpenetration of IR theory and the historiography of IO in a vital mutual effect that can now, indeed, be said to have relaunched serious study of international historical thought in IR as a whole.

## THE CREATION OF THE UNITED NATIONS

The creation of the United Nations (UN) has been described in glowing terms as a dream come true: 'If it is true ... that a good way to find out about a people is to study its dreams, then the citizens of all the Great Powers can take a just pride in the very idea of a United Nations ... a dream of ending, once and for all, mankind's curse of war ... They [the Powers] called for the prevention of war, when necessary, through the enforcement of peace' (Hildebrand, 1990: ix). However, an excellent history of the Security Council, the part of the UN system that most differentiated it from the LON, describes that body as resembling *Fifteen Men on a Powder Keg* (Boyd, 1971). No sooner had the UN been set up than it was submerged beneath the realities of the Cold War (q.v.). This section of the chapter therefore looks at some of the key works on the process of the UN's creation and then at one particular area that showed up both the positive and negative sides of that creation and development – that of human rights.

Former Secretary of State Dean Acheson referred to his time at the centre of power in the United States as being *Present at the Creation* (Acheson, 1969). It was largely the vision of President Franklin Delano Roosevelt (predecessor to Acheson's President Truman) – who conceived a 'realistic Wilsonian' alternative to the LON, one that had 'teeth' in the form of a Council whose resolutions were binding over the entire UN – to replace the toothless League Council, whose declarations were purely advisory. The story of Roosevelt's vision has been told in many places, by his biographers (Dallek, 1979; Schlesinger, 1957–1960) as well as by historians, who see him as part of a pattern of American 'visions' of world order (Harper, 1996) or as a president with a personal crusade (e.g. Hoopes and Brinkley, 1997). The exact nature of this vision has been the subject of several forensic analyses, both by participants in the process, such as Assistant Secretary of State Adolf Berle (1961), State Department officials (the most thorough is Notter, 1949), the President himself (Roosevelt, 1950) and by historians (Williams, 1998; Ikenberry, 2001; Mazower, 2009b).

All agree that the UN was seen at the time of the Dumbarton Oaks and San Francisco conferences of 1944 and 1945 as one of the cornerstones of American power. The organization of both of these conferences was a largely American affair, held on American soil and with an American aim, a new form of League that would bring in all the major Powers under one roof. But the groundwork for this endeavour was a long and drawn-out process of Great Power diplomacy and postwar planning in a number of capitals, notably London and Moscow, as well as Washington. The 'summit diplomacy' that began with the signature of the Atlantic Charter in August of 1941 continued through the rest of the war, culminating with meetings between the 'Big Three' (the USA, USSR and Britain) at Quebec, Moscow, Tehran (all 1943) and Yalta (1945), or the 'Big Four' at Potsdam (1945). This led to horse trading about the design of the postwar world which largely led to Britain agreeing to pass the baton of global power to the United States (Reynolds 1981, 1991) and the USSR being given land rights over much of Eastern Europe, in return for their cooperation in the new world body (Hoopes and Brinkley, 1997).

Unfortunately for the vision of Roosevelt and the drafters of the Charter, the UN's promise was not fulfilled in many ways until the end of the Cold War. The two major differences between the LON's Covenant and the Charter of the UN were twofold. Herbert Nicholas commented that 'San Francisco differed from Versailles in its genuine respect for "open covenants openly arrived at"' (Nicholas, 1967: 8). There was genuine discussion at the conference about the options for peace, though it must be said that the final peace treaty was never signed, and the world had to be content with the summit diplomacy outlined above, where the

Powers carved up the world between them. The second major change was the establishment of the Security Council, with its veto power for the 'Big Five' (Britain, China, France, the USA and the USSR), which was intended to make those Powers act responsibly in the collective interest but also to give the UN real 'teeth' through 'Chapter VI and VII' binding sanctions and military action if necessary. The problem was that the paralysis of the Security Council until 1990 made many believe, with George Kennan, that the UN was a 'vainglorious and pretentious assertion of purpose … [that failed to address] … the real substance of international affairs' (Kennan, 1968/1972: 171–173). To be sure the UN has also generated a huge number of 'functional' organizations, especially in the powerful 'Bretton Woods' grouping (set up at the eponymous meeting of 1944) of the World Bank, International Monetary Fund and what is now (post-1995) the World Trade Organization. But is that enough to prove the UN can protect or even affect the world? The numerous efforts at reform of the system do not seem to have made much impact (Taylor, 1993), though maybe it would also be true to say that the UN mirrors the system in which it exists as a nominal sounding board and symbol for an aspiration to fairness and order.

## Human rights – the apotheosis of the individual in IO?

If there is any historical development that we can trace through the twentieth century and until now, it might be said to be the move from the sovereignty of the 'state' to that of the 'individual'. IOs have been the major vector of this change of emphasis, while also showing up the limitations of such aspirational politics. The nineteenth century left the legacy of seeing 'freedom' as being linked to the idea of the 'nation', so when Woodrow Wilson talked of 'self-determination' he linked the idea that a people having their own state would necessarily lead to democracy and the rule of law being extended to all citizens. He believed this to be the case in the United States, though it clearly was not entirely so, as generations of Soviet diplomats pointed out in the UN the repression of African Americans' most basic rights for most of the period since 1776 (Sellars, 2002). The role of the USA in pushing the human rights agenda in the UN has nonetheless been of paramount importance, with a particular personal link to President Roosevelt's first lady, Eleanor, when she pursued that goal in a very impressive manner after his death. The Universal Declaration of Human Rights was in many ways her personal triumph, though its contents have been discussed and variously attacked or lauded ever since its signature in 1948 (Borgwardt, 2005).

## BOX 6.2 HUMAN RIGHTS AND THE UNITED NATIONS

The link between the individual and the state as guarantor of rights is explicitly made in the Charter of the United Nations: 'The right of self-determination … is an essential condition for the effective guarantee and observance of individual human rights.' It is seen essentially as preceding and guaranteeing all other rights. James Mayall has written that in international law, even by 1990, 'sovereignty is now said to reside with the people, as an act of self-determination based on the will of the majority' (Mayall, 1990: 26–28). By the end of the Cold War the IOs were still living out the fiction that individuals would always have their rights guaranteed by the states they lived in. The central problematic today is that human rights are presumed by charter to be underpinned by states whereas in practice states are often the worst abusers of those same rights (Forsythe, 2006). The UN came to play a significant role in the internal affairs of states through election monitoring and even setting up the system of government itself in many countries, well before the end of the Cold War (Bailey, 1994).

But in 1945 the Charter of the United Nations, signed at San Francisco, did for the first time in an international treaty document clearly encourage and 'reaffirm faith in human rights…, it guaranteed fundamental freedoms for all without distinction as to race, sex, language or religion' (Article 13), and in Article 55 it gave the UN the task of promoting these rights and freedoms. The problem was that it gave very scant machinery, and until the establishment of the High Commissioner for Human Rights in the 1990s (Ramcharan, 2002) the 'Human Rights Commission', later upgraded to a 'Centre' in 1981, was largely unknown and ineffectual, sandwiched as it was between the individual-centred Western view of human rights and the social and economic focus of the (then) East Bloc (Luard, 1982; Forsythe, 1985; Williams, 1988). This division was even cemented in 1966, in the Covenants on civil and political rights on one side and those for economic, social and cultural rights on the other (for a contemporary analysis, see Robertson, 1972).

## From collective security to humanitarian intervention

One of the key debates in IR since 1990 has centred on the idea and practice of the 'liberal peace', especially through the use of what has come to be known as 'humanitarian intervention' (HI). This has now arrived at the point where the General Assembly has accepted the findings of a thinktank, the International Commission on Intervention and State Sovereignty, and adopted the principle that there is a 'Responsibility to Protect' peoples within states where their own governments are deemed to be repressing their human rights (for detailed studies of this, see Wheeler, 2002; Bellamy, 2009). Insofar as this applies to the study of IO, it is worth reflecting how historians might be said to have looked at this development. Historians of the progress (or not) of human rights have tended to stress the state-centric, even power, orientation of their origins in institutional form after

1945. The current debate on HI is divided between anti- and pro-intervention camps and the different groups within these camps. Though there is no space to develop these complex themes here, one widely held view is that the UN has become a complicit actor in a form of Great Power intervention, even when that intervention may be said to be 'morally sound'. Michael Ignatieff, in his *Empire Lite*, summed this up when he wrote, 'The ostensible rule that sustains these nation-building projects may be humanitarian, but the real principle is imperial: the maintenance of order over barbarian threat' (2004: 22).

The roots of HI do indeed lie in two vital historical traditions, the first of which is liberal imperialism, as outlined above in our discussion of the nineteenth century – the idea of Rudyard Kipling's 'taking up the white man's burden' or the *mission civilisatrice*. The second tradition springs from the same roots in the nineteenth century and carries the other impetus behind IO: that of creating order and, hopefully, justice through the selective use of collective security or other forms of organized force against those who would disturb international order. The crucial period for the first testing of this dual impetus again is that of the period between about 1918 and 1945. Throughout this period, and indeed beyond it, the whole system of IO and postwar planning was geared to developing institutional order-creating and -maintaining institutions, the most important of which was that centred on the Security Council of the UN. We can see this impetus in the 'reconstruction' attempts of the LON (Williams, 2006) and, more importantly, in the work of the first proper UN organization, UNRRA, set up officially in 1944. The roots of UNRRA were in the State Department, organized by Roosevelt's close confidant Herbert Lehman, and closely modelled on New Deal ideas and practices (Williams, 2006: chapter 4).

As we have seen, the Security Council was supposed to act as the 'Four [or Five] Policemen' to stop threats to order. But when that same council was frozen into inability to act by the Cold War, the order-building machinery was itself frozen. The only possible compromise was 'peacekeeping', a compromise between collective security and 'fire-fighting' developed by the Secretary General Dag Hammarskjold in the 1950s (Diehl, 1994 is a good introduction, but see also James, 1990). As shown by its first test (in the Suez Crisis of 1956), peacekeeping relied on the consent of all forces in a given battle zone; the UN was not supposed to be 'making' peace and was not given the resources or the mandate to do so (Aulén, 1969; Sheldon, 1987; Rikhye, 1984).

With the end of the Cold War, and the consequent ending of the routine use of the veto on the Security Council by the USSR and/or the USA, a more robust form of collective security was again possible. The concrete evidence of this came in 1991 with the first really universal Collective Security mission to expel Iraqi forces from Kuwait, which had been occupied in August 1990. This operation saw units from over a hundred countries and no vetoes being used in the Security Council for the first time since Korea in 1950 – itself an aberration, as the USSR had absented itself in protest against other US actions. The success of 'Desert Storm' in Kuwait both encouraged non-Security Council Permanent Five states that the rule of international law would not be upheld by force if necessary, and also alarmed many of them when it became apparent that the success of 1991 might well lead to intervention being used to uphold one or more Powers' wishes for non-security reasons, especially the abuse of human rights, as defined by the West (Taylor and Groom, 2000).

## BOX 6.3 HUMANITARIAN INTERVENTION (HI) AND THE UNITED NATIONS

HI has become synonymous with a liberal desire to 'cure' the world of human rights abuses, as was seen in Kosovo in 1999, where no SC mandate was accorded for a NATO-led war against Serbia and, more importantly in Afghanistan and Iraq (2001 and 2003), where 'regime change' seemingly was the major justification for the invasions by (mainly) US troops, with no clear SC agreement, and arguably flagrant abuse of the UN Charter and its norm of non-intervention (Wheeler, 2002; Williams, 2006). It has also become clear that the kind of forces (usually not regular troops), the kinds of actions these troops undertake (usually of a savage and ill-disciplined kind, with no respect for the 'laws' of war) and the motivations of all sides have become much more suspect than was the case before 1990 make any form of UN intervention very difficult indeed (Kaldor, 1999; Shawcross, 2000). It is not just a question of 'good' UN against 'bad' insurgents; by becoming sucked into specific countries' humanitarian agendas, the UN has laid itself open to accusation that it is partial and thus a fair target for insurgents.

The 'HI agenda' gets its main support from politicians' thinktanks in the West that favour a muscled liberal response to human rights abuses, and especially in the USA and the UK, who are (ably helped mainly by Canada) engaged in a hard fight in Iraq and Afghanistan. The question that many commentators have asked is whether this is a new form of imperialism dressed up as HI. The links between the American 'neo-conservatives' and supporters of HI has been noted in both the UK and the USA (see notably – for the UK – the debate between Cooper, 2004 and Kampfner, 2004). In the USA writers like Noam Chomsky attack what they see as US patterns of imperial design, or the influence of Central European militant liberal philosophers like Leo Strauss (Norton, 2005). 'Neo-conservative' historians like Robert Kagan defend such actions as the defence of civilization itself (Kagan, 2006b, 2008), while other Americans, often on the Republican Right, attack such beliefs as hubristic and damaging to US national interest (Halper and Clarke, 2004, 2007).

## European Union

Attempts to understand the emergence of the European Union also reflect some of the trends in international history examined above. Mayne and Pinder, in their *Federal Union: The Pioneers* (1990), argued that it was the great (and small) thinkers that underpinned the elaboration of European ideas. This in turn was seen as having sowed the true foundations of European unity, a view that was echoed in collections such as that of Stirk (1989). Others, such as Milward, favoured a more state-centric approach. In his *Reconstruction of Western Europe, 1945–51*, Milward (1984) argued that the nation-state in Europe was 'saved' by the process of economic integration, and was in no way being 'eroded' by the process towards union. The process of European Union post-1945 was based on the self-interest of the European states and permitted their survival. Milward further argued that other explanations of European integration, such as Deutsch's 'community' theory (1953), have 'not been studied in any systematic way'. Hence, '[i]f historical research into the history of European integration is now to have its own proper agenda, including its own theoretical hypotheses', it should not reject earlier explanations, but neither, implicitly, should it totally embrace them. Prominent among the earlier theorists were the functionalists, who attributed European integration mainly to economic and technocratic pressures, and the 'idealists', who saw human agency at the centre of the process.

Some still look to a 'Great Power' explanation of European integration. Wallace (1997) argued that theorists of integration 'underplay the immense importance of the American presence in shaping the structure of post-war Western Europe', citing wartime planning, the Marshall Plan and the generalized dependence on the United States. 'Western Europe was "America's Europe"', he concluded. Perry Anderson takes Milward's and Wallace's case further, suggesting that the influence of Washington was crucial. Milward himself suggested that the 'unpropitious' origins of Europe were at least partly 'the offspring of American disillusionment with both the dangerous political disunity of the European continent and naive progressivist optimism'. In the last part of that sentence, Milward dismissed much of the thinking of the 1920s and 1930s, such as that of Coudenhove-Kalergi (1948, though *Pan-Europa* was first published in German in 1923), and also much of the political posturing on Europe of the interwar years captured, for example, in the Briand Plan of the early 1930s. Keohane (1984), a political scientist, stressed the need both for early leadership in creating any institutional framework and for maintaining that leadership. Lundestad (1998a) went further, arguing, 'The United States promoted the integration of Western Europe, rather strongly until the mid-1960s, [although] less strongly after that.' He went as far as to argue that the United States continued from 1945 to act as an 'imperial' power in Europe, purely out of self-interest; the United States 'did not pursue its pro-integrationist policy primarily for the sake of Western Europeans.' Its self-interest lay in avoiding the need to intervene, for a third time in this century, to 'prevent Europe from being dominated by a hostile power'. Lundestad also argued that integration was the cheapest option for the United States to protect its own security – cheapest in lives and in money. Lundestad left 'empire' in lower case and inverted commas, and pointed to many elements of 'predominance': 'Washington was able to organize NATO, control the larger part of crucial Germany, keep the Communists out of power, include the region in the American-organized system of freer trade, and gradually enhance the influence of American culture.' Although he immediately backtracked on his own term (i.e. 'empire'), he still approvingly quoted Maier, who wrote about the 'analog of empire', more Greek than Roman.

## CONCLUSION

As we have hopefully shown, the reality of IO and its aspirations to bring about world peace and harmony in many fields is now apparent in ways that were not so clear a mere hundred years ago. For, as Michael Howard has reminded us, quoting Sir Henry Maine: 'War appears to be as old as mankind, but peace is a modern invention' (2000: 1). The idea that we could 'end' war is redolent with paradox. Since 1928 and the Briand–Kellogg Pact, signed within the League of Nations (LON), war has been an 'illegal' way of resolving conflicts between states. This was reasserted in the Charter of the United Nations in 1945. Two world wars of indescribable destruction bracket these aspirational documents. Moreover, whenever we have tried to ban some aspect of war, such as with attempts at disarmament, we have ended up with more arms, better arms and more destructive wars. One very good example is the attempt to get rid of nuclear weapons. When limits were arrived at to limit the number of missiles in the Strategic Arms Limitation talks (SALT) of 1975, both the USA and the USSR resorted to putting multiple re-entry vehicles (MIRVs) on their previously single nuclear missile warheads. There are now weapons of a more conventional kind that can devastate an area as big as a whole football pitch, yet it is inconceivable that these could be used by most of the very states that hold such weapons of mass or lesser destruction. Those who are killing each other in large numbers these days tend to use high-tech versions of the bow and arrow, the kalashnikov rifle, the rocket-propelled grenade, or even weapons that make the bow and arrow look high-tech, like the machete in Rwanda in the massacres of 1994. Part of the legacy of the Treaty of Westphalia was a 'gentlemanly' settling of accounts on the battlefield and in the conference chamber. The aim of IO has been to put some flesh on these very basic normative bones.

Some vectors of IO influence and power have been there since at least the beginning of the twentieth century. Halper and Clarke point to the pivotal role of thinktanks in developing agendas that the USA, in particular, plays out in the corridors of power in the UN in New York (Halper and Clarke, 2007; see also Parmar, 2004). The accusation that the UN is the plaything of imperial interests, and indeed is based on and derives its force form such historical tradition of Empire, is hard to deny, be they British, American or other (Mazower, 2008, is a very good recent addition to this literature). Therefore, maybe the lesson of IO is that all power finds its way to direct itself into channels that are useful to the powerful. If the UN does not prove ultimately useful to the Powers of today, it may well go the same way as the LON. We must not be surprised if that proves to be the case. But if history has one lesson on IO, it is that the next generation of such bodies will be born out of a new, probably global, war.

# CHAPTER 7

# Identity

## Concept, category and organizing principle

There are few concepts that have as many historical derivations and contemporary definitions as identity. The purpose of this chapter is to familiarize international history and international relations (IHIR) audiences with these definitions and their origins. It does so by approaching identity in three ways. First, identity is understood as a *concept* that signifies both sameness and difference. Second, identity operates as an organizing *category* by which difference and similarity (usually in cultural and political terms) group people into social collectives. Third, identity functions as a *legitimating principle* that both motivates and justifies individual and group demands for a range of self-determination and recognition: political, economic, class, gender, ethnicity or religious-based, etc. Or, as Rogers Brubaker suggests, identities are 'at once categories of social and political practice and categories of social and political analysis' (Brubaker, 2004: 31).

Identity refers to the attributes or qualities by which an entity is recognized. What is difficult is that 'entities' – meaning actors, groups, people, states, nations – are themselves recognized in two ways, first by virtue of what makes them a group, principally by what they have in common between themselves that allows them to be identified as a group, and second, by what this group has that differentiates it from other groups, the unique attributes that are not shared by others. Identity is thus a paradoxical combination of an entity's unique qualities and qualities shared with other entities (including the very possession of an identity). Identity renders an actor at once both unlike and alike, to all other actors.

Identity is used by psychologists and social psychologists to refer to the form of self-representation used by an individual or group of individuals to refer to themselves (usually in relation to others); by historians as a force by which a group of people feel themselves bound together at the level of a city, region, nation or state, in social, cultural or political terms; by theorists of nationalism as the key driver in creating the modern European nation-state; and by political scientists and IR theorists as an endogenous dynamic that promotes group coherence, the subsequent definition of interests which may impact on state behaviour.

Notwithstanding this rather glorious disciplinary panoply of identity's myriad uses, what should remain clear is the difference between *the actor* to which identity is attributed (an individual, group or community); *the terms* in which an identity is attributed to this actor (its individuality, uniqueness, distinctiveness, commonality); *the types* of identity attributed to an actor (political, cultural, national, ethnic, civic, etc); and *process of constructing or embodying* an identity used in service of these types and terms undertaken by one or many in the service of individual or group goals (nationalism, patriotism, loyalty, partisanship, chauvinism, membership, etc.). Thus, while IHIR audiences may be most familiar with states and nations that seek to display their uniqueness in terms of collective identity as exhibited in forms of nationalism, there are dozens of other variants of actors, terms and types of identity processes. Taken in context, national identity has simply 're-invigorated the very possibility of collective identity in an age of nationalism' (Reicher and Hopkins, 2001: 4).

Both IH and IR use composites of all these types of identity, and the twenty-first century has brought forth a host of new forms of self-identification and challenges to such forms. It is therefore impossible to state categorically which type of identity is typically found within IH and IR, apart from a very broad political sense of self-definition. That sense of self is constituted by a host of different dynamics, each of which can readily be understood from a wide array of different disciplines. Sociology and psychology no longer possess an analytical monopoly on the facets and origins of identity; indeed, thorough historical enquiry and the categorizing strengths of IR theory may be better placed to adequately deconstruct both long-held tensions between state and national identities, and contemporary 'identity politics' including the most recent incarnation of non-Western and even anti-Western political identities emerging from the Muslim world.

The 'state vs nation' dichotomy is a particularly central spat found in both IH and IR, and requires some consideration by students and scholars alike. As will be seen below, only determined historical enquiry can help to identify the civic forces that result in state identities, cultural forces that result in national identities, and the broader forces that result in a nested series of other identities that generally characterize most contemporary groups. The 'input' of such state–nation linkages is generally the raw material of the history of a state that is drawn upon in establishing both state and nation, but in very different ways, and is thus all-important from the IH perspective. Equally, the 'output' of state–nation linkages is a clear determinant of state behaviour and thus a feature of the international structure and thus crucial from the IR perspective. These processes have similar features for all groups but manifest themselves in dramatically different ways, even across groups that appear largely alike in historical, political and even cultural composition.

Identity invites both the historian and the IR theorist to separate neatly civic from cultural, state from national, instrumental interests and ensuing international behaviour from domestic perceptions and cultural attitudes. But identity is rarely so simple. Virtually every facet of what constitutes an individual is reproduced writ large at the collective level and deployed at the international level; self-identification and the associated processes of defining oneself as a group and defending one's values and interests in the form of a definable political entity defies almost any logic apart from the apparent triad of identity–interests–policy (and not necessarily in that order). Equally, identity as a method of identifying with these same groups at the international level should not be dismissed as an IR afterthought; the 'international community' exists as a structural identity simply because the states and individuals that populate this community largely behave as if such a community exists. IHIR thus needs to retain the traditional bottom-up investigation of the self-referential role of key groups within states, and newer top-down examinations of identity building at the international level, constituted across states and between people.

## HISTORY AND IDENTITY

As a phenomenon of the early twenty-first century, it is important to study identity for a number of reasons. A number of major shifts in political affairs have raised the prominence and problems of identity as one of the most potent organizing principles of modern politics: the end of the Cold War, and the redefinition of Eastern bloc states and their societies and borders; the rapid development of European integration that has promoted new types of identity by constructing an economic and political union between twenty-seven states, and simultaneously reconfirmed ancient ones; and the shift from regional and inter-national economies to global ones.

At first glance, identity may not appear a key feature of international history or IR in the same sense as war or sovereignty. The latter are respectively key phases or attributes by which both states and the international system came into being. Likewise diplomatic history denotes the processes of state interaction, whilst international organizations represent a new trans-national actor to the taxonomy of the international structure. Identity cannot be charted with as precise a history as any of these subjects, because it denotes forms of self reference across a range of entities, both human and institutional. Identity is increasingly accepted as a convenient variable denoting qualities of groupness or allegiance that can be drawn upon by a number of disciplines, but many scholars in IH and IR still regard identity as of no specific interest in itself. Like nationalism, identity remains 'a convenient domain in which to study more general phenomena' (Reicher and Hopkins, 2001: 2).

However, from the perspective of both international history and international relations, this chapter argues that identity is arguably the most enduring and ubiquitous force of all; analyses that fail to take account of it are visibly diminished. As an organizing principle, identity applies enduringly to individuals, groups, states and even the system of states. As a category, identity classifies polities culturally and politically, economically and socially; it differentiates between the *content of the nation* and the *form of the state*, and between the internal body politic, the nature of its borders and the external quality of outsiders. Finally, as a concept, identity explains individual motivation, group choices and state behaviour. As an organizing principle, identity is therefore surprisingly flexible, serving multiple ends, and derived from multiple disciplines.

For international history, identity charts the rise of instrumental obligation and cultural allegiance that underwrite the growth of societies and states. For IR, identity reveals the principles by which cultural imperatives obtain politically, the constitution of collective interests and the use of policy to achieve those ends. For both streams of thought, therefore, identity is the organizing principle on which both a state's internal cohesion and the manner of its external relations is based. The explanatory power of identity lies in demonstrating how national societies, institutions and state unit are first and foremost bounded entities and, second, vehicles of both authority and allegiance; this effectively renders identity the social counterpart of sovereignty. Since the end of the Cold War, identity has been visibly deployed in the form of nationalism: 'the ideology through which people act to reproduce nation-states as nations' and political entities (Reicher and Hopkins, 2001: 3), witnessed by a surge of European nationalisms in nation-states from the Balkans to the Black Sea. Some of these nationalisms have produced large-scale violence that has brought about the creation of wholly new states from old entities, as with the creation of Kosovo. Other nationalisms have ratcheted up tensions that have flared into open but brief conflict (as with Georgia in 2008) or that linger quietly on the sidelines in 'cold conflicts' (as between Armenia and Azerbaijan, or Armenia and Turkey). For many others, identity remains a tacit, unacknowledged component of their lived realities, offering only periodic glimpses into wider structures of belonging. Which is all the more reason, therefore, to include identity in a text that can reasonably explore its historical and analytical offerings.

## IDENTITY FROM A HISTORICAL PERSPECTIVE

The prime requirement behind the construction and continuance of all groups is a sense of 'self'. Individual identity is the first unit; they grow into familial groups, which widen further into societal, communal groups. A collective identity is the first, most basic building block to societal construction, and social development, ranging from small communities to the largest unit of the nation-state. As the historian Tosh argues, 'social groupings need a *record* of prior experience, but they also require a *picture* of the past which services to explain or justify the present, often at the cost of historical accuracy' (Tosh, 2010: 3). These records and pictures contain both strategic and symbolic elements, which in turn constitute the collective identity of the contemporary state. The national society that inhabits the state identifies both with the state and (more visibly) with each other on the basis of a shared interpretation of key events and experiences, as detailed in Box 7.1.

## BOX 7.1 SHARED MODES OF NATIONAL EXPERIENCE

- Origins (primordial or constructed): America's First Nations and/versus Founding Fathers; the Persian Empire origins of Iran; Ottoman Empire origins of Armenia; the contested Macedonian origins of Greece and the Former Yugoslav Republic of Macedonia; the 1947 creation of Pakistan and (contemporary) Bangladesh from British India.
- Watershed moments symbolizing destruction and rebirth, e.g. 1519 conquest of Aztec empire by Hernán Cortés; the French Revolution of 1789; the dropping of atomic bombs on Hiroshima and Nagasaki, Japan in August 1945; the 1992 Canadian referendum on Quebec secession; the 1993 separation of the Czech and Slovak republics.
- Dealing with change, e.g. the end of colonial rule in Asia and Africa from the 1960s onwards; the collapse of Communism in Russia, eastern and central Europe and Caspian states from 1989 onwards; moderate views of the political challenges facing Israel during the First (1987–1993) and Second (2000–2005) Intifadas; the separation of church and state and widened electoral franchise in virtually every contemporary state.
- Confirmation of changelessness, e.g. Orthodox views of the religious origins of Israel during the First (1987–1993) and Second (2000–2005) Intifadas; political attitudes in North Korea during the Beijing Olympics of 2008, contemporary Russia, the persistence of poverty in the majority of sub-Saharan African states.

Taken together, origins, watershed moments and the challenges of dealing with change and rejecting change help to construct groups, and over time animate their interests in cultural and political forms. For historians, identity operates in two key ways. First, in a *long-term and passive method*, identity provides broad storylines of the national self, the national 'us', storylines which provide linear shape to the substance of national history, allowing it to have an effective beginning, a series of rises and falls and, in some cases, an end. Second, identity operates in a *short-term and dynamic method* via a series of snapshots: key moments in history that convey in abbreviated fashion the quintessence of the national identity.

The storyline operates by providing a long-term structure in which detailed narratives of national society is layered; it provides the foundation for national history as a repository of key national characteristics, which is used to educate younger generations and frequently to assimilate non-nationals. Snapshots provide populace and policymakers alike with 'off the shelf' templates in which the national identity has been drawn on in a given situation, national interests derived, and fundaments of public and foreign policy constituted and enacted. National history and national identity are in fact so overlapping that the history of a nation-state is effectively the storyline of the national 'self', permeated over time by challenges and successes. The state's composition, and the content of its policies, are largely products of past decisions, structures, trends, attitudes; so much so that breaking with them takes considerable effort, and justification. Indeed, breaking with past history generally implies distancing oneself from the very 'self' of the nation.

IR scholars therefore need to make use of identity as a key feature of history by grasping a few key nuances. First, the difference between a broad historical awareness of the past (as a repository) and the selectivity of the past embodied in social memory, in which national history helps policymakers made expedient use of national historical identity in service of political ends. IR scholars need to distinguish between written accounts of national histories providing a given perspective of national identity, versus the selective use of national storylines in the service of a political goal. Written accounts of national identity provide us with the passive foundation; this foundation becomes animated as social memory when key aspects are extracted to create or sustain a given policy (including the manufacturing of another identity or narrative). Thus, accounts of identity as derived from history are quite separate from the process by which identity catalyses collective cohesion and subsequent action.

## IDENTITY IN HISTORY: VISIONS OF THE 'SELF'

It would be impossible to provide a decent historical survey of even major instances of identity as a concept, category and organizing principle. Suffice it to say that IHIR students should not simply rehash Thucydides and the Peloponnesian Wars in getting to grips with a group-based example of Self/Other, but be more adventurous in seeking out instances of identity as a motivating factor for cultural and political ends, including, for example:

- The use of ethnicity and 'Otherness' in the Egyptian imperial conquest of their chief rival, Nubia. Here, ethnicity is a surprisingly mobile and permeable mode, challenging its later essentialist interpretations.
- As explored by Herodotus, Euripides and Strabo, various Athenian rituals like that of Artemis Tauropolos, in which a series of polarities were established to demonstrate a coming of age for groups of individuals: childhood vs adulthood, animal vs human, territorial heartland vs the periphery of Empire, and barbarian ethnicity vs Greek norms.
- The role of Roman *civitas* (community) vs the non-Roman *natio* (peoples/races) of the Empire, including well-known examples in Gaul and Britain, and lesser-known instances of the Jewish Diaspora, and the role of a non-ethnic, a-territorial identity, including the role of social networks and the vehicle of religion to promote an identity.

Engaging with these and others, one can quickly grasp the sheer number of actors to whom identity is attributed, and by whom identity is conferred. From the European perspective, Classical Greek, biblical and Roman sources provide the readiest examples. Indeed, ancient Greece and its contemporary civilizations had units that operated in an ascending range: the citizen, the family, the city, the country, the empire. Each of these bequeaths terms that are familiar today.

## BOX 7.2 HELPFUL DEIFINITIONS

- *demos* the population of a political entity; the populace of a district; the common people; city people
- *ethnikos* foreign; people with their own standards and beliefs (ethics)
- *ethnos* the people; the nation; a class; the country people; outsiders
- *ethos* how a people behave
- *natio* those among whom one is born

Most central was the city, the focus of commerce, worship and loyalty, worthy of the supreme sacrifice. This focus was subsequently widened by Greeks in the postclassical period. Both Cynics and Stoics are representative of a cosmopolitan world in which cities and municipal identities gradually lost their political independence, and where individuals began to conceive of themselves as citizens of the world, identifying not with local forms of self like cities and local regions, but with broader political, economic and social forces linking them as humans.

Moving into the Roman era, St Paul gives a good early example of the sheer complexity of identity that had sprung up around the concept of citizenship, and the form of political protection that this implied:

"I myself am a Jew," Paul went on. "I was born in Tarsus in Cilicia, but I was brought up here in the city, I received my training at the feet of Gamaliel and I was schooled in the strictest observance of our father's Law …" 22:23–25 – As they were yelling and ripping their clothes and hurling dust into the air, the colonel gave orders to bring Paul into the barracks and directed that he should be examined by scourging, so that he might discover the reason for such an uproar against him. But when they had strapped him up, Paul spoke to the centurion standing by, "Is it legal for you to flog a man who is a Roman citizen, and untried at that?" 22:26 – On hearing this the centurion went in to the colonel and reported to him, saying, "Do you realise what you were about to do? This man is a Roman citizen!" 22:27 – Then the colonel himself came up to Paul, and said, "Tell me, are you a Roman citizen?" And he said, "Yes." 22:28 – Whereupon the colonel replied, "It cost me a good deal to get my citizenship." "Ah," replied Paul, "but I was born a citizen." 22:29 – Then those who had been about to examine him left hurriedly, while even the colonel himself was alarmed at discovering that Paul was a Roman and that he had had him bound.

(*Acts of the Apostles*, 22:3–29)

Roman references to identity stem from two Latin terms *natio* and *civitas*, meaning birth/nation/people and community respectively. The structure of Roman law provides a context in which *natio* can refer to any group of people, or when contrasted against *civitas*, an inferior or marginalized race of people, as demonstrated in Cicero's *Philippics Against Mark Antony*:

*Omnes nationes servitutem ferre possunt: nostra civitas non potest.*
All races are able to bear enslavement, but our community cannot.

(Cicero, 1918)

With the rise of Christianity and the Respublica Christiana, Christianity switched from being the 'other' to the Roman 'self', to the chief 'Self' juxtaposed to non-Christian others. A parallel development to Christianity (as a rather transcendent 'self') was the rise of specific territorial units with which people readily identified, from city-states to kingdoms or towns, and the growth of area-specific languages by which to increase the sense of 'groupness' across a large number of people. The idea of 'nation' as a combination of land and linguistic-based identity is well expressed by Liutprand, the Bishop of Cremona in 968; rebuffing the ambitions of the Holy Roman Emperor, the Bishop declared that

The land … which you say belongs to your empire belongs, as the nationality and language of the people proves, to the kingdom of Italy.

(http://medieval.ucdavis.edu/20A/Luitprand.html, accessed June 2011)

However, a nation did not necessarily rely on land and language. By the twelfth century, the term was used in reference to community of learning, as demonstrated by the use of *natio* to describe the group of students at the University of Paris. However, what bound these students as a group was their land of birth, their common language, and a common body of law. Students could be divided thus into French, Saxon and Bavarian *nations*. Other medieval views of identity were wonderfully complex, because they were derived from the myriad forms of political organization that existed in Europe between the twelfth century and the standardizing tendencies inherent in the Peace of Westphalia (1648). As made clear in Chapter 4, various types of political authorities vied with each other over the constitution and application of sovereignty in terms of both authority and power. This produced a whole range of sacred and secular polities, from the Holy Roman Empire and the Papacy as imperial examples, to assorted kingdoms, duchies, principalities, free and cathedral cities, towns, guilds and charters. Each of these existed as a self-contained unit capable of conferring a measure of strategic protection and cultural affiliation on its members in a way that produced a host of discrete Selves drawn frequently in opposition to the claims of Others.

The variety of terms produced multiple understandings, complicated further by the difficulties of translating terms from one language to another, and indeed between different contexts. One of the final letters written by Niccolò Machiavelli reveals both the potency of identity in creating feelings of allegiance, and its complexity in defining the object of that allegiance. Machiavelli writes in 1527, '*amo patria mia più dell'anima*' ('I love my native city more than I love my soul'; in Xenos, 1996: 218). *Patria* has variously been translated as city, fatherland, homeland, country, or even city walls. The actual object may indeed be less significant than the dynamic of identity itself as realized by Machiavelli. The *patria* clearly represents something worthy of considerable sacrifice; a symbol of liberty, heritage and culture, a way of life that may demand the sacrifice of other lives. *Patria* denotes a location and a longing; or as Viroli argues, 'the patria is both a mode of life and a culture, it is a particular mode of life and a culture which is based on the values of liberty and civil equality', a location and a way of life that promotes the uniqueness of that location (in Xenos, 1996: 219).

Enlightenment views were similarly supportive of the cosmopolitan perspective, advocating a universalist, humanist ethos, rather than a particularist or individualist one. Political frontiers were the exercise and outcome of rulers, not the ruled; they were instrumental for the sovereign state but not substantive in constructing an accompanying political identity. Enlightenment cosmopolites viewed political identity as distinctly at odds with their universalist ethos; believing instead that 'identity is a matter of language, literature, folkways, and, in a broad sense, culture, without necessarily carrying political weight' (Brown, 2001: 120).

The key 'Early Modern' development (covering the sixteenth to the eighteenth centuries) is the transformation of territorial states from loose amalgams of authority and populace to the chief vehicle for territory-based authority, resource-based power and collective identities. This period saw the gradual replacement of dynastic or absolutist kingdoms and empires first by 'national' monarchies and then by constitutional republican states. These changes arose from two parallel drivers: an institutional shift in understanding sovereignty as the new benchmark for all claims of authority, and a sociological shift in transitioning from local (familial, kin-based, municipal) forms of allegiance to far wider forms of identification, i.e. a national group within the *territorial bounds* of the sovereign state, and additionally, on the *cultural grounds* of the group's particular uniqueness. The 'Late Modern' development (nineteenth and twentieth centuries) saw developing state-based entities transformed once again into a standardized sovereign unit complete with political and legal attributes; national identity functioned both to confirm the cultural and social legitimacy of settled states as an appropriate collective unit, or a method by which to demand a state, on the basis of self-determination.

## LIBERAL PERSPECTIVES

Rarely cited, **John Locke's** 'theory of mind' is arguably the progenitor of modern identity theory, and the philosophical basis for political and sociological processes of group identity. Simply put, Locke (generally referred to as an empiricist in his style of thought) was the first philosopher to define the idea of the 'self' through the process of consciousness. Beginning from first principles, in which the human mind is to begin with a *tabula rasa* (blank slate), Locke rejected the previous school of Cartesian philosophy, which was based on the premise that humans innately know key ideas and logical precepts, and argued instead that ideas derive solely from our various external experiences and are not inbuilt or innate. Human ideas can thus originate only from two sources: sensory and reflective. Locke's 'self' is thus entirely conscious: both self-aware and self-reflective, which he defines as:

> that conscious thinking thing (whatever substance, made up of whether spiritual, or material, simple, or compounded, it matters not) which is sensible, or conscious of pleasure and pain, capable of happiness or misery, and so is concerned for itself, as far as that consciousness extends.
>
> (Locke 1690/1997: 307)

Locke's three chief works deal with some aspect of human or collective identity (*An Essay Concerning Human Understanding*, 1690), as well as education (*Some Thoughts Concerning Education*, 1693) and government (*Two Treatises of Government*, 1689/1764). Particularly crucial for ensuing understandings of how identity actually operates is Locke's argument that identity is explicit and not latent if it is to operate as an organizing principle for a group. Groups are self-defining entities and this process can only occur with genuine self-awareness and progressive self-reflexivity. Locke thus pinpointed a truism about identity that only crystallized into workable analysis three hundred years later. As Walker Connor explains, 'many of the problems associated with defining a group are attributable precisely to the fact that it is a self-defining group. That is why scholars … have consistently used terms such as self-awareness and self-consciousness when analysing and describing the nation' (1994: 104).

In addition, Locke makes three observations critical to understanding the role of identity in defining the individuality and behaviour of individuals and groups. First, the use of sense and reflection (in early years, via education) to build up an association of ideas upon which a person's sense of self is first based. Second, this process of associationism (which had an enduring impact on contemporary psychology, educational theory) operates collectively, endowing a given group with key ideas about who they are in and of themselves, and who they are relative to others (the Self/Other dichotomy). Third, as the main content of human ideas is balanced roughly between reason and tolerance on the one hand, and the desire for selfish gains on the other, the optimum method by which individuals should flourish politically is in a state that is contractually organized between a ruler and the ruled. The rights of people to pursue their authentic human nature is captured in brief phrase that has since become immortalized in the US Constitution, namely that all have the right to 'Life, health, Liberty, or Possessions' (Locke, 1689/1764: 164). The optimum method to support these rights was in the structure of a state in which both the particularist forces of a given society could flourish (civil society) and the accompanying legal and political requirements could be addressed by a state government. Locke therefore represents something of a watershed in identifying both the sovereign rights of man, and the structure most likely to promote these rights in defence of the individual and group 'Self'.

Locke, along with Kant and Rousseau, represented the liberal tradition of a contractarian view of society that challenged older, absolutist, top-down methods of enforcing rule on the ruled. Instead, their view was of a broad social identity, grounded by a conceptual contract between the ruler and ruled; operating in every state unit, the people themselves thus had a great deal in common as to what held them together as subjects, citizens, etc. Based on his perspectives of autonomy and freedom, Kant clarified these ideas further in his writings on self-determination. Freedom for Kant is the claim laid by individuals and groups to be free from undue external influence, both physical and metaphysical. Freedom is promoted by the ability to adhere to a moral code (or law), rather than being forced to live, work or think in a way that runs counter to one's authentic nature. Thus, the state of being free is one of autonomy: freedom from external constraint as a result of 'giving the law to oneself' (Kant, 1993: 44). At the collective level, this suggests that a given group could lay claim to this form of autonomy; enabling them to both label external influence over them as unnatural to their authentic existence and demand the opportunity to give the law to themselves within their own community of governance. The Kantian argument for self-determination can be derived from the following observation:

> If the will seeks the law that is to determine it anywhere but in the fitness of its maxims for its own legislation of universal laws, and if it thus goes outside of itself and seeks this law in the character of any of its objects, then heteronomy [being beholden to outside influences] always results.
>
> (Kant, 1993: 45)

Kant's observances on the principle of self-determination had a profound impact on later philosophers, political movements (including the French Revolution), as well as providing the raw material for later scholars of nationalism (e.g. Elie Kedourie) and contemporary politicians (e.g. Woodrow Wilson), all of whom produced variants on Kant's original claim by arguing that a group of people need only consider themselves to be a definable national unit to claim the right to exist within a defensible state entity.

Like Locke, the writings of Hegel on the role of identity are generally neglected in favour of his treatises on the state. Philosophers and historians are familiar with Hegel's view of the state as the greatest of human accomplishments, a structure that attained the ideal balance between individual, group and national society. What is less well-known is the logic by which the state first attains this ideal balance. According to Hegel, the answer lies in achieving an equilibrium between the Self and its opposite, the Other. Thus states can only exist on the condition that other states exist (a core component of sovereign equality and international recognition), while individuals require an Other in order to determine the full extent of the Self (the Self/Other dichotomy). Thus, Hegel's *The Philosophy of Right* (1945) highlights the processes by which states develop their particularist characteristics specifically by differentiating themselves from other states, both in a given instance and over time.

## POLITICAL AND CULTURAL NATIONS

In addition to the political philosophy of the eighteenth century, identity emerged in an increasingly clear and prevalent way as an organizing principle of the Westphalian state unit. Within the social sciences, identity is the chief method by which a group of people identify themselves culturally, and register their preferences politically. The state unit emerged as the dominant political unit to undertake these objectives. Identity is thus directly connected to the civic aims and cultural requirements of a given group of people as embodied in a sovereign state. The eighteenth century is a crucial era for IHIR scholars because it contains philosophical practical examples of identity operating as both a *political device* in the service of the state, and a *cultural tool* in the service of the nation. The French Revolution exemplifies the increasing potency of identity to serve political needs, while German romanticism views popular sovereignty as serving cultural needs. The result is two visible types of identity: one political, buttressing the creation of a civic state; and one cultural, fashioning and articulating the nation.

The method by which the French state decides upon its sovereignty has knock-on effects for its identity. As decided by the French Constitution of 1791, sovereignty was first a national issue, decided upon by Parliament, which represented only a small portion of enfranchised citizens. The 1793 Constitution, however, transformed sovereignty into a popular issue, on the basis of wider enfranchisement and more direct forms of democratic representation. National sovereignty was *representative of* the people – a civic form in which the people were identified with at a distance, by people on their behalf. Popular sovereignty was a manifestation of claims to authority made by the people – a civic form that rested on a broader interpretation of their identity as citizens of the French nation, operating in a way that overlapped civic objectives with cultural ones. Emmanuel Joseph or 'Abbot' Sieyès, a theorist and pamphleteer of the French Revolution, was one of the first architects of this distinction. Suggesting that nations sequentially preceded states, Sieyès defined a *nation* as a subject of natural (rather than manmade) law, a body of people that existed before the creation of the political state as an objective sovereign entity (Sewell Jr, 1994: 9). The *people* were the national inhabitants of the subsequently formed sovereign state, contractually instituted on the basis of a constitution. The state lays claim to sovereignty; its people in turn lay claim to themselves as a nation and, as such, identify with their state.

## CULTURAL NATIONS

There are a number of different interpretations of the role of cultural identity in either constructing or receiving the nation. Robust interpretations suggest that a visible ethnic component comprises the core of a nation and provides a clear, immutable sense of identity strongly disposed to constructing itself in opposition to any series of others. This identity is dedicated to preserving its cultural particularism without necessarily resorting to the use of a state structure. Weaker interpretations suggest that, even if the state is successfully established subsequent to a nation, there will always remain some requirement for a national society to consider itself separate and unique from others, on the basis of its history, its achievements and failures, its symbols, its interests, ethics and principles.

Are there genuine cultural nations? Again, it depends on the criteria. If culture is being used as a method to justify group coherence rather than group difference, then culture is simply one of a number of attributes by which a national community identifies itself relative to others. This is quite common in most contemporary nation-states. However, there are groupings who even now do possess a discernible ethnic core and/or a potent national narrative regarding their common ancestry, be it familial, territorial, temporal or as a result of constant external forces. The sense of shared past origin produces a shared common destiny, and generally is accompanied by visible homogeneity in both its cultural and civic elements. The sense of being an ingroup can be further reinforced through language, religion, ethical and ideological heritage, amicable or hostile relationships with immediate neighbours, and success or failure in pursuing their political aims.

The cultural nation is from this perspective an originator. However, it is also a reactive force, as best evidenced by the zeal for cultural nations that swept Europe and America in reaction to Napoleon's usurpations of the founding principles of the French Revolution. Rejecting the uniquely civic principles of liberty, equality and brotherhood, true national groupings were deemed to require more essentialist, more authentic roots in order to withstand the forces of modernity and the impact of foreign conquest: the nation should not merely be defensible, but devotional, a source of idealized, even romanticized allegiance and loyalty. German romantic nationalists like Herder followed precisely this line, rejecting civicism and rationalism in the form of progress and even equality in favour of heritage and history. Liberal principles of equality as espoused by the American and French revolutions were rejected on the basis that – in quantitative terms – they represented merely the aggregate of the rights of all its citizens, and no more. This was, in the view of German nationalists, entirely unrepresentative of both the transcendent quality of the nation and the particularist traits of its people. A qualitative view of the identity of a nation, rather than state, based on the sum of their claims, produced a far more potent understanding of the specific characteristics of the people (or *Volk*), manifested in their overall cultural spirit (*Volkgeist*), as argued by Herder. The nation, in this way, was greater than the sum of its parts, an objective, organic entity rather than a series of subjective group desires. Cultural perspectives of national identity thus represent a distinct challenge to eighteenth-century liberalism and provided fuel for much nineteenth-century theorizing on nationalism. This eventually produced a neat division between the idea of Herder's 'cultural nation' (*Kulturnation*), and Hegel's *Staatsnation*, which transferred the cultural requirements of a national community into the state unit. Another key theme from this period was that of communication, as evidenced by the writings of Max Weber.

While much in the cultural school appears compelling, it is generally unconvincing. Herder and Hegel's qualities of a common language, common territory and common economic and cultural life representing a transhistorical *Geist* are largely improbable fictions that occur in only a minority of cases. Both historical and contemporary nation-states have rarely been repositories of a single language;

there are dozens of examples of states with two or more official languages, and equally, where a major lingua franca, like English, Spanish or Arabic encompasses a whole range of given political identities far beyond a given state. Languages are an effective vehicle for national identity only because they are first, and consciously '*elevated* to the symbol of the nation' (Connor, 1994: 44). Equally, common territory is an unlikely category. Many irredentist national limits frequently spill over and beyond state borders, while many state borders stop short of perceived national frontiers, and many states are multi-territorial in being spread across a variety of geographic features (e.g. archipelagos). Territory is also an unhelpful marker of identity for the landless, like diasporas or migrants or the permanently displaced. More frequently, territory denotes an unattainable quality of otherness, rather than a settled place for a national self (Said, 1979). In this respect, territory – like language – is 'more a symbolic means of mobilization than essential to nationhood' (Reicher and Hopkins, 2001: 10). Common economic and national characters are still less convincing. The former had virtually disappeared with the rise of economic interdependence between states and commercial entities and the sheer scope and scale of globalization. National characteristics are without question an abiding form of self-reference, but they are selectively chosen by both public and politician alike, and reflect generational, regional, social, economic and psychological biases in their retelling, and as such exist as a convenient but arguably abbreviated method of encapsulating the social mores and cultural codes advocated as reflective of a majority.

## CONCEPTUALIZING GROUP IDENTITY: THEORIES OF NATIONALISM

Conceptual developments in the twentieth century attempted to categorize these previous histories by grouping them into discrete theories of nationalism, based on the particular role played by identity. As a topic of academic enquiry, theories of nationalism emerged, assembled by a range of scholars, including historians, culturalists and anthropologists, and which are of direct relevance to the disciplines of sociology, political theory and IR. Evidence of this can be seen from the links between the three main questions asked by theories of nationalism – When/ Where/Why did nations begin? – to the logical consequences of nation formation on social, political and structural behaviour. This encourages IHIR scholars to ask, at the first instance, how a person's individual identity is first connected to a social group, and then to larger cultural (and then political) units. Culturalist orientations of IR continue this theme, examining what role culture plays in informing a group of how it wishes to be identified; foreign policy analysis takes over by investigating how sources of identity impact on the needs and values of a group in a way that produces specific interests, and results in observable policy behaviour. Identity – in all its many definitions and incarnations – runs like a thread throughout the fabric of all social science enquiries in which a given 'self' is the chief unit of analysis.

Within theories of nationalism, identity operates as either a thin or thick *bearer* of the cultural needs and political objectives of a given society, as expressed domestically and internationally. Developed across the twentieth century, these theories can be divided chronologically into three schools, each with their own particular interpretation of the role of identity and the use of nationalism for political ends.

## East is east: the genesis school

The 'genesis' school emerged from the work done by Hans Kohn (*The Idea of Nationalism*, 1945) and Carlton (*The Historical Evolution of Modern Nationalism*, 1931) immediately after World War II, based on the major forces of nationalism that had produced both of the previous world wars. Kohn and Carlton were pioneers who established the central tenets of the modernist position and, in so doing, laid the conceptual perimeters for the next fifty years of academic enquiry about nationalism and identity. Kohn set the stage by distinguishing between Western and Eastern nationalism. Western nationalism was understood to originate in popular sovereignty movements of the English Civil War and the French Revolution in a process whereby the population identifies itself en masse *as* a nation, and then subsequently *with* an existing political structure. For Kohn, this sequence 'serves as the justificatory foundation of the modern state in an age when the political and cultural integration of the entire population is assumed' (Xenos, 1996: 213). Eastern nationalism occurs less evenly as a force that precedes the state, but which constructs it only to further cultural rather than political forms of representation. Thus, as Kohn argues,

> in Central and Eastern Europe and in Asia, nationalism arose not only later, but also generally at a more backward stage of social and political development: the frontiers of an existing state and of a rising nationality rarely coincided; nationalism, there, grew in protest against and in conflict with the existing state pattern – not primarily to transform it into a people's state, but to redraw the political boundaries in conformity with ethnographic demands.
>
> (Kohn, 1945: 329)

Kohn's viewpoint is by contemporary standards now rather archaic, even chauvinistic. His political and cultural categories are emphatically different, with no leeway for overlap or ambiguity. However, this needs to be tempered by the context in which he and others were writing; the era immediately following World War II was given over to explaining the inexplicable in the rise of eastern fascism and the triumph of Western nationalism. Contemporary revisions of Kohn have used an alternative set of polarities – that of civic vs ethnic nationalism. Pursued by scholars including Ignatieff (1993), Viroli (1995) and Greenfeld (1992), the temptation to assign territories to these attributes produces European and North American examples of civic nationalism, and Eastern, Asian and African examples of ethnic nationalism.

## The modernist school: the rise and role of the state

The second or 'modernist' school emerged during the 1950s and 1960s based on the work of three key scholars: Ernest Gellner (*Nations and Nationalism*, 1983), Elie Kedourie (*Nationalism*, 1960) and Karl Deutsch (*Nationalism and Social Communication: An Inquiry into the Foundations of Nationality*, 1953). This school has in common that its scholars approached identity as a moving process built up over time, challenged and constructed by individuals and groups, and used in the conscious service of contemporary state-building. Each of these three authors makes this same point from a different angle.

Gellner argues that a swiftly industrializing Europe effectively required two things: a mobile workforce and the ability to communicate via a standardized language. From there, people could gain a sense of themselves which would be first based on their contemporary surroundings and only subsequently attached to older, cultural senses of self (Gellner, *Culture, Identity and Politics*, 1987). Kedourie uses the history of ideas as evidence for his central argument that nationalism is essentially a 'doctrine invented in Europe at the beginning of the nineteenth century' (Kedourie 1960: 10). Within the writings of nationalist scholars, language is viewed as catalytic by both Karl Deutsch and, rather more famously, by neo-modernist scholars of nationalism like Benedict Anderson (Anderson, 1983). Standardized oral and print languages provide the linguistic bedrock for key groups of people, who are able to communicate their values and needs with those who speak the same tongue – this promotes a sense of self that helps to crystallize the group as a whole and sharpen their sense of who they are (and what they want) relative to others. Cultural outputs of this group in oral, written or performative form are all increasingly sophisticated representations of the same sense of a 'group self'. Boosted by the spread of industrialization, the rise of contact among increasing numbers of people of the same national group prompts the growth of mass literacy in providing the 'necessary infrastructure through which culture might be more broadly shared' as a form of national consciousness, and the foundation to subsequent sociopolitical identities (Mann, 1995: 45).

This perspective is distinctly uneasy with Kohn's process of labelling various nationalisms in an 'either/or' framework. Nations do not simply arise in a natural fashion. However, they do not dismiss the existence or importance of culture for human groups. As Jacquin-Berdal argues, they question whether 'such groupings would be self-consciously formed around cultural criteria prior to the age of nationalism' (2000: 56). In other words, it is unlikely that societies have a cultural sense of themselves in the absence of any other political knowledge, which helps put those cultural understandings to use in a way that transcends the group's original form of self-understanding. The objective of the modernist school is therefore

> To unmask the processes which have led to the saliency of culture as *the* universal socio-political organiser. The modernists' objective is to understand why and when the fact of belonging to a nation, or any culturally defined homogenous

community, became felt as an imperative and conceived as the only 'natural' support of one's own socio-political identity.

(Jacquin-Berdal, in Vandersluis, 2000: 53)

The key point, then, is to ask what key factors actually bring about the nation. For the purposes of this chapter, IR scholars need to ask the following questions of the modernist school: What role does identity play at individual and collective level in forming both cultural and political senses of self? What are the implications for the particular sequence in which this takes place (i.e. nation to state, or state to nation)? and How does identity affect the ability of the resulting state to generate both a national history and a set of core behaviours in which identity plays a key role?

Modernists acknowledge the role of culture, and the driving force of language in prompting group consciousness, but they argue that groups still require an administrative structure to provide the political form that can internally contain and externally realize such cultural content. The administrative unit most likely to be chosen for cultural reasons and political ends is, of course, the state. The question is whether the state is a force for good or ill as regards the ultimate ends of nationalists. Is the state is a vehicle for the preservation and expansion of national consciousness? Or is the state a more insidious unit, turning the power of cultural self-identification to its own ends, subverting the original and authentic dynamics of a given identity, binding it artificially within geographical areas that are ill suited to the territorial origins of its people, and eroding its uniquely particularist content through practices of standardization in order to fit the generic mould of other sovereign states?

The modernist response is that the majority of national identifiers (territory, history, national symbols, etc.), as well as the national majorities and minorities, require and generally thrive within the standard state unit. Assuming the state has the minimum sovereign requirements of set borders, identifiable populace, a centralized and viable (though not necessarily representative) government, and external equality afforded by recognition, it can both *protect* the unique qualities of its national culture and *promote* the cause of the national identity in the form of the national interest and subsequent policy decisions. Paradoxically, the specificity of the nation – as both distinct from, and identical to, all other social groupings – can only be fully realized in the standardized unit of the state. While the particular blend of nation and state differs tremendously, even within the relatively small geographic area of Western Europe, the outcome, however uneven and even artificial, for both historians, political theorists and IR theorists, is the contemporary nation-state.

## Ethnicity redux: the primordialists

The third or 'primordialist' school challenged directly the precepts of the modernist school; arguing that the true nature of identity was far older, far more intangible and complex and its use less readily available to actors. Boosted by the wave of post-colonial independence movements sweeping across the Third World in the 1970s, scholars like Walker Connor (*Ethnonationalism: The Quest for Understanding*, 1994) and ethno-nationalists like Anthony Smith (*The Ethnic Revival*, 1981, and *The Ethnic Origins of Nations*, 1986) argued that, in ignoring the role of ethnic identity, the modernist school had missed a fundamental element driving the complex relation between individuals and societies, and between nations and states. Connor, Smith and others argued this failure to appreciate ethnicity meant that modernist theories of nationalism 'underrated the emotional appeal of nationalism and were thus unable to foresee and explain its re-emergence' (Jacquin-Berdal, 2000: 52).

Primordialists base their view of the nation on the assumption of a pre-existing, timeless and generally immutable group, lodged homogenously and permanently in one geographical location. The attributes of a pre-existing, generally homogenous group, with an inherently immutable identity in the face of change, forms the core view of the primordialist school. Generally, identity is immutable because it is ethnic. Identity – at individual or collective level – simply cannot be fashioned as one would fashion and then don a suit. One neither receives identity as a reflection of the modern era, nor uses it in instrumental fashion. Its fabric consists of threads that bind one inherently, irrevocably, undeniably, to one's past. In primordialism, identity fashions people; it is not fashioned by people. This is not only the true form of identity-building, but the 'true nationalism' by which the majority of national societies are themselves fashioned.

Nations are not – contrary to Gellner – mere inventions; accordingly, national identity is not – contrary to Eric Hobsbawm – the invention of tradition in the service of political pragmatism. Nations are not only authentic in terms of their culture, but valid representations of the political will of their national society. While the modernist school contends that the state and the nation are 'invented, imagined, constructed, or fabricated', the centrality of ethnicity as the prime mode of determining the indivisibility of a national identity demonstrates for these scholars 'that nations are not artificial creations, that they are in fact grounded in genuine cultural communities which pre-date the era of nationalism' (Jacquin-Berdal, 2000: 52).

## CONTEMPORARY SYNTHESIS: THE NATION-STATE

What complicates this division is that political identities (which view the state as the prime structure) and cultural identities (fixed upon a nation) are simplistic reductions of the intricate and uneven real-life examples of past and present groupings. Worse still, these identities are interchangeable. Principles and symbols based on territory and history apply equally well to state and nation. The concept of a common language, a centralized government, generations of received norms and values and a repository of national history are neither inherently cultural nor political in and of themselves. What transforms these *accoutrements of identity* from *concepts* and *categories* that organize people into groups based on similarity and difference through *organizing principles* is the perception of them regarding their ultimate use in pursuing cultural or political ends. Cultural and political divisions are, of course, helpful in providing an initial taxonomy of forms of national identity, but they are only a first step on a more complicated journey regarding the use of tangible and intangible forces in pursuance of group goals. This explains why people who do not share all the attributes understood to be specifically 'national' can still feel as if they belong to a group (and vice versa). Simply put, if people believe in the power of these attributes to the extent that they impact on their behaviour, then identity has a causal effect independent of the concepts and categories that make it up.

That being said, historians are correct to point out that the most potent core of either cultural or political forms of identity is the use of a national history (however questionable its accuracy) in providing explanations for how a national community first came together. At the heart of the national narrative one usually finds reference to essentialist qualities that the group alone holds in common, including a shared origin, and a sense of common ancestry. Again, however, shared origins need only be intersubjectively shared to have as potent an effect as groups who share a genuinely ethnic connection. Equally, political theorists are correct in identifying symbols or strategies by which a group's identity translates into principles of order, values that produce specific interests, and interests which promote particular behaviour. These behavioural outcomes can be civic in producing administrative structures, or cultural in preserving a particular attribute, narrative or aspect of heritage. When the constitutive force of history combines with the causal impact of group order, the outcome is a group whose cultural particularisms generally obtain as political interests in the form of the sovereign state and, through the process, policy-based behaviour. The outcome may contain elements of a political nation and/or a cultural nation, but it is in sum a '*Willensnation*', a 'nation by sheer will'.

Perhaps because these oppositions are so uncomfortable, the majority of IR theory tends not to engage with the detailed descriptions of the cultural, social and political background of the state and its national derivations, preferring instead the catch-all sobriquet of nation-state. This has the benefit of including both the ethnic/cultural/symbolic aspects of national consciousness that drive a people to feel themselves to be a group and the civic/political/strategic aspects of administrative and sovereign facets by which a people can legitimate governing themselves as a group. There are some considerable drawbacks. The main drawback depends upon one's disciplinary inclination; IR scholars are generally so used to dealing with states that the nation itself tends to be ignored, along with endogenous dynamics that are visibly – if unevenly – responsible for internal and external behaviour. Historians, particularly those focusing on nationalism, tend to ignore the administrative milieu and take the state itself for granted.

The final stage of identity is still occurring. It is a time of dislocation, rupture, disjuncture, in which old loyalties have been thrown into question, familiar symbols changed or eroded, and new forms of authority raised. Transnational organizations, economic interdependence, epistemic communities and even virtual entities all crowd around the older Westphalian unit, challenging the original state-based method of cultural expressions through political forms. But yet states last. They are undeniably enduring precisely because they confer identity, order and authority, and they do so in terms of spatial and temporal markers: the most basic tools for constructing identity. For Chris Brown, 'it is highly unlikely that, for most of the world's inhabitants, [these new forms] will be able to act as more than supplementary backups for the more traditional identity-conferring territorial units' (2001: 134). Contemporary theorists of nationalism now engage with both modernist viewpoints and the primordialist camp. As Salam observes, the result of both is that

> Whereas the nation was once looked upon as an unproblematic and transhistorical phenomenon ... this new scholarship ... is defined by a common acceptance of the nation as an 'imagined community', a collectivity based on shared historical memories and cultural experiences, not blood or soil ... National identity does not reflect [solely] a prior, primordial collective self; rather it is part of a fluid network of representations distinguished by its privileged place – one owed to the primacy of the territorial, sovereign nation-state.
>
> (Abdel Salam, 2001: 307)

## BOX 7.3 THE EUROPEAN UNION

The EU provides an uneasy example of attempting to construct a modernist identity in which citizens identify with the Union, whilst retaining their older 'original' national identities. This is a difficult task for two reasons. First, it is unlikely that people can do much more than simply *identify* the Union; they will rarely identify *with* it in the deeper sense of identifying *with* their national society. Second, the project of integration within the Union has had a paradoxical – though not exactly surprising outcome – in which efforts to 'reduce the significance of political frontiers within Europe [have] ... increased the salience of the border between the Union and the rest of the world', as well as heightened tensions between the member states themselves about their enduring importance (Brown, 2001: 118).

Europe is at once a gigantic civil society operating on cosmopolitan principles in which the four freedoms successfully reduce national differences; and an extended exercise in reasserting communitarian differences by permitting states to withhold key national competences that give meaning and cohesion to them as individual states. The EU attempts to transcend civil society, but its institutions are not yet strong or symbolic enough for people to identify with them in a way that transcends their national identities. The EU touts unity in diversity, but this is a contradiction in terms at least where identity is concerned. Identity is about difference. It is unlikely that an EU identity could transcend, and eventually displace, national identities; the very attempt to erase borders has paradoxically drawn greater attention to the need to retain them as political tools of difference, not strategies of similarity.

Such difficulties, however, have not prevented EU institutions and even EU member states from efforts to identify and engage with a European *demos*: the European people who can identify the EU, but still identify with their national and only subsequently European heritage. Inspiring this *demos* on key aspects of integration seems a challenge; the European population is not only notoriously suspicious of the alleged 'democratic deficit' but is unsure of the distinction between the means of EU decision-making processes and the ends of European integration. One place to begin may be simply identifying features held in common, in transnational fashion, on key aspects of heritage, education, communication and, above all, citizenship before weightier and more divisive issues regarding the internal market and external policy can be included. There is implicit acceptance but ironically little real knowledge of the guiding norms of the EU, including democracy, human rights, rule of law, as well as neoliberal principles of economic governance, and more contemporary practical norms including environmental protection and crisis management.

## IDENTITY IN IR THEORY: REALISTS VS LIBERALS

As will be seen, with some notable exceptions, IR has come rather late to the use of identity as a variable, concept and category. This is odd, as identity in any of these three forms assists IR in a number of key ways. First, it helps distinguish between political/internal and international/external dimensions. It is trendy in some camps (e.g. Christopher Hill, 2003) to suggest the two are now so intimately blended that they equate to an inter-mestic environment. This may describe some of the foreign policy dynamics in which state interests are informed by both domestic and foreign imperatives, but these two spheres are still distinct enough to retain their own identity sets. This can be broken down further into various inside–outside investigations (Walker, 1993) of national Selves and foreign Others, as well as the rights and requirements arising from processes of inclusion–exclusion (Linklater, 1998).

Second, identity is effectively the bearer of state sovereignty – it provides both an internal and external dimension, a negative method of engaging with external challenges – and a positive way of asserting internal authority. Third, identity, linked constitutively to the national interest, is a foreign policy catalyst. Identity is the conceptual foundation by which states define themselves, defend their interests and action the outcome in public and foreign policy (Hadfield, 2010). As such, identity represents the unit of the state, explains the nature of all the various dyads that make up the modern nation-state (cultural–political, civic–ethnic, primordial–constructed) and provides insights into state behaviour. Identity studies have challenged the body of pre-Cold War neo-realist thinking and its view of an abstract, reified, self-contained and uncomplicated state unit by suggesting that the process by which actors identify, constitute themselves within nation and state units, and are in turn constituted by these units directly connects to the construction of the state, the choice of its national interests, and the motivation and orientation of its foreign policy.

What explains such difficulties? Simply put, IR suffers from the same problems as IH and indeed every other discipline within the social sciences and humanities that has attempted to deal with identity: there are too many understandings of it on offer. Ironically, the definitional virility of identity initially produced a degree of analytical impotence within IR that lasted (with a few exceptions) until immediately after the Cold War. Due to this wide spectrum of understanding and usage, a brief overview of how identity connects with each of the major schools of thought within IR is therefore in order.

Identity for *realists*, for example, is an existent but rather uninteresting form of sociopolitical force by which a given populace engages with, and is in turn engaged by, forms of civic allegiance at municipal, regional and national levels. Their engagement is purely instrumental, i.e. allegiance to a given state and government supports the majority of their individual and collective interests, allowing specific governments to direct and deploy the means of a reliable workforce for the political, economic or territorial ends of the state. Identity is visible across all states at the domestic level in the form of citizenship, and visible between states in the form of sovereignty, as the generic status accorded exclusively to states *by* states. Because realists view states as unified and cohesive entities, their perspective of identity is as a generic force by which society inheres to a territory. They may draw upon historical and cultural modes of belonging to deepen this inherence, but the primary form of identification is a functional one and indicates merely that people inhere to political units in similar ways, for similar reasons. At the external level, such processes also explain why states themselves (alike in their internal compositions) behave similarly or, in IR terms, are functionally non-differentiated.

*Liberal* views are agreeably wider and countenance not only broader types of civic identity on the basis of class, modes of industry and methods of governing a people, but recognize that exogenous forms of self-recognition yield clearer ideas of humanism, idealism and varieties of commercial interchange. The liberal emphasis on the individual suggests that identities are not received or instrumental, but largely unique to a given group. Differences between people in the form of culture are of value in themselves, and to be respected. Conversely, the liberal emphasis on the universal qualities shared by all human beings suggests that people of every nation – despite their cultural differences – effectively share the same status and are entitled to the same rights (best exemplified in the doctrine of human rights). The paradox of identity as a mode of dissimilarity and similarity is most clearly seen within liberalism as a combination of unique forms of individuation and universal modes of treatment. Liberalism is thus torn between acknowledging the core facets of human identity as ultimately cosmopolitan in nature, and the distinguishing features by which that identity is made known to others: in national, social, gendered, ethnic and religious differences.

Within IR, the realist–liberal split over political affiliation and ensuring forms of allegiance, responsibility and even identity reached something of a zenith in the cosmopolitan–communitarian clash (under the aegis of normative theory). However, these two categories are historically representative of far older streams of political thought, which have rather more to say about identity itself. This dichotomy is a helpful organizing device that allows students and scholars to engage with these earlier historic traditions, and the varying ways in which identity is understood and applied.

Liberal political theory, derived from classic liberal thought, supports a universalist, *cosmopolitan perspective* in which political life operates on the basis of the social contract between ruler and ruled; the state becomes the natural container for this contract. What is of key value is not the state as a vessel, or the relationship between states, but what its contents have in common. What all individuals share – regardless of their specific social, cultural or national differences – is their basic humanity. As Brown argues,

> From a liberal perspective, the only true and foundational identity we possess derives from our common membership in the human race… We might well possess, by chance or choice, a series of other identities … but these are essentially secondary. The fact that they are secondary does not mean they are unimportant … so long as our primary identity as sharers of a common humanity is not compromised thereby.
>
> (Brown, 2001: 127–128)

Humans are classified primarily by what they most share in common, not by arbitrary methods of difference based on income, ethnicity or territory. The community in which humans live and grow is equally arbitrary; the state and its borders are a random series of structures to group people; they are not symbols by which people necessarily desire to be grouped or identified. Borders are not identifying devices either – as instrumentalist features, they do not drive identity formation. People construct themselves based on their humanity, and only subsequently on their surroundings; they are not made by such surroundings, because they are fundamentally contingent.

As a critical view of liberalism, *Marxism* suggests that the key unifying factor for all humans is their economic position as a result of their placement within the industrial order, and the social class to which they belong in consequence. Other identities like nationality, religion or ethnicity may tie, but ultimately do not bind. However, as manifestations of the unequal capitalist system, even class identities are regarded by Marxism as transitional rather than primordial, and would falter in the face of a reconstructed, identity-free communist system.

For approaches derived from realist theory support a particularist, *communitarian perspective*, the state, and its borders are of paramount importance, containing within in it a unique, self-contained community. From this view, identifying with others solely on the basis of a generic human identity is unrealistic because we are disposed to categorize people into groups on the basis of their inherent difference. And it is unsustainable simply because humans are inevitably the specific product of a particular culture. Winnowing out the precise aspect of humanity foundational to the panoply of other identities is an impossible task simply because our specific cultural and social identity overwhelmingly shapes and contains our broader human identity. Operating on the basis of human identity is too broad, too unworkable, too neutral; too close indeed to being without an identity. An identity, after all, is way of articulating a given characteristic, using specific signifiers to identify people based on their attributes. Humanity is too non-specific a signifier.

There are four consequences to the communitarian perspective. First, symbols and forces derived from our local community take on particular potency – in our ability to recognize, identify and defend them, we attach to them and them to us. Second, the process of constituting ourselves on the particularist is inevitably political – it serves our ends in a way that may originate in culture, but ultimately obtains in a political form. Third, that process of constitution generally binds a people strongly to the place within which they first constitute themselves. The place, and its boundaries, take on a significance precisely because the people that spring from this place invariably develop a territory-based sense of self which produces a sense of a common destiny within the community, making a group rather than an assortment of individuals. Fourth, constituting oneself within one community logically implies that one cannot be constituted elsewhere. Identity denotes who a Self is and, equally, who it is not. Identity therefore denotes similarity and difference in equal (though not always predictable) measure.

The main clash, therefore, between the two schools is between the equality of those across contingent borders; and the differences (and possibly superior attributes) of those contained by, and defined by borders. Cosmopolitans can readily dispose of borders and presumably engage with broader, universalizing dynamics as well as locating their identity in forms of civil, rather than national society. For communitarians, 'the maintenance of borders is central to identity formation and preservation, within and between communities'; they abhor a borderless world because it suggests a world 'in which human identity itself was put in question' (Brown, 2001: 130). The implications for identity are clear. For liberal political theory, the dominant cosmopolitan discourse cannot engage with either the particularist nature of identity or with the process of identity conferral from a state to a society, or vice versa. The danger here is that because it regards national borders, domestic symbols and even aspects of sovereignty and as 'no great moral or normative significance', easily 'replaced, rearranged, and refocused more or less at will', cosmopolitan discourse weakens its overall ability to engage with the state as the most enduring unit of authority and identity (Brown, 2001: 130). It cannot register the supreme importance of abiding qualities, including national narratives, collective attributes, and even behavioural preferences that are largely formed within the state, and deployed without. Cosmopolitan discourse may engage with the rising tide of political, economic and sociocultural changes, but as a school of thought, it fails to appreciate how such changes are actually understood and managed (as either opportunity or challenge) by individuals and groups. It also fails to engage with the conservative tendency to see virtually every value in normative and ethnocentric terms. Liberty, freedom and egalitarian principles are all filtered through a local lens, because people operate on the basis of intersubjective understandings (even if in pursuance of instrumental ends).

Communitarian viewpoints do not simply have more to say about identity; they have greater explanatory power to engage with both strategic and symbolic aspects of group formation, with both traditional forms of loyalty and the reasons behind claims for new modes of representation, precisely because they have a conceptual and empirical baseline from which to extend their analyses. Brown makes this point also, by arguing first that 'communitarianism has a clearer sense of the importance of borders and of systems of inclusion and exclusion more generally for political life', and that, in consequence, 'political identity is foundational to politics rather than a secondary phenomenon' (Brown, 2001: 135).

## Identity in IR theory: constructivist and critical paradigms

The next paradigm within IR treats identity less as a troublesome definition (qua realism) or a helpful if troubling organizing category (qua liberalism). Constructivism grapples more effectively with identity as a concept describing both material and intangible forces by which political and social realities are constructed. Despite groundwork by sociologists like Berger and Luckmann laid in the late 1960s, a new ontology emerged with real force within IR only when the end of the Cold War finally broke the seemingly inexorable grip of realism and neo-realism as a method of analysis of state interest and behaviour. States became reclassified as agents, operating on behalf of the needs and identities of the collectives that inhabit them, and recast as agents both located in, and fundamentally part of, the international structure (Berger and Luckmann, 1966). Agents, either individuals or states, literally create their social environment, which in turn takes on objective reality of its own. Within this constructed social reality, agents are first socialized into, and then gradually internalize, this external reality, which is in turn transformed into a subjective reality for them in a process known as mutual constitution.

The central importance in the use of identity within IR is the work of Alexander Wendt, who applied sociologically based explanations to provide insights (and critiques) of the international neo-realist/neo-liberal international structure, and in the process transformed identity as a 'viable variable' of IR analysis. Wendt's 1992 article 'Anarchy is what states make of it' broke new ground in raising the profile of identities, but does not employ a historic perspective to explain the origin or changing nature of identities; whilst not a priori, Wendt's treatment of identity is rather more categoric than conceptual. Identities are part of the institutional 'portfolio' that states carry and deploy in determining their interests and policies with each other. Helpfully, Wendt suggests that states interact as people, on the basis of meanings in an international system whose key structures are intersubjective as well as material. He views identities and interests as socially constructed, and state endowed with a limited degree of self-reference; but apart from regarding the state as a corporate identity, views identities as instrumental bearers of interests rather than constitutive and causal drivers of interests, policy and ultimately behaviour.

Other forms of constructivism, particularly the more critical variants, are less focused on the instrumental role played by values, norms and identities in explaining cooperative or conflictual behaviour between states at the structural or institutional level, and more interested by the extent to which interests and actions of collective and individual actors are literally fashioned by identity, and the multiple conditioning contexts from which identities (themselves multiple and contested forms of self-representation) spring.

The advent of poststructuralism has pushed this debate still further, encouraging theorists to look critically at mainstream forms of political and social identity, to deconstruct these forms and their underlying contexts, to examine both the 'nested and contested' qualities that contemporary citizens deploy in different circumstances to obtain specific and changing preferences. The central argument from the 1970s onwards has been to think of identity not merely as a given self, but also as a form of difference, as a related or opposition 'other' by which a given self is defined. When moral (like human rights) or political categories like political self-assertion or citizenship, or territorial distinctions like 'inside' or 'outside', are applied to the Self/Other duality, identity is transformed into an analytical concept around which complex political and social methods of identification and behaviour are constructed. Just as different histories exist to challenge scholars to look beyond the state to its forms of government, beyond the individual to their social class, gender, ethnicity and religion, so IR theory has gradually equipped itself with tools – largely underwritten by the role of identity – by which to analyse a host of contested intersubjective selves and others, beyond the abstract unit of the state.

## CONCLUSION

Identity is now at the stage of a semi-accepted variable in IR, one which comes with complicated historical, sociological and cultural baggage, but which can no longer be ignored (Hadfield, 2010). Two key developments have taken place. First is the introduction of cultural themes as acceptable IR variables by key IR scholars. As initially identified by Lapid and Kratochwil, the 'ship of culture' now seems to be sailing more easily through IR waters (Hudson, in Lapid, 1996: 3) with the effect that theories of state, and theories of foreign policy, both previously content to utilize culture 'as an explanation of last resort', are now prepared to 'move forward in the study of cultural effect in foreign policy', the construction of states, and the analysis of state behaviour (Hudson, in Lapid, 1996: 3). The second is the quiet but substantive growth of neoclassical realism. This is a new school of thought that introduces a wider methodology (through the use of an intervening variable), which allows scholars to capture many more historical, cultural and social dynamics (including identity) in their analysis of state behaviour. First identified and categorized in 1998 by Gideon Rose as a new canon of foreign policy theories, subsequent analysis suggests that neoclassical realism uses both systemic and domestic-level variables, but by 'focusing expressly on domestic dynamics to explain the external behavior of a state' (1998: 146) can feasibly and persuasively include national identities and their various cultural and political incarnations:

> As a theory of foreign policy, its top-down methodology is guided by the burgeoning research agenda of neoclassical realism, and illustrates the role played by national identity as an intervening variable between domestic foreign policy making and the opportunities and threats of the external environment against which foreign policy ambitions are drawn. As a theory of state, its bottom-up approach unpacks the forces that national identity wields in shaping unique cultural and political senses of self reference and 'nationhood' internal to the state and its national interests. This hermeneutical framework transforms national identity from a misaligned category of last of resort to a sound theory of both state and foreign policy analysis.
>
> (Hadfield, 2010: 30)

Whether through the unsettling social and linguistic deconstructions afforded by poststructuralism, the use of identity by mainstream constructivists as a manageable and dynamic state portfolio or the more recent dualistic combination of exogenous and endogenous forces of self-identification permitted by neoclassical realism, identity is now a clear contender for analytical acceptance, if not predominance, within IR. It has had a much easier acceptance as a working category and series of self-referential concepts within IH. Ideas, images of visions of individual and collective identities spring more readily from the pages of IH than the sometime laborious work about agents and structures within IR's various and expanding school of thought. The romantic view of the nation as espoused by Herder and Hegel is appealing to look at but lacks empirical credibility when tested against historical examples. A more pragmatic view – in which identity in either primordial or constructed form is merely one of a number of vehicles for national states to articulate other identities, legitimate its interests and establishing the contours of policy – may be easier to grapple with, at least for those in IH. As articulated by Reicher and Hopkins, Montesquieu's view of the nation-state is both compelling and enduring in this respect:

> The national whole has a threefold nature: it is historical, it is a layering of diverse causalities, and it provides the conditions for its own transcendence into more exclusive categorizations.
>
> (quoted in Reicher and Hopkins, 2001: 12)

# Bibliography

Abdel Salam, A. H., and De Waal, Alexander (2001) *The Phoenix State: Civil Society and the Future of Sudan*. Ewing Township, NJ: The Red Sea Press Inc, Justice Africa/Committee of the Civil Project.

Acheson, Dean (1969) *Present at the Creation: My Years with the State Department*. New York: Norton.

Adamthwaite, Anthony (1995) *Grandeur and Misery: France's Bid for Power in Europe, 1914–1940*. London: Arnold.

Addams, Jane (1922) *Peace and Bread in Time of War*. New York: Macmillan.

Addams, Jane (1960) *Jane Addams: A Centennial Reader*. New York: Macmillan.

Addams, Jane (1964) *Democracy and Social Ethics*. Cambridge, MA: Harvard University Press.

Alanbrooke, Field Marshal Lord (2001) *War Diaries 1939–1945*, ed. Alex Danchev and Daniel Todman. London: Phoenix Press.

Aldrich, Robert (1996) *Greater France: A History of French Overseas Expansion: Short History of French Overseas Expansion*. London: Palgrave Macmillan.

Alexandrowicz, C. H. (1967) *An Introduction to the History of the Law of Nations in the East Indies*. Oxford: Clarendon.

Alexandrowicz, C. H. (1973) *The European–African Confrontation: A Study in Treaty Making*. Amsterdam: Sijthoff.

Allawi, Ali A. (2007) *The Occupation of Iraq: Winning the War, Losing the Peace*. New Haven/London: Yale University Press.

Allison, Graham (1971) *Essence of Decision: Explaining the Cuban Missile Crisis*. London: Longman.

Alperovitz, Gar (1965) *Atomic Diplomacy: Hiroshima and Potsdam*. New York: Vintage.

Alperovitz, Gar (1995) *The Decision to Use the Atomic Bomb and the Architecture of an American Myth*. New York: Alfred A. Knopf.

Ambrose, Stephen (1983) *Eisenhower: Soldier, General of the Army, President-Elect (1893–1952)*. New York: Simon & Schuster.

Amin, Samir (1992) *Empire of Chaos*. New York: Monthly Review Press.

Amitai-Preiss, R., and Morgan, David O. (eds) (1999) *The Mongol Empire and its Legacy*. Leiden: Brill.

Amrith, S., and Sluga, G. (2008) New Histories of the United Nations. *Journal of World History*, 19(3, September), 251–274.

Anderson, Benedict (1983) *Imagined Communities*. London: Verso.

Anderson, David (2005) *Histories of the Hanged: Britain's Dirty War in Kenya and the End of Empire*. London: Weidenfeld & Nicolson.

Anderson, David (2009) *The Cold War in Africa*. London: Faber and Faber.

Andrew, Christopher (2009) *The Defence of the Realm: The Authorized History of MI5*. London: Allen Lane.

Andrew, Christopher, and Gordievsky, Oleg (1990) *KGB: The Inside Story of its Foreign Operations from Lenin to Gorbachev*. New York: Harper.

Andrew, Christopher, and Mitrokhin, Vasili (1999) *The Mitrokhin Archive: The KGB in Europe and the West*. New York: Basic Books.

Andrews, Kenneth (1984) *Trade, Plunder and Settlement: Maritime Enterprise and the Genesis of the British Empire, 1480–1630*. Cambridge: Cambridge University Press.

Angell, Norman (1910) *The Great Illusion: A Study of the Relation of Military Power in Nations to Their Economic and Social Advantage*. London: William Heinemann. Revised editions 1911, 1912.

Angell, Norman (1921) *The Fruits of Victory*. London: W. Collins Sons & Co. Ltd.

Anghie, Antony (1999) Finding the Peripheries: Sovereignty and Colonialism in Nineteenth Century International Law. *Harvard International Law Journal*, Winter, 1–68.

Angold, Michael (1997) *The Byzantine Empire, 1025–1204: A Political History*, 2nd edition. London: Longman.

Anstey, Roger (1966) *King Leopold's Legacy: The Congo under Belgian Rule 1908–1960*. Oxford: Oxford University Press.

Anthony, Constance G. (2008) American Democratic Interventionism: Romancing the Iconic Woodrow Wilson. *International Studies Perspectives*, 9(3), 239–253.

Applebaum, Anne (2003) *Gulag: A History*. New York: Doubleday.

Aquinas, Thomas (1938) *On the Governance of Rulers*, 2nd edition. London: Institute of Mediaeval Studies/Sheed and Ward.

Arcidiacono, Bruno (2011) *Cinq Types de paix: Une histoire des plans de pacification perpétuelle (XVIIe–XXe siècles)*. Paris: Presses Universitaires de France.

Arendt, Hannah (1958) *The Origins of Totalitarianism*. NY: Harcourt, Brace Jovanovich.

Aristotle, with Sir Richard Baker (1995) *Politics.* Oxford: Oxford University Press.

Armstrong, David, Lloyd, Lorna, and Redmond, John (1996/2004) *From Versailles to Maastricht: International Organisation in the Twentieth Century.* London: Macmillan.

Armstrong, David (1993) *Revolution and World Order: The Revolutionary State in International Society.* Oxford: Clarendon Press.

Aron, Raymond (1962) *Paix et guerre entre les nations*, Paris: Calmann-Lévy.

Aron, Raymond (1966) *Peace and War: A theory of international relations.* London: Weidenfeld & Nicolson.

Ashcroft, Bill, Griffiths, Gareth, and Tiffin, Helen (1989) *The Empire Writes Back: Theory and Practice in Post-Colonial Literatures.* London: Routledge.

Ashley, Richard (1981) Political Realism and Human Interests. *International Studies Quarterly*, 25(2), 204–237.

Ashworth, Lucian (1999) *Creating International Studies: Angell, Mitrany and the Liberal Tradition.* Aldershot: Ashgate.

Ashworth, Lucian (2002) Did the Realist–Idealist Great Debate Really Happen? *International Relations*, 16(1), 33–51.

Ashworth, Lucian (2006) Where are the Idealists in Interwar International Relations? *Review of International Studies*, 32, 291–308.

Ashworth, Lucian (2007) *International Relations Theory and the Labour Party: Intellectuals and Policymaking from 1918–1945.* London: I. B. Tauris.

Ashworth, Lucian (2010) Geopolitics and the Birth of the American Empire: Mackinder, Whittlesey and the Victory of the West. Paper presented to International Studies Association, New Orleans.

Ashworth, Lucian M. (2011) Feminism, War and the Prospects for Peace. *International Feminist Journal of Politics*, 13(1), 25–43.

Ashworth, Lucian (2012) Mapping a New World. Geography and the Inter-war Study of International Relations. *International Studies Quarterly*, 56(2, June).

Aslan, Reza (ed.) (2011) *Tablet and Pen: Literary Landscapes from the Modern Middle East.* New York: W. W. Norton.

Aspaturian, Vernon V. (1971) *Process and Power in Soviet Foreign Policy.* Boston: Little, Brown.

Aulén, Gustaf (1969) *Dag Hammarskjöld's White Book: An Analysis of 'Markings'.* Philadelphia: Fortress.

Austin, J. (1869) *Lectures on Jurisprudence: or The Philosophy of Positive Law*, 3rd edition, revised and edited by Robert Campbell. London: John Murray.

Bailey, Sidney (1994) *The UN Security Council and Human Rights.* London: Macmillan.

Barkan, Elazar (2001) *The Guilt of Nations: Restitution and Negotiating Historical Injustices.* Baltimore, MD: Johns Hopkins University Press.

Barker, Ernest (1906) *The Political Thought of Plato and Aristotle.* New York: G. P. Putnam's Sons/London: Methuen.

Barraclough, Geoffrey (1979) *Main Trends in History.* New York: Meir.

Barros, James (1970) *The League of Nations and the Great Powers: The Greek–Bulgarian Incident, 1925.* Oxford: Clarendon Press.

Bartelson, Jens (1995) *A Genealogy of Sovereignty*. Cambridge: Cambridge University Press.

Bartlett, C. J. (1994) *The Global Conflict, 1880–1970: The International Rivalry of the Great Powers, 1880–1990*. London: Longman.

Bass, Gary (2004) Jus Post Bellum. *Philosophy & Public Affairs*, 32(4), 384–412.

Bass, Herbert J. (ed.) (1970) *The State of American History*. Chicago: Quadrangle Books.

Bassett, John Spencer (1928) *The League of Nations: A Chapter in World Politics*. New York: Longmans.

Baudrillard, Jean (1994) *The Illusion of the End*. Oxford: Polity Press.

Baylis, John, Wirtz, James, Cohen, Eliot, and Gray, Colin (2002) *Strategy in the Contemporary World: An Introduction to Strategic Studies*. Oxford: Oxford University Press.

Bayly, Christopher (2004) *The Birth of the Modern World 1780–1914. Global Connections and Comparisons*. Oxford: Blackwell.

Becque, Paul (2009) Toynbee and the Limits of Reason: Arnold J. Toynbee's Search for a Middle Way. Ph.D. thesis, University of Kent.

Beer, Max (1933) *The League on Trial*. London: George Allen and Unwin.

Beetham, David (1985) *Max Weber and the Theory of Modern Politics*, 2nd edition. Cambridge and New York: Polity Press.

Beevor, Antony (2002) *Stalingrad*. London: Penguin.

Beevor, Antony (2007a) *The Battle for Spain: The Spanish Civil War 1936–1939*. London: Penguin.

Beevor, Antony (2007b) *Berlin: The Downfall 1945*. London: Penguin.

Bell, Duncan (2005) Unity and Difference: John Robert Seeley and the Political Theology of International Relations. *Review of International Studies*, 31 (3, March), 559–579.

Bell, Duncan (2007) *The Idea of a Greater Britain: Empire and the Future of World Order, 1860–1900*. Princeton: Princeton University Press.

Bell, P. M. H. (2001) *The World Since 1945: An International History*. London: Arnold.

Bellamy, Alex (2006) *Just Wars: From Cicero to Iraq*. Cambridge: Polity Press.

Bellamy, Alex (2009) *Responsibility to Protect: The Global Effort to End Mass Atrocities*. Cambridge: Polity Press.

Bellamy, Alex, Williams, Paul, and Griffin, Stuart (2010) *Understanding Peacekeeping*, 2nd edition. Cambridge: Polity Press.

Belloc (1898) *The Modern Traveller*. London: Edward Arnold.

Beloff, Max (1950) Historians in a Revolutionary Age. *Foreign Affairs*, 29, 248–262.

Ben-Ghiat, Ruth, and Fuller, Mia (2005) *Italian Colonialism*. London: Palgrave.

Bentley, Michael (1977) *The Liberal Mind 1914–1929*. Cambridge: Cambridge University Press.

Bentley, Michael (ed.) (1997) *Companion to Historiography*. London: Routledge.

Bentley, Michael (1999) *Modern Historiography: An Introduction*. London: Routledge.

Berger, Peter L., and Luckmann, Thomas (1967) *The Social Construction of Reality: A Treatise in the Sociology of Knowledge*. Garden City: Anchor Books.

Berger, Stefan, Feldner, Heiko, and Passmore, Kevin (2003) *Writing History: Theory and Practice*. London: Hodder.

Berle, Adolf (1961) *Navigating the Rapids, 1918–1971; From the Diaries of Adolf A. Berle*. New York: Harcourt, Brace, Jovanovich.

Bernal, Martin (1987) *Black Athena: The Afroasiatic Roots of Classical Civilization*. Rutgers University Press.

Berridge, Geoff (2010) *Diplomacy*, 4th edition. Basingstoke: Palgrave.

Beschloss, Michael (2002) *The Conquerors: Roosevelt, Truman and the Destruction of Hitler's Germany, 1941–1945*. New York: Simon and Schuster.

Bhabha, Homi (1994) *The Location of Culture*. London: Routledge.

Biersteker, Thomas J., and Weber, Cynthia (eds) (1996) *State Sovereignty as Social Construct*. Cambridge: Cambridge University Press.

Biran, Michael (2005) *The Empire of the Qara Khitai in Eurasian History*. Cambridge: Cambridge University Press.

Birgerson, Susanne Michele (ed.) (2002) *After the Breakup of a Multi-Ethnic Empire: Russia, Successor States and Eurasian Security*. Westport, CN: Praeger.

Birn, Donald (1981) *The League of Nations*. Oxford: Clarendon Press.

Blainey, Geoffrey (1988) *The Causes of War*, 3rd edition. New York: Free Press.

Bleiker, Roland (2001) The Aesthetic Turn in International Political Theory. *Millennium: Journal of International Studies*, 30(3), 509–533.

Bloch, Marc (1992) *The Historian's Craft*. Manchester: Manchester University Press.

Bodin, Jean (1576/1986) *Les Six Livres de la République* (usually translated as *The Six Books of the Commonwealth*). Paris: Fayard, 1986.

Boemeke, Manfred F., Feldman, Gerald D., and Gläser, Elisabeth (eds) (1998) *The Treaty of Versailles: A Reassessment After 75 Years*. Washington, DC: German Historical Institute.

Boobbyer, Philip (2000) *The Stalin Era*. London: Routledge.

Boobbyer, Philip (2005) *Conscience, Dissent and Reform in Soviet Russia*. London: Routledge.

Booth, Ken (ed.) (1998) *Statecraft and Security: The Cold War and Beyond*. Cambridge: Cambridge University Press.

Booth, Ken, and Smith, Steve (eds) (1995) *International Relations Theory Today*. University Park, PA: Pennsylvania State University Press.

Borgwardt, Elizabeth (2005) *A New Deal for the World: America's Vision for Human Rights*. Cambridge, MA: Belknap Press.

Bosanquet, Bernard (1899) *The Philosophical Theory of the State*. London: Macmillan.

Bossuet (1862–1866) *Oeuvres complètes*. 31 vols, ed. F. Lachat. Paris.

Bourgeois, Léon (1896) *Solidarité*. Paris: Colin.

Bourgeois, Léon (1910) *Pour la Société des Nations*. Paris: Charpentier.

Bourgeois, Léon (1919) *Le Pacte de 1919 et la Société des Nations*. Paris: Charpentier.

Bourgeois, Léon (1923) *L'Oeuvre de la Société des Nations, 1920–1923*. Paris: Payot.

Bourke, Joanna (2000) *An Intimate History of Killing: Face-to-Face Killing in the Twentieth Century*. London: Granta.

Bourne, John, and Sheffield, Gary (2005) *Douglas Haig: War Diaries and Letters 1914–1918*. London: Weidenfeld & Nicolson.

Bourne, K., and Watt, D. C. (1967) *Studies in International History*. London: Longman.

Bowle, John (1961) *Western Political Thought*. Jonathan Cape: London.

Boyd, Andrew (1971) *Fifteen Men on a Powder Keg: A History of the UN Security Council*. New York: Stein and Day.

Boyne, John (2007) *The Boy in the Striped Pyjamas*. London: David Fickling Books/ Random House.

Bozeman, Adda B. (1960) *Politics and Culture in International History*. Princeton: Princeton University Press.

Braddick, Michael (2008) *God's Fury, England's Fire: A New History of the English Civil Wars*. London: Penguin.

Bradshaw, Cherry (2008) *Bloody Nations (Ethics and Global Politics)*. Aldershot: Ashgate.

Braithwaite, Rodric (2011) *Afgantsy: The Russians in Afghanistan, 1979–1989*. London: Profile.

Braudel, Fernand (1980) *On History*. London/Chicago: Weidenfeld & Nicolson/ University of Chicago Press.

Braudel, Fernand (1972–1974) *The Mediterranean and the Mediterranean World in the Age of Philip II*. New York: Harper and Row.

Brendon, Piers (2000) *The Dark Valley: A Panorama of the 1930s*. London: Jonathan Cape.

British Bombing Survey Unit (1998) *The Strategic Air War against Germany, 1939– 1945*. London: Taylor & Francis.

Brock, Peter (2000) *Varieties of Pacifism: A Survey from Antiquity to the Outset of the Twentieth Century*, 4th edition. Syracuse, NY: Syracuse University Press.

Brock, Peter, and Young, Nigel (1999) *Pacifism in the Twentieth Century*. Syracuse, NY: Syracuse University Press.

Bromley, Simon (2008) *American Power and the Prospects for International Order*. Cambridge: Polity.

Brown, Christopher (1992) *International Relations Theory: New Normative Approaches*. Brighton: Harvester/Wheatsheaf.

Brown, Christopher (2001) *Understanding International Relations*. London: Palgrave.

Brown, Christopher, Nardin, Terry, and Rengger, Nicholas (eds) (2002) *International Relations in Political Thought Texts from the Ancient Greeks to the First World War*. Cambridge: Cambridge University Press.

Brown, Peter (1971) *The World of Late Antiquity: From Marcus Aurelius to Muhammad*. London: Thames and Hudson.

Brown, Peter (2003) *The Rise of Western Christendom: Triumph and Diversity, 200–1000*, 2nd edition. Oxford: Blackwell.

Brownlie, Ian (1998), *Principles of Public International Law*, 5th edition. Oxford: Clarendon Press.

Brubaker, Rogers (2004) *Ethnicity Without Groups*. Cambridge, MA: Harvard University Press.

Bryce, James (1864) *The Holy Roman Empire*. Oxford: Shripton.

Bryce, James (1901) *Studies in History and Jurisprudence*, 2 vols. New York/London: Oxford University Press/H. Frowde.

Bull, Hedley (2002) *The Anarchical Society: A Study of Order in World Politics*, 3rd edition, forewords by Andrew Hurrell and Stanley Hoffman. London: Palgrave.

Bullock, Alan (1962) *Hitler: A Study in Tyranny*. London: Penguin.

Bullock, Alan (1991) *Hitler and Stalin: Parallel Lives*. London: HarperCollins.

Bunselmayer, R. E. (1975) *The Cost of the War, 1914–1919: British Economic War Aims and the Origins of Reparation*. Hampden, CN: Shoestring Press.

Burgess, John William (1893) *Political Science and Comparative Constitutional Law*. Boston: Ginn & Co.

Burke, Edmund (1791/1968) *Reflections on the Revolution in France*. London: Penguin.

Burkman, Thomas W. (2008) *Japan and the League of Nations: Empire and World Order, 1914–1938*. University of Hawaii Press.

Burleigh, Michael (2000) *The Third Reich: A New History*. London: Pan/Macmillan.

Burrin, Philippe (1995) *La France à l'heure Allemande 1940–1944*. Paris: Editions du Seuil.

Burton, Margaret (1941) *The Assembly of the League of Nations*. Chicago: University of Chicago Press.

Byman, Daniel J., and Pollack, Kenneth M. (2001) Let Us Now Praise Great Men: Bringing the Statesman Back In. *International Security*, 25 (Spring), 107–146.

Caesar, Julius, and Hammond, Carolyn (58–50 BCE/2008) *The Gallic War: Seven Commentaries on the Gallic War with an Eighth Commentary by Aulus Hirtius*. Oxford: Oxford University Press.

Cain, Peter, and Hopkins, Anthony (2001) *British Imperialism, 1688–2000*, 2nd edition. London: Pearson.

Callahan, Michael D. (2004) *A Sacred Trust: The League of Nations and Africa, 1929–1946*. Sussex Academic Press.

Callil, Carmen (2006) *Bad Faith: A Forgotten History of Family and Fatherland*. New York: Vintage.

Callinicos, Alex (1995) *Theories and Narratives: Reflections on the Philosophy of History*. Oxford: Polity Press.

Calvert, Peter (1997) *Revolution and International Politics*, 2nd edition. London: Continuum.

Calvocoressi, Peter (1996) *World Politics since 1945*, 7th edition. London: Penguin.

Cameron, Averil (1993) *The Later Roman Empire, AD 284–430*. London: Fontana.

Cannadine, David (2001) *Ornamentalism: How the British Saw Their Empire*. London: Allen Lane.

Cannadine, David (ed.) (2004) *What is History Now?* London: Palgrave Macmillan.

Carlton, J. H. Hayes (1931) *The Historical Evolution of Modern Nationalism.* New York: Macmillan.

Carlyle, R. W., and Carlyle, A. W. (1950) *A History of Medieval Political Theory in the West.* London: Thomas Blackwood.

Carnegie Endowment for International Peace (1914/1993) *The Other Balkan Wars.* Introduction by G. F. Kennan. Washington: Carnegie Endowment.

Carr, Edward Hallett (1939) *The Twenty Years' Crisis: An Introduction to International Relations.* London: Macmillan. Revised editions 1945, 1991.

Carr, Edward Hallett (1942) *The Conditions of Peace.* London, Macmillan.

Carr, Edward Hallett (1945) *Nationalism and After.* London, Macmillan.

Carr, Edward Hallett (1950–1978) *A History of Soviet Russia*, 14 vols. London: Macmillan.

Carr, E. H. (1952) *The Bolshevik Revolution, 1917–1923*, 2 vols; (1954) *The Interregnum, 1923–1924*; (1959) *Socialism in One country, 1924–1926*; (1971, 1978), and, with R.W. Davies (1979) *Foundations of a Planned Economy*, all London: Macmillan.

Carr, E. H. (1953) Victorian History. *Times Literary Supplement*, 19 June, xiii.

Carr, E. H. (1961) *What is History?* London: Pelican.

Carr, E. H., with Davies, R. W. (1979) *Foundations of a Planned Economy*, 3 vols. London: Macmillan.

Carruthers, Susan L. (1995) *Winning Hearts and Minds: British Governments, the Media, and Colonial Counter-Insurgency, 1944–1960.* London: Leicester University Press.

Caute, David (1988) *The Fellow Travellers: Intellectual Friends of Communism.* New Haven, CT: Yale University Press.

Caute, David (2003) *The Dancer Defects: The Struggle for Cultural Supremacy during the Cold War.* Oxford: Oxford University Press.

Cesarani, David (1998) *Britain and the Holocaust*, London: Holocaust Educational Trust.

Campbell, Brian (1994) *The Roman Army, 31 BC–AD 337.* London: Routledge.

Ceadel, Martin (1980) *Pacifism in Britain, 1914–1945.* Oxford: Clarendon Press.

Ceadel, Martin (1987) *Thinking about Peace and War.* Oxford: Oxford University Press.

Ceadel, Martin (1996) *The Origins of War Prevention: The British Peace Movement and International Relations, 1730–1854.* Oxford: Clarendon Press.

Ceadel, Martin (2009) *Living the Great Illusion: Sir Norman Angell, 1872–1967.* Oxford: Oxford University Press.

Cecil, Lord Robert (1941) *A Great Experiment: An Autobiography.* New York: Oxford University Press.

Cecil, Lord Robert (1949) *All the Way.* London: Hodder & Stoughton.

Céline, Louis-Ferdinand (1932/1999) *Voyage au bout de la nuit.* Paris: Flammarion/ Folio. English translation (2009) *Journey to the End of the Night.* New York: One World Classics.

Chafer, Tony (2002) *The End of Empire in French West Africa: France's Successful Decolonization.* Oxford: Berg.

Chan, Steve (1997) In Search of Democratic Peace: Problems and Promise. *Mershon International Studies Review*, 41, 59–91.

Chan, Stephen, and Williams, Andrew (1994) *Renegade States: The Evolution of Revolutionary Foreign Policy*. Manchester: Manchester University Press.

Charney, Jonathon (1998) The Impact on the International Legal System of the Growth of International Courts and Tribunals. *NYU International Law and Politics*, 31(4), 697–708.

Chomsky, Noam (1999) *The New Military Humanism: The Lessons from Kosovo*. London: Pluto.

Chomsky, Noam (2003) *Hegemony or Survival*. London: Penguin.

Chomsky, Noam (2007) *Failed States*. London: Penguin.

Christian, David (1998) *A History of Russia, Central Asia and Mongolia*. vol. 1, *Inner Eurasia from Prehistory to the Mongol Empire*. Oxford: Blackwell.

Churchill, Winston (1949) *The Second World War Volume II – Their Finest Hour*. London: Cassell and Co. Ltd.

Cicero, Marcus Tullius (1918) Orationes in Catilinam. In Albert Curtis Clark (ed.), *Collegii Reginae Socius, Oxonii. e Typographeo Clarendoniano*. Oxford: Scriptorum Classicorum Bibliotheca Oxoniensis.

Cimbala, S. J. (2001) *Clausewitz and Chaos: Friction in War and Military Policy*. Westport, CT: Praeger.

Claeys, Gregory (2010) *Imperial Sceptics: British Critics of Empire, 1850–1920*. Cambridge: Cambridge University Press.

Clark, Albert Curtis (1933) The *Acts of the Apostles: A Critical Edition*. Oxford: Clarendon Press.

Clarke, Michael (2001) Review Article. War in the New International Order. *International Affairs*, 77(3), 663–671.

Claude, Inis J. L., Jr (1964) *Swords into Ploughshares: The Problems and Progress of International Organization*. New York: Random House.

Clausewitz, Carl von (1976, unfinished 1830) *On War*, ed. Michael Howard, Peter Paret and Beatrice Heuser. Oxford: Oxford University Press. Introduction by Anatol Rapoport (1968). London: Penguin.

Clavin, Patricia (2005) Defining Transnationalism. *Contemporary European History*, 14(4), 421–439.

Clavin, Patricia (2010) Manner, Place: Writing Modern European History in Global, Transnational and International Contexts. *European History Quarterly*, 40 (October), 624–640.

Clavin, Patricia, and Wessels, Jens-Wilhelm (2005) Transnationalism and the League of Nations: Understanding the Work of its Economic and Financial Organization. *Contemporary European History*, 14(4), 465–492.

Clemens, Diane (1970) *Yalta*. Oxford: Oxford University Press.

Codding, George (1952) *The International Telecommunication Union: An Experiment in International Cooperation*. Leiden: Brill.

Cohen, Stephen F. (1971) *Bukharin and the Bolshevik Revolution: A Political Biography, 1888–1938*. Oxford: Oxford University Press.

Coleman, Christopher, and Starkey, David (eds) (1986) *Revolution Reassessed: Revisions in the History of Tudor Government and Administration*. Oxford: Oxford University Press.

Coleman, Terry (2001) *Nelson: The Man and the Legend*. London: Bloomsbury.

Collingwood, R. G. (1994) *The Idea of History: With Lectures 1926–1928*. Oxford: Oxford University Press.

Colville, Sir John (2004) *Fringes of Power: Downing Street Diaries, 1939–1955*. London: Weidenfeld and Nicolson.

Coker, Christopher (1997) How Wars End. *Millennium*, 26(3), 615–629.

Coker, Christopher (1998) *The Decline of the West*. London: Hurst.

Coker, Christopher (2000) Review. *RUSI Journal*, 145, 78.

Coker, Christopher (2001) *Humane Warfare: The New Ethics of Postmodern War*. London: Routledge.

Coker, Christopher (2007) *The Warrior Ethos: Military Culture and the War on Terror*. LSE International Studies Series. London: Routledge.

Connor, Walker (1994) *Ethnonationalism: The Quest for Understanding*. Princeton, NJ: Princeton University Press.

Conquest, Robert (1968) *The Great Terror: Stalin's Purge of the 1930s*. London: Penguin.

Conquest, Robert (2007) *The Great Terror: A Reassessment: 40th Anniversary Edition*. New York: Oxford University Press.

Cooley, T. M. (1890) *A Treatise on the Constitutional Limitations which Rest upon the Legislative Power of the States of the American Union*, 6th edition, with large additions giving the results of the recent cases by Alexis C. Angell. Boston: Little, Brown.

Cooper, Robert (2004) *The Breaking of Nations: Order and Chaos in the Twenty-First Century*. London: Atlantic Books.

Corbett, Julian Stafford (1914/2009) *Naval and Military Essays*. Cambridge: Cambridge University Press. Reissued 2009.

Cormick, John (2007) *The European Superpower*. London: Palgrave Macmillan.

Corrigan, Gordon (2007) *Mud, Blood and Poppycock: This Will Overturn Everything You Thought You Knew about Britain and the First World War*. London: Cassell Military Paperbacks.

Cortright, David (2008) *Peace: A History of Movements and Ideas*. Cambridge: Cambridge University Press.

Coudenhove-Kalergi, Richard (1948) *Europe Seeks Unity: With a Preface by William C. Bullitt*. New York: New York Institute of Public Affairs and Regional Studies, New York University.

Cowling, Maurice (1971) *The Impact of Labour 1920–1924*. Cambridge: Cambridge University Press.

Cowling, Maurice (1975) *The Impact of Hitler 1933–1940*. Cambridge: Cambridge University Press.

Cox, Mick (ed.) (1998) *Rethinking the Soviet Collapse*. London: Pinter.

Cox, Michael (ed.) (2000) *E. H. Carr: A Critical Appraisal*. London: Palgrave.

Craig, Gordon A. (1983) The Historian and the Study of International Relations. *American Historical Review*, 88 (February), 1–11.

Cramer, Christopher (2006) *Civil War is Not a Stupid Thing: Accounting for Violence in Developing Countries*. London: C. Hurst.

Crampton, R. J. (1994, 2011) *Eastern Europe in the Twentieth Century*. London: Routledge.

Croxton, Derek, and Tischer, Anushka (2001) *The Peace of Westphalia: A Historical Dictionary*. Westport, CT: Greenwood.

Cull, Nicholas J. (2008) *The Cold War and the United States Information Agency: American Propaganda and Public Diplomacy, 1945–1989*. Cambridge: Cambridge University Press.

Dallek, Robert (1979) *Franklin Delano Roosevelt and American Foreign Policy, 1932–1945*. New York: Oxford University Press.

Darwin, John (2007) *After Tamerlane: The Global History of Empire*. London: Allen Lane.

Daum, Andreas W., Gardner, Lloyd C., and Mansbach, Wilfried (2003) *America, The Vietnam War and the World, Comparative and International Perspectives*. Cambridge: Cambridge University Press.

Davies, David (2002) *A Brief History of Fighting Ships: Ships of the Line and Napoleonic Sea Battles, 1793–1815*. London: Constable and Robinson.

Davies, R. W. (1980) *The Industrialization of Soviet Russia: The Socialist Offensive, The Collectivization of Soviet Agriculture, 1919–1930*, vol. 1. London: Macmillan.

De Groot, Gerard J. (2000) *The First World War*. London: Palgrave.

De Groot, Gerald J. (2004) *The Bomb: A Life*. London: Jonathan Cape.

De Hartog, Leo (1996) *Russia and the Mongol Yoke: The History of the Russian Principalities and the Golden Horde, 1221–1502*. London: British Academic Press/I. B. Tauris.

de Vigny, Alfred (1835/1953) *The Military Necessity*. London: Cresset Press. First published in 1835 as *Servitude et grandeur militaires*.

De Visscher, Charles (1957) *Theory and Reality in Public International Law*. Princeton, NJ: Princeton University Press.

Deighton, Anne (1993) *The Impossible Peace: Britain, the Division of Germany and the Origins of the Cold War*. Oxford: Clarendon Press.

Dekar, Paul R. (2005) *Creating the Beloved Community: A Journey with the Fellowship of Reconciliation*. Telford, PA: Cascadia Publishing.

Dell, Robert (1941) *The Geneva Racket*. London: Robert Hale.

Der Derian, James (1987) *On Diplomacy: A Genealogy of Western Estrangement*. Oxford: Blackwell.

Deutsch, Karl Wolfgang (1953) *Nationalism and Social Communication: An Inquiry into the Foundations of Nationality*. Cambridge, MA: MIT Press.

Deutscher, Isaac (1954/2003) *The Trotsky Trilogy: The Prophet Armed: Trotsky 1879–1921*. London: Verso.

Deutscher, Isaac (1959/2003) *The Prophet Unarmed: 1921–1929*. London: Verso.

Deutscher, Isaac (1963/2003) *The Prophet Outcast: 1929–1940*. London: Verso.

Devin, Guillaume (2008) Que reste-t-il du fonctionnalisme international? Relire David Mitrany (1888–1975). *Critique Internationale*, 38 (January–March), 137–152.

Dicey, A. V. (1902) *Introduction to the Study of the Law of the Constitution*, 6th edition. London/New York: Macmillan.

Diehl, Paul (1994) *International Peacekeeping*. Baltimore, MD: Johns Hopkins Press.

Donelan, Michael (2007) *Honor in Foreign Policy: A History and Discussion*. London: Palgrave Macmillan.

Dougherty, James E., and Pfaltzgraff, Robert L. (1971) *Contending Theories of International Relations*, New York: J. P. Lippincott.

Dowden, Richard (2009) *Africa: Altered States, Ordinary Miracles*. London: Portobello.

Doyle, Michael (1983a) Kant, Liberal Legacies and Foreign Affairs. *Philosophy and Public Affairs*, 12(3, Summer), 205–235.

Doyle, Michael (1983b) Kant, Liberal Legacies and Foreign Affairs Part II. *Philosophy and Public Affairs*, 12(4, Autumn), 323–353.

Doyle, Michael (1986) *Empires*. Ithaca, NY: Cornell University Press.

Doyle, Michael (1997) *Ways of War and Peace*. New York: W.W. Norton.

Dudziak, Mary (2010) War, Law and the History of Time. *California Law Review*. University of Southern California Law Legal Studies Paper No. 09-6.

Dunbabin, J. P. D. (1993) The League of Nations' Place in the International System. *History*, 421–442.

Dunbabin, J. P. D. (1994a/2008) *The Cold War: The Great Powers and their Allies*. London: Longman.

Dunbabin, J. P. D. (1994b) *International Relations since 1945*, 2 vols. London: Pearson/Longman.

Dunne, Timothy (1998) *Inventing International Society: A History of the English School*. London: Macmillan, St Antony's Series.

Dunne, Timothy (1999) The British School of International Relations. In Jack Hayward, Brian Barry and Archie Brown (eds), *The British Study of Politics in the Twentieth Century*. Oxford: British Academy/Oxford University Press, pp. 395–424.

Dunne, Timothy (2005) International Society and World Society: How Does it all Hang Together? *Millennium*, 35(1), 157–170.

Dunne, Tim, Schmidt, Brian C., and Lamy, Steven L. (2010) Realism and Liberalism. In Steven L. Lamy, John Baylis, Steve Smith and Patricia Owens (eds), *Introduction to Global Politics*. Oxford: Oxford University Press, pp. 63–91.

Duroselle, Jean-Baptiste (1979) *Politique extérieure de la France: la décadence*. Paris: Imprimerie Nationale.

Duroselle, Jean-Baptiste (1981) *Tout empire périra. Théorie des relations internationales*. Paris: Publications de la Sorbonne.

Durrheim, Kevin (1997) Peace Talk and Violence: An Analysis of the Power of Peace. In Ann Levett, Amanda Kottler, Erica Burman and Ian Parker (eds), *Culture, Power and Difference: Discourse Analysis in South Africa*. London: Zed Books Ltd/University of Cape Town Press, pp. 31–43.

Edmonds, Robin (1991) *The Big Three*. London: Penguin.

Egerton, George (1974) The Lloyd George Government and the Creation of the League of Nations. *American Historical Review*, 79(2 April), 419–444.

Egerton, George (1978) *Great Britain and the Creation of the League of Nations: Strategy, Politics, and International Organization, 1914–1919*. Chapel Hill: University of North Carolina Press.

Eliot, J. H. (2007) *Empires of the Atlantic World: Britain and Spain in America, 1492–1830*. New Haven, CT: Yale University Press.

Elkins, Caroline (2005) *Britain's Gulag: The Brutal End of the Empire in Kenya*. London: Jonathan Cape.

Ellis, Joseph (2002) *Founding Brothers: The Revolutionary Generation*. New York: Random House.

Elton, Geoffrey (1953) *The Tudor Revolution in Government: Administrative Changes in the Reign of Henry VIII*. Cambridge: Cambridge University Press.

Englund, Peter (2002) *The Battle That Shook Europe: Poltava and the Birth of the Russian Empire*. London: I. B. Tauris.

Enloe, Cynthia (1993/2000) *The Morning After: Sexual Politics at the End of the Cold War*. Berkeley/London: University of California Press. New edition Berkeley/London: University of California Press.

Etherington, Mark (2005) *Revolt on the Tigris: The Al-Sadr Uprising and the Governing of Iraq*. London: Hurst and Co.

Evans, Richard (1987) *Rethinking German History: Nineteenth Century Germany and the Origins of the Third Reich*. London: Routledge.

Evans, Richard J. (2000a) *In Defence of History*. London: Granta.

Evans, Richard (2000b) *Rereading German History: From Unification to Reunification, 1800–1996*. London: Routledge.

Evans, Richard (2003) *The Coming of the Third Reich*. London: Penguin.

Faroghi, Suraiya (2005) *The Ottoman Empire and the World Around It*. London: I. B. Tauris.

Faulks, Sebastian (1993) *Birdsong*. London: Vintage.

Fawcett, Louise (2005) *International Relations of the Middle East*. Oxford: Oxford University Press.

Feis, Herbert (1957) *Churchill, Roosevelt, Stalin*. Princeton, NJ: Princeton University Press.

Feis, Herbert (1970) *From Trust to Terror*. New York: Norton.

Fejto, François (1974) *A History of the People's Democracies: Eastern Europe since Stalin*. London: Penguin.

Feldherr, Andrew (ed.) (2009) *The Cambridge Companion to the Roman Historians*. Cambridge: Cambridge University Press.

Ferguson, Niall (1995) *Paper and Iron: Hamburg Business and German Politics in the Era of Inflation, 1897–1927*. Cambridge: Cambridge University Press.

Ferguson, Niall (1997) *Virtual History: Alternatives and Counterfactuals*. New York: Basic Books.

Ferguson, Niall (1998) *The Pity of War*. London: Allen Lane.

Ferguson, Niall (2003a) *Empire: The Rise and Demise of the British World Order and the Lessons for Global Power*. New York: Basic Books.

Ferguson, Niall (2003b) *Empire: How Britain Made the Modern World*, London: Allen Lane/Penguin.

Ferguson, Niall (2004) *Colossus: The Rise And Fall of the American Empire*. London: Allen Lane/Penguin.

Ferguson, Yale H. (2008) Approaches to Defining 'Empire' and Characterizing United States Influence in the World. *International Studies Perspectives*, 9(3), 272–280.

Fernandez-Armesto, Felipe (1995) *Millennium: A History of the Last Thousand Years*. London: Bantam.

Fernandez-Armesto, Felipe (1997) *Truth: A History*. London: Bantam.

Fernandez-Armesto, Felipe (2000) *Civilizations*. London: Macmillan.

Fernandez-Armesto, Felipe (2006) *Pathfinders: A Global History of Exploration*. Oxford: Oxford University Press.

Ferrell, Robert H. (1952) *Peace in Their Time: The Origins of the Kellogg–Briand Pact*. New Haven, CN: Yale University Press.

Feuer, Lewis S. (1989) *Imperialism and the Anti-Imperialist Mind*. New Brunswick: Transaction Publishers.

Figes, Orlando (1997) *A People's Tragedy: The Russian Revolution, 1891–1924*. London: Pimlico.

Figes, Orlando (2003) *Natasha's Dance: A Cultural History of Russia*. London: Penguin.

Figes, Orlando (2010) *Crimea: The Last Crusade*. London: Allen Lane.

Figgis, J. N. (1913) *Churches in the Modern State*. London: Longman.

Findley, Carter Vaughn (2005) *The Turks in World History*. Oxford: Oxford University Press.

Finkel, Caroline (2006) *Osman's Dream: The Story of the Ottoman Empire 1300–1923*. London: John Murray.

Foggon, George (1988) The Origin and Development of the ILO and International Labour Organisations. In Paul Taylor and A. J. R. Groom (eds), *International Institutions at Work*. London: Pinter.

Förster, Steig, Mommsen, Wolfgang, J., and Robinson, Ronald (eds) (1988) *Bismarck, Europe and Africa: The Berlin Africa Conference, 1884–1885 and the Onset of Partition*. London: Oxford University Press.

Forsythe, David (1985) The United Nations and Human Rights, 1945–1985. *Political Science Quarterly*, 100 (2, Summer).

Forsythe, David (2006) *Human Rights in International Relations*, 2nd edition. Cambridge: Cambridge University Press.

Fowler, W. W. (1893/1919) *The City-State of the Greeks and Romans: A Survey Introductory to the study of Ancient History*. London: Macmillan.

Franke, Herbert, and Twitchett, Dennis (1994) *The Cambridge History of China*, vol. 6, *Alien Regimes and Border States, 907–1368*. Cambridge: Cambridge University Press.

Franklin, Ruth (2011) *A Thousand Darknesses: Lies and Truth in Holocaust Fiction*. Oxford: Oxford University Press.

Fraser, Peter (1966) *Joseph Chamberlain*. London: Cassell.

Freeman, Charles (1996). *Egypt, Greece and Rome*. Oxford: Oxford University Press.

Freidel, Frank (1990) *Franklin D. Roosevelt: A Rendezvous with Destiny*. New York: Little, Brown.

Fremont-Barnes, Anthony (2007) *The Indian Mutiny 1857–58*. London: Osprey.

French, Shannon (2003) *The Code of the Warrior: Exploring Warrior Values Past and Present*, Lanham, MD/Boulder, CO: Rowman & Littlefield.

Friedländer, Saul (1966) *Pius XII and the Third Reich: A Documentation*, trans. Charles Fullman. New York: Knopf.

Friedländer, Saul (1997) *Nazi Germany and the Jews, 1933–1939*. New York: HarperCollins.

Friedländer, Saul (2007) *The Years of Extermination: Nazi Germany and the Jews, 1939–1945*. London: HarperCollins.

Friedländer, Saul (2009) *Nazi Germany and the Jews, 1933–1945*, abridged Orna Kenan. London: Phoenix.

Fromkin, D. (2000) *A Peace to End All Peace: The Fall of the Ottoman Empire and the Creation of the Modern Middle East*. London: Phoenix.

Fry, Michael G. (1977) *Lloyd George and Foreign Policy*, vol. 1, *The Education of a Statesman, 1890–1916*. Montreal, Canada: McGill-Queen's University Press.

Fry, Michael G. (1987) *History and International Studies*. Washington, DC: American Historical Association, Institutional Services Program.

Fry, Michael G. (2011) *And Fortune Fled: David Lloyd George, The First Democratic Statesman, 1916–1922*. New York/Oxford: Peter Lang.

Fry, Michael G., and Gilbert, Arthur (1982) A Historian and Linkage Politics; Arno Mayer. *International Studies Quarterly* (26, September), 425–444.

Fukuyama, Francis (1992) *The End of History and the Last Man*. New York: Free Press.

Fulbrook, Mary (1995) *Anatomy of a Dictatorship: Inside the GDR, 1949–1989*. Oxford: Oxford University Press.

Fulbrook, Mary (2005) *The People's State: East German Society from Hitler to Honecker*. New Haven, CT: Yale University Press.

Fuller, J. F. C. (1948) *The Second World War, 1939–1945: A Strategical and Tactical History*. London: Eyre & Spottiswoode.

Fussell, Paul (1975) *The Great War and Modern Memory*. Oxford: Oxford University Press.

Gaddis, John Lewis (1984) The Emerging Post-Revisionist Synthesis on the Origins of the Cold War. *Diplomatic History*, 7(3), 171–190.

Gaddis, John Lewis (1986) The Long Peace: Elements of Stability in the Postwar International System. *International Security*, 10(4, Spring), 99–142.

Gaddis, John Lewis (1987) *The Long Peace: Inquiries into the History of the Cold War*. Oxford: Oxford University Press.

Gaddis, John Lewis (1992/1993) International Relations Theory and the End of the Cold War. *International Security*, 17(3, Winter), 5–58.

Gaddis, John Lewis (1997) *We Now Know: Rethinking Cold War History*. Oxford: Oxford University Press.

Gaddis, John Lewis (2005) *The Cold War: A New History*. London: Penguin.

Galambos, Louis, et al. (eds) (1989) *The Papers of Dwight David Eisenhower*, vols 12 and 13, *NATO and the Campaign of 1952*. Baltimore, MD: Johns Hopkins University Press.

Galeotti, Mark (1995) *Afghanistan: The Soviet Union's Last War*. London: Frank Cass.

Gallagher, John, and Seal, Anil (2004) *The Decline, Revival and Fall of the British Empire*. Cambridge: Cambridge University Press.

Gallie, W. B. (1978) *Philosophers of Peace and War*. Cambridge: Cambridge University Press.

Gat, Azar (1992) *The Development of Military Thought: The Nineteenth Century*. Oxford: Oxford University Press.

Gearson, John, and Schake, Kori (eds) (2002) *The Berlin Wall Crisis: Perspectives on Cold War Alliances*. Basingstoke: Palgrave Macmillan.

Gellner, E. (1983) *Nations and Nationalism*. Ithaca NY: Cornell University Press.

Gellner, Ernest (1987) *Culture, Identity and Politics*. Cambridge/New York: Cambridge University Press.

Gellner, D., and Singer, J. D. (2000) *Nations at War: A Scientific Study of International Conflict, 1816–1992*. Cambridge: Cambridge University Press.

Gentile, Emilio (2008) *L'Apocalypse de la modernité*. Paris: Aubier.

George, Alexander (1993) *Bridging the Gap: Theory and Practice in Foreign Policy*. Washington, DC: United States Institute of Peace.

George, Alexander (1997) Knowledge for Statecraft: The Challenge for Political Science and History. *International Security*, 22(1, Summer).

Gibbon, Edward (1776/1981) *The Decline and Fall of the Roman Empire*. London: Penguin.

Gibbon, Edward (1830) *History of the Later Roman Empire and Its Fall*. Philadelphia: B. F. French.

Giddings, Franklin Henry (1896) *The Principles of Sociology: An Analysis of the Phenomena of Association and of Social Organization*, 3rd edition, reprinted with minor corrections. New York: Macmillan.

Gierke, O. (1880) *Johannes Althusius und die Entwicklung der naturrechtlichen Staatstheorien*. Breslau.

Gilbert, Martin (1991) *Auschwitz and the Allies*. London: Mandarin.

Gilbert, Martin (1992) *Churchill: A Life*. New York: Henry Holt.

Gilligan, Chris (1997) Peace or Pacification Process? A Brief Critique of the Peace Process. In Chris Gilligan and Jon Tonge (eds), *Peace or War? Understanding the Peace Process in Northern Ireland*. Aldershot: Ashgate.

Glendinning, Victoria (2006) *Leonard Woolf*. New York: Simon & Schuster.

Goodman, Martin (2007) *Rome and Jerusalem: The Clash of Ancient Civilizations*. London: Allen Lane.

Goldhagen, Daniel (1997) *Hitler's Willing Executioners: Ordinary Germans and the Holocaust*. London: Abacus.

Goldstein, Erik (1991) *Winning the Peace: British Diplomatic Strategy, Peace Planning, and the Paris Peace Conference, 1916–1920*. Oxford: Oxford University Press.

Goldstein, Erik (1992) *Wars and Peace Treaties, 1816–1991*. London: Routledge.

Goldstein, Erik (2002) *The First World War's Peace Settlements: International Relations, 1918–1925*. London: Longman.

Goldsworthy, Adrian (2009) *How Rome Fell: Death of a Superpower*. New Haven and London: Yale University Press. Published in 2009 as *The Fall of the West: The Slow Death of the Roman Superpower*. London: Phoenix/Orion.

Gorbachev, Mikhail (1999) *On My Country and the World*. New York: Columbia University Press.

Gorki, Maxim (1907/1949) *Mother*. Moscow: Raduga Publishers.

Goulding, Marrack (2003) *Peacemonger*. Baltimore, MD: Johns Hopkins University Press.

Gowing, Margaret (1964) *Britain and Atomic Energy, 1939–1945*. London: Macmillan.

Gramsci, Antonio (1971) *Selections from the Prison Notebooks of Antonio Gramsci*. London: International Publishers.

Grant, John P. (ed). and Barker, Craig J. (2004) *Parry and Grant Encyclopaedic Dictionary of International Law*, 2nd edition. New York: Oceana Publications, Inc.

Gray, Chris Hables (1998) *Postmodern War: The New Politics of Conflict*. Place: Guilford Press.

Gray, Colin (1999) *Modern Strategy*. Oxford: Oxford University Press.

Gray, Colin (2002) *Defining and Achieving Decisive Victory*. Carlisle, PA: Strategic Studies Institute/US Army War College.

Gray, Colin (2005) *Another Bloody Century*, London: Wiedenfeld & Nicolson.

Gray, William Glenn (2003) *Germany's Cold War: The Global Campaign to Isolate East Germany, 1949–1969*. University of North Carolina Press.

Green, John Richard (1892), *Works*. London: Longman, Green and Co.

Greenfeld, Liah (1992), *Nationalism: Five Roads to Modernity*. Cambridge, MA: Harvard University Press.

Grimmelshausen, Johann (1668/1999) *Simplicissimus: The Adventures of Simplicius Simplicissimus*. Sawtry: Dedalus.

Grob-Fitzgibbon, Benjamin (2011) *Imperial Endgame: Britain's Dirty Wars and the End of Empire*. London: Palgrave Macmillan.

Groom, A. J. R., and Taylor, Paul (1975) *Functionalism*. London: Hodder Arnold.

Haas, Ernst B. (1964) *Beyond the Nation State: Functionalism and International Organization*. Palo Alto, CA: Stanford University Press.

Haas, Ernst B. (1968) *The Uniting of Europe: Political, Social and Economic Forces, 1950–57*. Palo Alto, CA: Stanford University Press.

Haas, Peter M. (ed.) (1997) *Knowledge, Power and International Policy*. Columbia: South Carolina University Press.

Haber, Stephen D., Kennedy, David M., and Krasner, Stephen G. (1997) Brothers under the Skin: Diplomatic History and International Relations. *International Security*, Special Issue, 22(1, Summer).

Hadfield, Amelia (2010), *British Foreign Policy, National Identity, and Neoclassical Realism*. Lanham, MD: Rowman and Littlefield.

Halle, Louis (1967) *The Cold War as History*. New York: Harper and Row.

Halper, Stefan and Clarke, Jonathan (2004) *America Alone: The Neo-Conservatives and the Global Order*. Cambridge: Cambridge University Press.

Halper, Stefan and Clarke, Jonathan (2007) *The Silence of the Rational Center: Why American Foreign Policy is Failing*. New York: Perseus Books.

Hamilton, Nigel (2001) *The Full Monty: Montgomery of Alamein 1887–1942*. London: Allen Lane.

Hanson, Neil (2008) *First Blitz: The Secret German Plan to Raze London to the Ground in 1918*. London: Corgi.

Hanson, Victor Davis (2009) *The Western Way of War: Infantry Battle in Classical Greece*. 2nd revised edition. Berkeley: University of California Press.

Hardt, Michael, and Negri, Antonio (2000) *Empire*. Cambridge, MA: Harvard University Press.

Harper, John Lamberton (1996) *American Visions of Europe: Franklin D. Roosevelt, George F. Kennan, and Dean G. Acheson* Cambridge: Cambridge University Press.

Haslam, Jonathan (1999) *The Vices Of Integrity: E. H. Carr, 1892–1982*. London/New York: Verso.

Hathaway, Robert M. (1981) *Ambiguous Partnership: Britain and America, 1944–1947*. New York: Columbia University Press.

Hayek, Friedrich (1944/2001) *The Road to Serfdom*, London: Routledge Classics.

Hayner, Patricia (2002) *Unspeakable Truths: Facing the Challenge of Truth Commissions*. New York: Routledge.

Heater, Derek (1994) *National Self-Determination: Woodrow Wilson and His Legacy*. London: Macmillan.

Heather, Peter (2005) *The Fall of the Roman Empire*. London: Macmillan.

Hegel, Georg Wilhelm Friedrich (1945) *The Philosophy of Right*, trans. with notes by Thomas Malcolm Knox. Oxford: Clarendon Press.

Heidegger, Martin (2004), *On the Essence of Language: The Metaphysics of Language and the Essencing of the Word; Concerning Herder's Treatise On the Origin of Language*, trans. Wanda Torres Gregory and Yvonne Unna. Albany: State University of New York Press.

Hell, Stefan (2010) *Siam and the League of Nations: Modernisation, Sovereignty and Multilateral Diplomacy 1920–1940*. Bangkok: River Press.

Hemleben, Sylvester J. (1943) *Plans for World Peace through Six Centuries*. Chicago: University of Chicago Press.

Henig, Ruth (1973) *The League of Nations*. Edinburgh: Oliver and Boyd.

Henig, Ruth (1995) *Versailles and After, 1919–33*. London: Routledge.

Herder, Johann Gottfried (1967) *Herder's Social and Political Thought: From Enlightenment to Nationalism*, trans. F. M Barnard. Oxford: Clarendon Press.

Herder, Johann Gottfried (1968) *Reflections on the Philosophy of the History of Mankind*, trans. Frank E. Manuel. Chicago: University of Chicago Press.

Herder, Johann Gottfried (2003) *Herder on Nationality, Humanity, and History*, trans. F. M. Barnard. Montreal/Kingston: McGill-Queen's University Press.

Herder, Johann Gottfried (2007) *Herder: Philosophical Writings*, ed. Desmond M. Clarke and Michael N. Forster. Cambridge: Cambridge University Press.

Herman, Gabriel (2006) *Morality and Behaviour in Democratic Athens: A Social History*. Cambridge: Cambridge University Press.

Herodotus (440 BCE/1996) *The Histories*. London: Penguin.

Herrin, Judith (1989) *The Formation of Christendom*, revised, illustrated paperback edition. Princeton University Press/London: Fontana.

Herrin, Judith (2007) *Byzantium: The Surprising Life of a Medieval Empire*. London: Penguin.

Herzstein, Robert Edwin (1982) *When Nazi Dreams Come True: The Horrifying Story of the Nazi Blueprint for Europe*. London: Sphere/Abacus.

Heuser, Beatrice (2002) *Reading Clausewitz*. London: Pimlico.

Hildebrand, Robert C. (1990) *Dumbarton Oaks: The Origins of the United Nations and the Search for Post-War Security*. Chapel Hill: University of North Carolina Press.

Hill, Christopher (2003) *The Changing Politics of Foreign Policy*. London: Palgrave.

Hinsley, Francis Harry (1966) *Sovereignty*. London: C. A. Watts and Co.

Hinsley, Francis Harry (1967) *Power and the Pursuit of Peace*. Cambridge: Cambridge University Press.

Hinsley, Francis Harry (ed.) (1977) *British Foreign Policy under Sir Edward Grey*. Cambridge: Cambridge University Press.

Hinsley, Francis Harry (1988) *British Intelligence in the Second World War*. Cambridge: Cambridge University Press.

Hirst, Margaret E. (1923) *The Quakers in Peace and War: An Account of their Peace Principles and Practice*. London/New York: Swarthmore Press/George H. Doran Co.

Hitler, Adolf (1924/1939) *Mein Kampf*, trans. James Murphy, 4th edition. Hurst & Blackett Ltd (see also, among many others, the 1992 version edited by Donald Cameron Watt. London: Pimlico).

Hobsbawm, Eric (1995) *The Age of Extremes – The Short Twentieth Century 1914–1991*, London, Abacus.

Hobson, J. A. (1902/2005) *Imperialism: A Study*. London: Cosimo Classics.

Hobson, John (2004) *The Eastern Origins of Western Civilization*. Cambridge: Cambridge University Press.

Hoffman, Stanley (1977) An American Social Science: International Relations. *Daedalus*, 106, 41–60.

Hogan, Michael J. (1989) *The Marshall Plan: America, Britain, and the Reconstruction of Western Europe, 1947–1952*. Cambridge: Cambridge University Press.

Hogan, Michael J. (1991) Corporatism. In M. J. Hogan and T. G. Paterson (eds), *Explaining the History of American Foreign Relations*. Cambridge: Cambridge University Press, pp. 226–236.

Hogan, Michael J. (ed.) (1992) *The End of the Cold War: Its Meanings and Implications*. Cambridge: Cambridge University Press.

Hogan, Michael J., and Paterson, Thomas G. (1991) *Explaining the History of American Foreign Relations*. Cambridge: Cambridge University Press.

Holbrooke, Richard (1998) *To End a War*. New York: Random House.

Holland, Robert, Williams, Susan, and Barringer, Terry (eds) (2010) *The Iconography of Independence: Freedoms at Midnight*. London: Routledge.

Holloway, David (1996) *Stalin and the Bomb: The Soviet Union and Atomic Energy, 1939–1956*. New Haven: Yale University Press.

Holsti, Kalevi Jaakko (2004) *Taming the Sovereigns: Institutional Change in International Politics*. Cambridge: Cambridge University Press.

Hoopes, Townsend and Brinkley, Douglas (1997) *FDR and the Creation of the UN*. New Haven: Yale University Press.

Hopkins, Anthony G. (2002) *Globalization in World History*. London: Pimlico.

Hopkirk, Peter (1992) *The Great Game: The Struggle for Empire in Central Asia*. London: Kodansha International.

Horne, Alistair (1978) *A Savage War of Peace: Algeria 1954–1962*. New York: Viking.

Howard, Michael (1976) *War in European History*. Oxford: Oxford University Press.

Howard, Michael (2000) *The Invention of Peace: Reflections on War and International Order*. New Haven/London: Yale University Press.

Howard, Michael (2001) Mistake to Declare this a War. *Royal United Services Institute Journal*, 146(6, December).

Howard, Michael (2008) *War and the Liberal Conscience*. London: Hurst.

Howe, Stephen (ed.) (2010) *The New Imperial Histories Reader*. London: Routledge.

Hudson, Valerie, and Den Boer, Andrea (2005) *Bare Branches: The Security Implications of Asia's Surplus Male Population*. Cambridge, MA: MIT Press.

Hunt, Michael H. (1992) The Long Crisis in US Diplomatic History: Coming to Closure. *Diplomatic History*, 16(1, January), 115–140.

Huntington, Samuel (1973) Transnational Organizations in World Politics. *World Politics*, 25(3, April), 333–368.

Huntington, Samuel P. (1988) The US – Decline or Renewal? *Foreign Affairs* (Winter).

Hussey, Barry (2010) Realism, Disciplinary History and European Studies: From Integration Theory to Normative Power Europe. Ph.D. thesis, University of Limerick.

Hyam, Ronald (2002) *Britain's Imperial Century, 1815–1914: A Study of Empire and Expansion*. London: Palgrave Macmillan.

Ignatieff, Michael (1993) *Blood and Belonging: Journeys into the New Nationalism*. London: BBC Books/Chatto & Windus.

Ignatieff, Michael (1999) *The Warrior's Honor: Ethnic War and the Modern Conscience*. London: Vintage.

Ignatieff, Michael (2004) *Empire Lite: Nation Building in Bosnia, Kosovo, Afghanistan*. New York: Vintage.

Ikenberry, G. John (1996) The Myth of Post-War Chaos. *Foreign Affairs* (May/June).

Ikenberry, G. John (2001) *After Victory: Institutions, Strategic Restraint and the Rebuilding of Order after Major Wars*. Princeton: Princeton University Press.

Ikenberry, G. John (2006) *Liberal Order and Imperial Ambitions*. Cambridge: Polity Press.

Iriye, Akira (1979) Culture and Power, International Relations as Intercultural Relations, *Diplomatic History*, 3, 115–128.

Iriye, Akira (1987) *The Origins of the Second World War in Asia and the Pacific*. London: Longman.

Iriye, Akira, and Saunier, Pierre-Yves (eds) (2009) *The Palgrave Dictionary of Transnational History*. Basingstoke: Palgrave Macmillan.

Israel, Jonathan (1995) *The Dutch Republic: Its Rise, Greatness, and Fall, 1477–1806*. Oxford: Oxford University Press.

Jabri, Viv (1994) *Discourses on Violence*. Manchester: Manchester University Press.

Jackson, Ashley (2009) *Mad Dogs and Englishmen*. London: Quercus.

Jackson, Ian (2001) *The Economic Cold War: America, Britain and East–West Trade, 1948–63*. London: Palgrave.

Jackson, Peter (2005) *The Mongols and the West*. Harlow: Pearson.

Jackson, R. H. (1990) *Quasi-States: Sovereignty, International Relations and the Third World*. Cambridge: Cambridge University Press.

Jacquin-Berdal, D. (2000) State and War in the Formation of the Eritrean National Identity. in S. O. Vandersluis (ed.), *The State and Identity Construction in International Relations*. London: Palgrave Macmillan.

James, Alan (1990) *Peacekeeping in International Politics*. London: Macmillan.

James, Harold (2006) *The Roman Predicament: How the Rules of International Order Created the Politics of Empire*. Princeton, NJ: Princeton University Press.

Jenkins, Keith (1991) *Rethinking History*. London: Routledge.

Jenkins, Keith (1995) *On 'What is History': From Carr and Elton to Rorty and White*. London: Routledge.

Jenkins, Keith (1997) *The Postmodern History Reader*. London: Routledge.

Jenkins, Roy (2001) *Churchill*. London: Pan Books.

Jilek, Lubor (2004/2005) Pan-Europe de Coudenhove-Kalergi: l'homme, le projet et le movement paneuropéen. *Human Security*, 9, 205–209.

Joas, Hans (2003) *War and Modernity*. Cambridge: Polity Press.

Johnson, Gaynor (2011) *Lord Robert Cecil, Viscount Cecil of Chelwood*. Basingstoke: Ashgate Gower.

Joint Warfare Publication (2004) The Military Contribution to Peace Support Operations, JWP3-50, 2nd edition. http://pksoi.army.mil/doctrine_concepts/documents/UK/jwp3_50.pdf

Joll, James (1968) *1914. The Unspoken Assumptions*. London: Weidenfeld & Nicolson.

Joll, James and Martel, Gordon (2007) *The Origins of the First World War*, 3rd edition. Harlow: Pearson.

Jones, Charles (1998) *E. H. Carr and International Relations: A Duty To Lie*. New York: Cambridge University Press.

Jones, Heather (2009) International or Transnational? Humanitarian Action During the First World War. *European Review of History*, 16(5, October), 697–713.

Jordanova, Ludmilla (2000) *History in Practice*. London: Hodder.

Joyce, James Avery (1978) *Broken Star: The Story of the League of Nations, 1919–1939*. Swansea: Christopher Davies.

Judd, Denis (1977) *Radical Joe: A Life of Joseph Chamberlain*. London: Hamish Hamilton.

Judd, Denis (1997) *Empire: The British Imperial Experience, from 1765 to the Present*. London: Fontana.

Jünger, Ernst (1948) *The Peace*. Hinsdale, IL: Henry Regnery Company.

Jünger, Ernst (2004) *Storm of Steel*, trans. Michael Hofman. London: Penguin.

Kacowicz, Arie M., et al. (2000) *Stable Peace among Nations*. London: Rowman and Littlefield.

Kagan, Robert (2006a) *Dangerous Nation: America and the World 1600–1898*. London: Atlantic Books.

Kagan, Robert (2006b) *Paradise and Power: America and Europe in the New World Order*. London: Atlantic Books.

Kagan, Robert (2008) *The Return of History and the End of Dreams*. New York: Knopf.

Kaldor, Mary (1999) *New and Old Wars: Organized Violence in a Global Era*. Cambridge: Polity.

Kalyvas, Stathis N. (2006) *The Logic of Violence in Civil War*. Cambridge: Cambridge University Press.

Kampfner, John (2004) *Blair's Wars*. London: Simon and Schuster/Free Press.

Kant, Immanuel (1795/1983) *Perpetual Peace and Other Essays*, trans. Ted Humphrey. Indianapolis: Hackett.

Kant, Immanuel (1993) *Grounding for the Metaphysics of Morals with On a Supposed Right to Lie Because of Philanthropic Concerns*, 3rd edition, trans. James W. Ellington. Indianapolis: Hackett Publishing Company.

Kapoor, Ilan (2004) Hyper-Self-Reflexive Development? Spivak on Representing the Third World 'Other'. *Third World Quarterly*, 25(4), 627–647.

Karsh, Ephraim (1988) *Neutrality and Small States*. London: Routledge.

Katyal, Neal K., and Tribe, Laurence H. (2002) Waging War, Deciding Guilt: Trying the Military Tribunals. *Yale Law Journal*, 111, 1259–1310.

Kavanagh, Denis (1991) Why Political Science Needs History. *Political Studies*, 39(3, September), 479–495.

Kedourie, E. (1960) *Nationalism*. Oxford: Blackwell.

Keegan, John (1976) *The Face of Battle: A Study of Agincourt, Waterloo and the Somme*. London: Penguin.

Keegan, John (1994) *A History of Warfare*. New York: Vintage.

Keegan, John (2009) *The American Civil War: A Military History*. New York: Alfred A. Knopf.

Kegley, C. W., and Raymond, G. (2001) *Exorcising the Ghost of Westphalia: Building World Order in the New Millennium*. Saddle River, NJ: Prentice Hall.

Kennan, George (1947) The Sources of Soviet Conduct. *Foreign Affairs*, 25(4, July), 566–582.

Kennan, George (1951/1984) *American Diplomacy, 1900–1950*. Chicago: University of Chicago Press.

Kennan, George F. (1968/1972) *Memoirs, 1950–1963*. Boston: Little, Brown.

Kennedy, Paul (1980) *The Rise of Anglo-German Antagonism, 1860–1914*. London: Prometheus.

Kennedy, Paul (1988) *The Rise and Fall of Great Powers: Economic Change and Military Conflict from 1500 to 2000*. London: Unwin Hyman.

Kennedy-Pipe, Caroline (1995) *Stalin's Cold War: Soviet Strategies in Europe, 1943–1956*. Manchester: Manchester University Press.

Kent, Bruce (1989) *The Spoils of War: The Politics, Economics and Diplomacy of Reparations, 1918–1922*. Oxford: Clarendon Press.

Keohane, Robert (1984) *After Hegemony*. Princeton: Princeton University Press.

Keohane, Robert, and Nye, Joseph (eds) (1981) *Transnational Relations and World Politics*. Cambridge, MA: Harvard University Press.

Kersaudy, François (1981) *Churchill and de Gaulle*. London: Collins.

Kershaw, Ian (1998) *Hitler, 1889–1936: Hubris*. London: Penguin.

Kershaw, Ian (2000a) *Hitler, 1936–1945: Nemesis*. London: Penguin.

Kershaw, Ian (2000b) *The Nazi Dictatorship*. London: Edward Arnold.

Keylor, William (2000) *The Twentieth Century World: An International History*. New York: Oxford University Press.

Keynes, John Maynard (1920/2011) *The Economic Consequences of the Peace*. London and New York: Macmillan/Wilder.

Khazhdan, A. P., and Epstein, Ann Wharton (1985) *Change in Byzantine Culture in the Eleventh and Twelfth Centuries*. Berkeley: University of California Press.

Kier, Elizabeth (1999) *Imagining War: French and British Military Doctrine between the Wars*. Princeton: Princeton University Press.

Kiernan, Ben (2007) *Blood and Soil: A World History of Genocide and Extermination from Sparta to Darfur*. New Haven, CT: Yale University Press.

King, Charles (2000) *The Moldovans: Romania, Russia, and the Politics of Culture*. Studies of Nationalities. Stanford, CA: Hoover Institution.

Kinross, Patrick Balfour (1979) *The Ottoman Centuries: The Rise and Fall of the Turkish Empire*. London: William Morrow.

Kissinger, Henry (1964) *A World Restored*. New York: Grosset and Dunlap.

Kissinger, Henry (1994) *Diplomacy*. New York: Simon and Schuster.

Kitchen, Martin (2009) *Rommel's Desert War: Waging World War II in North Africa, 1941–1943*. Cambridge: Cambridge University Press.

Kitching, Carolyn J. (1999) *Britain and the Problem of International Disarmament, 1919–1934*. London: Routledge.

Kitto, H. D. F. (1992) *The Greeks*. London: Penguin.

Knock, Thomas J. (1992) *To End All Wars: Woodrow Wilson and the Quest for a New World Order*. New York: Oxford University Press.

Knutsen, Tjorborn (1999) *The Rise and Fall of World Orders*. Manchester: Manchester University Press.

Kohn, H. (1945) *The Idea of Nationalism*. Macmillan: New York.

Koliopoulos, John, and Veremis, Thanos (2002) *Greece: The Modern Sequel: From 1821 to the Present*. London: C. Hurst and Co.

Kolko, Gabriel, (1990) *The Politics of War: The World and United States Foreign Policy, 1943–1945*. New York: Pantheon.

Koskenniemi, Martti (2002) *The Gentle Civilizer of Nations: The Rise and Fall of International Law 1870–1960*. Cambridge: Cambridge University Press.

Koskenniemi, Martti (2005), *From Apology to Utopia: The Structure of International Legal Argument*. Cambridge: Cambridge University Press.

Krasner, S. D. (2009) *Power, the State, and Sovereignty: Essays on International Relations*. Routledge.

Krauthammer, Charles (1990/1991) The Unipolar Moment. *Foreign Affairs* (Winter).

Kreijen, Gerard (2004) *State Failure, Sovereignty and Effectiveness: legal lessons from the decolonization of Sub-Saharan Africa*, foreword by Sir Robert Y. Jennings. Leiden/Boston: M. Nijhoff.

Kuehl, Warren F., and Dunn, Lynne K. (1997) *Keeping the Covenant: American Internationalists and the League of Nations, 1920–1939*. Kent, OH: Kent State University Press.

Kuitenbrouwer, Maarten (1991) *The Netherlands and the Rise of Modern Imperialism: Colonies and Foreign Policy, 1870–1902*. New York/Oxford: Berg Publishers.

Kuklick, Bruce (1972) *American Policy and the Division of Germany: The Clash with Russia over Reparations*. New York: Cornell University Press.

Kupchan, Charles (2003) *The End of the American Era: US Foreign Policy and the Geopolitics of the Twenty-First Century*. New York: Vintage.

Lacouture, Jean (1991) *De Gaulle: The Ruler, 1945–1970*. London: Harvill.

LaFeber, Walter (1993) *Inevitable Revolutions: United States in Central America*. New York: W. W. Norton.

Laity, Paul (2001) *The British Peace Movement, 1870–1914*. Cambridge: Cambridge University Press.

Lake, David A. (2008) The New American Empire? *International Studies Perspectives*, 9(3), 281–289.

Lal, Deepak (2004) *In Praise of Empires: Globalization and Order*. London: Palgrave.

Landau, Ronnie S. (1998) *Studying the Holocaust: Issues, Readings, and Documents*. London: Routledge.

Landau, Ronnie S. (2006) *The Nazi Holocaust: Its History and Meaning*. London: I. B. Tauris.

Langhorne, Richard (1981) *The Collapse of the Concert of Europe. International Politics, 1897–1914*. London: Macmillan.

Langhorne, Richard (1982) The Establishment of the Idea and Practice of the International Conference, 1648–1830. *Studies in History and Politics*, 2.

Langhorne, Richard (1986) Reflections on the significance of the Congress of Vienna. *Review of International Studies*, 12.

Lapid, Yosef (1996) Culture's Ship? Returns and Departures in International Relations Theory. In Yosef Lapid and Friedrich Kratochwil (eds), *The Return of Culture and Identity in IR Theory*. Boulder, CO: Lynne Rienner.

Lapid, Yosef, and Kratochwil, Friedrich (eds) (1996) *The Return of Culture and Identity in IR Theory*. Boulder, CO: Lynne Rienner.

Laqueur, Walter (2003) *A History of Zionism*. London: Tauris Parke.

Larson, Arthur C., and Jenks, Wilfred (1965) *Sovereignty Within the Law*. Dobbs Ferry, NY: Oceana/London: Stevens.

Layne, Christopher (1994) Kant or Cant: The Myth of Democratic Peace. *International Security*, 19(2, Autumn), 5–49.

Lebow, Richard Ned (2006) *The Tragic Vision of Politics*. Cambridge: Cambridge University Press.

Lebow, Richard Ned (2008) *A Cultural History of International Relations*. Cambridge: Cambridge University Press.

Lebow, Richard Ned, and Stein, Janice Gross (1994) *We All Lost the Cold War*. Princeton: Princeton University Press.

Leffler, Melvyn P., and Painter, David A. (eds) (1994) *Origins of the Cold War: An International History*. London: Routledge.

Leffler, Melvyn, and Westad, Odd Arne (eds) (2009) *The Cambridge History of the Cold War*, vol. 1. Cambridge: Cambridge University Press.

Lemkin, Raphael (1944) *Axis Rule in Occupied Europe*. Washington, DC: Carnegie Endowment for International Peace.

Lenin, Vladimir Ilyich (1916/2000) *Imperialism, the Highest Stage of Capitalism*. New Delhi: Left Word Books.

Lentin, Anthony (1984) *Guilt at Versailles: Lloyd George and the Pre-History of Appeasement*. London, Methuen.

Leuchtenberg, William E. (2009) *Herbert Hoover*. New York: Henry Holt and Co.

Levi, Primo (2007) *Survival in Auschwitz: If This is a Man*. www.bnpublishing.com

Levy, Jack S. (1988) Domestic Politics and War. *Journal of Interdisciplinary History*, 18(4), The Origin and Prevention of Major Wars (Spring), 653–673.

Levy, Jack (1994) The Theoretical Foundations of Paul W. Schroeder's International System. *International History Review*, 16(4, November), 715–744.

Levy, Jack (1997) Too Important to Leave to the Other: History and Political Science in the Study of International Relations. *International Security*, 22(1, Summer).

Lewis, Joanna (2007) Nasty, Brutish and in Shorts? British Colonial Rule, Violence and the Historians of Mau Mau. *Round Table*, 96(389), 201, 223.

Liddell Hart, Basil (1932/1944) *The British Way in Warfare*. London: Faber and Faber.

Liebknecht, Wilhelm (1917/1973) *Militarism and Anti Militarism*. Cambridge: Rivers Press.

Lieven, Dominic (2000) *Empire: The Russian Empire and Its Rivals*. London: John Murray.

Lindqvist, Sven (2001) *A History of Bombing*. London: Granta.

Link, Arthur Stanley (1971) *The Higher Idealism of Woodrow Wilson*. Nashville, TN: Vanderbilt University Press.

Link, Arthur Stanley (1972) *Woodrow Wilson and the Progressive Era, 1910–1917*. New York: HarperCollins.

Link, Arthur Stanley (1979) *Woodrow Wilson, Revolution, War and Peace*. Arlington Heights, IL: Harlan Davidson Inc.

Linklater, Andrew (1998) *The Transformation of Political Community: Ethical Foundations of the Post-Westphalian Era*. Cambridge: Polity Press.

Linn, James W. (1935) *Jane Addams: A Biography*. New York, Appleton-Century.

Lipgens, Walter (ed.) (1984) *Documents on the History of European Integration*, vol. 1, *Continental Plans for European Union 1939–1945*. Berlin: Walter De Gruyter.

Lipstadt, Deborah (1993) *Denying the Holocaust – The Growing Assault on Truth and Memory*. Harmondsworth: Penguin.

Livy (2006) *Hannibal's War, Books 21–31*. Oxford: Oxford University Press.

Lloyd, Lorna (1997) *Peace through Law. Britain and the International Court in the 1920s*, Boydell & Brewer for the Royal Historical Society.

Lloyd George, David (1932) *The Truth about Reparations and War Debts*. London: William Heinemann.

Lloyd George, David (1938) *The Truth about the Peace Treaties*. London: Gollancz.

Locke, John (1689/1764) *Two Treatises of Government*, ed. Thomas Hollis. London: A. Millar et al.

Locke, John (1690/1997) *An Essay Concerning Human Understanding*, ed. Roger Woolhouse. London: Penguin.

Locke, John (1693/1996) *Some Thoughts Concerning Education*. London/New York: Thoemmes Press, facsimile of 1693 edition.

London, Louise (2001) *Whitehall and the Jews, 1933–1948: British Immigration Policy and the Holocaust*. Cambridge: Cambridge University Press.

Long, David, and Wilson, Peter (eds) (1995) *Thinkers of the Twenty Years' Crisis*. Oxford: Clarendon Press.

Louis, William Roger (1967) *Great Britain and Germany's Lost Colonies 1914–1919*. Oxford: Clarendon Press.

Louis, William Roger (2006) *Ends of British Imperialism: The Scramble for Empire, Suez and Decolonization: Collected Essays*. London: I. B. Tauris.

Lovell, Julia (2011) *The Opium War: Drugs, Dreams and the Making of China*. London: Picador.

Lowes Dickinson, G. (1917) *The Choice before Us*. London: George Allen and Unwin.

Lowes Dickinson, G. (1926) *The International Anarchy, 1904–1914*. London: George Allen and Unwin.

Loyd, Anthony (2000) *My War Gone by, I Miss it So*. London: Anchor.

Luard, Evan (1982) *A History of the United Nations*, 2 vols. London: Macmillan.

Lucan (1999) *Civil War*. Oxford: Oxford University Press.

Lucas, W. Scott (1991) *Divided We Stand: Britain, the US and the Suez Crisis*. London: Hodder and Stoughton.

Lucas, W. Scott (1996) *The Lion's Last War: Britain and the Suez Crisis*. Manchester: Manchester University Press.

Lukacs, John (1976) *The Last European War, September 1939–December 1941*. New York: Anchor Press.

Lukes, Steven (2005) *Power: A Radical View*, 2nd edition. London: Palgrave Macmillan.

Lundestad, Geir (1998a) *'Empire' by Integration: The United States and European Integration, 1945–1997*. Oxford: Oxford University Press.

Lundestad, Geir (1998b/2005) *The United States and Western Europe since 1945: From Empire by Invitation to Transatlantic Drift*. Oxford: Oxford University Press.

Lundestad, Geir, and Njolstad, Olav (2002) War and Peace in the 20th Century and Beyond. *Proceedings of the Nobel Centennial Symposium*. New Jersey/London/Singapore/Hong Kong: World Scientific Publishing Co.

Luttwak, Edvard N. (1987/2001/2002) *Strategy: The Logic of War and Peace*. Cambridge, MA: Harvard University Press.

Luttwak, Edvard N. (1991) Give War a Chance. *Foreign Affairs* (July/August).

Lynch, Allen (1987) *The Soviet Study of International Relations*. Cambridge: Cambridge University Press.

Lynch, Allen (1986) *The Cold War is Over: Again*. Boulder, CO: Westview.

Lyon, Peter (1963) *Neutralism*. Leicester: University of Leicester Press.

McCarthy, Thomas (2009) *Race, Empire and the Idea of Human Development*. Cambridge: Cambridge University Press.

McDonald, Patrick J. (2009) *The Invisible Hand of Peace: Capitalism, The War Machine, and International Relations Theory*. Cambridge: Cambridge University Press.

Macdonald, R. St J., and Johnstone, Douglas M. (eds) (1983/1986) *The Structure and Process of International Law: Essays in Legal Philosophy Doctrine and Theory*. Dordrecht/Boston: Martinus Nijhoff.

Macdonald Fraser, George (1971) *The Steel Bonnets: Story of the Anglo-Scottish Reivers*. London: HarperCollins.

McGerr, Michael (1991) The Price of the 'New Transnational History'. *American Historical Review*, 96(4, October), 1056–1067.

Mac Ginty, Roger, and Williams, Andrew (2009) *Conflict and Development*. London: Routledge.

McIntyre, W. David (2001) *A Guide to the Contemporary Commonwealth*. London: Palgrave.

McIntyre, W. David (2009) *The Britannic Vision: Historians and the Making of the British Commonwealth, 1907–1948*. London: Palgrave.

McKercher, Brian (ed.) (1990) *Anglo-American Relations in the 1920s: The Struggle for Dominance*. London: Macmillan.

McLellan, David (1976) *Karl Marx: His Life and Thought*. London: Paladin.

McPherson, James (2001) *Battle Cry of Freedom: The Civil War Era*. London: Penguin.

Machel, Graca (2001) *Impact of War on Children*. London: Hurst and Co.

Mack Smith, Denis (2001) *Mussolini*, new edition. Weidenfeld & Nicolson.

Macmillan, Margaret (2001) *Peacemakers: The Paris Conference of 1919 and its Attempt to End War*. London: John Murray.

Madariaga, Salvador de (1929) *Disarmament*. Oxford: Oxford University Press.

Maier, Charles S. (1988) *Recasting Bourgeois Europe*. Princeton: Princeton University Press.

Maier, Charles (ed.) (1996) *The Cold War in Europe: Era of a Divided Continent*, 3rd edition. Princeton: Princeton University Press.

Maine, Henry (1864) Minute on the Kathiawar States (1864) Printed in *Life and Speeches*, and *Early History of Institutions* (1875).

Maine, Henry Sumner (1875) *Early History of Institutions*. London: John Murray.

Maine, Henry Sumner (1906) *Ancient Law: Its Connection with the Early History of Society and its Relation to Modern Ideas*, 1st edition, with Fredrick Pollock's notes. London: John Murray.

Malmborg, Mikael af (2003) *Neutrality and State-building in Sweden*. London: Palgrave Macmillan.

Mandelbaum, Michael (2002) *The Ideas that Conquered the World: Peace, Democracy and Free Markets in the Twenty-First Century*. Oxford: Public Affairs.

Mann, Michael (1986) *The Sources of Social Power*, vol. 1, *A History of Power from the Beginning to 1760 AD*. Cambridge: Cambridge University Press.

Mann, Michael (1993) *The Sources of Social Power*, vol. 2, *The Rise of Classes and Nation-States, 1760–1914*. Cambridge: Cambridge University Press.

Mann, Michael (1995) A Political Theory of Nationalism and its Excesses. In Sukumar Periwal (ed.), *Notions of Nationalism*. Budapest: Central European University Press.

Manners, Ian, and Whitman, Richard G. (2000) *The Foreign Policies of European Union Member States*. Manchester: Manchester University Press.

Mansfield, Edward, and Snyder, Jack (2005) *Electing to Fight – Why Emerging Democracies go to War*. Cambridge, MA: MIT Press.

Mantoux, Paul (1946) *The Carthaginian Peace: The Economic Consequences of Mr Keynes*. Oxford: Oxford University Press.

Markwell, Donald (2006) *John Maynard Keynes and International Relations: Economic Paths to War and Peace*. Oxford: Oxford University Press.

Marriott, J. A. R. (1937) *Commonwealth or Anarchy: A Survey of Projects of Peace from the 16th to the 20th Centuries*. London: Philip Allen.

Martin, Gilbert (1991) *Churchill: A Life*, 1st edition. London: William Heinemann.

Martin, Raymond (1993) Objectivity and Meaning in Historical Studies: Toward a Post-Analytic View. *History and Theory*, 32(1).

Marx, Karl (1999/1867) *Capital: A New Abridgement*, ed. David McLellan. Cambridge: Cambridge University Press.

Mastanduno, Michael (1992) *Economic Containment: CoCom and the Politics of East–West Trade*. Ithaca, NY: Cornell University Press.

Mawdsley, Ewan (2008) *The Russian Civil War*. Edinburgh: Birlinn.

May, Alex (1995) The Round Table, 1910–1966. Unpublished D.Phil. thesis, University of Oxford.

May, Ernest B. (1984) Writing Contemporary International History. *Diplomatic History*, 8 (Spring), 103–113.

Mayall, James (1990) *Nationalism and International Society*. Cambridge: Cambridge University Press.

Mayne, Richard, and Pinder, John (1990) *Federal Union: The Pioneers*. London: Macmillan.

Mazower, Mark (2008) *Networks of Power in Modern Greece: Essays in Honour of John Campbell*. London: C. Hurst and Co.

Mazower, Mark (2009a) *Hitler's Empire: Nazi Rule in Occupied Europe*. London: Penguin.

Mazower, Mark (2009b) *No Enchanted Palace: The End of Empire and the Ideological Origins of the United Nations*. Princeton: Princeton University Press.

Meacham, Jon (2003) *Franklin and Winston: A Portrait of a Friendship*. London: Granta.

Mead, Walter Russell (2002) *Special Providence: American Foreign Policy and How It Changed the World*. London: Routledge.

Mearsheimer, John (1991) Back to the Future: Instability in Europe after the Cold War. In Sean Lynn-Jones (ed.), *The Cold War and After: Prospects for Peace*. Cambridge, MA: MIT Press.

Medlicott, W. M. (1955) The Scope and Study of International History. *International Affairs*, 31 (October).

Medlicott, W. N. (1956) *Bismarck, Gladstone and the Concert of Europe*. London: University of London/Athlone Press.

Medlicott, W. N. (1963) *The Congress of Berlin and After: A Diplomatic History of the Near Eastern Settlement, 1878–1880*, 2nd edition. London: Frank Cass.

Mercer, Jonathon (1995) Anarchy and Identity. *International Organisation*, 49(2), 229–252.

Merriam, Charles Edward (1900) *History of the Theory of Sovereignty since Rousseau*. New York: Columbia University Press.

Meskill, John (1973) History of China. In John Meskill and J. Mason Gentzler, *An Introduction to Chinese Civilization*. New York: Columbia University Press.

Miller, David Hunter (1925) *The Geneva Protocol*. New York: Macmillan.

Miller, David Hunter (1928) *The Drafting of the Covenant*. New York: G. P. Putnam's Sons.

Miller, J. D. B. (1986) *Norman Angell and the Futility of War: Peace and the Public Mind*. London: Macmillan.

Milward, Alan (1984) *The Reconstruction of Western Europe, 1945–51*. London: Routledge.

Mitchell, George J. (1999) *Making Peace*. Berkeley/London: University of California Press.

Mitrany, David (1933) *The Progress of International Government*. New Haven, CN: Yale University Press.

Mitrany, David (1943/1966) *A Working Peace System*. Reprinted with a new introduction by Hans Morgenthau. Chicago: Quadrangle Books.

Molnar, Miklos (1975) *Marx, Engels et la politique internationale*. Paris, Presses Universitaires de France.

Mombauer, Annika (2002) *The Origins of the First World War: Controversies and Consensus*. London: Longman.

Montefiore, Simon Sebag (2005a) *Potemkin: Catherine the Great's Imperial Partner*. New York: Vintage.

Montefiore, Simon Sebag (2005b) *Stalin: The Court of the Red Tsar*. New York: Vintage.

Montefiore, Simon Sebag (2011) *Jerusalem: The Biography*. Weidenfeld & Nicolson.

Mommsen, Theodor (1968) *The Provinces of the Roman Empire: The European Provinces*. Chicago: University of Chicago Press.

Momssen, Theodor (1996/1854–1856) *History of Rome*, abridged edition. London: Routledge/Thoemmes Press.

Momssen, Theodor (2008) *Mommsen's History of Rome*, abridged edition. London: Wildside Press.

Moorehead, Caroline (1999) *Dunant's Dream: War, Switzerland and The History of the Red Cross*. London: HarperCollins.

Moorhead, John (2001) *The Roman Empire Divided, 400–700*. London: Longman.

Morefield, Jeanne (2005) *Covenants without Swords: Idealist Liberalism and the Spirit of Empire*. Princeton: Princeton University Press.

Morel, E. D. (1915) *Ten Years of Secret Diplomacy: An Unheeded Warning*. London: National Labour Press.

Morgan, Philip D., and Hawkins, Sean (eds) (2004) *Black Experience and the Empire*. Oxford: Oxford University Press.

Morgan, David (2007) *The Mongols*, 2nd edition. Oxford: Blackwell.

Morgenthau, Hans (1945) The Machiavellian Utopia. *Ethics*, 55(2, January), 145–147.

Morgenthau, Hans (1948) *Politics among Nations: The Struggle for Power and Peace*. New York: McGraw Hill.

Morgenthau, Henry (1929) *I Was Sent to Athens*. Garden City, NY: Doubleday, Doran.

Morgenthau, Henry (2003) *Ambassador Morgenthau's Story*. Detroit: Wayne State University.

Morton, Brian (2008) *Woodrow Wilson*. London: Haus Publishing.

Müller, Michael, and Torp, Cornelius (2009) Conceptualising Transnational Spaces in History. *European Review of History*, 16(5, October), 609–617.

Mulligan, William (2010) *The Origins of the First World War*. Cambridge: Cambridge University Press.

Münkler, Herfried (2007) *Empires: The Logic of World Domination from Ancient Rome to the United States*. Cambridge: Polity.

Murphy, Craig (1994) *International Organization and Industrial Change*. Cambridge: Polity.

Murray, Gilbert (1928) *The Ordeal of this Generation: The War, the League and the Future*. London: George Allen and Unwin.

Murray, Gilbert (1948) *From the League to the UN*. Oxford: Oxford University Press.

Nasson, Bill (2004) *Britannia's Empire: Making a British World*. London: Tempus.

Nau, Henry R. (1990) *The Myth of America's Decline – Leading the World Economy into the 1990s*. New York: Oxford University Press.

Navari, Cornelia (1995) David Mitrany and International Functionalism, in David Long and Peter Wilson (eds.), *Thinkers of the Twenty Years. Crisis: Inter-War Idealism Reassessed*. Oxford: Clarendon Press.

Nef, John U. (1968) *War and Human Progress*. New York: Free Press.

Negash, Tekaste, and Tronvoll, Kjetil (2001) *Brothers at War: Making Sense of the Eritrean–Ethiopian War*. Athens: Ohio University Press/Swallow Press.

Nicholas, Herbert (1967) *The United Nations as a Political Institution*. Oxford: Oxford University Press.

Nicolson, Harold (1946) *The Congress of Vienna: A Study in Allied Unity: 1812–1822*, London: Constable and Co.

Nicolson, Harold (2005) *The Harold Nicolson Diaries, 1907–1964*, ed. Nigel Nicolson. London, Phoenix.

Noel-Baker, Philip (1925) *The Geneva Protocol*. London: King.

Noel-Baker, Philip (1926/1972) *Disarmament*. London: Garland Publishing.

Norman, Richard, (1995) *Ethics, Killing and War*. Cambridge: Cambridge University Press.

Northedge, F. S. (1986) *The League of Nations: Its Life and Times, 1920–1946*. New York: Holmes & Meier.

Norton, Anne (2005) *Leo Strauss and the Politics of American Empire*. New Haven, CT: Yale University Press.

Norwich, John Julius (1990) *Byzantium: The Early Centuries*, vol. 1. London: Penguin.

Norwich, John Julius (1992) *Byzantium: The Apogee*. New York: Alfred A. Knopf.

Norwich, John Julius (1995) *Byzantium: The Decline and Fall*. New York: Viking.

Notter, Harley (1949) *Post-War Foreign Policy Preparation, 1939–1945*. Washington, DC: US Department of State.

Nunn, Wilfrid (1932/2007) *Tigris Gunboats: The Forgotten War in Iraq, 1914–1917*. London: Chatham Publishing. 2007 edition with a new introduction by Sir Jeremy Greenstock.

Nye, Joseph (1991) *Bound to Lead: The Changing Nature of American Power*. New York: Basic Books.

Nzongola-Ntalaja, Georges (2002) *The Congo from Leopold to Kabila: A People's History*. London: Zed Books.

Oakeshott, Michael (1990) *Experience and Its Modes*. Cambridge: Cambridge University Press.

Olson, William C., and Groom, A. J. R. (1991) *International Relations Then and Now: Origins and Trends in Interpretation*. London: HarperCollins.

Orend, Brian (2007) Jus Post Bellum: The Perspective of a Just-War Theorist. *Leiden Journal of International Law*, 20(3), 571–591.

Orwell, George (1945/2011) *Animal Farm*. London: Penguin.

Osiander, Andreas (1994) *The States System of Europe, 1640–1990*. Oxford: Clarendon Press.

Ostrower, Gary B. (1996) *The League of Nations: From 1919 to 1929*. New York: Avery Publishing Group.

Overy, Richard (2002) *Interrogation: The Nazi Elite in Allied Hands*. Harmondsworth: Penguin. First published 1945.

Overy, Richard (2004) *The Dictators: Hitler's Germany, Stalin's Russia*. London: Allen Lane.

Overy, Richard (2009) *The Morbid Age: Britain and the Crisis of Civilization, 1919–1939*. London: Penguin.

Owen, John W. (1997) *Liberal Peace, Liberal War: American Politics and International Security*. Ithaca, NY: Cornell University Press.

Owen, John W., IV (2005) Iraq and the Democratic Peace. *Foreign Affairs* (November–December).

Pagden, Anthony (2010) Imperialism, Liberalism and the Quest for Perpetual Peace. In Stephen Howe (ed.), *The New Imperial Histories Reader*. London: Routledge, pp. 437–447.

Paine, Thomas (2009) *Thomas Paine: Collected Writings: Common Sense/The Crisis/Rights of Man/The Age of Reason*. New York: Classic House.

Paine, Thomas (2010) *Dissertation on First Principles of Government*. Gale ECCO: Print Editions.

Parchami, Ali (2009) *Hegemonic Peace and Empire. The Pax Romana, Britannica, and Americana (War, History and Politics)*. London: Routledge.

Paris, Roland (2004) *At War's End: Building Peace after Civil Conflict*. Cambridge: Cambridge University Press.

Parker, W.H. (1982) *Mackinder: Geography as an Aid to Statecraft*. Oxford: Oxford University Press.

Parmar, Inderjeet (2004) *Think Tanks and Power in Foreign Policy: A Comparative Study of the Role and Influence of the Council on Foreign Relations and the Royal Institute of International Affairs, 1939–1945*. London: Palgrave.

Patch, William L. Jr (1998) *Heinrich Bruning and the Dissolution of the Weimar Republic*. Cambridge: Cambridge University Press.

Paul, Derek (1997) Peace Studies at Bradford. *Peace Magazine*, 13(6, November–December).

Paul, T. V., Wirtz, James J., and Fortman, Michel (2004) *Order and Balance of Power*. Stanford, CA: Stanford University Press.

Penn, William (1693/1912) *An Essay towards the Present and Future Peace of Europe*. The American Peace Society, online at: http://www.archive.org/details/anessaytowardsp00penngoog

Perrie, Maureen, and Pavlov, Andrei (2003) *Ivan the Terrible (Profiles in Power)*. Harlow, UK: Longman.

Persico, Joseph (2001) *Roosevelt's Secret War: FDR and World War II Espionage*. New York: Random House.

Persico, Joseph (2004) *Eleventh Month, Eleventh Day, Eleventh Hour: The War to End All Wars and Its Violent End*. London: Hutchinson.

Philips, David L. (2005) *Losing Iraq: Inside the Post-war Reconstruction Fiasco*. New York: Basic Books.

Philpott, D. (2001) *Revolutions in Sovereignty: How Ideas Shaped Modern International Relations*. Princeton: Princeton University Press.

Pick, Daniel (1993) *War Machine: the Rationalization of Slaughter in the Modern Age*. New Haven: Yale University Press.

Pink, Gerhard P. (1942) The Conference of Ambassadors (Paris 1920 – 1931). *Geneva Studies*, 12(4–5).

Pipes, Richard (1995) *Russia Under the Bolshevik Regime*. New York: Vintage Books, Random House Inc.

Plato (2010) *Laws*. New York: Classic Books International.

Plesch, Dan (2010) *America, Hitler and the UN – How the Allies Won the War and Forged a Peace.* London: I. B. Tauris.

Pomeroy, Sarah B. (1999) *Ancient Greece: A Political, Social, and Cultural History.* Oxford: Oxford University Press.

Ponting, Clive (2000) *World History: A New Perspective.* London: Chatto and Windus.

Popovski, Vesselin, Reichberg, Gregory M., and Turner, Nicholas (eds) (2009) *World Religions and the Norms of War.* Tokyo: United Nations University Press.

Porter, Andrew (1994) *European Imperialism, 1860–1914 (Studies in European History).* London: Palgrave.

Porter, Bernard (1968/2007) *Critics of Empire: British Radical Attitudes towards Colonialism in Africa, 1895–1914*, 2nd edition. London: I. B. Tauris.

Porter, Bernard (2004) *The Lion's Share: A Short History of British Imperialism 1850–1990.* London: Pearson.

Porter, Bernard (2006) *Empire and Superempire: Britain, America and the World.* New Haven, CT: Yale University Press.

Power, Eileen (n.d.) The Opening of the Land Routes to Cathay. In Arthur Percival Newton, *Travel and Travellers of the Middle Ages.* n.p.

Preston, R. A., Wise, S. F., and Werner, H. O. (1956) *Men in Arms: A History of Warfare and its Interrelationships with Western Society.* Boston: Atlantic.

Ramcharan, Bertrand (2002) *The United Nations High Commissioner for Human Rights: The Challenges of International Protection.* The Hague: Martinus Nijhoff.

Ray, James Lee (1992) *Global Politics.* Boston: Houghton Mifflin.

Reicher, Stephen, and Hopkins, Nick (2001) *Self and Nation: Categorization, Contestation and Mobilization.* London: Sage.

Reid, Walter (2006) *Douglas Haig: Architect of Victory.* Edinburgh: Berlinn.

Reves, Emery (1945) *The Anatomy of Peace*: New York/London: Harper & Brothers Publishers.

Reynolds, David (1981) *The Creation of the Anglo-American Alliance, 1937–1941: A Study in Competitive Co-operation.* Chapel Hill: University of North Carolina Press.

Reynolds, David (1991) *Britannia Overruled: British Policy and World Power in the Twentieth Century.* London: Longman.

Reynolds, David (2000) *One World Divisible: A Global History Since 1945.* New York: W. W. Norton.

Reynolds, David (2006) *From World War to Cold War: Churchill, Roosevelt, and the International History of the 1940s.* Oxford: Oxford University Press.

Reynolds, David (2007) *Summits: Six Meetings That Shaped the Twentieth Century.* London: Allen Lane.

Rhodes, Richard (1998) *The Making of the Atomic Bomb.* New York: Simon & Schuster.

Richmond, Oliver (2005) *The Transformation of Peace.* Basingstoke: Palgrave.

Richmond, Oliver, and Franks, Jason (2009) *Liberal Peace Transitions: Between Statebuilding and Peacebuilding.* Edinburgh: Edinburgh University Press.

Rigby, Andrew (2001) *Justice and Reconciliation: After the Violence.* London: Lynne Rienner.

Rikhye, Indar Jit (1984) *The Theory and Practice of Peacekeeping*. New York: International Peace Academy.

Robbins, Keith (1976) *The Abolition of War: The 'Peace Movement' in Britain, 1914–1919*. Cardiff: University of Wales Press.

Roberts, Andrew (2006) *A History of the English-Speaking Peoples since 1900*. London: Weidenfeld & Nicolson.

Roberts, J. M. (1999) *Twentieth Century: A History of the World 1901 to the Present*. London: Penguin.

Robertson, A. H. (1972) *Human Rights in the World: An Introduction to the Study of the International Protection of Human Rights*. Manchester: Manchester University Press.

Robinson, P. (ed.) (2003) *Just War in Comparative Perspective*. Aldershot: Ashgate.

Robinson, R., Gallagher, J., and Denny, A. (1961) *Africa and the Victorians – The Climax of Imperialism*. New York: Garden City.

Rodger, N. A. M. (2006) *The Command of the Ocean: A Naval History of Britain 1649–1815*. London: Penguin.

Rofe, J. Simon (2007) *Franklin D. Roosevelt's Foreign Policy and the Welles Mission*. New York: Palgrave.

Rofe, J. Simon (2012) The Roosevelt Administration's Dilemma during the 'Phony War': Pre-War Post-War Planning and the case of the Advisory Committee on Problems in Foreign Relations, *Diplomacy and Statecraft* Vol. 22:3 2012.

Roosevelt, Franklin Delano (1950) *FDR: His Personal Letters*. New York: Duell, Sloane and Pearce.

Rosamond, Ben (2000) *Theories of European Integration*. London: Palgrave Macmillan.

Rosenman, Samuel L. (1950) *The Public Papers and Addresses of Franklin D. Roosevelt*. London: Macmillan & Co. Ltd.

Rothschild, Joseph, and Wingfield, Nancy M. (2007) *Return to Diversity. A Political History of East Central Europe since World War II*. New York: Oxford University Press.

Rougemont, Denis de (1961) *Vingt-huit siècles d'Europe*. Paris: Payot.

Rousseau, Jean-Jacques (1964) Que l'état de guerre naît de l'état social. *Oeuvres complètes*, vol. 3. Paris: Gallimard.

Said, Edward (1979) *Orientalism*. New York: Vintage.

Said, Edward (1993) *Culture and Imperialism*. New York: Vintage.

Sainsbury, Keith (1985) *The Turning Point*. Oxford: Oxford University Press.

Sainsbury, Keith (1996) *Churchill and Roosevelt at War: The War They Fought and the Peace They Hoped to Make*. London: Macmillan.

Saint-Simon, Claude Henri de (1814) *De la réorganization de la société européenne*. Paris: Adrien Egron.

Sakwa, Richard (2008) *Russian Politics and Society*, 4th edition. London: Routledge.

Sallust (2007) *Catiline's War, The Jugurthine War, Histories*. London: Penguin.

Sancery, Elizabeth (1999) (quoting Amiral Lanxade, Ethique et opérations militaires, *L'Armement: Revue de la Delegation Generale pour l'Armement*, September 1995, p. 9), Ph.D. thesis, University of Kent.

Sancery, Elizabeth (2001) Rethinking the Management of United Nations Peacekeeping Operations: Implications for Command and Control. University of Kent.

Sanders, J. J. (1971) *The History of the Mongol Conquests*. Philadelphia: University of Pennsylvania Press.

Sarolea, Charles (2009) *Europe and the League of Nations*. Charleston, NC: BiblioBazaar.

Sassoon, Siegfried (1974) *Memoirs of an Infantry Officer*. London: Faber and Faber.

Schlesinger, Arthur M., Jr (1957–1960), *The Age of Roosevelt*, 3 vols. Boston: Houghton Mifflin.

Schmidt, Brian C. (1998a) Lessons from the Past: Reassessing the Interwar Disciplinary History of International Relations. *International Studies Quarterly*, 42, 433–459.

Schmidt, Brian C. (1998b) *The Political Discourse of Anarchy*. Albany, NY: State University of New York Press.

Scholte, Jan Art (1994) New Border Crossings: Christopher Thorne and International History. *SHAFR Newsletter*, 25(2, June), 1–28.

Schöpflin, George (2000) *Nations, Identity, Power*. London: Hurst.

Schroeder, Paul W. (1994) *The Transformation of European Politics, 1763–1848*. New York: Oxford University Press.

Schroeder, Paul W. (1997) History and International Relations Theory: Not Use or Abuse, but Fit or Misfit. *International Security*, 22(1) (Summer), 64–74.

Schuker, Stephen A. (1976) *The End of French Predominance in Europe: The Financial Crisis of 1924 and the Adoption of the Dawes Plan*. Chapel Hill: University of North Carolina Press.

Schulzinger, Robert (1975) *The Making of the Diplomatic Mind*. Middletown, CN: Wesleyan University Press.

Scott, Franklin Daniel (1989) *Sweden, the Nation's History*. Carbondale, IL: Southern Illinois University Press.

Scott-Smith, Giles, and Krabbendam, Hans (2003) *The Cultural Cold War in Western Europe, 1945–1960*. London: Frank Cass.

Seib, Philip (2006) *Broadcasts from the Blitz: How Edward R. Murrow Helped Lead America into War*. Dulles, VA: Potomac Books.

Sellars, Kirsten (2002) *The Rise and Rise of Human Rights*. Thrupp: Sutton Publishing.

Service, Robert (2004) *Stalin: A Biography*. London: Macmillan.

Seth, Sanjay (2009) Historical Sociology and Postcolonial theory: Two Strategies for Challenging Eurocentrism. *International Political Sociology*, 3(3, September), 334–338.

Sewell, William H., Jr (1994) *A Rhetoric of Bourgeois Revolution: The Abbé Sieyes and 'What Is the Third Estate?'* Durham, NC: Duke University Press.

Sharp, Alan (1991) *The Versailles Settlement: Peacemaking in Paris*. London: Macmillan.

Sharp, Alan (2008a) *David Lloyd George*. London: Haus Publishing.

Sharp, Alan (2008b) *The Versailles Settlement: Peacemaking After the First World War, 1919–1923*. London: Palgrave Macmillan.

Sharp, Alan (ed.) (2010) *Consequences of Peace: The Versailles Settlement – Aftermath and Legacy*. London: Haus Publishing.

Sharp, Paul (2009) *Diplomatic Theory of International Relations*. Cambridge: Cambridge University Press.

Sharp, Paul, and Wiseman, Geoff (eds) (2007) *The Diplomatic Corps as an Institution of International Society*. New York: Palgrave Macmillan.

Shaw, Timothy (2008) *Commonwealth: Inter- and Non-State Contributions to Global Governance*. London: Routledge.

Shawcross, William (2000) *Deliver Us from Evil: Warlords and Peacekeepers in a World of Endless Conflict*. London: Bloomsbury.

Sheffield, Gary (2002) *Forgotten Victory: The First World War, Myths and Realities*. London: Review.

Sheffield, Gary (2011) *The Chief: Douglas Haig and the British Army*. London: Aurum.

Sheldon, Richard (1987) *Hammarskjöld*. New York: Chelsea House Publishers.

Shennan, Andrew (1989) *Rethinking France: Plans for Renewal, 1940–1946*. Oxford: Clarendon Press.

Sherman, Nancy (2006) *Stoic Warriors: The Ancient Philosophy behind the Military Mind*. Oxford: Oxford University Press.

Simms, Brendan (2007) *Three Victories and a Defeat: The Rise and Fall of the First British Empire, 1714–1783*. London: Allen Lane.

Skidelsky, Robert (1990) *Oswald Mosley*. London: Macmillan.

Skidelsky, Robert (2000) *John Maynard Keynes: Fighting for Britain, 1937–1946*. London: Macmillan.

Skidelsky, Robert (2003) *John Maynard Keynes: 1883–1946: Economist, Philosopher, Statesman*. London: Macmillan.

Skinner, Quentin (1985) *The Return of Grand Theory in the Human Sciences*. Cambridge: Cambridge University Press.

Skocpol, Theda (1979) *States and Social Revolutions*. Cambridge: Cambridge University Press.

Small, Melvin, and Singer, David J. (1976) The War Proneness of Democratic Regimes, 1816–1965. *Jerusalem Journal of International Relations*, 1, 50–69.

Smart, Nick (2003) *British Strategy and Politics during the Phony War: Before the Balloon Went Up*, London: Praeger.

Smith, Adam (1776/1982) *The Wealth of Nations*. London: Penguin.

Smith, Anthony D. (1981) *The Ethnic Revival*. Cambridge: Cambridge University Press.

Smith, Anthony D. (1986) *The Ethnic Origins of Nations*. Oxford: Blackwell.

Smith, Neil (2003) *American Empire: Roosevelt's Geographer and the Prelude to Globalization*. Berkeley: University of California Press.

Smith, R. B. (1987) *An International History of the Vietnam War: Revolution versus Containment, 1955–1961*. London: Palgrave Macmillan.

Smith, R. B. (1988) *An International History of the Vietnam War: The Struggle for South-East Asia, 1961–65*. London: Palgrave Macmillan.

Smith, Rupert (2005) *The Utility of Force: The Art of War in the Modern World*. London: Allen Lane.

Smith, Thomas W. (1999) *History and International Relations*. London: Routledge.

Solzhenitsyn, Aleksandr (1973) *The Gulag Archipelago*. New York: Harper and Row.

Solzhenitsyn, Aleksandr (2000) *One Day in the Life of Ivan Denisovich*. trans. and introduction Ralph Parker. London: Penguin.

Sorel, Georges (1941) *Reflections on Violence*. New York: Peter Smith.

Spilsbury, Julian (2008) *The Indian Mutiny*. London: Phoenix.

Spivak, Gayatri Chakravorty (1988) Can the Subaltern Speak? In C. Nelson and L. Grossman (eds), *Marxism and the Interpretation of Culture*. Basingstoke: Macmillan.

Stahn, Carsten, and Kleffner, Jann K. (eds) (2008) *Jus Post Bellum – Towards a Law of Transition from Conflict to Peace*. Cambridge: Cambridge University Press.

Stein, Peter, Thomas, J. A. C., and Lewis, A. D. E. (eds) *Studies in Justinian's Institutes in memory of J. A. C. Thomas*. London: Sweet & Maxwell.

Steiner, Zara (1969) *The Foreign Office and Foreign Policy*. Cambridge: Cambridge University Press.

Stelzer, Irwin (ed.) (2004) *The Neocon Reader*. New York: Grove Press.

Stern, Fritz (1974) *The Politics of Cultural Despair: A Study in the Rise of Germanic Ideology*. Berkeley: University of California Press.

Stern, Fritz (1999) *Einstein's German World*. Princeton: Princeton University Press

Stettinius, Edward R. (1950) *Roosevelt and the Russians: The Yalta Conference*. London: Jonathan Cape.

Stevenson, David (1988) *The First World War and International Politics*. Oxford: Oxford University Press.

Stevenson, David (1996) *Armaments and the Coming of War in Europe, 1904–1914*. Oxford: Clarendon Press.

Stevenson, David (2005) *1914–1918: The History of the First World War*. London: Penguin.

Stirk, Peter M. R. (ed.) (1989) *European Unity in Context: The Interwar Period*. London: Pinter.

Stoessinger, John G. (2007) *Why Nations Go to War*, 10th edition. London: Wadsworth Publishing.

Stokes, Gale (1993) *The Walls Came Tumbling Down. The Collapse of Communism in Eastern Europe*. New York: Oxford University Press.

Stone, Norman (2011) *Turkey: A Short History*. London: Thames and Hudson.

Stuart, Douglas T. (2008) *Creating the National Security State: A History of the Law that Transformed America*. Princeton/Oxford: Princeton University Press.

Stueck, William Whitney (1997) *The Korean War: An International History*. Princeton: Princeton University Press.

Suganami, Hidemi (1996) *On the Causes of War*. New York: Oxford University Press.

Sun Tzu (1998) *The Art of War*. Ware: Wordsworth.

Swartz, Marvin (1971) *The Union of Democratic Control in British Politics during the First World War*. Oxford: Clarendon Press.

Sylvest, Casper (2009a) *British Liberal Internationalism, 1880–1930: Making Progress?* Manchester: Manchester University Press.

Sylvest, Casper (2009b) James Bryce and the Two Faces of Nationalism. In Ian Hall and Lisa Hill (eds), *British International Thought from Hobbes to Namier*. New York: Palgrave.

Tacitus, Cornelius (1971) *The Agricola and the Germania*. London: Penguin.

Taleb, Nassim Nicholas (2007) *The Black Swan: The Impact of the Highly Improbable*. London: Allen Lane.

Talmon, Jacob. L. (1952) *The Origins of Totalitarian Democracy*. London: Mercury.

Taylor, Paul (1964) Functionalism: The Theory of David Mitrany. In Paul Taylor and A. J. R. Groom (eds), *International Organisation*. London: Pinter.

Taylor, Paul (1993) *International Organization in the Modern World*. London: Pinter.

Taylor, Paul, and Groom, A. J. R. (eds) (1988) *International Institutions at Work*. London: Pinter.

Taylor, Paul, and Groom, A. J. R. (2000) *The United Nations at the Millennium: The Principal Organs*. London: Continuum.

Thelen, David (1999) The Nation and Beyond: Transnational Perspectives on United States History. *Journal of American History*, 86(3), 12.

Thomas, Martin (2005) *The French Empire Between the Wars: Imperialism, Politics and Society*. Manchester: Manchester University Press.

Thomas, Martin, Moore, Bob, and Butler, L. J. (2008) *Crises of Empire: Decolonization and Europe's Imperial States, 1918–1975*. London: Routledge.

Thompson, Andrew (2005) *The Empire Strikes Back? The Impact on Britain from the Mid-Nineteenth Century*. London: Longman.

Thompson, Kenneth W. (1985) *Toynbee's Philosophy of World History and Politics*. Louisiana: Louisiana State University Press.

Thompson, A., and Snidal, D. (2000) International Organization. In B. Bouckaert and G. De. Geest (eds), *Encyclopedia of Law and Economics*, Vol. 1, *The History and Methodology of Law and Economics*. Cheltenham: Edward Elgar.

Thorne, Christopher (1967) *The Approach of War, 1938–1939*. London: Macmillan.

Thorne, Christopher (1973) *The Limits of Foreign Policy: The West, The League and the Far Eastern Crisis of 1931–33*. New York: Putnam.

Thorne, Christopher (1978) *Allies of a Kind*. London: Hamish Hamilton.

Thorne, Christopher (1983) International Relations and the Promptings of History. *Review of International Studies*, 9 (April), 123–136.

Thorne, Christopher (1985) *The Issue of War: States, Societies and the Far Eastern Conflict of 1941–1945*. New York: Hamilton.

Thorne, Christopher (1988) *Border Crossings: Studies in International History*. Oxford: Blackwell.

Thucydides (431 BCE/1954) *The History of the Peloponnesian War*, revised edition. ed. M. I. Finley, trans. Rex Warner. London: Penguin.

Tilly, Charles (1975) *The Formation of National States in Western Europe*. Princeton: Princeton University Press.

Tilly, Charles (1990) *Coercion, Capital and European States, A.D. 990–1990 (Studies in Social Discontinuity)*. Oxford: Basil Blackwell.

Todorov, Tzvetan (1999) *Facing the Extreme: Moral Life in the Concentration Camps*. London: Weidenfeld & Nicolson.

Todorov, Tzvetan (2000) *Mémoire du mal: Tentation du bien: Enquête sur le siècle*. Paris: Robert Laffont.

Tosh, John (2009) *The Pursuit of the Past*. London: Longman.

Tosh, John (2010) *The Pursuit of History: Aims, Methods and New Directions in the Study of Modern History*, 5th edition. New York: Pearson Longman.

Toynbee, Arnold (1974) *A Study of History, Abridgement of Vols I–X*. Oxford: Oxford University Press.

Towle, Philip (2009) *Going to War*. London: Palgrave Macmillan.

Trachtenberg, Mark (1980) *A Constructed Peace: The Making of the European Settlement, 1945–1963*. Princeton: Princeton University Press.

Trevelyan, G. M. (1944) *English Social History: A Survey of Six Centuries from Chaucer to Queen Victoria*. London: Longman.

Troubetzkoy, Alexis S. (2006) *A Brief History of the Crimean War*. London: Robinson.

Tuck, Richard (1999) *The Rights of War and Peace: Political Thought and the International Order from Grotius to Kant*. Oxford: Oxford University Press.

Tyler, Christian (2003) *Wild West China: The Taming of Xinjiang*. London: John Murray.

Tyrell, Ian (2007) *Transnational Nation: United States History in Global Perspective Since 1789*. London: Palgrave Macmillan.

Ulam, Adam (1968) *Expansion and Coexistence: Soviet Foreign Policy, 1917–1973*, 2nd edition. New York: Holt.

Ulam, Adam (1984) *Dangerous Relations: The Soviet Union in World Politics, 1970–1982*. Oxford: Oxford University Press.

Ullmann, W. (1949) The Development of the Medieval Idea of Sovereignty. *English Historical Review*, 64.

Urban, Mark (1988) *War in Afghanistan*. London: Macmillan.

Urquhart, Brian (1987) *A Life in Peace and War*. New York: Harper and Row.

Van Creveld, Martin (2011) *The Age of Air Power*. New York: Public Affairs.

Van Evera, Stephen (1999) *Causes of War: Power and the Roots of Conflict*. Ithaca, NY: Cornell University Press.

Van Kleffens, E. N. (1953) Sovereignty in International Law. *Recueil des Cours*, 82, 1–132.

Vandersluis, Sarah-Owen (2000) *The State and Identity Construction in International Relations*. London: Palgrave Macmillan.

Vandersluis, Sarah-Owen, and Yeros, Paris (2000) *Poverty in World Politics: Whose Global Era?* London, Palgrave Macmillan.

Veblen, Thorstein (1912/1994) *The Theory of the Leisure Class: An Economic Study of Institutions*. Chicago: University of Chicago Press.

Vedrine, Hubert (2007) *History Strikes Back: How States, Nations and Conflicts are Shaping the 21st Century*, trans. Philip H. Gordon. Washington, DC: Brookings Institution Press.

Vegetius (Flavius Vegetius Renatus) (2001) *Vegetius: Epitome of Military Science*, trans. N. P. Milner. Liverpool: Liverpool University Press.

Vellacott, Jo (1980) *Bertrand Russell and the Pacifists in the First World War*. Brighton: Harvester Press.

Vernadsky, George (1979) *The Mongols in Russia*. New Haven: Yale University Press.

Vinen, Richard (2002) *A History in Fragments: Europe in the Twentieth Century*. London: Abacus.

Virilio, Paul (1989) *War and Cinema: The Logistics of Perception*. London: Verso.

Viroli, Maurizio (1995) *For Love of Country: An Essay on Patriotism and Nationalism*. Oxford: Clarendon Press.

Visser, Reidar (2005) *Basra, the Failed Gulf State: Separatism and Nationalism in Southern Iraq*. Munster: LitVerlag.

Vogt, Joseph (1993) *The Decline of Rome*. London: Weidenfeld.

Walker, Rob (1993) *Inside/Outside: International Relations as Political Theory*. Cambridge: Cambridge University Press.

Waite, Terry (1994) *Taken on Trust*. Coronet: London.

Wallace, William (1997) The Nation-State: Rescue or Retreat. In Peter Gowan and Perry Anderson (eds), *The Question of Europe*. London: Verso.

Wallerstein, Immanuel (1974) *The Modern World System*. New York: Academic Press.

Wallerstein, Immanuel (1980) *The Modern World System II: Mercantilism and the Consolidation of the European World-Economy, 1600–1750*. New York: Academic Press.

Wallerstein, Immanuel (1987) The United States and the World 'Crisis'. In T. Boswell and A. Bergesen (eds), *America's Changing Role in the World System*. New York: Praeger.

Walt, Stephen M. (1998) International Relations: One World, Many Theories. *Foreign Policy*, 110, special edition, Frontiers of Knowledge, 29–32, 34–46.

Walters, F. P. (1952) *A History of the League of Nations*, 2 vols. Oxford: Oxford University Press.

Waltz, Kenneth (1959) *Man, The State and War*. New York: Columbia University Press.

Walzer, Michael (1992/2000) *Just and Unjust Wars: A Moral Argument with Historical Illustrations*, 2nd edition. New York: Basic Books.

Ward-Perkins, Bryan (2005) *The Fall of Rome and the End of Civilization*. Oxford: Oxford University Press.

Washington, George (1790) State of the Union Address http://www.presidency. ucsb.edu/ws/index.php?pid=29431#axzz1lzTblmb7

Watson, David Robin (1974) *Clemenceau, A Political Biography*. London: Eyre Methuen.

Watson, David Robin (2008) *Clemenceau*. London: Haus Publishing.

Watt, Donald Cameron (1983) *What About the People? Abstraction and Reality in History and the Social Sciences*. London: London School of Economics and Political Science.

Watts, Barry D. (2004) *Clausewitzian Friction and Future War* (McNair Paper no. 68). Washington, DC: Institute for National Strategic Studies.

Weill-Raynal, Etienne (1947) *Les Réparations allemandes et la France, 1918–1936*. Paris: Nouvelles Editions Latines.

Wells, Herbert George (1898) *The War of the Worlds*. London: William Heinemann.

Welsh, Jennifer (1995) *Edmund Burke and International Relations*. London: Macmillan/St Martin's Press.

Wendt, Alexander (1992) Anarchy is what States Make of it: The Social Construction of Power Politics. *International Organization* 46(2, Spring), 396–397.

Wendt, Alexander (1995) Constructing International Politics, *International Security*, 20(1, Summer), 71–81.

Wesseling, Henk (1996) *Divide and Rule: The Partition of Africa 1880–1914*, trans. Arnold J. Pomerans. Westport, CT: Praeger.

Westad, Odd Arne (2000) The New International History of the Cold War. *Diplomatic History*, 24(4), 551–556.

Westad, Odd Arne (2006) *Global Cold War: Third World Interventions and the Making of our Times*. Cambridge: Cambridge University Press.

Wheeler, Nicholas (2002) *Saving Strangers: Humanitarian Intervention in International Society*, 2nd edition. Oxford: Oxford University Press.

White, Hayden (1975) *Metahistory: The Historical Imagination in Nineteenth Century Europe*. Baltimore, MD: Johns Hopkins University Press.

Whittow, Mark (1996) *The Making of Orthodox Byzantium, 600–1025*. Houndsmills: Palgrave.

Whitworth, Wendy (2003) *Survival: Holocaust Survivors Tell Their Story*. London: Quill.

Wiesel, Elie, and Wiesel, Marion (2008) *Night*. London: Penguin.

Wight, Martin (2005) *Four Seminal Thinkers in International Theory: Machiavelli, Grotius, Kant and Mazzini*, ed. Gabrielle Wight and Brian Porter. Oxford: Oxford University Press.

Williams, Andrew (1988) The United Nations and Human Rights. In P. Taylor and A. J. R. Groom (eds), *International Institutions at Work*. London: Pinter, pp. 114–129.

Williams, Andrew (1989) *Labour and Russia: The Attitude of the Labour Party to the USSR, 1924–1934*. Manchester: Manchester University Press.

Williams, Andrew (1992) *Trading with the Bolsheviks: The Politics of East–West Trade, 1918–1939*, Manchester: Manchester University Press.

Williams, Andrew (1998) *Failed Imagination? New World Orders of the Twentieth Century*, 2nd edition 2007. Manchester: Manchester University Press.

Williams, Andrew (2006) *Liberalism and War: The Victors and the Vanquished*. London: Routledge.

Williams, Robert E., Jr, and Caldwell, Dan (2006) Jus Post Bellum: Just War Theory and the Principles of Just Peace. *International Studies Perspectives*, 7(4), 309–320.

Williams, William Appleman (1962) *The Tragedy of American Diplomacy*. New York: Dell.

Willoughby, W. W. (1896) *An Examination of the Nature of the State: A Study in Political Philosophy*. New York: Macmillan.

Wills, John E. (2001) *1688: A Global History*. New York: W. W. Norton.

Wilson, A. N. (1997) *Hilaire Belloc: A Biography*. London: Mandarin.

Wilson, A. N. (2006) *After the Victorians: The World Our Parents Knew*. New York: Random House.

Wilson, Peter (2003) *The International Theory of Leonard Woolf: A Study in Twentieth Century Idealism*. London: Palgrave Macmillan.

Wilson, Peter (2008) Leonard Woolf: Still Not out of the Jungle? *The Round Table: The Commonwealth Journal of International Affairs*, 97(394), 147–160.

Winock, Michel (2007) *Clemenceau*. Paris: Perrin.

Wint, Guy (1999) *The Penguin History of the Second World War*. London: Penguin.

Winter, Jay (1995) *Sites of Memory, Sites of Mourning. The Great War in European Cultural History*. Cambridge: Cambridge University Press.

Winter, Jay, and Prost, Antoine (2005) *The Great War in History: Debates and Controversies, 1914 to the Present*. Cambridge: Cambridge University Press.

Wohl, Robert (1979) *The Generation of 1914*. Cambridge, MA: Harvard University Press.

Woodhouse, C. M. (1999) *Modern Greece: A Short History*. London: Faber and Faber.

Woods, Ngaire (1996) *Explaining IR since 1945*. Oxford: Oxford University Press.

Wormell, Deborah (1980) *Sir John Seeley and the Uses of History*. Cambridge: Cambridge University Press.

Wright, Quincy (1921) *Limitation of Armament*. Washington: Institute of International Education.

Wright, Quincy (1935) *The Causes of War and the Conditions of Peace*. London: Longmans, Green and Co.

Wright, Quincy (1942) *A Study of War*. Chicago: University of Chicago Press.

Wright-Mills, C. (1959) *The Sociological Imagination*. New York: Basic Books.

Xenos, Nicholas (1996) Civic Nationalism: Oxymoron? *Critical Review*, 10(2, Summer).

Yehuda, Bauer (2002) *Rethinking the Holocaust*. New Haven, CN: Yale University Press.

Yergin, Daniel (1977) *Shattered Peace: The Origins of the Cold War and the National Security State*. Boston, MA: Houghton Mifflin.

Young, Robert (1990) *White Mythologies: Writing History and the West*. London: Routledge.

Zamoyski, Adam (2008) *Rites of Peace: The Fall of Napoleon and the Congress of Vienna*. New York: HarperPerennial.

Zimmern, Alfred (1931) *The Study of International Relations: An Inaugural Lecture, Delivered before the University of Oxford, on 20 February 1931.* Oxford: Clarendon Press.

Zimmern, Alfred (1936) *The League of Nations and the Rule of Law, 1918–1935.* London: Macmillan.

Zubok, Vladimir, and Pleshakov, Constantine (1997) *Inside the Kremlin's Cold War: From Stalin to Khrushchev*, Cambridge, MA: Harvard University Press.

Zullo, Alan, and Bovsun, Mara (2005) *Survivors: True Stories of Children in the Holocaust.* London: Scholastic.

# INDEX